Buddhism

FOR

DUMMIES®

Buddhism For Dummies®

Timeline of Buddhist History

Date(s)	Historical Event(s)
563–483 BCE	Life of Shakyamuni Buddha, founder of Buddhism (624–544 according to Theravada tradition).
268–239 BCE	Reign of King Ashoka, patron of Buddhism; sends first Buddhists to Sri Lanka in 246 BCE.
1st century BCE	Buddhist teachings written down for the first time.
100 BCE to 100 CE	Rise of Mahayana Buddhism.
78–101 CE	Reign of King Kanishka; Mahayana Buddhism spreads to Central Asia.
1st century CE	Buddhism first enters China.
520	First Zen patriarch Bodhidharma arrives in China.
538	Buddhism enters Japan from Korea.
7th to 8th century	Vajrayana Buddhism established in Tibet.
11th to 14th century	Theravada Buddhism established in Southeast Asia.
1199	Nalanda University destroyed; demise of Buddhism in India.
13th century	Zen, Pure Land, and Nichiren Buddhism established in Japan.
1881	Pali Text Society founded.
1893	World Parliament of Religions (Chicago).
1956	Celebration of 2,500 years of Buddhism.

Buddhism by the Numbers

3 Jewels of Refuge

Buddha

Dharma (the teachings)

Sangha (the Buddhist community)

3 higher trainings

Morality

Concentration

Wisdom

4 noble truths

Suffering

Cause of suffering

Cessation of suffering

Eight-fold path to the cessation of suffering

4 marks of Buddha's teachings

Compounded phenomena are impermanent

Ordinary phenomena are unsatisfactory

All phenomena are insubstantial (selfless)

Nirvana is peace

5 aggregates (skandhas)

Form

Feeling

Recognition

Karmic formations

Consciousness

(continued)

Buddhism For Dummies®

Buddhism by the Numbers (continued)

6 Mahayana perfections

Generosity (giving)

Moral discipline (ethics)

Patience

Effort, energy

Meditative concentration

Wisdom

10 Theravada perfections

Generosity

Moral discipline

Patience

Effort

Meditative concentration

Wisdom

Renunciation

Truthfulness

Loving-kindness

Equanimity

8-fold path

Right view

Right intention

Right speech

Right action

Right livelihood

Right effort

Right mindfulness

Right concentration

10 non-virtuous actions

Body

Killing

Stealing

Sexual misconduct

Speech

Lying

Divisive speech

Harsh speech

Idle gossip

Mind

Covetousness

Ill will

Wrong views

12 links of dependent arising

Ignorance

Karmic formations

Consciousness

Name and form

Six senses

Contact

Feeling

Craving

Grasping

Becoming

Birth

Aging and death

For Dummies: Bestselling Book Series for Beginners

Buddhism
FOR
DUMMIES®

by Jonathan Landaw and Stephan Bodian

WILEY

Wiley Publishing, Inc.

Buddhism For Dummies®

Published by
Wiley Publishing, Inc.
111 River St.
Hoboken, NJ 07030-5774
www.wiley.com

About the Authors

Jonathan Landaw was born in Paterson, New Jersey, in 1944 and attended Dartmouth College in New Hampshire. While there he took a course in Asian religions taught by one of the leading authorities on Chinese thought, Professor Wing-tsit Chan. This course provided Jon with his first formal exposure to the teachings of the East and sparked his lifelong interest in Buddhism. This interest remained dormant while Jon attended graduate school in English literature at the University of California in Berkeley and then served in the Peace Corps teaching English language in Iran for three years. Not long after his stint in the Peace Corps, he was living overseas again, this time in northern India and Nepal, where he stayed throughout most of the 1970s. There he first encountered and was inspired by the living tradition of Buddhism as preserved by the refugee community that had recently fled from Chinese oppression in Tibet. By 1972 Jon was studying Buddhism full-time and working as English editor of the texts being produced by the Translation Bureau of His Holiness the Dalai Lama at the Library of Tibetan Works and Archives in Dharamsala, India. Although he received training in other traditions of Buddhism during this time, the majority of his study and practice has been under the guidance of Tibetan lamas, most particularly Geshe Ngawang Dhargyey (1925–1995), Lama Thubten Yeshe (1935–1984), and Lama Zopa Rinpoche. In 1977 Jon returned to the West, though he's managed to make periodic visits back to India and Nepal since then. While living in England, the Netherlands, and now in the United States, he has continued his studies and his work editing Buddhist books for publication. He has also authored books of his own, including *Prince Siddhartha,* the story of Buddha's life retold for children, and *Images of Enlightenment,* an introduction to the sacred art of Tibet. In addition, he's been leading meditation courses at Buddhist centers worldwide for more than 25 years. He now resides in Capitola, California, with his wife and three children.

Stephan Bodian began practicing Zen meditation in 1969 and was ordained a monk in 1974 after studying about Buddhism and other Asian religions at Columbia University. He had the extraordinary good fortune to train under the guidance of several Zen masters, including Shunryu Suzuki Roshi, Kobun Chino Roshi, and Taizan Maezumi Roshi. In 1982, after a period as head monk and director of training at the Zen Center of Los Angeles, he left the monastic life to study psychology. Shortly thereafter he married and helped raise a family.

During this period he continued his spiritual practice, studying with several Tibetan teachers, including Sogyal Rinpoche and Namkhai Norbu Rinpoche. In 1988 he met his guru, Jean Klein, a master of Advaita Vedanta and Kashmiri yoga, with whom he spent ten years inquiring into the nature of truth.

Eventually Stephan completed his Zen training and received dharma transmission (authorization to teach) from his teacher, Adyashanti, in a lineage dating back to the historical Buddha.

In addition to authoring several previous books, including *Meditation For Dummies,* and numerous magazine articles, Stephan was editor-in-chief of the magazine *Yoga Journal* for 10 years. Currently he practices as a licensed psychotherapist, personal coach, writing consultant, and spiritual counselor, while offering intensives and retreats dedicated to spiritual awakening. You can reach him at www.meditationsource.com.

Dedication

To my mother, Ida M. Landaw, for her boundless love and support. And to the memory of my father, Louis Landaw, and of my beloved spiritual friend, Lama Thubten Yeshe.

— Jon Landaw

To my teachers, with boundless gratitude; and to the awakening of all beings everywhere.

— Stephan Bodian

Authors' Acknowledgments

Although it would be impossible for me to name everyone who had a hand in this work, several people's contributions must be acknowledged. First I have to thank my coauthor, Stephan Bodian, for his expertise and sound judgment in giving this book a balance and breadth of view it never would have had without him.

I would also like to acknowledge Carol Susan Roth, my literary agent for this work, Tracy Boggier of Wiley Publishing for overseeing its production, and our copy editor, Mike Baker, for his many helpful suggestions. And to our generous and supportive project editor, Allyson Grove, I owe more thanks than I can easily express.

I'd also like to thank Andy Weber for his beautiful line drawings, and Dolma Beresford of Nomad Pictures for providing a number of the photographs. In addition, I'd like to express my appreciation to T. Yeshe, former Buddhist nun and for many years a teacher associated with the Foundation for the Preservation of the Mahayana Tradition; Katherine Thanas, abbot of the Santa Cruz Zen Center; and Bob Stahl, former Theravada monk and current mindfulness-based stress reduction teacher at El Camino Hospital and the Santa Cruz Medical Clinic for reading and offering welcome suggestions to the manuscript, and to Venerable Ajahn Amaro and Richard Kollmar for their timely contributions.

I also wish to express my gratitude to the following for their invaluable aid in providing me with a computer and the assistance to use it properly: Susan Marfield, Victoria Clark, Yorgos Hadzis, Sharon Gross, Dennis Wilson, and Elizabeth Hull.

I would also like to mention Dr. Kevin Zhu and his assistants at the Five Branches Institute in Santa Cruz and my dear friend Karuna Cayton for helping me through some particularly rough patches, and George and Betsy Cameron whose generosity is a constant source of amazement to me. And to all those teachers who have guided me along the spiritual path, I can only offer this present work in the hope that it reflects a small portion of the insight and compassion they have always demonstrated. And lastly, to Truus Philipsen, and our children, Lisa, Anna, and Kevin: thank you for being in my life.

— Jon Landaw

Any grasp of Buddhist wisdom I bring to this book can be attributed to the grace of my beloved teachers and the support of my loving friends and colleagues. In particular, I would like to thank my first Zen teacher, Kobun Chino Otogawa, who introduced me to the depths of dharma and acted as spiritual mentor and elder brother during my formative years as a practitioner; my guru, Jean Klein, who embodied the teachings of the great Zen masters and kindled the first awakening; and Adyashanti — dharma brother, heart friend — in whose presence the truth finally burst into flame.

On a day-to-day level, my dear friends have been a constant source of encouragement, especially my Thursday group; old friends Katie Darling, Barbara Green, John Welwood, and Roy Wiskar; and above all my wife, Lis, without whose constant love and support at every level this book would never have come into being. My heartfelt thanks to you all!

I would also like to thank Reverend David Matsumoto, Venerable Ajahn Amaro, and Dechen Bartso for taking the time to answer my detailed questions about Buddhist practice, and Venerable Ajahn Munindo, Reverend Bill Eijun Eidson, Rosalie Curtis, and Liza Matthews for contributing invaluable images to this book.

— Stephan Bodian

Publisher's Acknowledgments

We're proud of this book; please send us your comments through our Dummies online registration form located at www.dummies.com/register/.

Some of the people who helped bring this book to market include the following:

Acquisitions, Editorial, and Media Development

Project Editor: Allyson Grove

Acquisitions Editor: Tracy Boggier

Copy Editor: Mike Baker

Technical Editors: T. Yeshe, Katherine Thanas, Bob Stahl

Editorial Manager: Jennifer Ehrlich

Media Development Manager: Laura VanWinkle

Editorial Assistant: Elizabeth Rea

Cartoons: Rich Tennant, www.the5thwave.com

Cover Photo: ©David Samuel Robbins/CORBIS

Production

Project Coordinator: Nancee Reeves

Layout and Graphics: Seth Conley, Carrie Foster, Tiffany Muth, Barry Offringa, Jeremy Unger

Proofreaders: Laura Albert, TECHBOOKS Production Services

Indexer: Johnna VanHoose

Illustrations: ® Andy Weber Studios

Special Help: Kurt Bateman, Laura Peterson, Kimberly Skeel

Publishing and Editorial for Consumer Dummies

Diane Graves Steele, Vice President and Publisher, Consumer Dummies

Joyce Pepple, Acquisitions Director, Consumer Dummies

Kristin A. Cocks, Product Development Director, Consumer Dummies

Michael Spring, Vice President and Publisher, Travel

Brice Gosnell, Associate Publisher, Travel

Suzanne Jannetta, Editorial Director, Travel

Publishing for Technology Dummies

Andy Cummings, Vice President and Publisher, Dummies Technology/General User

Composition Services

Gerry Fahey, Vice President of Production Services

Debbie Stailey, Director of Composition Services

Contents at a Glance

Table of Contents

Introduction

· ·

*B*uddhism is much more widely known today than it was 30 years ago when we first became involved in it. Dozens of books on the subject line the shelves at your local bookstore, and hundreds of Buddhist centers are located throughout North America where you can find out about Buddhism directly from members of its various traditions. Buddhism even seems to be seeping into the general culture; you commonly hear casual references to it in movies and on TV.

But, even with all the increased recognition, we still wonder how much the general public actually knows and understands about Buddhism. Despite the number of books on the subject, we suspect that, except for those folks who have pursued their interest fairly seriously, most people still have only a vague idea of what Buddhism is all about.

About This Book

So what do you do if you want to understand more about Buddhism in general, but the books you've looked at so far are too narrow — covering, for example, only one particular school, aspect, or practice — and you're not ready to take a class at your local Buddhist center (supposing you even have one)? Well, the book you have in your hands may be just what you're looking for.

In this book, we try to cover the main themes and currents of Buddhism without overwhelming you with too much technical jargon. (In the places that we do use technical terms, we explain them as clearly and succinctly as we can, and even provide a glossary you can use to refresh your memory.) Because we believe that Buddha meant his teachings to be taken as practical advice — advice that's as relevant to the human condition today as it was 2,500 years ago when he first gave it — we've tried to avoid taking a purely theoretical approach to Buddhism in favor of one that shows you how you can apply its insights to your everyday life.

Conventions Used in This Book

In assigning dates, we use BCE (before the Common Era) and CE (in the Common Era) in place of the BC and AD that are probably more familiar to many people. These relatively new designations are coming into wider use and, being religiously neutral, seem to be more appropriate for a book of this nature. And don't be concerned if the dates given differ a little from dates you find in other books on Buddhism. Historians disagree about quite a few of these dates, so we simply adopted those that seemed most reasonable to us.

Also, throughout this book, we cite (not too often, we hope) Buddhist technical terms and personal names from the ancient Indian languages Pali and Sanskrit (in which the Buddhist scriptures were first written) and from a smattering of other Asian languages such as Chinese, Japanese, and Tibetan. Wherever possible, we simplify the spelling of these words to reflect their approximate pronunciation, and we omit most of the marks that scholars of these languages typically employ when writing them using the Latin alphabet. If any scholars happen to be reading this book, they should have no trouble identifying these terms even without their accustomed markings; for everyone else, we think that the simpler, clearer presentation is more user friendly.

How This Book Is Organized

Buddhism is a huge subject. Not only were Buddha's own teachings extensive (filling more than 100 volumes in translation), but a succession of brilliant commentators in India and other countries also added their thoughts and interpretations to them. This process produced a large body of writings and led to the development of different Buddhist schools and traditions. In addition, as Buddhism moved from country to country, it took on different flavors. The Buddhism of Japan, for example, is different from the Buddhism of Thailand, and you can even find a number of distinct forms of practice within Japan itself.

In a work like this, we can't possibly do justice to all these various aspects of Buddhist thought and practice. Instead, we combine a general overview of the different traditions and schools with a more in-depth discussion of the most important themes — those themes that characterize Buddhism as a whole. Then, in the list of recommended readings in Appendix B, we provide the names of books and other resources you can consult to research the aspects of Buddhism that you want to explore further.

To make our presentation as clear and useful as possible, we group the topics into the following parts, each having its own unifying theme.

Part I: Introducing Buddhism

We begin with an overview of Buddhism as a whole, showing how it can be regarded as a religion, a philosophy of life, and a practical approach to dealing with life's problems — all rolled into one. Then, because the mind is so central to Buddhism, we take a look at how the mind creates both happiness and suffering, and how the centrally important Buddhist practices of wisdom and compassion can bring you into contact with your inner spiritual resources.

Part II: Buddhism Past and Present

History doesn't have to be a boring subject, especially when it deals with the lives and deeds of extraordinary people. In this part, we look at the history of Buddhism, beginning with the life of its founder, Shakyamuni Buddha, including a summary of his earliest and most basic teachings. We then explore how Buddhism developed in India and then evolved further as it spread from country to country across Asia. Finally, we show you how Theravada, Vajrayana, and Zen Buddhism grew to become the three main Buddhist traditions practiced in the West.

Part III: Buddhism in Practice

In this part, we address a number of practical questions: How does someone become a Buddhist? What does being a Buddhist involve? How does Buddhism affect the way you live your life? In short, what do Buddhists actually do? To answer these questions, we look at the ways people can benefit from what Buddhism has to offer. We explore meditation and show you some of the ways you can practice it. We examine how followers of various traditions bring Buddhism into their everyday lives. And we conclude by taking you on a tour of the major Buddhist pilgrimage sites.

Part IV: Traveling the Buddhist Path

Buddha's teachings are vast and contain a wide variety of different practices. In this part, we show you how all these different methods fit together. We examine the different interpretations of enlightenment and show you how you can apply the Buddhist teachings at each stage along the spiritual path. Finally, we take a look at how enlightenment expresses itself in the lives of four contemporary Buddhist masters.

Part V: The Part of Tens

If you like to receive information in bite-sized, easily digestible chunks, then this is the part for you. We discuss (and try to dispel) ten common misconceptions about Buddhism and present ten ways that Buddhist insights can be applied to your life. All this at no extra charge.

Part VI: Appendixes

Finally, in the appendixes, we provide some information that should help round out your understanding and appreciation of Buddhism. Here you will find a glossary containing many of the most commonly used Buddhist terms, as well as a list of resources you can consult if you want to find out more about the different aspects of Buddhism that you encounter in this book.

Icons Used in This Book

To draw your attention to bits of information that we think are particularly important or interesting, we use the following icons throughout the text.

The information next to this icon is worth repeating. We may use this icon to highlight a thought expressed elsewhere in the book or simply to point out something we think is especially important for you to keep in mind.

This icon contains suggestions for ways you can get a deeper understanding of the aspect of Buddhism being discussed.

Don't be unduly alarmed by this icon. We use it to draw your attention to areas where misunderstandings can arise so that you can avoid tripping up.

Next to this icon are quotations from famous Buddhist masters of the past — including Buddha himself — that illustrate the aspect of Buddhism being discussed.

This icon alerts you that we're retelling a traditional Buddhist story or perhaps relating an incident of a more personal nature.

Where to Go from Here

You can approach this book in several different ways. The Table of Contents and Index are detailed enough that you can find specific topics of interest and turn directly to them if you want. Or, because each chapter of the book is quite self-contained, you can start reading anywhere and skip around at your leisure. The cross references we provide point out where you can find additional information on selected topics.

You can also read this book in the ordinary, straightforward manner: In other words, start at the beginning and, when you reach the end, stop. Finally, if you're like some people, you can open the book at the end and, after many detours, make your way back to the beginning. We hope that, whichever approach you follow, you find the material informative and enjoyable.

Part I
Introducing Buddhism

The 5th Wave — By Rich Tennant

"So, relief from suffering is found by following an Eightfold Path? The path I've followed for relief from suffering has generally gone past several large shopping malls."

In this part . . .

Want to find out what *Buddhism* actually means, and whether it's a religion, a philosophy, a psychology, or something else. Well, look no further than the pages contained in this part for the answers to these questions. We also introduce you to the Buddhist understanding of the mind and its importance and tell you about the treasures inside of you that Buddhism wants to help you discover. That seems well worth the price of admission, doesn't it?

Chapter 1

What Is Buddhism?

Not too long ago, the West was virtually unfamiliar with Buddhism. Back in the 1950s and '60s, for example, you could've gone about your life scarcely hearing it mentioned. Sure, you may have come across Buddhist concepts in school in the writings of American Transcendentalists like Thoreau and Emerson (who read English translations of Buddhist texts in the mid-19th century). But the fact is that if you were like the majority of middle-class individuals, you may have grown up, grown old, and died without ever meeting a practicing Buddhist — except perhaps in an Asian restaurant.

If you wanted to find out about Buddhism, your resource options were few and far between. Aside from a rare course in Eastern philosophy at a large university, you would have to dig deep into the shelves and stacks at your local library to discover anything more than the most basic facts about Buddhism. The few books that you could get your hands on tended to treat Buddhism as if it were an exotic relic from some long-ago and far-away land, like some dusty Buddha statue in a dark corner of the Asian section of a museum. And good luck if you wanted to find a Buddhist center where you could study and practice.

Today the situation couldn't be more different. Buddhist terms seem to pop up everywhere. You can find them in ordinary conversation ("It's just your *karma*"), on television (*Dharma* and Greg), and even in the names of rock groups (*Nirvana*). Famous Hollywood stars, avant-garde composers, pop singers, and even one highly successful professional basketball coach practice one form of Buddhism or another. (We're thinking of Richard Gere, Philip Glass, Tina Turner, and Phil Jackson, but you may be able to come up with a different list of celebrities on your own.)

Bookstores and libraries everywhere boast a wide range of Buddhist titles, some of which — like the Dalai Lama's *Art of Happiness* (Riverhead Books) — regularly top the *New York Times* best-seller lists. And centers where people can study and practice Buddhism are now located in most metropolitan areas (and many smaller cities as well).

What caused such a dramatic change in just a few decades? Certainly Buddhism has become more available as Asian Buddhist teachers and their disciples have carried the tradition to North America and Europe. (For more on the influx of Buddhism to the West, see Chapter 5.) But there's more to the story than increased availability. In this chapter, we try to account for the appeal this ancient tradition has in today's largely secular world by looking at some of the features responsible for its growing popularity.

Figuring Out Whether Buddhism Is a Religion

Wondering whether Buddhism is actually a religion may seem odd. After all, if you consult any list of the world's major religious traditions, you inevitably find Buddhism mentioned prominently alongside Christianity, Islam, Hinduism, Judaism, and the rest. No one ever questions whether these other traditions are religions. But this question *does* come up again and again in relation to Buddhism. Why is that?

Ask most people what comes to mind when they think of "religion," and they'll probably mention something about the belief in God. Our dictionary agrees. *Webster's New World College Dictionary* defines *religion* as a "belief in a divine or superhuman power or powers to be obeyed and worshiped as the creator(s) and ruler(s) of the universe."

If this definition were the only definition of religion, you'd definitely have to count Buddhism out! Why? Well, we have two reasons:

- ✔ **No God:** Worship of a supernatural power isn't the central concern of Buddhism. God (as this word is ordinarily used) is completely absent from Buddhist teachings — so much so that some people half-jokingly call Buddhism a good religion for atheists!

- ✔ **Not a belief system:** Buddhism isn't primarily a system of belief. Although it does contain certain fundamental principles (as we discuss throughout Part III), most Buddhist teachers actively encourage their students to adopt an attitude that is the *opposite* of belief or blind faith.

Buddhist teachers advise you to be skeptical about teachings you receive, even if they come directly from Buddha himself. (For more about the founder of Buddhism, see Chapter 3.) Don't passively accept what you hear or read, or automatically reject it either. Use your intelligence instead. See for yourself if the teachings make sense in terms of your own experience and the experience of others. Then, as the Dalai Lama of Tibet (see Chapter 15) often advises, "If you find that the teachings suit you, apply them to your life as much as you can. If they don't suit you, just leave them be."

This non-dogmatic approach (one that doesn't have a rigid system of doctrines or beliefs) agrees with both the spirit and the letter of Buddha's own teachings. In one of his most famous pronouncements, Buddha declared, "Do not accept anything I say as true simply because I have said it. Instead, test it as you would gold to see if it is genuine or not. If, after examining my teachings, you find that they are true, put them into practice. But do not do so simply out of respect for me."

Buddhism therefore encourages you to use the entire range of your mental, emotional, and spiritual abilities and intelligence — instead of merely placing your blind faith in what past authorities have said. This attitude makes Buddhism especially attractive to many westerners; although it's 2,500 years old, it appeals to the postmodern spirit of skepticism and scientific investigation.

If Buddhism is *not* primarily a belief system and is *not* centered upon the worship of a supreme deity, then why is it classified as a religion at all? Because like all religions, Buddhism gives people who practice it a way of finding answers to the deeper questions of life, such as "Who am I?" "Why am I here?" "What is the meaning of life?" "Why do we suffer?" and "How can I achieve lasting happiness?"

In addition to fundamental teachings on the nature of reality, Buddhism offers a *methodology* — a set of techniques and practices — that enables its followers to experience a deeper level of reality directly for themselves. In Buddhist terms, this experience involves waking up to the truth of your authentic being, your innermost nature. The experience of awakening is the ultimate goal of all Buddhist teachings. (For more on awakening, or enlightenment as it's often called, see Chapter 10.) Some schools do emphasize awakening more than others (and a few even relegate it to the background in their scheme of priorities), but in every tradition, it's the final goal of human existence — whether achieved in this life or in lives to come.

By the way, you don't have to join a Buddhist organization to benefit from the teachings and practices of Buddhism. For more info on the different stages of involvement in Buddhism, see Chapter 6.

Recognizing the Role of Buddha: The Awakened One

The Buddhist religion is founded upon the teachings given 2,500 years ago by one of the great spiritual figures of human history, Shakyamuni Buddha. As we explain in more detail in Chapter 3, he was born into the ruling family of the Shakya clan in northern India and was expected to someday succeed his father as king. Instead, Prince Siddhartha (as he was known at the time) quit the royal life at the age of 29 after he saw the reality of the extensive suffering and dissatisfaction in the world. He then set out to find a way to overcome this suffering.

Finally, at age 35, Prince Siddhartha achieved his goal. Seated under what became known as the *Bodhi tree* — the tree of enlightenment — he achieved the complete awakening of Buddhahood. From this time on, he was known as *Shakyamuni Buddha,* the fully awakened sage (*muni*) of the Shakya clan (see Figure 1-1).

Buddha: Human or divine?

Newcomers to Buddhism often ask the question: "What kind of being was Shakyamuni Buddha — a man, a god, or something else?" Buddha himself stated, and all Buddhist traditions agree, that like every other enlightened being who has ever appeared in the past (or who ever *will* appear in the future), he was once an ordinary, unenlightened human being with the same hang-ups and problems as everyone else. No one ever started out as a Buddha; no one was ever enlightened from the beginning. And Shakyamuni was no exception.

Only through great effort exerted over a long period of time — over many lifetimes, in fact — did he succeed in removing all the different layers that covered up the clear nature of his consciousness, thereby "awakening" to Buddhahood, or full enlightenment.

Where the Buddhist traditions differ is over this question: "When did Shakyamuni actually attain enlightenment?" Some Buddhist traditions say that he accomplished this feat exactly as we discuss it in this chapter — at age 35 while seated under the Bodhi tree 2,500 years ago. Others maintain that he reached Buddhahood a long time before that in the far distant past. According to this second interpretation, the Buddha who came to be known as Shakyamuni had attained enlightenment long before he was born as Prince Siddhartha. His entire existence on this earth, from his birth to his passing away, was a conscious demonstration to others of how the spiritual path should be followed. In other words, it was all an act performed to inspire others to develop themselves spiritually as he did.

More important than the question of when Shakyamuni achieved enlightenment is the fact that sincere Buddhist practitioners can emulate Shakyamuni's example to the best of their ability. If you were an aspiring practitioner, for example, you may ask yourself, "If Shakyamuni was originally no different from me, how can I follow in his footsteps and find the satisfaction and fulfillment he found?"

Figure 1-1:
Shakyamuni
Buddha.

He spent the remaining 45 years of his life wandering across northern India teaching anyone who was interested about the path that leads to freedom from suffering in the full enlightenment of a Buddha. (Part III offers an overview of this entire path.) After a lifetime of compassionate service to others, he passed away at the age of 80.

The Buddhist spiritual community (*sangha*) took great pains to preserve and transmit his teachings as purely as possible so they could be passed on from one generation to the next. These extensive teachings were eventually written down, producing a vast collection (or *canon*) of more than a hundred volumes of Buddha's own discourses (*sutras*) and twice that number of commentaries (*shastras*) by later Indian masters. (See Chapters 4 and 5 for more about how these teachings spread and evolved.)

Over the centuries the sangha also erected monuments (*stupas*) in honor of the major events in their teacher's life, which allowed later practitioners to make pilgrimage to these honored sites (see Figure 1-2) and receive the inspiration of the Compassionate Buddha directly for themselves. (Chapters 8 and 9 have more information on Buddhist devotional practices and rituals.)

Figure 1-2:
Pilgrims
visiting the
Bodhi tree.

Photo © Ian Cumming/Tibet Images.

Thanks to the efforts of each generation of teachers and their disciples, the lineage of Buddha's teachings (known as *dharma*) has remained fundamentally unbroken up to the present day. That's why after 2,500 years Buddhism is still a living tradition, capable of bestowing peace, happiness, and fulfillment upon anyone who practices it sincerely.

Because Buddha was a mere mortal, not a living god or some mythical super-hero (see the "Buddha: Human or divine?" sidebar in this chapter), he's always been more than a distant figure to Buddhists; he's a vital example of what each and every one of us can achieve if we devote ourselves whole-heartedly to the study and practice of the dharma he taught. In fact, one of the primary truths he awakened to under the Bodhi tree was that all beings have the potential to become Buddhas. Or, as some traditions put it, all beings are already essentially Buddhas — they merely need to wake up to this fact.

Understanding the Philosophy of Buddhism

Socrates, one of the fathers of Western philosophy, claimed that the unexam-ined life isn't worth living, and most Buddhists would certainly agree with him. Because of the importance they place on logical reasoning and rational examination, many Buddhist traditions and schools have a strong philosophi-cal flavor. Others place more emphasis on the direct, non-conceptual investi-gation and examination that take place during the practice of meditation. In either approach, direct personal experience based on self-awareness is con-sidered key. (For more on the Buddhist practice of meditation, see Chapter 7.)

Although Buddhism emphasizes direct investigation and experience, it does put forth certain philosophical tenets that sketch out a basic understanding of human existence and serve as guidelines and inspirations for practice and study. Over the centuries, Buddhism actually grew into a variety of schools and traditions, each of which had its own more or less elaborate and distinct understanding of what Buddha taught. (For the story of these different tradi-tions, see Chapters 4 and 5.) In addition to the discourses memorized during the founder's lifetime and recorded after his death, numerous other scrip-tures emerged many centuries later that were attributed to him.

Despite all its philosophical sophistication, however, Buddhism remains at heart an extremely practical religion. Buddha has often been called the Great Physician for good reason: He always avoided abstract speculation and made identifying the cause of human suffering and providing ways to eliminate it his chief concern. (See the sidebar, "The parable of the poisoned arrow," for details.) Likewise, the dharma he taught is known as powerful medicine to cure the deeper dissatisfaction that afflicts us all. Buddha's first and best-known teaching, the *four noble truths* (see Chapter 3), outlines the cause of suffering and the means for eliminating it. All subsequent teachings merely expand and elaborate upon these fundamental truths.

At the core of all genuine dharma teachings is the understanding that suffering and dissatisfaction originate in the way your mind responds and reacts to life's circumstances — not in the raw facts of life. In particular, Buddhism teaches that your mind causes you suffering by attaching to permanence and constructing a separate self where in fact neither exists. (For more on the central teachings of impermanence and no-self, see Chapter 2.)

Reality is constantly changing; as the Greek philosopher Heraclitus said, you can't step into the same river twice. Success and failure, gain and loss, comfort and discomfort — they all come and go. And you have only limited control over the changes. But you can exert some control over (and ultimately clarify) your chattering, misguided mind, which distorts your perceptions, mightily resists the way things are, and causes you extraordinary stress and suffering in the process.

Happiness, Buddha once said, is actually quite simple: The secret is to want what you have and not want what you don't have. Simple though it may be, it's definitely not easy. Have you ever tried to reign in your restless and unruly mind, even for a moment? Have you ever tried to tame your anger or your jealousy, control your fear, or remain calm and undisturbed in the middle of life's inevitable ups and downs? If you have, you've no doubt discovered how difficult even the simplest self-control or self-awareness can be. To benefit from the medicine Buddha prescribed, you have to take it — which means, you have to put it into practice for yourself. (See Chapter 17 for ten practical suggestions for putting Buddha's teachings to use in your everyday life, and check out Chapter 14 for additional hands-on advice.)

Appreciating the Practice of Buddhism

Anyone interested in benefiting from Buddhism — rather than simply discovering a few interesting facts about it — has to ask, "How do I take this spiritual medicine? How can I apply the teachings of Shakyamuni to my life in such a way that my restlessness and dissatisfaction can be reduced, neutralized, and eventually extinguished?" The answer is spiritual practice, which takes three forms in Buddhism:

- ✔ Ethical behavior
- ✔ Meditation (and the wisdom that follows)
- ✔ Devotion

ANECDOTE

The parable of the poisoned arrow

Because intellectual activity has had such a significant place in Buddhist history, it would indeed be tempting to classify Buddhism as a philosophy rather than a religion. But Shakyamuni Buddha himself warned against getting so caught up in philosophical speculation that you lose sight of the ultimate aim of his teachings. This attitude is clearly illustrated in the oft-told story of a monk named Malunkyaputta (we'll just call him the Venerable Mal for short), who approached Buddha one day complaining that he had never addressed certain philosophical questions such as "Does the universe have a beginning or an end?" and "Does the Buddha exist after death?" Venerable Mal declared that if Buddha wouldn't answer these questions once and for all, he would abandon his training as a Buddhist monk and return to his former life as a layman.

In response, Shakyamuni described the following hypothetical situation. Suppose, he said, a man has been wounded by a poisoned arrow. His concerned relatives find a skillful surgeon who can remove the arrow, but the wounded man refuses to let the doctor operate until he has received satisfactory answers to a long list of questions. "I will not have the arrow taken out," the wounded man declares, "until I know the caste to which the man who wounded me belongs, his name, his height, the village he comes from, the wood from which the arrow was made, and so forth." Clearly, such a foolish person would die long before his questions could ever be answered.

"In the same way," Shakyamuni advised Venerable Mal, "anyone who says, 'I will not follow the spiritual life until Buddha has explained to me whether the universe is eternal or not or whether Buddha exists after death' would die long before he could ever receive satisfying answers to his questions." The truly spiritual or religious life doesn't depend at all on how these questions are answered. For, as Shakyamuni then pointed out, "Whether or not the universe is eternal, you're still faced with birth, old age, death, sorrow, grief, and despair, for which I'm now prescribing the antidote."

Living an ethical life

Ethical behavior has been an essential component of the Buddhist spiritual path since the historical Buddha first cautioned his monks and nuns to refrain from certain behaviors because they distracted them from their pursuit of truth. During Buddha's lifetime, his followers collected and codified these guidelines, which eventually became the moral code (*vinaya*) that, in more or less the same form, has continued to shape the monastic life for more than 2,500 years. (The term *monastic* describes both monks and nuns.) From this code emerged briefer guidelines for lay practitioners (non-monastic Buddhists), which have remained remarkably similar from tradition to tradition. (For more on ethical behavior, see Chapter 12.)

Far from establishing an absolute standard of right and wrong, ethical guidelines in Buddhism have an entirely practical purpose — to keep practitioners focused on the goal of their practice, which is a liberating insight into the nature of reality. During his 45 years of teaching, Buddha found that certain activities contributed to increased craving, attachment, restlessness, and dissatisfaction and led to interpersonal conflict in the community at large. By contrast, other behaviors helped keep the mind peaceful and focused and contributed to a more supportive atmosphere for spiritual reflection and realization. From these observations, rather than from any abstract moral point of view, the ethical guidelines emerged.

Examining your life through meditation

In the popular imagination, Buddhism is definitely the religion of meditation. After all, who hasn't seen statues of Buddha sitting cross-legged, eyes half closed, deeply immersed in spiritual reflection — or picked up one of the many titles available these days devoted to teaching the basics of Buddhist meditation?

But many people misunderstand the role meditation plays in Buddhism. They falsely assume that you're meant to withdraw from the affairs of ordinary life into a peaceful, detached, and unaffected inner realm until you no longer feel any emotion or concern about the things that once mattered to you. Nothing, however, could be farther from the truth. (We cover other misconceptions about Buddhism and Buddhist practice in Chapter 16.)

The real purpose of meditation in Buddhism isn't to calm the mind (though this result may happen and is certainly conducive to the meditative process), nor is it to become detached and uncaring. Rather, the purpose is to experience the profound and ultimately liberating insight into the nature of reality and yourself that we talk about in the "Understanding the Philosophy of Buddhism" section earlier in this chapter — an insight that shows you who you are and what life is about and frees you from suffering once and for all. (For more on this insight, known as spiritual realization or enlightenment, see Chapter 10.)

Meditation facilitates this insight by bringing focused, ongoing attention to the workings of your mind and heart. In the early stages of meditation, you spend most of your time being aware of your experience as much as you can — an almost universal Buddhist practice known as *mindfulness*. You may also cultivate positive, beneficial heart qualities like loving-kindness and compassion or practice visualizations of beneficial figures and energies. But in the end, the goal of all Buddhist meditation is to find out who you are and thereby bring your restless seeking and dissatisfaction to an end. (For more on meditation, see Chapter 7.)

Expressing devotion

Although Buddha didn't teach it explicitly, devotion has long been a central Buddhist practice. No doubt it began with the spontaneous devotion Buddha's own followers felt for their gentle, wise, and compassionate teacher. After his death, followers with a devotional bent directed their reverence toward the enlightened elders of the monastic community and toward Buddha's remains, which were preserved in monuments known as stupas (see Figure 1-2).

As Buddhism spread throughout India and ultimately to other lands, the primary object of devotion became the *Three Jewels* of Buddha, dharma, and sangha — the great teacher (and his successors), the teachings themselves, and the community of practitioners who preserve and uphold the teachings. To this day all Buddhists, both lay and monastic, *take refuge* in the Three Jewels (also known as the Three Treasures or Triple Gem). (For more on taking refuge, see Chapter 6.)

Eventually, in certain traditions of Buddhism, the natural human tendency to revere and idealize gave rise to a host of transcendent figures that embodied especially desirable spiritual qualities. By expressing heartfelt devotion to these figures and then imagining yourself merging with them and thereby assuming their awakened qualities, you can gradually change your negative qualities into positive ones and ultimately gain complete enlightenment for the benefit of yourself and others — or so these traditions teach.

Study and reflection help clarify the Buddhist teachings, but devotion forges a heartfelt connection with the tradition, allowing you to express your love and appreciation for the teachers (and teachings) and to experience their love and compassion in return. Even traditions like Zen, which seem to de-emphasize devotion in favor of insight, have a strong devotional undercurrent that gets expressed in rituals and ceremonies but isn't always visible to newcomers. For lay Buddhist practitioners who may not have the time or inclination to meditate, devotion to the Three Jewels may even become their main practice. In fact, some traditions, like Pure Land Buddhism, are primarily devotional. (For more on the different traditions of Buddhism, including Zen and Pure Land, see Chapter 5.)

Dedicating Your Life to the Benefit of All Beings

When you get right down to it, Buddhism teaches that you and the people around you are fundamentally interconnected and interdependent — that each apparently separate being or thing, you included, is merely a unique expression of one vast, indivisible reality. With this perspective in mind (and heart), Buddhism encourages you to dedicate your spiritual efforts not only to yourself and your loved ones, but also to the benefit and enlightenment of *all* beings (who are in fact inseparable from you).

Many Buddhist traditions teach their followers to actively cultivate love and compassion for others — not only those they care about but also those who disturb them or toward whom they may feel hostility (in other words, enemies). In fact, some traditions believe that this dedication to the welfare of all forms the foundation of the spiritual path upon which all other practices are based. Other traditions allow the love and compassion to arise naturally as insight deepens and wisdom ripens, while instructing practitioners to dedicate the merits of their meditations and rituals to all beings.

Whatever the method, the teachings here essentially agree that all beings are inseparable, and some traditions even counsel that, in the end, you won't be able to achieve lasting happiness and peace of mind until all beings are happy and peaceful too. From this realization arises the vow of the *bodhisattva* (Sanskrit for "awakening being") who dedicates his or her life to the enlightenment of all (see Chapter 14). Until all beings are liberated, the bodhisattva believes, my work on this Earth is not yet done. Though not every Buddhist tradition views the bodhisattva in quite the same way, all would agree that this spirit lies at the very heart of Buddhism.

Chapter 2

Understanding Your Mind: The Creator of All Experience

*I*n Chapter 1, we introduce Buddhism by contrasting what it *isn't* — a strict, rigid system of religious beliefs — with what it actually *is* — a practical, experience-based method for transforming your life.

At the heart of this transformation is your mind. But *mind* is a rather slippery term: Although the word pops up in conversation all the time — "She's got a sharp mind," "My mind's not very clear today," "Are you out of your mind?" and so on — its definition isn't easy to pin down.

In this chapter, we talk a little about what Buddhism has to say about the mind, paying particular attention to the ways in which the various functions of the mind shape everything from your spiritual progress to the most ordinary, everyday life experiences.

Recognizing How Your Mind Shapes Your Experience

On many occasions, Buddha himself said that your mind creates, shapes, and experiences everything that happens to you, without a single exception. That's why, from the Buddhist point of view, what goes on inside you (in your mind) is much more important in determining whether you're happy or miserable than any of the outer circumstances of your life.

Hold it right there. Does what you just read sound reasonable? Do the inner workings of your mind really have a greater effect on you than, say, your possessions or your surroundings? After all, big companies and advertising agencies spend billions of dollars every year trying to convince you that the opposite is true! In their eyes, your best shot at achieving happiness is to buy whatever they're selling. They appeal to what Jon likes to call the "if only" mentality: If only you drove a fancier car, lived in a bigger house, gargled with a stronger mouthwash, and used a softer toilet paper — then you'd be truly happy. Even if you don't believe everything advertisers tell you, don't you believe that the external conditions of your life determine how well-off you are?

You should get into the habit of asking yourself these types of questions when you come across new information. Investigating points brought up in a book that you're reading or in teachings you receive isn't an intellectual game or idle pastime. If done properly, such questioning becomes a vital part of your spiritual development. As Buddha himself indicated, merely accepting certain statements as true while rejecting others as false without examining them closely doesn't accomplish very much.

In this case, examination is particularly important because the questions concern the best way to live your life. Should your pursuit of happiness focus mainly on the accumulation of possessions and other "externals"? Or is primarily devoting yourself to putting your inner house in order the better way to go?

To get a feel for how you might go about examining this issue, consider the following situation. Two friends of yours, call them Jennifer and Karen, take a vacation together to Tahiti. They stay in the same luxurious guesthouse, eat the same food prepared by the same master chef, lounge on the same pristine beaches, and engage in the same recreational activities. But, when they get home and tell you about their trip, their stories sound like they vacationed in two completely different worlds! For Jennifer, Tahiti was heaven on Earth, but for Karen, it was pure hell. For every wonderful experience Jennifer brings up, Karen tells you about two awful ones. This situation is hypothetical, of course, but doesn't it sound familiar? Hasn't something like this happened to you or your friends?

Consider one more scenario. During wartime, two friends get thrown into a prison camp. As in the previous example, both guys end up in identical situations, but this time, the outward conditions are miserable. One soldier experiences extreme mental torment due to the horrible physical conditions and ends up bitter and broken in spirit; the other manages to rise above his surroundings, even becoming a source of strength for the other prisoners. True stories like this scenario aren't rare, so how can you account for them?

These examples (and relevant ones from your own experience) demonstrate that the outer circumstances of your life aren't the only factors — or even the most important ones — in determining whether you're content or not. If external conditions were more important than the condition of your mind, both Jennifer and Karen would've loved Tahiti, both prisoners would have been equally miserable, and no rich and famous person would ever contemplate suicide.

The more closely you look, the more clearly you'll see (if the Buddhist teachings are correct on this point) that your mental attitude is what mainly determines the quality of your life. We're not saying that your outer circumstances count for nothing, nor are we implying that a person has to give away all of his or her possessions to be a sincere spiritual seeker. But, without developing your *inner* resources of peace and mental stability, no amount of worldly success — whether measured in terms of wealth, fame, power, or relationships — can ever bring real satisfaction. Or, as someone once said, "Money can't buy happiness; it can only allow you to select your particular form of misery."

Contrasting the Body and Mind

Even if you have a general idea what the mind is, you may have a difficult time identifying it exactly. After all, you can't point to something and say, "This is my mind." Why not? Because your mind isn't a material thing made up of atoms and molecules. Unlike your brain, heart, or any other bodily organ, your mind has no color, shape, weight, or other physical attribute.

But, as long as you're alive, your body and mind remain intimately interconnected and have a powerful influence on one another. For example, everyone knows that drinking too much alcohol can have a potent, harmful effect on the mind. The physical properties of alcohol dull your mental capacities, lower your inhibitions, and may even cause you to hallucinate.

The mind-body influence works the other way around as well. Worrying too much, for example, can contribute to many physical ailments, including stomach ulcers, colitis (inflammation of the large intestine), and high blood pressure. This connection hasn't been lost on medical professionals. Everyday, more and more of them recognize that a patient's mental state can have an enormous effect on his or her recovery from disease. Many hospitals now provide a variety of mind-body treatment options, including hypnotherapy, support groups, and individual counseling, to help their patients heal more rapidly and completely. And a quick trip to your local bookstore presents you with even more evidence of the mind's role in the health of the body —

dozens of books about the healing influence of visualizations, affirmations, and a positive state of mind line the shelves. A well-known writer even helped cure himself of cancer by watching one Marx Brothers movie after another! In his case, laughter really was the best medicine.

They're interconnected, but the body and mind aren't the same thing. If they were, your mental states would be nothing more than the nerve cells, electrical activity, and chemical reactions of your brain. But is this definition an adequate and satisfying explanation for what actually goes on in your mind? Can such varied and richly colored experiences as falling in love, feeling embarrassed, and receiving a flash of artistic inspiration be reduced to molecular interactions?

Buddhism teaches that your body (including your brain) has a physical form, but your mind (which is conscious of all your experiences) is formless. That's why you can't see your mind or touch it. But being formless doesn't prevent your mind from doing what only it can do — enabling you to be aware! In fact, the job of the mind is just that: to be aware (or conscious). This awareness operates on many different levels, from the mundane (you're aware of the words on this page, for example) to the extraordinary (like when a person with "heightened" awareness can read another person's mind or know about events that are taking place somewhere else in the world).

Approaching the Mind from Three Different Buddhist Perspectives

The various Buddhist traditions have their own particular way of talking about the mind and its role in spiritual development. To give you some idea of the richness and variety of these views, we briefly mention the approach of the three main Buddhist traditions in the West today:

 ✔ The Theravada Buddhist tradition of Southeast Asia follows the detailed analysis of the mind given in the *abhidharma,* or "higher learning," section of Buddha's teachings. (For more on all three sections, or "baskets," of Buddha's teachings, see Chapter 4.) These extensive teachings divide the mind's functions into different categories, such as primary and secondary, skillful and unskillful, and so on. This psychological analysis can help you precisely understand which of the many different mental functions (one abhidharma system identifies nearly 50 of them!) are arising in your mind at any given moment. The more skillful you become in identifying the complex and ever-changing nature of these mental functions as they arise, the more thoroughly you can cut through the harmful illusion of a solid, unchanging ego-identity (as we explain in Chapter 13) and achieve spiritual liberation.

✔ Many serious followers of the Vajrayana Buddhist tradition also study the abhidharma teachings dealing with the mind, the many different mental functions, and so forth. In addition, the Vajrayana offers techniques for contacting what it calls the *mind of clear light,* a blissful state of consciousness residing at the core of your being, which is far more powerful than any ordinary state of mind. By gaining control of this hidden treasure, skillful meditators (or *yogis* of clear light) can burn through mental obstructions rapidly and completely. This act brings them face to face with ultimate reality and eventually to the supreme enlightenment of Buddhahood itself.

✔ According to the Japanese Zen Buddhist tradition, *big mind,* or *Buddha nature,* pervades the whole universe. Everything you experience, both inside and outside yourself, is nothing other than this Mind (with a capital *m*). By contrast, the *small mind,* the analytical, conceptual mind, tends to identify itself as a limited, separate ego or self. Spiritual awakening involves a shift in identity from small mind to big Mind.

We talk more about the approaches of these three main traditions throughout this book (especially in Chapter 5). But, for now, we want to point out one thing. Despite their many differences, these three traditions agree in one important respect. They each say that you have a choice in the way that you experience your life: Your mind can be obscured or unobscured, limited or vast. The first option involves frustration and dissatisfaction; the second brings freedom and fulfillment. The so-called spiritual path enables you to shift your vision of life from the obscured to the unobscured, the limited to the vast.

Identifying Some Ways Your Mind Works

Any discussion of something as broad as consciousness or awareness can quickly become too vague and abstract. So join us in taking a closer look, first of all, at two ways in which your mind ordinarily allows you to become aware of your world: *perception* and *conception.*

✔ **Perception:** When you wake up in the morning, your mind starts looking out at the world through a window — your senses. We talk more about these physical senses in the "Recognizing the six major types of consciousness" section later in this chapter, but for now, just consider your eyesight. Imagine you just spent a night in an unfamiliar hotel room. As you wipe the sleep from your eyes in the morning and look around, you don't immediately see the various items in your hotel room. Instead of the painting on the wall, for instance, you simply see an arrangement of different shapes and colors. That's all your eyes directly perceive: shapes and colors. Then conception steps to the plate.

✔ **Conception:** Some time after perception occurs (it may be just a split second or considerably longer), you identify the arrangement of shapes and colors as a painting. As soon as you make the connection, the way is open for you to generate a host of additional ideas about this painting. "I like it." "That's the worst painting I've ever seen." "I think it's an original." "Maybe it's a reproduction." "I wonder how much it costs." "I think it'd look good in my bedroom." If you like the painting so much that you purchase it, the next time you look at it you may also think, "This is *my* painting." Conceptions — a *good* painting, a *bad* painting, an *expensive* painting, *my* painting — are interpretations that your mind makes.

As this simple example illustrates, a two-step process is at work here. The first step is bare perception; your visual consciousness simply becomes aware of some raw sensory data. But, soon afterward, the conceptualizing part of your mind dresses up the bare perception in a huge assortment of notions, ideas, preferences, and other dualistic judgments. (Conceptions are called *dualistic* because you can't think of some things as "good" without automatically thinking of others as "bad." This dualistic way of regarding everything is where attachment and aversion begin, and attachment and aversion are the cause of all your problems, according to Buddhism. For more details, see the section, "Wisdom: Removing the veils of misconception," later in this chapter.)

However, a brief moment exists before the conceptualizing mind comes into play when your mind has a glimpse of the object itself, just as it is, with no attached judgments, interpretations, or stories. Continuing the hotel-room painting example, you behold the painting directly, non-dualistically, in this brief moment. This is how the enlightened mind works — unburdened by concepts like good and bad, mine and yours, and so on. (See Chapter 10 for more on the meaning of enlightenment.) Spiritual training is largely a matter of practicing and learning to see things in this direct, non-conceptual manner.

Recognizing the six major types of consciousness

Because the human body comes equipped with five senses, you have five types of sensory awareness, sometimes referred to as the *five sensory consciousnesses.* In some Buddhist texts, they're given the following rather technical names, but their meaning is quite simple, so don't sweat the Latin-sounding names:

✔ **Auditory consciousness:** Perceives (or is aware of) sounds

✔ **Gustatory consciousness:** Perceives tastes (such as bitter, sweet, and sour)

✔ **Olfactory consciousness:** Perceives odors

> ✔ **Tactile consciousness:** Perceives bodily sensations (such as hot and cold, rough and smooth, and so on)
>
> ✔ **Visual consciousness:** Perceives colors and shapes

These five types of sensory awareness, or sensory consciousness, obviously depend upon the health of your body and your sense organs. But a sixth type of awareness does *not* rely so directly on your physical senses to function. This sixth consciousness is called mental consciousness. *Mental consciousness* can be aware of *all* the previously listed items — sights, sounds, odors, tastes, and sensations — and a lot more.

Seeing how certain factors affect mental consciousness

When people speak about the mind, they're generally referring to the sixth consciousness — mental consciousness. For example, if you think about your mother, even if she lives hundreds of miles away — or is no longer living — you may say, "My mother has been on my mind lately." And, if you think about her so strongly that her image appears to you, you're then *seeing* her — not with your *visual* consciousness but with your *mental* consciousness. Or, as the old expression goes, you see her in your *mind's eye.*

This sixth consciousness functions in many different ways and affects everything about you, including the five sensory consciousnesses. For example, *attention* — the ability to turn your mind in a particular direction — is just one of the many different qualities associated with mental consciousness.

Distorted appearances

Needless to say, the five types of sensory awareness depend on the conditions of their related sense organs. When you have a cold, for example, you may lose your sense of smell entirely; the olfactory consciousness continues to function well, but the nasal congestion interferes with your nose's ability to smell. Similarly, as every cook who has ever added too much salt to a soup knows, the tongue can become accustomed to certain tastes. Here's one more: Press your finger against the side of your eye socket in a certain place, then look up into the night sky, and you may see *two* moons instead of one. These are just a few examples that demonstrate how you can't always trust the way things appear to your mind. If you add the various distortions created by your preconceptions and expectations to the mix, you can see that clear, undistorted perceptions aren't as common as you may have thought.

While you're awake, all five types of sensory awareness continually receive information from your environment in the form of raw sensory data, but the amount of attention your mind pays to each piece of information in this constant stream of data can vary quite a bit.

As you read this book, for instance, you pay attention to the shape of the letters and words on the page with your visual consciousness. But how aware are you of the tactile (touch) sensations being produced as the chair (couch, bench, or patio swing) that you're sitting on makes contact with your buttocks? Pause for a moment and think about this. Until we directed your attention to these sensations just now, you were probably oblivious to them. (Of course, the situation would be different if you suddenly sat on a splinter. You wouldn't need anyone's help raising *that* kind of sensation to full awareness.)

This brief demonstration just goes to show that the quality of your sensory awareness varies greatly depending upon many factors. In some cases — such as when you look at optical illusions — you can completely mistake what you perceive. Sense impressions are notoriously unreliable. But under certain very specific circumstances, you may experience a truly astonishing level of heightened sensory awareness. For example, professional athletes often speak about being in the zone. When this happens, all the action (and time itself) seems to slow down, no matter how furious it may be. Athletes claim that they can see everything clearly, as if events were in super-slow motion. The entire playing field and all the other players come into sharp focus. This is when miraculous things can happen.

Such dramatic changes result from an increase in your concentration, another aspect or function of your mental consciousness. *Concentration* is the mind's ability to remain unwaveringly on any object toward which you turn your attention. Like other mental abilities, concentration can be developed (for tips on developing your concentration, turn your attention to Chapter 7). Most of the time your concentration is rather scattered — soft and fuzzy like the light of an ordinary light bulb. But when your concentration becomes sharply focused, it resembles the penetrating light of a laser beam. Some master meditators achieve a particularly concentrated state of mind, *samadhi,* in which their mind is capable of gaining profound insights into reality. (People report that when Einstein was occupied with a particular theoretical problem, he would slip into a *samadhi*-like state of mind for long stretches of time. While in this state, he would remain motionless, oblivious to what was happening around him.)

Feeling around for your emotions

So far, in this introduction to the mind, we've emphasized certain mental activities — such as investigating, concentrating, and conceptualizing — but these activities are certainly not the only functions of the mind. Mental consciousness also includes your attitudes and emotional states, both positive and negative.

Mind, head, and heart

In the West, the tendency is to think of the various aspects of mental consciousness as residing in one of two locations: the head or the heart. Functions such as knowing, thinking, reasoning, remembering, and analyzing — in other words, functions that most people generally think of as mental in nature — are assigned to the head. If someone has sharp academic intelligence, for example, she's often called "a real brain." When people try to figure out a difficult problem or remember something they've forgotten, they often scratch their heads, as if this activity can somehow help them jump start their thought processes.

The emotional center of your being, on the other hand, is often assigned to the heart. When caught in the grip of strong emotions, many people grab or beat their chest. Love, bravery, and a host of other feelings are commonly said to have their home there. In fact, the heart has become the symbol of romantic feelings (think of all those Valentine's Day cards), and the English word *courage* — a brave attitude of mind — is related to the French word *coeur*, meaning "heart."

(It's interesting to note that organs other than the heart have historically been considered the seat of different emotions. In Shakespeare's day, for example, people thought of the liver as the seat of passion. This usage survives today in the insult *lily-livered*, meaning "cowardly" or "timid." Additional expressions, such as "don't vent your spleen" or "you have a lot of gall," indicate that at one time or another specific emotions were associated with other internal organs.)

Note that this sharp distinction between the emotional nature of the heart and the more intellectual qualities associated with the brain and the head doesn't exist in Buddhism. The Sanskrit word *chitta* (which we talk about again in Chapter 14) is translated as "mind," "heart," "attitude," or "consciousness," depending upon its context. Similarly, the Japanese word *shin* can also be translated as both "mind" and "heart."

When Buddhists speak of mental development, they're not talking about becoming smarter. Mental development is about relaxing the hold that the "negative" states have on your mind and increasing the strength of your mind's "positive" qualities. (We put those words in quotation marks because "negative" and "positive" are just relative terms; don't think that one part of your mind is inherently "good" and another part inherently "bad.")

Tapping your emotional intelligence — to borrow a phrase that's become popular recently — is a large part of your mental and spiritual development.

Appreciating the Fundamental Purity of Your Mind

If you've read the previous sections of this chapter, you may have some questions at this point. For example, having recognized that the mind contains both negative *and* positive elements, you may be wondering whether it will always remain like this. Why should this situation ever change? Is there any reason to believe that the admirable qualities that everyone appreciates (such as benevolence) will ever replace those responsible for misery (such as ill-will)? In other words, can spiritual development ever really occur?

Seeing that delusions are baseless

To answer these questions, you first need to recognize that your mind is *always* changing. A powerfully negative state of mind, such as hatred, may arise one moment, but it's certain to subside. That's the very nature of things: They don't last. (As the popular saying goes, "The only thing constant is change.")

Furthermore, none of these negative, disturbing states of mind rests on a solid foundation. They're all based on misconceptions. In fact, jealousy, hatred, greed, and the like lead to suffering and dissatisfaction precisely because they're out of step with reality. They paint a misleading picture of the world. If you happen to find something attractive, the delusion of attachment exaggerates its good qualities until it appears perfect and utterly desirable. Then, if you happen to discover even the slightest flaw in that very same object, your anger and disappointment may make the object appear worthless or even repulsive in your eyes. What a roller coaster ride of emotions! A man who is totally infatuated with a woman, for example, can't find enough words to praise all her wonderful qualities. But, at the divorce proceedings a short time later, he can't come up with a single good thing to say about her.

Because the delusions have no firm foundation in reality, they can be overcome by wisdom. (Or, to put it another way, they can be penetrated by insight.) *Wisdom* is the positive, clarifying mental factor that shows you the way things actually are, not the way you falsely imagine them to be. The other positive states of mind and heart, such as love and compassion, aren't threatened by wisdom at all. In fact, they're strengthened by it.

Indeed, some traditions of Buddhism teach that wisdom, love, and compassion are inherent qualities that lie at the core of your being. These positive qualities are deeper and more reliable than the negative factors, which are understood to be overlays or veils. So change for the better isn't just possible, it's actually a return to your natural, underlying condition.

Finding the sun behind the clouds

From the Buddhist point of view, the underlying nature of the mind itself is essentially pure, uncontaminated, and unconditioned.

A powerful analogy is often used to illustrate this point. First, you need to whip up a memory of prolonged, cloudy weather. (Jon lived in northern England for a number of years, so he finds this exercise easy to do. He can remember someone once saying, "The weather wasn't so bad last week; it only rained twice — once for three days, and once for four!") In these miserable conditions, it sometimes feels like the sun has completely disappeared, that it no longer exists. But, as everyone knows, the sun hasn't really disappeared, no matter what the weather is like. The clouds merely block the sun from your vision. After the winds shift and the clouds part, you can see the sun again, shining as brightly as before.

In a similar fashion, beneath the clouds of delusion that may be disturbing you right now (whatever confused and uncomfortable feelings of greed, anger, jealousy, and the like that you may be experiencing at the moment), an essential purity still exists. This basic purity is unaffected and uncontaminated by obscuring delusions, no matter how violent they may be or how frequently they may disturb your peace of mind. This calm quality is reflected in the Zen expression: "Beneath the one who is busy is one who is not busy."

The spiritual path set forth in Buddha's teachings, therefore, consists mainly of penetrating the inauthentic, nonessential aspects of your experience so that the sunlight of your *Buddha nature* — the fundamental purity of your deepest level of consciousness — can shine forth without interruption. Sometimes folks use an analogy that is more down to earth: Following the spiritual path is likened to peeling away successive layers of an onion!

An important Mahayana Buddhist text entitled *The Peerless Continuum,* attributed to Maitreya Buddha (check out Chapter 3 for more about him), contains a series of poetic analogies for this fundamental purity. In the following analogy (adapted from a translation by Glenn Mullin), the Buddha nature shared by all beings is compared to a treasure lying hidden beneath a poor man's house.

> Under the floor of some poor man's house lies a treasure,
>
> But because he does not know of its existence
>
> He does not think he is rich.
>
> Similarly, inside one's mind lies truth itself
>
> Firm and unfading,
>
> Yet, because beings see it not, they experience
>
> A constant stream of misery.
>
> The treasure of truth lies within the house of the mind;
>
> Buddhas take pure birth into this world
>
> So that this treasure may be made known.

Tracing the Path of Wisdom and Loving-Compassion

How do you go about contacting, revealing, and fulfilling the fundamental purity at the core of your being? This is a big subject, to say the least. We discuss the process of uncovering and realizing your Buddha nature in detail throughout Part IV, but the following statements give you a quick summary:

✔ Cultivate the *wisdom* that unmasks ignorance, the root of all suffering

✔ Generate the *loving-compassion* that opens your heart to others

In a nutshell, the entire path to enlightenment is a *union of wisdom and compassion.* (This concept is often referred to as the *union of wisdom and means* because loving-compassion is the best means for helping others.) In Chapter 14, we explain more about wisdom and compassion, but the following sections should give you a fairly good idea of what they entail.

Wisdom: Removing the veils of misconception

Throughout his teachings, Buddha emphasized that every experience of suffering and dissatisfaction, *without exception,* has its root or source in ignorance.

But the term *ignorance* in this context doesn't simply mean *not* understanding or *not* knowing something, as when a person says, "I never studied trigonometry; I'm completely ignorant of that subject." Instead, ignorance at its most troublesome — the kind of ignorance that Buddha said was responsible for everyone's problems — is the condition of *mis*understanding or *mis*knowing the way that things actually exist. Simply put, this ignorance consists of all of the misconceptions that prevent you from seeing things as they really are. According to the Zen tradition, "All beings have the wisdom and virtue of the fully enlightened one. But because of their distorted views, they don't realize this fact."

When Jon's teacher and beloved spiritual friend, Lama Thubten Yeshe, first came to the United States in 1974, he sometimes used the example of the strained relations between blacks and whites (remember, this was before the term *African American* came into general use) to illustrate the destructive effects of ignorant misconceptions. He pointed out that when a white man and a black man encounter each other on the street, they don't actually see each other at all. All they see are their own *projections* — the distorted images from their own mind that they "project" onto the person they meet.

This blanket of projections — "All black people are like this." "All white people are like that." — prevents each man from seeing the other person *as he actually is,* in all his human complexity. The resulting atmosphere of mistrust, suspicion, and fear produces nothing but problems.

Buddha pointed out three specific types of misconception, or ignorance, that you need to peel away if you want to see things with the enlightened eye of wisdom and experience an end to your problems:

✔ Mistakenly believing that a source of suffering and dissatisfaction is actually a source of true happiness (as when an alcoholic thinks salvation can be found in a bottle)

✔ Mistakenly believing that something that changes from moment to moment is actually permanent, lasting, and unchanging (as when a person thinks his or her youthful good looks will last forever — cosmetic surgery notwithstanding)

✔ Mistakenly believing that people and things possess a substantial, independent, findable *self* — an individual nature of their own, separate from the whole

This last and most fundamental form of ignorance may not be easy to understand. Even the words used to explain it have specific meanings that aren't obvious to the casual observer. But don't worry. We explain this most subtle form of ignorance (and the preceding two) in more detail in Chapter 13.

Loving-compassion: Opening your heart to others

If you find the discussion of ignorance and misconceptions heavy going, this topic may be a welcome change. *Loving-compassion* is a trait that everyone admires — in fact, it may be the most immediately attractive character trait of those who have advanced along a genuine spiritual path, whether they're Buddhist or not.

Witnessing examples of enlightened compassion

Take the example of His Holiness, the Dalai Lama of Tibet (we talk more about him in Chapter 15). Many people consider the Dalai Lama to be a human embodiment of this warm and friendly attitude of loving-compassion. His smiling countenance and genuine concern for others — not to mention his hearty laughter! — may have done more to promote the values of true spiritual development than all the books published on Buddhism in the past several decades. And the reason why this single Tibetan monk has affected so many people from all walks of life is no secret. As he himself has stated many times, "My religion is kindness."

You won't find anything complex or mysterious about this kindness, or humanity, or loving-compassion, or whatever you want to call this warm feeling for others. Loving-compassion can arise spontaneously in all but the most damaged of human hearts. You feel it, for example, when you sense that a small child is in danger or hear an animal howling in pain. Without regard for yourself, and without thinking about it, you immediately want to separate these helpless victims from whatever harm they're experiencing.

The only difference between such spontaneous compassion and that of a fully enlightened being — a Buddha — is its scope. Although generating genuine concern for the welfare of pets, small children, and others you feel close to probably comes easy to you, can you say the same thing about your attitude toward everyone? Be honest with yourself: How do you feel when you hear that someone you dislike — perhaps someone who has recently insulted you — is experiencing a problem or has just had some bad luck? If you immediately feel like rejoicing, the scope of your loving-compassion is limited.

A fully enlightened being, such as Shakyamuni Buddha (one of whose epithets is the Compassionate One), no longer experiences such limitation or prejudice (see Chapter 3 for more about the historical Buddha). The compassionate concern he or she extends to others is not conditional. Whether those in difficulty have been friendly or unfriendly, supporters or sworn enemies, loving-compassion arises for them all equally and spontaneously.

Buddhists are certainly not the only ones who admire this unconditional, altruistic concern for others. The often-quoted commandment given by Jesus, "Love your enemy," is a powerful expression of this same unlimited outpouring from the heart.

Overcoming selfishness and transforming your mind

Praising the beauty of unconditional love and compassion is all well and good. After all, admiring loving-compassion is easy when you see it in the life and deeds of such outstanding spiritual figures as Buddha, Jesus Christ, the Dalai Lama, and Mother Teresa.

But you may be left wondering where all this leaves you. "I know I don't have unconditional love for everyone," you may be thinking. "But what should I do? Feel guilty about it? Should I fake it and pretend to be happy when my rival at work gets promoted instead of me?" Or perhaps you feel like throwing your hands up in despair, thinking, "No one like me could ever hope to live up to the example of people like the Dalai Lama or Mother Teresa. I guess I'm just no good." Or, if you're feeling particularly cynical, you may even think, "I know how selfish I am, and I don't believe anyone else is really any different. All this talk about caring for others and feeling unconditional love for everyone is just a lot of pious pretense. My philosophy is, 'Look out for number one!' I'm a realist, and all this spiritual nonsense is for fools."

How can these doubts, feelings of inadequacy, and objections be answered?

Spiritual progress doesn't happen without preparation. Buddha himself said that it took him *three countless eons* — you can think of that as more than enough time for this planet to come into and go out of existence — from the time he first turned his mind toward the spiritual path to the time he achieved full and complete enlightenment. So expecting instant results isn't realistic. (Many traditions of Buddhism do teach that you can wake up to your enlightened nature in an instant — but it still takes years to fully actualize or embody this awakening in everyday life. For more on the different approaches to enlightenment, see Chapter 10.)

To determine whether a particular path works for you, check to see if it leads to the results it advertises. We're not talking about experiencing blinding flashes of insight or discovering that you've suddenly gained miraculous powers. Simply, are you becoming freer, more relaxed, and more open as a result of following what Buddha — or anyone else, for that matter — has taught? Are your spontaneity and authenticity increasing, your self-preoccupation subsiding, your wisdom growing, your joy and compassion expanding? Results like this won't happen overnight, and you shouldn't obsess about your progress. But, after you've been practicing Buddhism regularly for six months or a year, check in to see how you're doing.

Fortunately, the Buddhist path contains the means for bringing about this desired self-transformation in the form of *meditation,* the heart of Buddhist practice. We give you a sampling of different meditative techniques and general discussions of the role of meditation in spiritual growth throughout this book. In Chapter 7, for example, you can find certain meditative techniques for dealing with the issue at hand — lessening selfishness and expanding the scope of your concern for others.

By putting meditative techniques into practice, you may discover that you do, in fact, have the power to shape the way you habitually react to others, to your surroundings, and even to yourself. With enough perseverance, you may find that you're no longer so compelled to speak, act, or even think in the limited patterns you're used to. Slowly but surely, you may find that you can liberate yourself from suffering and dissatisfaction.

And if, after some time, none of this happens — if you don't experience beneficial results at all — then simply put whatever you've read aside. After all, as the Dalai Lama often says, "You're under no obligation to follow Buddha's teachings. Just try to be a good person. That's enough."

Part II
Buddhism Past and Present

The 5th Wave   By Rich Tennant

BUDDHISM traveled to EUROPE via...
the SPICE ROUTE...   the SILK ROUTE...

...and the little known POGO ROUTE

In this part . . .

Come right in, ladies and gentlemen, and take an engaging and enlightening tour of the history of Buddhism, featuring the life of Buddha himself. Peruse this part and you can also discover Buddha's basic teachings and see how they evolved as Buddhism spread through Asia and made its way through history to the present day.

Chapter 3

Surveying the Life and Teachings of the Historical Buddha

In This Chapter

▶ Glimpsing the early life of Prince Siddhartha

▶ Leaving the royal life behind

▶ Becoming Buddha

▶ Practicing what he preached

Shakyamuni Buddha, the founder of Buddhism, is thought to have lived from 563 to 483 BCE (Before the Common Era, otherwise known as BC). Born Prince Siddhartha, the heir of a ruling family, he gave up the royal way of life in his search for an end to all suffering. This search eventually brought him to the foot of the famous Bodhi tree — *bodhi* means enlightenment — where he reached the full awakening of Buddhahood at the age of 35. This awakening earned him the name *Shakyamuni,* a title that means Enlightened Sage of the Shakyas. (Shakya was the name of the clan to which he belonged.) He then spent the remaining 45 years of his life teaching those who were drawn to the path that leads from suffering and dissatisfaction toward genuine spiritual fulfillment.

At one level, Buddhism is the record of these vast and profound spiritual teachings. (At another level, of course, it's the living embodiment of these teachings in the lives of spiritual practitioners through the ages, including right now.) But perhaps the most inspiring teachings that Shakyamuni Buddha ever gave were contained in the example of his own life. Just as in the case of Jesus, Shakyamuni's life story has been told over and over again during the past 2,500 years, and each culture that Buddhism has entered has responded to his life in its own distinctive way.

In this chapter, we give you a glimpse of Buddha's basic teachings and some of the most significant and inspiring episodes in his life story as it has been passed down through the ages. (The complete story is too extensive to include here. If you want to read more about Buddha's life, check out the list of books in Appendix B.) We also omit many (though not all) of the more miraculous details that appear in the traditional accounts of his life because we believe that, for a Western audience at least, the story reads better without them.

Revealing Buddha's Early Life

Even within the traditional forms of Buddhism, you can find different ways of interpreting the events in Buddha's life and the meaning of his enlightenment.

- ✔ Some traditions claim that the person who was honored as Shakyamuni actually achieved Buddhahood (that is, complete and supreme enlightenment) during a previous lifetime. He then hung out with a host of other Buddhas in a pure state of existence, appropriately called *Tushita* — "the place of happiness" — until the time came for him to descend to Earth and demonstrate to others the spiritual path that he'd already completed. From this point of view, his entire life on Earth was just a demonstration that he put on to show others how to liberate themselves from all limitations and achieve the fulfillment that everyone secretly longs for.

- ✔ According to another explanation, Shakyamuni definitely began his spiritual journey a long time before his 563 to 483 BCE lifetime and achieved significant levels of realization, but he didn't actually complete his journey until he sat under the Bodhi tree in the 35th year of his historical lifetime as the Indian prince Siddhartha.

- ✔ Still other traditions teach that Shakyamuni was an ordinary person like you and me who happened to have uniquely favorable life circumstances (that is, plenty of spare time and energy) and an unflagging dedication to achieve full spiritual realization. Like him, this version suggests, you too can attain enlightenment in a single lifetime.

Though some traditions elevate Buddha to mythic proportions and others view him as a regular guy, they all agree that he exemplifies the ultimate fulfillment of the human condition — complete liberation from confusion and suffering.

The various Buddhist traditions also broadly agree about the events of Shakyamuni's life. To begin with, they say, he was born the son and heir of King Shuddhodana of the North Indian Shakya clan.

An auspicious birth

The Shakya clan lived in the part of North India that borders the present-day kingdom of Nepal. The clan's leader, King Shuddhodana (shoe-*doe*-da-na), was unhappy because he didn't have an heir to his throne. Then one night, his wife, Queen Maya, had a dream in which a beautiful, white, six-tusked elephant appeared to her and dissolved into her body (see Figure 3-1).

Dealing with contradictions

The fact that you can interpret Buddha's life story in different ways raises an interesting point. When you have two different and contradictory ways of explaining something, most people assume that if one explanation is right, the other must be wrong. For example, when you solve the equation $2 + x = 5$, you have only one correct answer; anything other than 3 is wrong. If you're in the habit of applying this strict "mathematical" approach to everything, the different ways of viewing Buddha's life story may make you uneasy. "Only one of those interpretations can be correct," you may insist. "If he's a Buddha, either he reached enlightenment *during* his life as an Indian prince or *before* it. If one answer is right, the other must be wrong. So which is which?"

The Buddhist teachers we've met don't seem to feel uneasy at all about giving different explanations for the same event. We don't mean to imply that they're careless with the truth. A large part of their training involves keenly intelligent investigation of the nature of reality, so their thinking certainly isn't fuzzy. But they accept that the value of a particular explanation depends to a great extent on the intended beneficiary of that explanation. Because people have such different attitudes and inclinations from one another, the explanation that's best for one person may not be particularly helpful for another.

On one occasion many years ago, Jon had the chance to meet privately with the Dalai Lama and ask him some questions. (Chapter 15 has more on this extraordinary person.) During the interview, the Dalai Lama brought up the name of Tsongkhapa, a great Tibetan master, born more than 600 years ago, who had been the teacher of the very first Dalai Lama. Successive Dalai Lamas have always had the utmost respect and devotion for this particular master, and the current Dalai Lama — the 14th in this lineage — is no exception.

In general, Tibetans have great reverence for Tsongkhapa and regard him as a fully enlightened Buddha. They think of him as a human manifestation of Manjushri, the Buddha who embodies the wisdom of all enlightened beings. But on this occasion, the Dalai Lama said (to the best of Jon's memory), "I prefer to think of Tsongkhapa as a regular human being who, through great effort, was able to complete the spiritual path in his lifetime. I find this way of thinking about him more inspiring than thinking that he was born already enlightened."

The queen immediately awoke, and her body and mind were filled with much greater bliss than she'd ever experienced before. The wise men at court all recognized this dream as a sign that the queen was pregnant with a special child who'd someday grow up to be a great leader.

Toward the end of her pregnancy, the queen left her husband's palace in the capital city of Kapilavastu and, with her entourage, headed for her parents' home to give birth — a custom still followed by expectant mothers in many parts of India today. As they passed the beautiful gardens of Lumbini, the queen realized that she could give birth at any minute. So she entered the gardens and, supported by the branch of a tree, the queen gave birth to her son (see Figure 3-2).

Figure 3-1:
Queen
Maya
dreams of a
miraculous
elephant.

Figure 3-2:
Birth in the
Lumbini
gardens.

By all accounts, the child was extremely beautiful, though I'm sure you'd
expect nothing less from the protagonist of this story. Numerous promising
signs accompanied his birth, and in recognition of this, his proud father
named him *Siddhartha* (sid-*hart*-ta), which means "he through whom everything wonderful is accomplished."

Shortly after Siddhartha's birth, Asita (a-*see*-ta), a widely respected religious hermit, unexpectedly arrived in Kapilavastu. He, too, had seen the signs of an auspicious birth and had come to the royal household to check out the child for himself. King Shuddhodana greeted Asita with great courtesy and had the baby brought to him. Imagine, then, the proud parents' shock and fear when the old hermit burst into tears after taking a long look at their cherished boy.

But Asita quickly assured the royal couple that he hadn't seen anything wrong with the child, nor any signs that a disaster awaited him in the future. Quite the contrary! Asita said that the boy displayed remarkable qualities — qualities that would make him an even greater ruler than his father. And, if Siddhartha were to leave the royal life and become a seeker of the truth, he would become even greater than a mere emperor: He'd become the source of spiritual guidance for the entire world!

As for his tears, Asita said, he was weeping for himself. All his life, he had wanted only to follow the spiritual path. But now that he'd met the one person who could reveal this path to him, it was too late. Asita knew that by the time Siddhartha was old enough to begin teaching, he himself would already have died.

An overprotective father

Asita's prophesy both encouraged and bothered the king. He wanted nothing more than to have his son inherit his throne and bring added glory to the royal family. Afterward, when he was an old man like Asita, Siddhartha could retire to the religious life if he wanted. But the king's priorities were clear: His son was to become a powerful and universally admired monarch.

Although he showed signs of great intelligence early on, something in the young prince's character worried his father. The child, who was brought up by his aunt after his mother died, was extraordinarily kind and sensitive, too gentle to be a ruler of nations. He wasn't interested in the rough games of his playmates and preferred spending time caring for the animals that lived on the palace grounds. In one famous episode, the prince saved the life of a swan (see Figure 3-3) that his mean-spirited cousin, Devadatta (day-va-*dah*-ta) had shot. (Throughout Siddhartha's life, Devadatta keeps reappearing as his jealous rival.)

The king was afraid that Siddhartha's sensitive nature would lead him to abandon the royal life prematurely, so he did everything he could to keep the harsh realities of life hidden from his son. For example, if a servant fell ill, the king removed the individual from the palace until the illness had passed. According to the stories, one of the king's gardeners was responsible for clipping and removing any flower the moment it began to wilt. In this way, the prince would be spared the pain of encountering even natural signs of decay.

Figure 3-3:
Saving the
swan from
his cousin.

The prince marries: Imprisoned in palaces of pleasure

Eventually Siddhartha became old enough to think about getting married and raising his own family. The king was sure that these responsibilities would keep him from abandoning the royal life, so he arranged an event where his son could meet the eligible young women in the area. (Think of the ball held in Prince Charming's honor in *Cinderella,* and you'll get the idea.)

At this event, Siddhartha met Yashodhara (yah-*sho*-da-ra), the daughter of a neighboring king. It was love at first sight for both of them. (Later, when fully enlightened, Shakyamuni explained this instant attraction by saying that he and Yashodhara had been married to each other in a number of previous lifetimes. They'd even mated for life as tigers at one point along the way!) But before they could marry and live happily ever after, Siddhartha had to prove that he was worthy of Yashodhara by defeating rival suitors in contests of strength and martial skill. As you may have guessed, Siddhartha was victorious, and he and Yashodhara celebrated a joyous wedding.

Soon Siddhartha and his bride were living in the three pleasure palaces (one each for the hot, cool, and rainy seasons) that his father built for them. The palaces were all located in a vast park surrounded by a wall. In fact, the king had imprisoned Siddhartha in the palaces without the prince realizing it. Because everything and everyone inside these prisons were attractive and captivating, Siddhartha would surely never want to leave — at least, that was the king's plan. And, when Yashodhara gave birth to a son, Rahula (rah-*hu*-la), the plan seemed complete.

Forbidden knowledge revealed: The four visions

But even the best laid plans of courtiers and kings sometimes go astray. One day a palace musician serenaded Siddhartha and his wife with a song about the beauties and wonders of the world. Intrigued by the descriptions, the prince asked his father for permission to journey beyond the palace gates to see for himself what was out there.

By this time, Siddhartha was 29 years old, and his father realized that the time had come for him to see the kingdom he would someday rule. So the king gave permission for the excursion, but not before he arranged for the removal of all unpleasant sites in the area of town that his son would visit. Finally, when everything was prepared, the prince and his charioteer, Channa, rode into town.

At first the visit went very well. The people greeted Siddhartha with great joy and affection, and Siddhartha liked everything that he saw. But then Siddhartha and Channa ran into something that only the two of them seemed to notice — an unfortunate person who was bent over in pain and racked by cough and fever (see Figure 3-4).

Figure 3-4:
Sickness.

Siddhartha asked his charioteer to explain the meaning of this unexpected vision. "This is sickness, my lord," Channa replied. He then went on to explain that sooner or later nearly everyone experiences such disease and discomfort. The prince was startled upon realizing that at any time his family, friends, or companions, or he himself, could experience pain and misery. Suddenly, all his happiness and joy faded away, and the suffering he'd just seen, a suffering that threatened everyone, was all he could think about.

The next two times Siddhartha rode out into the city, he encountered even more disturbing sights — old age and death (see Figures 3-5 and 3-6). The prince was devastated. He wondered how people could act so carefree and happy with the threat of sickness, old age, and inevitable death hanging over their heads.

Figure 3-5:
Old age.

Finally, on his fourth excursion, he discovered what he had to do. On this occasion, he saw a homeless wanderer (see Figure 3-7). Despite his shabby appearance, the man possessed remarkable calm and determination. When the prince asked him who he was, the man replied, "I am one who has given up the household life to search for a way out of the suffering of the world." Siddhartha's destiny was suddenly revealed to him. He knew that he, too, would have to give up his way of life and devote himself completely to the spiritual quest.

Figure 3-6:
Death.

Figure 3-7:
A homeless
seeker of
truth.

Beginning the Quest

The four visions of sickness, old age, death, and a homeless seeker of truth (which we cover in the "Forbidden knowledge revealed: The four visions" section earlier in this chapter) mark the beginning of the prince's spiritual quest. Their importance to the history of Buddhism is undeniable, and depictions of Siddhartha's crucial encounters with them are often painted on the walls of Buddhist temples.

Renouncing the royal life

After Siddhartha knew that he could no longer stay cooped up within the confines of royal life, he went to his father and asked for his permission to leave. The king reacted as many fathers would in similar situations: He blew his stack! He absolutely forbade the prince from leaving and posted a guard at all the palace exits to prevent his departure.

But the prince was determined to go. Siddhartha wanted to hold his infant son in his arms before he left, but he decided against it, fearing that he'd accidentally awaken the sleeping Yashodhara (see Figure 3-8). He silently made his way past the sleeping musicians, dancing girls, and attendants and went outside where he roused Channa (his charioteer) and asked him to prepare his horse, telling him that he wanted to ride out that night. Channa was surprised, but he obeyed the prince.

Figure 3-8:
Bidding silent farewell to his wife and child.

All the people in the palace, including the guards, had fallen asleep (think of the scene in *Sleeping Beauty* where everyone is suddenly overcome by drowsiness), so Siddhartha was able to escape. He and Channa rode through the night, and when they stopped, the prince told Channa to take his horse and his royal jewelry and return to the palace without him. Channa began to cry and asked what he should tell the prince's family, who were sure to be devastated. "Tell them," Siddhartha replied, "that I have not left because I do not love them. It is because I *do* love them all that I must find a way to

Making sense of Buddha's story

Even in this *Reader's Digest* version of Prince Siddhartha's story, you may have already encountered a number of things that challenge your ability to take the account at face value. For example, how could someone as bright as Siddhartha reach the age of 29 and still know nothing about sickness, old age, and death? How could the precautions of even the most overprotective father have shielded him from these grim realities?

Yet despite these objections, the story rings true on a deep level. Even in this modern world of instant, worldwide communication and the information superhighway, people manage to avoid seeing what's right in front of their eyes. The homeless fill the streets, but they remain invisible to most people. In hospitals, where death is everywhere, a dying person's true condition is often kept from him or her. And we've even heard of some communities where funeral processions can take place only at night, to avoid freaking out the general public.

Denial is the name of the game (not to mention a river in Egypt), and you can see the game being played all around you. If and when the reality of life's miseries manages to break through this wall of denial, the experience can be devastating, even life-transforming. Like Siddhartha, many people do turn their attention away from worldly accomplishment and toward the spiritual path as the result of some unexpected experience of suffering or loss. Of course, very few people give up everything at the first glimpse of sickness and death and search for the truth like Siddhartha did.

overcome the sufferings of sickness, old age, and death. If I am successful, I shall return. If I am not, then death would have eventually parted us anyway." Channa could do nothing but return alone.

Siddhartha was now on his own, and the first thing he did was cast off the signs of royalty. He cut his long, flowing hair (see Figure 3-9), exchanged his silk clothing for the rough garb of a forest dweller, and, renouncing his former way of life completely, went in search of someone who could help him in his quest.

After his great renunciation (see the sidebar, "The meaning of renunciation," in this chapter, for more details), Siddhartha met and studied with two renowned spiritual teachers. Though he quickly mastered the meditation techniques they taught him, he realized that, though helpful, the techniques were insufficient to bring him the complete liberation from suffering that he desired. He'd have to go deeper.

Figure 3-9:
The great
renunciation.

Going to extremes: Six years of self-denial

Siddhartha heard of a forest in the kingdom of Magadha where *ascetics* (people who deny themselves even the smallest comforts of life) often gathered to practice and immediately decided to go there and join them. On the way, he caught the attention of the ruler of Magadha, King Bimbisara (bim-bi-*sa*-ra). The king was so impressed by the young man's demeanor and dedication that he immediately asked Siddhartha to stay and help him rule. But Siddhartha politely explained that he'd already given up one royal position and had no desire to assume another. Bimbisara then told Siddhartha that if he ever found what he was looking for, he should return and teach it to him.

When Siddhartha arrived at the forest, he found five other ascetics already engaged in strict practices. The ascetics hoped that by winning complete control over their senses and enduring extreme pain and hardship, they could overcome suffering through the sheer force of willpower. Siddhartha adopted these practices, and soon, his extraordinary concentration and determination convinced his new companions that if any one of them was going to reach the final goal, it would be the newcomer.

Thus began what later became known as the six-year fast. Siddhartha sat exposed to the elements day and night. He ate less and less, eventually consuming nothing but the few seeds that happened to blow into his lap. His body, once so glorious and attractive, became withered and shrunken. Eventually, the practice reduced Siddhartha to little more than a living skeleton, but still he persevered (see Figure 3-10 top picture).

Finally, one day Siddhartha took stock of himself. He discovered that, in his weakened condition, he couldn't think as clearly as before; therefore, he was further from his goal than when he'd started six years ago. Tired and dirty, he decided to refresh himself in the nearby river but nearly drowned before he could pull himself out. As Siddhartha lay on the bank recovering, he realized that if he were ever going to succeed, he'd have to follow the middle way between self-indulgence and extreme self-denial. (Later this phrase, the *middle way,* took on more and more meaning and became the name that Buddha himself often used when referring to his teachings. Even today, Buddhism is widely known as the middle way that avoids all extremes.)

Siddhartha sat up again, and the wife of a local herdsman soon entered the forest with an offering for the local spirits. Her name was Sujata (*sue*-ja-ta), and she had often prayed to the spirits of the forest for a baby boy. Now that she'd given birth to the child she desperately wanted, she came to the forest

The meaning of renunciation

Long hair was one of the major signs of Indian royalty, and Siddhartha's decision to cut it off symbolized his strong determination to change the entire pattern of his life and devote himself to the spiritual quest. Even today, the ceremony marking someone's formal decision to enter the Buddhist way of life often includes having a lock of his or her hair snipped off, in imitation of Buddha's great renunciation. If you choose to become ordained as a celibate monk or a nun, you have your entire head shaved as a sign that you have completely renounced the married life of a layperson.

But renunciation isn't really a matter of having your hair cut or changing your outward appearance in some other way. Nor does it mean that you necessarily have to give up all the things you enjoy. If you like going to the movies or watching football games on TV, for example, you don't have to give up these pleasures when you become a Buddhist. This fact may come as a surprise to some of you, because we occasionally hear people say, "I thought Buddhists were supposed to renounce all that."

Ultimately, renunciation isn't about giving up pleasure or enjoyment at all. In fact, it's quite the opposite! The true meaning of renunciation is the decision to give up suffering. The cause of suffering and dissatisfaction is attachment, and attachment is what you need to give up. If you can enjoy something without becoming attached to it — without letting it become an obstacle to your spiritual progress or a waste of your time and energy — you don't need to give it up.

with a bowl of specially prepared milk rice to thank the spirits for granting her wish. When she saw Siddhartha sitting there, she mistook him for the king of the spirits who helped her and presented the nourishing offering to him with great devotion (see Figure 3-10 bottom picture). When his five ascetic companions saw him accept this fine meal, they were deeply disappointed. Thinking that Siddhartha had abandoned his quest, they left the forest in disgust, determined to continue their practices somewhere else.

Figure 3-10:
The six-year
fast.

After he'd eaten, and his body regained its radiance and strength, Siddhartha thanked the woman. He told her that he wasn't the spirit she thought he was; he was just a human being searching for the path that would end all suffering. And, because of her offering, he felt that he was now strong enough to succeed.

Sitting in the Shade of the Old Bodhi Tree: The Defeat of Mara

Siddhartha crossed the river and made his way to a large fig tree that later became known as the Bodhi tree — the Tree of Enlightenment. With some bundles of grass that he received from a local grass-cutter, he prepared a cushion and sat down facing east. He did this with the confident determination that he wouldn't get up from that seat until he reached full and complete enlightenment.

The classical Buddhist texts describe what happened next with barely-contained excitement. The accounts say that the world held its breath as the moment that would transform history approached. Siddhartha sat under the Tree of Enlightenment, and the spirits of the air rejoiced.

But not everyone was overjoyed. Mara the Tempter, the embodiment of all the evil that plagues the mind, was terrified. He knew that if Siddhartha successfully gained enlightenment, the power that delusion holds over the world would be threatened. Traditional texts use very dramatic imagery to depict the events that follow. As Siddhartha sat in meditation, the sons and daughters of Mara — the whole host of demonic interferences — began their attack, trying to disturb his concentration. (Take a look at Figure 3-11. Siddhartha's seat has been left empty so you, the reader, can imagine sitting there and perhaps experience what it feels like to be surrounded by the forces of delusion.)

Violent storms of hatred arose, but beneath the Bodhi tree, all remained calm. The demonic forces unleashed a barrage of weapons, but they turned into flower petals that fell harmlessly at the feet of the determined meditator. Visions of the most enticing sensual delights then appeared to Siddhartha, along with images of his wife and son, but nothing could break his concentration.

The Bodhi tree today

You can still visit a Bodhi tree in Bodh Gaya (in Northeast India) that grows on the spot where Siddhartha attained enlightenment two-and-a-half millennia ago. It isn't the exact same tree, but it is a direct descendant of the original.

A few hundred years after the time of Buddha, during the reign of King Ashoka (turn to Chapter 4 for the exploits of this important monarch), Buddhism spread to the island nation now known as Sri Lanka (formerly Ceylon). At that time, a cutting from the Bodhi tree was planted on the island and became the focal point of a famous Buddhist shrine. Centuries later, when the original tree in Bodh Gaya had been destroyed, a cutting from Ceylon's Bodhi tree was brought back to India and planted at the original site. This tree toppled during restoration work begun in 1877, but a sapling from it was planted in its place. That's the tree you can still visit today.

Mara had just one weapon left — the seeds of doubt. Dismissing his legions, Mara appeared before Siddhartha and addressed him directly. "Show me one witness who can testify that you deserve to succeed where all others have failed," he demanded mockingly. Siddhartha responded wordlessly. He simply stretched forth his right hand and touched the earth (see Figure 3-12), because the earth itself was the witness that Siddhartha had practiced the virtues (over countless lifetimes) that would now empower his attainment of Buddhahood. Mara was defeated and faded away like a bad dream.

Figure 3-11:
Being attacked by the forces of delusion.

Figure 3-12:
The defeat
of Mara.

It was the night of the full moon in the fourth Indian month (which falls in May or June of our calendar). As the moon rose higher and higher in the sky, Siddhartha's meditative concentration deepened. The fire of his growing wisdom burnt away whatever layers of unknowing still obscured his mind. He directly and unmistakenly perceived the stream of his past lives and understood exactly how past actions lead to present results. He saw how attachment, the source of suffering, is rooted in ignorance. As his wisdom got rid of subtler and subtler levels of this ignorance, his mind grew increasingly luminous. Finally, as the moon was setting and the sun of the next day was rising, Siddhartha attained the ultimate goal — full and complete enlightenment. No longer a mere prince, he was now an Awakened One, a Buddha.

Benefiting Others: Buddha's Career in Full Gear

All the events in Buddha's life, from the moment of his birth as Prince Siddhartha up until his defeat of Mara under the Bodhi tree (as described in the preceding sections), were directed to one ultimate goal: the ability to help others free themselves from suffering. Now that he had achieved Buddhahood and gained the limitless wisdom, compassion, and skill to benefit others to the maximum extent, he was ready to begin his enlightened career in earnest. But was the world ready for him?

Providing spiritual guidance: Turning the wheel of dharma

For seven weeks, Shakyamuni Buddha (the former Siddhartha) remained in the vicinity of the Bodhi tree, absorbed in the limitless awareness only a fully awakened being experiences. According to traditional accounts, Buddha thought that because no one else was likely to exert the extraordinary effort required to achieve the goal he'd attained, enjoying the fruits of enlightenment himself would be the best way to go.

As if in response to this unspoken thought, the gods of heaven appeared to Shakyamuni and, on behalf of the world, begged him to reconsider: "While it is true that beings' minds are obscured, the coverings of some are less thick than others. Certainly there are those who can benefit from your realizations. For their sake, please teach us what you have learned." Buddha immediately agreed.

Shakyamuni had always intended to share with others whatever he discovered. His entire motivation, from the beginning, was the compassionate wish to benefit others in whatever way he could. His apparent hesitancy to teach was only a ploy; he knew that it wasn't proper or beneficial for a Buddha to teach those who didn't first express a sincere interest in gaining spiritual freedom. Without a readiness to learn and a willingness to change on the part of the student, even the most powerful teachings will be ineffective. For this reason, even today, most Buddhists generally refrain from teaching unless others request that they do so. In fact, in some traditions, disciples have to make such requests three times before the teacher will agree to give instruction.

When Buddha thought about which individuals would be ready to receive his initial teachings, he first considered the two teachers he had studied with but realized that they already had passed away. So he chose his five former companions who were continuing their strict ascetic practices without him in Sarnath — near the ancient Indian holy city of Benares.

The five ascetics were staying in the Deer Park at Sarnath when they saw Buddha approach. Still believing that he'd given up the spiritual quest, they resolved not to welcome back this "quitter." But they couldn't help noticing, even from a distance, that a profound change had come over him. He radiated such peaceful assurance and benevolence that they had to greet him with great respect and offer him a seat of honor among them. Then, in response to their request to reveal his experiences, he delivered his first formal teaching as an Awakened One, a Buddha.

Of all the activities of a Buddha, *turning the wheel of the dharma* (giving spiritual instruction) is number one because an enlightened being is most helpful to others when providing spiritual instruction. As Shakyamuni himself later pointed out, a Buddha can't remove another's suffering the way you can remove a thorn from another's flesh. (If he could, everyone's problems would already be gone; the compassionate Buddha certainly would've removed them all by now.) But what a Buddha *can* do — and do with matchless skill — is reveal the path to others in ways that are best suited to each person's individual makeup.

Not every teaching that a Buddha gives is verbal. A Buddha provides spiritual inspiration and instruction by his or her presence and can convey great meaning even through silent gestures (see the famous story of the origin of Zen Buddhism in Chapter 5). But, during his lifetime, Shakyamuni Buddha did deliver many formal discourses, the first of which he gave at the Deer Park in Sarnath. The theme of this discourse was the *four noble truths,* a theme that he elaborated on and refined in the countless other teachings he gave during the remaining 45 years of his life. (The "Understanding the Four Noble Truths" section later in this chapter delves into this subject in greater detail.)

Founding the sangha community

As Buddha had predicted, his five former companions were particularly ripe for spiritual instruction. Just a few words by Buddha were enough to trigger deep insights into his teachings. They gave up all activities that Buddha taught were harmful to the welfare of others and to their own spiritual evolution, took ordination as monks, and became the first members of the *sangha,* the Buddhist spiritual community.

As more and more people became inspired by Buddha's wisdom and compassion and benefited from his teachings, the sangha community grew larger and larger. This growth attracted the attention (and often aroused the jealousy) of other established teachers who, together with their own disciples, came to test and challenge Buddha. Recognizing that Buddha was indeed the real thing — a fully awakened master — many of the rival teachers and their followers became Buddha's disciples. The sangha grew by leaps and bounds, eventually numbering in the tens of thousands.

Who is the true brahmin?

If you'd been born in ancient India, you would've become a member of the caste — the priests, warriors, merchants, or menial workers — to which your parents belonged. Upward mobility didn't exist in this society; your birth determined everything. At the top of the heap were the priests, or *brahmins*. As a proud sign of their high rank, priests wore a special looped cord known as the *brahmin's thread*. Possession of such a thread automatically made the person wearing it an object of the highest respect.

Buddha himself was not a brahmin. As Prince Siddhartha, he had been born into the ruling warrior caste, one level below that of the priesthood. Buddha taught that an individual's moral character, not caste, determines his or her worth. So the true brahmin — the person worthy of the greatest respect — isn't the one wearing a special thread or born into a particular family. As he said, "He who is tolerant to the intolerant, peaceful to the violent, who is free from greed, who speaks words that are calm, helpful, and true and that offend no one — him I call a brahmin." These democratic sentiments, which sound so right to modern ears, were threatening to the status quo of his time. Twenty-five centuries later, they inspired many Indians (including the so-called "untouchables") who felt oppressed by the caste system to quit their traditional faith and adopt Buddhism.)

In many respects, this sangha community was quite revolutionary. Buddha accepted disciples from all levels of society and treated them with equal concern and respect. This behavior ran counter to the separation between high and low fostered by the rigid Indian caste system, which Buddha often preached against. His acceptance of women as disciples and his belief that they were as capable of spiritual development as men was equally unusual, given the male-dominated society of the time.

Knowing that the more conservative elements of Indian society would have great difficulty accepting a sangha that included women, Buddha hesitated for quite a while before ordaining any of his women followers. But eventually he established an order of nuns, and the aunt who raised him became its first member.

In addition to a growing community of monks and nuns, many laypeople also became followers of Shakyamuni Buddha. One of these individuals was King Bimbisara of Magadha, the monarch who'd offered to share his kingdom with Prince Siddhartha before the six-year fast began. When the king became a disciple and patron of Buddha, a large number of his subjects followed suit, and the Buddhist community suddenly grew even larger (see Chapter 4 for more on the growth of the Buddhist community in India).

Eventually Buddha returned to Kapilavastu, where he grew up and where many members of his family and clan still lived. Many of them became his followers, including his son, Rahula, who received ordination as a monk. His father, who'd wanted Prince Siddhartha to rule his kingdom, also became one of his son's disciples, though his pride in being known as the father of Buddha hampered his spiritual progress somewhat. Devadatta (Buddha's cousin and lifelong rival) also joined the community, but, jealous of Buddha's popularity, set himself up as a rival teacher, causing a split within the sangha. (For more about some of the other significant events in Buddha's life and teaching career, see Chapter 9 where we describe the major places of Buddhist pilgrimage.)

Listening to Buddha's final message: All things must pass

Finally, at the age of 80, after a lifetime of selfless, compassionate service to others, Shakyamuni decided that he'd helped everyone he could. So just as he'd taught others how to live with peaceful minds and open hearts, he would now demonstrate how to die the same way.

He told his faithful attendant Ananda that he wanted to return to the place of his birth for the final time. On their way, Shakyamuni and Ananda stopped at the village of Kushinagar where Buddha announced that this was the place where he'd breathe his last. Choosing a spot between two large trees, he laid down on his right side (in what's sometimes called the lion posture) and prepared to pass away. Yet, even on the last day of his life, Buddha continued helping others, clearing away the doubts an old man named Subhadda had about the teachings and leading him onto the path to liberation.

Finally, with many of his disciples and the people of the nearby villages gathered around him, Buddha spoke his final words, reminding them all of the essential truths he'd been teaching throughout his life:

> All things are impermanent,
>
> Work out your own salvation with diligence.

Entering deeper and deeper meditative states, Buddha passed away calmly on the anniversary of his enlightenment 45 years earlier. Many of his followers were overcome by grief. But some — those who understood his teachings well — remained at peace. His disciples cremated his remains (see Chapter 9 for more details) and placed his ashes within monuments (*stupas*) throughout the lands that he'd blessed with his presence.

Envisioning the Future

Shakyamuni Buddha never said he was unique.

When one of his disciples praised him extravagantly, claiming that no one anywhere was like him, Buddha admonished him, pointing out that the disciple had no way of knowing whether the statement was true. "Instead of praising me," Buddha suggested, "it would be far more beneficial for you simply to put my teachings into practice."

Shakyamuni also pointed out that Buddhas repeatedly appear in different times and in different places throughout the universe to help awaken those who are ready to benefit from spiritual instruction. For example, in the present age (or *kalpa,* meaning an exceedingly long period of time measured in millions of years), no less than 1,000 Buddhas are destined to appear. Their purpose is to introduce the dharma (or, as it is usually stated, "set the wheel of dharma in motion") where the teachings haven't yet appeared or have declined. (In addition to these 1,000 "founding" Buddhas, countless other men and women will realize Buddhahood by putting the dharma taught by these founders into practice. If you practice wholeheartedly, you could be one of them! But the wheel-turning Buddhas are the ones who get it all rolling.)

Presently, the Buddha in this kalpa is Shakyamuni because, even though he passed away 2,500 years ago, the dharma he introduced still exists and people continue to benefit from it. According to some Buddhist traditions, Shakyamuni is the fourth of the 1,000 wheel-turning Buddhas, and he predicted that one of his own disciples, Maitreya (see Figure 3-13), would be the fifth.

The advent of Maitreya

The name Maitreya comes from the Sanskrit word *maitri,* which means loving-kindness. Maitreya received his name because loving-kindness — the wish for others to be happy — was his main spiritual practice. (In Pali, the other ancient Indian language in which the Buddhist teachings were recorded, the term for this radiant, open-hearted quality is *metta.*)

According to some Buddhist traditions, Maitreya had already completed his own path and achieved Buddhahood long before he appeared on Earth as one of Shakyamuni's main disciples. Why would someone who already attained the Supreme goal of enlightenment play the part of another Buddha's student? The traditional explanation is that Maitreya was acting as a role model, demonstrating to Shakyamuni's other disciples how a compassionate *bodhisattva* — an enlightenment-bound being — should train under the guidance of his or her spiritual master. (According to other traditional accounts, however, Maitreya is a bodhisattva who, through continuous practice, will eventually discover the dharma for himself and become a Buddha.)

Even now, Maitreya remains a source of inspiration and hope for many of Shakyamuni's followers. Realizing that they may not be able to complete the spiritual path in their present lifetime, they pray to be reborn in the first circle of Maitreya's disciples when he reappears as a Buddha to complete their training under his guidance.

Different beliefs abound concerning when Maitreya is due to reappear on Earth. Some people think that he won't be here for several thousand years, but others say the wait is just a matter of a few hundred years. Still others — who perhaps share in the hopes surrounding the start of the new millennium and the dawning of the Aquarian age — believe he's already on Earth and will soon make his presence known.

Figure 3-13:
Maitreya,
the future
Buddha.

All this speculation aside, some traditional Buddhist sources say that Maitreya currently resides in the pure realm called Tushita. He'll remain in this cosmic way station (as Shakyamuni did before him) until the proper moment arrives for him to descend to the human realm to be born. (To indicate that this Buddha-in-waiting is prepared to come to the aid of the world, Maitreya is sometimes depicted as if he were just about to stand up. This sets him apart from other Buddhas, most of whom are shown seated in the cross-legged meditation posture described in Chapter 7.)

Degeneration, followed by hope

According to some accounts, the era of Shakyamuni's teachings is half over; in another 2,500 years, the dharma he introduced will disappear from this planet completely. As the times grow more and more degenerate — in other words, as hatred, greed, and ignorance increase in strength — the world will be transformed into a battlefield. Epidemic diseases and natural calamities will become more severe and frequent, and people will begin dying of old age while they're still relatively young.

When things become as bad as they are bound to get, and people have grown stunted and deformed by their overwhelming negativities, Maitreya will show himself. Although fully enlightened, he won't appear as a Buddha at first. He'll simply show up as someone taller and more attractive than everyone else. Impressed by his beauty, people will ask him how he got to be so good looking. He will reply, "Through the practice of morality, avoiding giving harm to any living being."

As more and more people are inspired to take up the practice of morality and loving-kindness, the age of degeneration will come to an end. Peacefulness will replace belligerence, and as a result, people's life span, health, and general good fortune will increase. Finally, when all the proper conditions are in place and potential disciples are sufficiently ripe for guidance, Maitreya will reappear as a glorious wheel-turning Buddha and usher in the next golden age of dharma.

Understanding the Four Noble Truths

In his first discourse at the Deer Park in Sarnath (see the "Providing spiritual guidance: Turning the wheel of dharma" section earlier in this chapter), Shakyamuni introduced the *four noble truths,* the basis of all the rest of his teachings. The more you understand these four truths, the better you can understand what Buddhism is all about. They are the truths of

The future lies in your hands

Some Buddhist teachings present an apocalyptic vision of the future, in which conditions of this planet go from bad to worse, but don't let such visions freak you out. For one thing, such accounts are just part of Buddhist mythology — you don't need to take them as unarguable truth. Some schools of Buddhism even ignore such mythic stories entirely. For another thing, according to the teachings on karma (which we discuss in Chapter 12), you have the power to choose whether to share in these miserable conditions or not. If your own mind is peaceful and loving, you'll create the conditions for a comfortable future no matter what happens.

In the Buddhist view, the world is limitless, containing many more possibilities than appear to ordinary thought and perception. For instance, from a simple historical perspective, Shakyamuni Buddha's life is over and done with: He has already been born, taught the dharma to others, and passed away. But according to Buddha's teachings, the universe contains countless world systems, and in many of these systems, Shakyamuni and others are currently performing the various beneficial deeds of an awakened being. Therefore, even if conditions on this planet deteriorate and his teachings disappear, people who have created sufficiently positive karma will be reborn in a world where the teachings still flourish and conditions are favorable for spiritual practice.

Of course, this possibility isn't a reason to sit back idly while things here get worse — as many folks seem to do nowadays — and let the world go to hell in a hand basket. Devoted followers of the compassionate Buddha don't give up on the world. Instead, they do whatever they can to turn back the tide of suffering and protect the environment and all the beings who live in it from disaster. The point, however, is that only a profound change in attitude and behavior can provide real protection from suffering, whether for an individual or an entire planet. Through the practice of insight and loving compassion, you can transform the world into a pure land, but if you allow selfishness and harmfulness to run rampant in your life, suffering is the inevitable result, both for yourself as an individual and for the world as a whole.

✔ Suffering

✔ The cause of suffering

✔ The cessation of suffering

✔ The path that leads to the cessation of suffering

The truth of suffering

The first of the four noble truths acknowledges the widespread experience of *duhkha*. This Sanskrit term (*dukkha* in Pali) is most commonly translated as "suffering," but it has a much broader range of meaning. In particular, *duhkha* conveys a sense of dissatisfaction about things not being the way you want them to be.

Certain experiences in life are so obviously painful and miserable that no one has any difficulty identifying them as suffering. For example, a headache isn't fun. When you have that familiar throbbing in your skull, sometimes all you can think about is how much you want the pain to go away. You demand relief immediately, if not sooner. And a headache is a relatively minor thing when compared to many physical illnesses.

Even when physical discomfort is absent, countless mental and emotional difficulties arise. In his teaching at Sarnath, Buddha specifically mentioned that these things are unpleasant:

- ✔ Meeting with what you dislike
- ✔ Being parted from what you like
- ✔ Not getting what you want

If you consider how much of your life (and the lives of the people you know) is occupied with just these three types of unpleasant experiences, you can start to realize that there's more than enough *duhkha* to go around.

But, if Shakyamuni Buddha was as compassionate as he's made out to be, why did he draw attention to something as distasteful as suffering and make it the *first* of the noble truths? Partly because humans have such a large capacity for self-deception. Like the person who refuses to admit to himself that he has a life-threatening disease until it's too late to do anything about it,

---

Taking myth and doctrine with a grain of salt

Throughout this book, but especially in this chapter, we mix the practical teachings of Buddha designed to help you deal with your suffering and confusion with the mythology that has accrued over several thousand years. Though the elaborate stories and myths may inspire you to put the teachings into practice, you don't have to believe them to practice Buddhism. In fact, Buddha himself didn't teach doctrine or dogma that he required his disciples to believe. Instead, he constantly encouraged them to question any concept to make sure that it agreed with their own experience and understanding. Then, he recommended putting the ideas into practice to make sure that they actually worked.

In one famous story, Buddha was asked a series of theoretical questions about reincarnation and the size of the universe. Instead of answering in his usual way, he remained silent. When pressed further, he told the following story. Suppose someone shoots you with an arrow that you know to be laced with a fast-acting poison. Do you spend time trying to find out the name and caste of the archer, where he comes from, and of what materials his bow and arrow were constructed? Of course not. Instead, you act as quickly as possible to remove the arrow and find an antidote to the poison.

In the same way, argued Buddha, it can be a waste of precious time to pursue the answer to hypothetical questions when you have been shot with the poison arrow of greed, hatred, and ignorance and have only so much time to put an end to your suffering!

The truth about the four truths

Many writers and teachers have their own favorite English translations for the key terms that crop up over and over again in the traditional Buddhist texts. For example, when talking about what is known as *dana* in both Pali and Sanskrit — the two major Indian Buddhist languages — one person may call it "generosity," another "charity," a third "giving," and a fourth may even opt for "open-handedness." Plenty of other examples of the translation question exist. For instance, although *patience, tolerance,* and *forbearance* mean quite different things in English, they've all been used to translate the Sanskrit term *kshanti,* one of the main antidotes to anger. Even the Sanskrit word *duhkha* (*dukkha* in Pali), which is central to Buddha's teachings and has generally been translated as "suffering," has also been rendered as "misery," "dissatisfaction," "stress," and even "oppression."

But very little variation is found from one writer to the next when it comes to the four noble truths. Almost everyone refers to them simply as the *four noble truths.* Yet something is misleading about this phrase. These words seem to imply that suffering, its cause, and so on are themselves noble, but this isn't the intended meaning at all. The word *noble* (*arya*) doesn't refer to the truths of suffering and so on, but to the individual who is spiritually advanced enough to see these truths directly.

In the Buddhist scheme of things, an *arya* (a noble one) is someone who has peeled away the layers of misconception blanketing his or her mind and can, therefore, for the first time, look upon ultimate reality directly (see Chapter 14). With this clear understanding, certain truths that previously had been hidden from view finally appear directly and unmistakenly. So the *four noble truths* are actually the *four* things that the *noble ones* see as *true*. But people stick with the more compact term *four noble truths* for obvious reasons!

many people will do almost anything to avoid taking a close look at themselves and the way they truly live their lives. They just stumble along from one unsatisfactory situation to the next. Whenever they get a whiff of the flawed nature of their existence, they shrug it off and reach for another drink — or another cigarette, or TV show, or some similar distraction.

Buddha's intention was to help people wake up from their denial. By mentioning suffering and dissatisfaction so prominently, he wasn't trying to bum anyone out. Instead, he knew that when you squarely face the truth of your suffering, an extraordinary thing can happen: You can cut right through it! As a number of contemporary teachers have pointed out, even though pain is inevitable in life, suffering itself is entirely optional. Although you may not be able to choose what happens to you, you can definitely take control of your response. And this makes all the difference in the world.

Also, keep in mind that even suffering can have its good points. Sometimes, when things are going along relatively smoothly for you, you can more easily ignore the difficulties of others. But, when you yourself encounter these same difficulties, you're more likely to open your heart and experience empathy. As your heart opens, your loving-compassion also grows stronger. If you can use your difficulties to help generate genuine and deeply felt compassion for others — one of the most beautiful and liberating of all spiritual qualities — then your suffering was definitely worthwhile.

The truth of suffering's cause

Having pointed out how pervasive suffering is, Buddha then addresses the unspoken question, "Where does all this misery come from? What is its origin, its cause?" To answer this question, he states the second noble truth: All suffering, without exception, comes from desirous attachment. In other words, as long as you allow insatiable desires for this and that to lead you around by the nose, you'll be dragged from one unsatisfactory life situation to the next, never knowing true peace and satisfaction.

What Buddha is saying, in essence, is that if you want to find the true source of your problems, you have to look inside yourself. Suffering isn't a punishment inflicted upon you by other people, life circumstances, or some supernatural force outside yourself. Nor does suffering come to you for no reason at all; suffering isn't a random occurrence in a meaningless universe governed by the laws of chance (even if it has become fashionable to think so). Instead, the suffering or dissatisfaction you experience is directly related to attitudes that arise within your own heart and mind. (See Chapter 12 where we discuss the karmic laws of cause and effect in more detail.)

You can get an idea of the relationship between attachment and dissatisfaction by thinking of some common, everyday occurrences. For example, many people head for the nearest mall when they feel restless or dissatisfied. They look for something, anything, that can fill up the hollow feeling inside of them. Perhaps they spot a shirt and think how great it'll look on them. They begin to fantasize, imagining how this piece of cloth will bolster their self-esteem, make them attractive to others, and perhaps even help them catch the man or woman of their dreams and change the course of their lives!

This example may seem exaggerated, but that's exactly what desirous attachment does. It exaggerates everything. You cling to your possessions, your appearance, and other people's opinions of you in the hopes of satisfying a deep, inner longing. But the more you cling, the more disappointed you become. Why? Because everything is constantly changing, and nothing can possibly live up to the unrealistic expectations you place on it. You may walk out of that mall holding the new dress or sweater you just bought, but you're really grasping onto an illusion. And sooner or later — usually sooner — the illusion will let you down.

So the problem isn't the piece of clothing, or even the fact that you find it attractive and derive pleasure from it. The problem is your attachment to it and the unrealistic expectations this attachment can cultivate. All the grief you experience afterwards — when the dress or shirt reveals its impermanent nature by fading, fraying, or going out of style — is the direct result of your clinging.

When Buddha spoke about desire, or clinging, as the cause of suffering, he was thinking of a lot more than the effects of mall fever. Ultimately he was talking about the way all unenlightened beings (that is, all those who've not yet fully awakened to reality; see Chapter 10 for more on the meaning of enlightenment) grasp onto an unrealistic image of who and what they are. Behind the thought, "I hope I look attractive in that shirt," is a much deeper level of grasping onto one's overly concrete sense of *I* itself. By clinging to this false sense of self, you not only set yourself up for disappointment and suffering as you go through this life, but you also condemn yourself to wander endlessly from one unsatisfactory life to the next. (Head over to Chapter 13 for more on this cycle of dissatisfaction and Buddha's solution for breaking free of it.)

The truth of suffering's cessation

The third of the noble truths is Buddha's bold declaration that there is indeed an end to suffering. (What a welcome relief after the first two rather sobering truths of suffering and its cause!) We're not just talking about a brief vacation from the cycle of dissatisfaction, but a complete cessation. Buddha was confident in this declaration because he had experienced this liberation and saw clearly that nothing prevents everyone else from doing the same.

The solution lies in uprooting desirous attachment from your heart and mind. A simple way of putting this: Let go! Let go of all unrealistic expectations. Let go of all harmful behavior. Let go of your clinging attitude toward people, possessions, and even your own body. Let go, finally, of yourself! Buddha taught that removing all ignorantly produced attachment from your mind in this way is like damming a river at its source: The flow of unwanted suffering will dry up by itself.

Distinguishing between attachment and desire

Many people mistakenly believe that Buddhism is down on desire. If it were, there wouldn't be any Buddhists left! The problem, according to Buddha, lies not with your preferences and wishes, but with your relationship to them. If you don't get what you want, do you get angry or depressed? Or have you developed the inner resilience and detachment necessary to accept life the way it presents itself?

After all, you have only limited control over your circumstances, so the more attached you are to having things be a certain way, the more you will inevitably suffer. The secret to a happy life, taught Buddha, is to want what you have and not want what you don't have. A simple formula, perhaps — but one that can take a lifetime of spiritual practice to master!

We know, we know, giving up attachment isn't simple. You've been grasping onto an unrealistic sense of self far longer than you can remember, so breaking this habit isn't going to be easy. But it can be done, and Buddha is proof. Two and a half millennia have passed since Shakyamuni walked this Earth, but his enlightened example still inspires people. And, if you meet those who have trained themselves well in the methods Buddha taught — the same methods he followed — you may be fortunate enough to see that "letting go" leads to some pretty inspiring results. (Even better — you can follow these methods and experience the same results firsthand.)

The truth of the path

The fourth and final noble truth contains the do-it-yourself instruction manual that leads to the cessation of suffering and the experiences of spiritual liberation and enlightenment that go along with it. (See Chapter 10 for more about the various levels of spiritual attainment.) These instructions are presented in terms of the eight-fold path, symbolized by the eight spokes of the wheel of dharma (see Figure 3-14), which we outline later in this section.

Figure 3-14:
The eight-
spoked
wheel of
dharma.

The spiritual life, whether Buddhist or otherwise, is often referred to as a path because it leads you where, in your heart of hearts, you want to go. But don't make the mistake of thinking that this path is outside of you. Like the cause of suffering, the path that leads to the highest spiritual goals is within you — in what you think, say, and do.

Also, even though you may be following a path, you're not really going anywhere. It's not as if suffering is somewhere over here and liberation is in some other country. Some Buddhist traditions stress this point by speaking about the "pathless path" or the "path without a goal." These paradoxical phrases serve to emphasize the immediacy of spiritual experience and help free you from the expectation — which can itself be a hindrance — that enlightenment is somewhere other than right here, right now.

With these caveats in mind, here are the eight divisions of the path leading to the cessation of suffering:

- **Right view:** The path begins when you see for yourself that suffering and dissatisfaction infect the entirety of ordinary, unenlightened existence. If you want to improve your situation, you need to cultivate the insightful wisdom that maintains this correct view clearly.

- **Right intention:** Right intention — or right thought — involves giving up selfish attitudes that lead to further suffering and replacing them with their opposites. In place of thoughts that cause harm to yourself and others, you cultivate the intention to bring happiness to all.

- **Right speech:** Because what you say can have a powerful effect on others and affect your own spiritual evolution as well, cultivating right speech is important. This cultivation involves speaking words that are true, pleasing to listen to, and most important, beneficial to others.

- **Right action:** Just as right speech means to avoid causing harm with what you say, right action means avoiding causing harm with what you do. So in place of physically hurting others through your actions, you seek to help and protect them.

- **Right livelihood:** You can earn your living in many different ways, but if you're intent on gaining more than just material wealth, avoid occupations that involve harm and deception. Naturally, a profession in which you can be of service to others is an excellent way of supporting yourself. But, even if you don't have that kind of job, you can still make sure that your dealings with others are honest and kind.

- **Right effort:** This type of effort concerns your spiritual practices. Instead of being lazy, exert continuous, yet relaxed (some would say "effortless") effort to be aware of what's arising in your mind. If it's negative, don't let it overwhelm you; if it's positive, rejoice!

- **Right mindfulness:** Mindfulness — playing close attention to what's happening right now — is essential at all levels of spiritual practice. Instead of holding onto thoughts of the past or fantasizing about the future, keep your attention focused on the present moment. This advice applies not only to your meditation practice, but to your everyday activities as well. In fact, with strong mindfulness, your everyday activities themselves actually become a form of meditation.

✔ **Right concentration:** In order to develop deep insight into the nature of reality, the focus of your mind must become sharp and free of distraction and dullness. Through practicing right concentration, you will eventually be able to place your full attention on any object you choose, and keep it there without wavering. The ability to focus your attention in this way is what enables you to gain life-altering insight into the true nature of things. Without right concentration, whatever understanding you have will remain superficial and ineffectual.

There, in brief, are all the elements of the spiritual path. How Buddha and later masters elaborated upon them and shaped them into the various Buddhist traditions that have appeared over the past 2,500 years is explained in Chapters 4 and 5 and 11 through 14.

Chapter 4

Charting the Development of Buddhism in India

*B*uddhism began 2,500 years ago with one person's experience of spiritual awakening while sitting quietly under a tree. During his lifetime, Shakyamuni Buddha had contact with thousands of people, and by the time of his passing, the influence of his teachings extended throughout a handful of kingdoms in North India. But, in the centuries that followed, Buddhism spread throughout India and the rest of Asia. And today, millions and millions of people around the world practice Buddhism in one form or another — though, interestingly enough, it has only recently been reintroduced into India itself 800 years after disappearing from the country where it was born.

Buddha himself didn't practice "Buddhism" — he merely taught what he called the *dharma,* the truth of existence. His disciples and their successors interpreted, clarified, and ultimately diversified Buddha's teachings, creating a variety of Buddhist schools and traditions that took the dharma in directions Buddha himself may not have anticipated.

In this chapter, we chronicle the growth and development of Buddhism. We concentrate on the changes Buddha's teachings underwent as they spread throughout India (and then to Sri Lanka) in the first centuries after his passing. In Chapter 5, we follow Buddhism as it transformed and adapted to the cultures of Southeast Asia, China, Korea, Japan, Tibet, and finally the West.

You may wonder what relevance the ancient history of Buddhism has today. But, as you read this abbreviated account of its development, we think that you'll discover issues and themes that have timeless significance — things that keep reappearing in Buddhist practice and thought wherever and whenever the religion takes root. Besides, it's a fascinating story.

Convening the First Buddhist Council

Before Buddha died — or, as Buddhist scriptures put it, before he entered *parinirvana* (final liberation) — he told his disciples not to worry about being leaderless after he was gone. He said that the dharma teachings themselves would be their guide. So, after Buddha's passing, the Venerable Mahakashyapa, the monk chosen by Buddha to preside over the community of monks, gathered 500 of Buddha's most spiritually advanced disciples to collect and preserve the precious teachings that make up the dharma.

Gathering the council

This important gathering, known in Buddhist history as the First Council, was held at Rajgir, the capital of the kingdom of Magadha (see Chapter 9 for present-day Rajgir pilgrimage info). At the council, Mahakashyapa selected some of Buddha's foremost disciples to recite from memory the teachings they had heard. Because Ananda, Buddha's cousin, who had been his personal attendant and constant companion for more than 30 years, had heard more of the Master's discourses than anyone else, he went first.

The 500th arhat

When Mahakashyapa convened the First Council, he invited 500 of Buddha's most advanced disciples to attend. These invitees were monks who had experienced *nirvana* (liberation), thereby becoming *arhats:* those who have completely overcome suffering and its causes (see Chapter 10 for more on the stages leading up to arhatship). But there was a problem: Ananda, who was renowned for his powers of memorization and (as Buddha's personal attendant for more than 30 years) had heard more of Buddha's discourses than anyone else, was not yet an arhat. He still had not reached nirvana, and was therefore not qualified to attend this special council.

To deal with this situation, Mahakashyapa apparently instructed Ananda to engage in intensive meditation practice until he'd completed his training. Some legends claim that Mahakashyapa pushed Ananda into a kind of spiritual crisis before sending him off by reminding him of some of the mistakes he'd made while attending Buddha. Other versions say that Ananda confessed his shortcomings after his training was done. In any case, Ananda's efforts apparently paid off. After just a few hours of concentrated meditation (as the culmination of many years of practice), he experienced complete liberation and returned to join the assembly.

The joys of memorization

Most people nowadays find it incredible that Ananda and the other disciples had such amazing powers of memorization that they could hold whole volumes of Buddha's teachings in their heads. While not trying to diminish their accomplishment in any way, certain aspects of Buddha's discourses helped his listeners learn them by heart. For example, he repeated certain key phrases over again — so much so, in fact, that many English editors of these discourses eliminate much of this repetition because it doesn't suit the modern reader's taste. Occasionally, Buddha also summarized some of the longer passages in rhythmical verse, which was also a great aid in memorization.

Although Buddha's early disciples certainly possessed extraordinary mental faculties, their powers of memorization aren't unattainable today — although the world we live in does make it challenging. Just a few centuries ago in Europe, university students and scholars — and even ordinary school children — with brains no different from yours and ours had to commit long poems and other literary works to memory. And, until recently, members of preliterate societies throughout the world have been able to recite long passages of their native epics by heart. But, with the growing reliance on the written word since the advent of printing and the media saturation of the modern world, the ability to memorize seems to be vanishing. Maybe, if everyone turned off the TV long enough, the full power of memory would return.

It is interesting to note that this tradition of reciting Buddha's teachings by heart was revived in Burma in the second half of the 20th century. An American Buddhist who's been living in Burma for more than 22 years has reported meeting one of these "reciting monks" who told him that it takes more than eight hours a day of recitation for one and a half months to recite the entire Buddhist collection of teachings!

Ananda began each recitation with the words "Thus I have heard," to indicate that he himself had been present at the teaching he was about to relate — no second-hand information here. Then he mentioned where Buddha gave that particular discourse — for example, at Buddha's rainy-season residence near Shravasti (see Chapter 9) — and who was in the audience on that particular occasion. After setting the scene in this way, Ananda then recited from memory what Buddha had taught. Monks who had also been present at that particular teaching were asked to confirm that Ananda's recitation was accurate. When they agreed, the recitation was accepted, and Mahakashyapa directed the assembly to commit it to memory.

Categorizing the teachings: The three baskets

The First Council formally divided Buddha's dharma discourses into the three "baskets" (*pitaka*) that make up the principal categories of the Buddhist canon, or collection of teachings, to this day. Here are the *three baskets* (*tipitaka* in Pali; *tripitaka* in Sanskrit) the First Council came up with:

✔ **The Basket of Discourses** (*Sutta Pitaka* in Pali; *Sutra Pitaka* in Sanskrit). Recited by Ananda, this extensive collection contains the advice that Buddha gave about the practice of meditation and related topics. The principal discourses in this basket demonstrate how you can train your mind to gain the insights that lead eventually to *nirvana* — the complete release from suffering.

For example, within the *Sutta Pitaka,* you can find the teaching known as the *Greater Discourse on the Foundations of Mindfulness* (Pali: *Mahasatipatthana Sutta*), which contains essential instructions for gaining a clear, unmistaken realization of the four noble truths (check out Chapter 3 for more insight into these truths). Meditators from many different Buddhist traditions (especially the Theravada) continue to use the practices described in this discourse.

✔ **The Basket of Discipline** (called the *Vinaya Pitaka* in both Pali and Sanskrit). Recited by a monk named Upali (who'd been a barber in Kapilavastu before joining Buddha), this collection contains the more than 225 rules of conduct that Buddha passed along to his monastic community.

Buddha generally formulated these rules spontaneously, in response to new situations. In other words, whenever he noticed his followers behaving in a way that was either contrary to the spirit of the dharma or that could bring discredit to the sangha (community of monks and nuns), he established the appropriate rule to govern that behavior. For example, the monk Sudinna once confessed to having sexual relations with his former wife (in order, it is said, to provide an heir who could inherit his family's property). Buddha first rebuked him, pointing out that such behavior was unbecoming a member of the sangha and leads to further attachment to the world of sensual desires, rather than liberation from it. Then Buddha established the rule that forbids individuals following the monastic way of life from engaging in any sexual behavior whatsoever. (See Chapter 12 for more on the basic rules of conduct for both monastics and lay people.)

✔ **The Basket of Higher Knowledge** (*Abhidhamma Pitaka* in Pali; *Abhidharma Pitaka* in Sanskrit). After Ananda and Upali finished recounting what they remembered at the First Council (by the way, some accounts state that Upali recited first), Mahakashyapa addressed the assembly. The subject of his recitation was what you might call Buddhist phenomenology — that is, a scientific analysis of reality from Buddha's point of view.

Buddha often pointed out that the kind of philosophical speculation that was widespread in India at the time ("Does the world have a beginning or an end?" for example) didn't lead anywhere. But he did want his followers to have as detailed a conceptual understanding of their world as possible. In particular, he wanted them to know how the mind works, the way suffering arises, and how suffering can be eliminated. During his teachings, therefore, Buddha often gave detailed lists of the elements that make up both mental and physical reality as he perceived them with his penetrating insight. (One example is the list of 12 links outlining the way ignorance perpetuates suffering, which we present in Chapter 13.) At the First Council, Mahakashyapa repeated all the detailed lists he'd heard Buddha mention. From these lists grew the extensive teachings on psychology, philosophy, and related matters that make up Buddhist "higher knowledge" studies.

Spreading the Teachings — Peacefully

When Mahakashyapa passed away not long after the First Council, Ananda became head of the Buddhist order. During the 40 years of his leadership, Buddhism spread throughout India as monks dispersed in all directions, following Buddha's advice to teach "for the welfare of the many, out of compassion for the world." Some monks "specialized" in teaching one particular part of the Tripitaka ("three baskets"); others, like Buddha himself, could teach all aspects of the dharma.

Ananda himself taught thousands of disciples, setting them firmly on the path to liberation. He and the other sangha leaders that followed — sometimes referred to as the early Buddhist patriarchs — did a lot to help Buddhism grow. The early leaders founded many monastic communities, which produced new members for the sangha, and brought a large number of lay disciples into the Buddhist fold.

To the credit of those involved in the rapid growth during the early years, the spread of Buddhism occurred peacefully. People became Buddhists because they wanted to, not because they were forced to.

The following scenario is typical of the way interest in Buddhism grew. A pair of simply clad monks entered a village in the early morning, having spent the previous night outdoors in the nearby forest. Carrying begging bowls, they walked from house to house on their daily alms round, silently receiving whatever food people offered them, and then returned to the outskirts of town. Villagers who were sufficiently impressed by the calm, self-controlled demeanor of these monks often approached them after the monks had finished their one meal of the day and requested instruction. Some villagers even asked how they could join the Buddhist order.

Following the example of Buddha, the monks responded to these requests in ways that seemed suitable — freely sharing whatever teachings they'd memorized and understood before moving on in their homeless wandering to the next village. The fact that these monks spoke respectfully with all members of society, whether they were of a high caste or low, helped increase their standing with the general population, and the number of Buddhists grew correspondingly.

A Fork in the Road: Managing a Developing Split in the Buddhist Community

Though peaceful, the Buddhist fold wasn't free from differences, and even the occasional controversy. As Buddhist communities in India became larger and more widespread, different styles of practice emerged. For example, some monks favored a strict interpretation of the rules of discipline, while others took a somewhat more liberal approach.

Convening the Second Council

To deal with the various concerns that were dividing the sangha community, a second Buddhist council was held in Vaishali about 100 years after the first. In the different accounts of this meeting — both those written by Western historians and those given by the various Buddhist traditions themselves — you find quite a bit of disagreement about exactly what took place there.

But everyone does agree that the Second Council led to the first major schism, or split, within the Buddhist community. Depending on which account you follow, several thousand monks were either expelled from the council or left voluntarily because they felt that the others were interpreting the spirit of Buddha's teachings too narrowly.

Two major Buddhist groups emerged from the Second Council. They called themselves:

- **The Elders** (Sanskrit: *Sthavira;* Pali: *Thera*): Considered themselves the keepers of Buddha's original teachings

- **The Great Community** (*Mahasanghika* in Sanskrit): Held a more liberal interpretation of Buddha's word that, they believed, matched his original intentions

We mention these two ancient groups because their spiritual descendents eventually evolved into the two major traditions of Buddhism still followed today. These traditions are

- **Theravada:** The name means "Way of the Elders," and this tradition is sometimes called the Southern tradition because it spread mainly to South Asian countries such as Sri Lanka, Burma, and Thailand.

- **Mahayana:** The various Northern traditions practiced in China, Korea, Japan, Tibet, Mongolia, and so on comprise the "Great Vehicle."

Advancing the teachings in different ways

The way the various traditions divided and evolved, especially in the early centuries of Buddhism's development, is a complicated subject, to say the least. Because the subject is complex and views of it are shaded by the tradition each individual follows, we present only the most basic outline of the process. If you want to research this matter in more detail, we suggest that you check out different books on the subject — such as *The Buddhist Handbook* by John Snelling (Inner Traditions International) and *The Story of Buddhism* by Donald Lopez (HarperSanFrancisco) — and then attempt to unravel this complex story for yourself.

Within a couple of centuries of Buddha's passing, at least 18 separate Buddhist schools (and perhaps twice that number) were active throughout India. Each had its own version of what Buddha taught and its own way of interpreting and practicing these teachings. As chaotic as the situation may seem, the existence of these different schools wasn't necessarily a bad thing (especially because the different schools apparently never actually fought with one another — other than in philosophical debate).

You shouldn't be too surprised to hear about divisions and subdivisions in the Buddhist community in those early years. After all, Buddha himself didn't teach all his followers in exactly the same way. Taking into account differences in their interests and intellectual capacities, he taught in the manner that would most benefit each audience. As a result, his teachings — especially those regarding the nature of the *self* (see Chapter 13 where we tackle the issue of self) — can be interpreted in a variety of ways. It's only natural that later generations of Buddhists would group themselves into schools identifying with the philosophical position that best suited their own understanding.

Besides purely philosophical differences, other differences emerged among Buddhists, some concerning standards of acceptable behavior and others based on language. Buddha encouraged his followers to make the teachings they themselves had heard and understood widely available to others, and he exhorted them to do so in their native language. In this way, everyone (not just the literate and highly educated) could benefit from the dharma. India was a land of many different languages, as it is today, and these linguistic differences also helped give each school its own character or flavor.

Making Buddhism a Religion of the People: The Emperor Ashoka's Influence

In the third century BCE, a figure appeared on the Indian scene who had a dramatic effect on the entire course of Buddhist history. This figure was

Emperor Ashoka, the third ruler of the powerful Mauryan dynasty established by his grandfather.

Ashoka was the individual most responsible for setting Buddhism on the road to becoming a world religion.

Transforming his approach

In the beginning of his reign (approximately 268 BCE), Ashoka followed the same warlike, expansionist policies as his father and grandfather before him. His conquests were so extensive that he eventually ruled an empire stretching over a vast portion of the Indian subcontinent.

But his bloody campaign to put down a rebellion in what is now the eastern state of Orissa involved such an enormous loss of life that Ashoka was horrified by his own actions. Deeply regretting all the suffering he caused, he underwent a profound spiritual transformation. Having become acquainted with the Buddhist teachings through a monk he met, Ashoka made the momentous decision to rule his empire according to the Buddhist principles of nonviolence and compassion.

Ashoka set out to put these lofty principles into practice on an unprecedented scale. For example,

- He gave up military conquest and instead devoted himself to the welfare of his people.
- He established schools and hospitals and even had wells dug along the main roads for the relief of travelers.
- In the spirit of respect and toleration, he gave royal support to many different religious institutions — not just the Buddhist ones.
- Because of his special interest in promoting the Buddhist moral code, he ordered edicts to be carved on pillars and rocks throughout his empire exhorting his people to behave toward others with generosity, humility, and honesty.

Ashoka also promoted the practice of *pilgrimage,* visiting the various sites that Buddha had blessed with his presence (travel over to Chapter 9 for more on pilgrimages), and ordered the construction of thousands of monuments (*stupas*) to the Compassionate One. With his devotion as their example, many of Ashoka's subjects developed interest in Buddhism as well, and the number of individuals professing the Buddhist faith rose dramatically, especially among the ordinary lay people.

Before Ashoka, Buddhism appealed largely to people who were well educated or highly placed in society. Afterward, it became much more a religion of the people.

Promoting Buddhism beyond India

Emperor Ashoka also sent emissaries in all directions from India to spread the word of Buddha. Some of them supposedly reached lands as far west as Egypt, Syria, and Macedonia, though no evidence indicates that they had much of an impact in these areas.

The mission to Sri Lanka, however, turned out to be a huge success. Two of the emissaries to this island nation were a Buddhist monk and nun said to be Ashoka's children. They were well received by the local ruler, King Tissa, and invited to the royal city of Anuradhapura where a great monastery was later established. Ashoka's daughter brought with her a cutting from the original Bodhi tree under which Buddha had achieved enlightenment some 300 years earlier, and the descendent of the tree that grew from this cutting remains a popular pilgrimage site in Sri Lanka to this day. (Check out Chapter 3 for the story of the Bodhi tree.)

How original is "original" Buddhism?

Some members of the Theravada tradition like to refer to this tradition as "original" Buddhism, implying that it's free from the later additions (and, by implication, possible distortions) that affect other (specifically Mahayana) traditions. No one can deny that the Pali canon followed by the Theravadins is the oldest written version of Buddha's teachings in the world. And even Buddhists from the Mahayana traditions accept these Pali writings as an accurate reflection — remember that Buddha didn't actually speak in Pali — of what Buddha taught.

Does this mean that the Pali canon is *all* that Buddha had to say? Keep in mind that Buddha taught for 45 years to a wide variety of disciples and that these teachings were preserved for several hundred years in oral form only. Given these complex factors, some scholars have wondered whether anyone can really know for certain what Buddha taught at all. Similar disagreement and controversy still rage around the teachings of the historical Jesus.

But wait, there's more. The Theravada is only one of at least 18 schools that passed on their versions of Buddha's teachings for many centuries. Add all these factors up, and you can see why it's unlikely that any one Buddhist tradition, no matter how ancient, could have succeeded in recording and preserving all of Shakyamuni's original teachings. By comparison, consider the Christian tradition again: Though every Christian denomination agrees on the contents of the New Testament, each has its own favorite English translations of certain passages and its own interpretation of what the text actually means. But, unless you're a true believer, you're unlikely to view a single interpretation as the one and only true gospel as Jesus himself preached it.

At Anuradhapura, Buddha's teachings were written down for the first time. For the previous 400 years or so in India, different collections of these teachings had been passed down orally, in various languages and dialects, from one generation to the next. But in the first century BCE (some historians say 88 BCE precisely), a version of these teachings was finally put into writing in Sri Lanka.

The particular form of the Tripitaka (the "three baskets" we mention in the "Categorizing the teachings: The three baskets" section earlier in the chapter) transcribed at that time was the one preserved in the Theravada tradition, which arrived in Sri Lanka with Ashoka's children, and which eventually spread throughout Southeast Asia. Its language was Pali, one of India's more ancient languages.

Even now, more than 2,000 years later, many people turn to the Pali canon of the Theravada Buddhist tradition (a complete English translation was published last century by the Pali Text Society) when they want a taste of "original" Buddhism. (Peruse the "How original is 'original' Buddhism" sidebar for more details.)

Two Levels of Practice in Early Buddhism

When you visit a country that subscribes to the Theravada Buddhist tradition, like Thailand, where people still practice many of the customs from the early days of Buddhism, you can get a feeling for how Buddhism must've impacted Indian society in its early years.

Members of the Buddhist order (the sangha) relied on villagers and townspeople for their basic necessities of life, and the laity relied on members of the sangha for spiritual instruction and the performance of religious rites. You can still see this interaction today, even in Thailand's overgrown capitol of Bangkok. Early every morning, monks carrying begging bowls emerge from their neighborhood temples into the city's streets, where members of the local populace wait to make food offerings to them. After the monks complete their alms rounds, they return to their temples. Later, some of the same families who gave food may gather at one of the local temples to request that the monks offer prayers or teachings on their behalf.

An important element in this interaction between monks and laity is what is known as the *collection of merit*. As Buddha taught, virtuous actions — such as the practice of generosity — create a store of positive energy, or merit (*punya* in both Pali and Sanskrit). This meritorious energy brings about positive results in the future in accordance with the karmic law of cause and effect (see Chapter 12 for more on karma). The person to whom you present offerings — the object, or recipient, of your virtuous actions — is known as your *field of merit,* and the more worthy your field, the more merit you create.

Because fully ordained monks (and nuns, in the few places where their lineage still exists) are among the most worthy of all fields of merit, making offerings to them is a powerful way of quickly collecting vast stores of merit. Therefore, when a woman standing in front of her house places food in the alms bowl of a monk from a nearby temple, she feels that she herself is the one who truly benefits from this act of generosity, because she receives the merit. And the merit she collects, she hopes, will bring her happiness in the future, specifically a rebirth in one of the more fortunate realms of existence (see Chapter 13 where we explain the various realms in which beings live).

This example of the interaction between monks and the laity neatly illustrates two levels of Buddhist practice that existed side-by-side in the early days of Buddhism in India — and that still exist in many places throughout the Buddhist world.

- ✔ On one level of Buddhist practice was the renounced style of the monastic community. Monks and nuns, ideally speaking, gave up family, possessions, and worldly ambition in their quest for complete liberation from suffering. They shaved their heads and donned robes, thereby eliminating (or at least minimizing) anything in their lives that would distract them from their ultimate goal, and devoted themselves primarily to the strict observance of moral precepts (check out Chapter 12 for more on these precepts) and the practice of meditation. (Chapter 7 deals with meditation in detail.)

- ✔ The other level of Buddhist practice (traditionally regarded as inferior from a spiritual perspective) was followed by many of the devoted lay people. Though some lay people have always practiced meditation, individuals (called householders) who chose to live an ordinary life and raise a family were believed to be passing up the chance to win liberation in this lifetime.

  Instead, a layperson was mainly limited to amassing enough merit — largely by supporting people who were committed to the monastic way of life — so that he or she could achieve happiness later in this life and a favorable rebirth in the future. Then, if the future rebirth was particularly fortunate, an individual might be able to devote himself or herself to the pure practices of a fully ordained sangha member at that time.

Witnessing Shifting Allegiances and New Ideals

This rather sharp division of the Buddhist faithful into two groups — one seeking freedom from the wheel of suffering (the pattern of recurring misery and dissatisfaction known as cyclic existence, or *samsara*) and the other hoping only for temporary comfort within it and perhaps the chance for a better rebirth in the future — had a profound effect on the way Buddhism developed, changed, and spread.

The existing system required that the ordained sangha community continued to be highly respected by the laity. The early arhats, such as Ananda and the patriarchs who followed (see the "Convening the First Buddhist Council" section earlier in this chapter), were undoubtedly worthy of the highest esteem. But not everyone wearing the robes of a monk or a priest is a model of virtue, which is painfully evident in many religious traditions today, Buddhist and non-Buddhist alike.

If the householders in a particular Indian town, for example, lost faith in the local Buddhist monks — finding them distant, insincere, lazy, or even corrupt — they eventually withdrew their support, and the monastic system would begin to crumble in that area.

Turning to the stupas

Historical evidence indicates that some lay people shifted their allegiance, and their support, from the monastic community to the growing number of *stupas* (monuments) located throughout India (see the "Making Buddhism a Religion of the People: The Emperor Ashoka's Influence" section earlier in the chapter).

The faithful regarded these monuments, originally built to house the relics of Buddha, as indistinguishable from Shakyamuni Buddha himself. A growing number of Buddhists, lay and monastic alike, congregated at these representations of supreme enlightenment, walking around them in the same way that Shakyamuni's own disciples, centuries before, had walked respectfully around Buddha before addressing him. (For more information on the location of some of these stupas, see Chapter 9.)

For many of those intent on collecting merit, the rewards of making offerings to these embodiments of Buddha's enlightened mind seemed even greater than supporting the sangha.

Taking a ride in the Great Vehicle: Mahayana Buddhism

Around the same time as the cult of stupas was growing, the second major form of Buddhist thought and practice — the Mahayana — began emerging in India. This approach called itself the "Great Vehicle" because it held out the promise of enlightenment to everyone, not just the monastic few. This spirit of inclusiveness appealed especially to those lay people whose spiritual needs weren't being met by the more restrictive, prevailing forms of practice.

At the center of this Mahayana conception is the figure of the *bodhisattva.* The Mahayanists didn't invent this term, but they did broaden its meaning. Prior to the rise of the Mahayana, most Buddhists believed that just one enlightenment-bound being, or bodhisattva (*bodhi* meaning enlightenment; *sattva* meaning being), existed in each era. This unique figure was destined to become the Buddha who would reveal the dharma for that particular age. In the *Jataka Tales* (the stories Buddha told of his previous lives), for example, the bodhisattva may appear one time as an animal and another time as a human, but each life brought him closer to his achievement of full enlightenment as Shakyamuni Buddha.

According to the Mahayana, anyone compassionate and dedicated enough to place the welfare of others before his or her own attainment of nirvana can achieve the same enlightenment as Shakyamuni. In other words, instead of working toward becoming an arhat and achieving liberation just for oneself, the compassionate bodhisattvas aim for Buddhahood to bring infinite benefit to all others. This points to another reason for the term Mahayana, or Great Vehicle: These teachings not only benefit a great number of beings, but they also lead the bodhisattva practitioners to the greatest possible achievement: supreme enlightenment.

For those individuals who lacked this supremely altruistic intention and were intent only on their own personal liberation, the Mahayanists coined the rather negative term *Hinayana,* or "Lesser Vehicle." We avoided using this term until now — and won't use it again after the next paragraph — because many writers have inaccurately applied this label to entire Buddhist traditions, such as the Theravada. This categorization is grossly unfair because practitioners of outstanding dedication and heart are found within the ranks of the Theravada. The Theravada tradition has always maintained that the wisdom that liberates you from suffering is the culmination of practicing both compassion and insight. Furthermore, the Theravada tradition has evolved considerably over the centuries, and nowadays most teachers in this tradition, especially in the West, place particularly strong emphasis on the cultivating compassion and loving-kindness for others, in addition to personal insight.

The terms *Mahayana* and *Hinayana* properly refer to attitudes that any practitioner of any tradition can hold at any time. As one of Jon's teachers pointed out, you can't tell if others are Mahayana or Hinayana by considering the scriptures they honor or the school they follow. People can only make this determination about themselves, and they can only do so by looking into the depths of their own heart. You may pride yourself on being a Mahayanist, for example, but if you're really only interested in your own welfare — or worse yet, the fleeting pleasures of the moment — you aren't even worthy of calling yourself a Hinayana practitioner. It is a very personal matter. As the American Vipassana teacher Joseph Goldstein has often said, "Whether the vehicles are small or large, they all get towed at the owner's expense."

Chronicling the Rise of the Mahayana Teachings

Even though books on Buddhism often speak about the Mahayana tradition in the singular, as if only one existed, a number of different Mahayana traditions rose to prominence starting around the first century CE — and almost certainly existed in some form even before then.

To be more precise, different Mahayana sutras (or discourses) began to circulate about that time, and each one expanded the Buddhist worldview in one way or another. These sutras (which were all written down in Sanskrit) claimed to be teachings of Shakyamuni Buddha that some of his disciples had preserved in secret and were now unveiling to address the needs of the historical moment. In many cases, their proponents asserted that these sutras presented the dharma in a deeper, more potent form than what had appeared before. We explain the most important of these teachings in the next few sections.

White Lotus of the True Dharma Sutra

Popularly known as the *Lotus Sutra,* this extensive Mahayana scripture has been very influential in India and, later, throughout the Far East and beyond. (To find out more about the way the *Lotus Sutra* and the other Buddhist teachings and traditions mentioned in this chapter spread throughout Asia and to the West, check out Chapter 5.)

This poetic and elaborately symbolic work (called *Saddharma-pundarika* in Sanskrit) presents a cosmic view of time and space and the spiritual path. As in a number of other scriptures, the events in this sutra start out at Vulture Peak near Rajgir (see Chapter 9), but they soon get a lot broader in scope. How much broader? We're talking all of existence here. Shakyamuni reveals a spectacular vision of the universe populated by countless Buddhas teaching dharma to their huge circles of disciples. He then explains that, although Buddhas like himself may teach paths that lead to lesser goals (such as individual liberation), all beings ultimately have only one final spiritual destination: the supreme enlightenment of Buddhahood.

Exposition of Vimalakirti

This work is one of the oldest and most beloved of all Mahayana scriptures, and it takes place at Vaishali (site of the Second Council; see the "Convening the Second Council" section earlier in this chapter). This scripture is so popular among lay people mainly because its central character, the layperson

Vimalakirti, has a more profound understanding of the dharma than even Shakyamuni's close disciple Shariputra, a monk renowned for his wisdom. This sutra (Sanskrit: *Vimalakirti-nirdesha*) also contains a famous gender-bending scene in which a goddess appears and temporarily transforms Shariputra into a woman, much to his wonder and embarrassment. This event demonstrates that all conceptual ideas, including male and female, lack ultimate reality.

Perfection of Wisdom Sutras

This collection of discourses — which, like the *Lotus Sutra*, takes place at Vulture Peak — presents the path to supreme awakening as the union of compassionate method and insightful wisdom (see Chapters 2 and 14 where the connection between compassion and wisdom is explained). Focusing on the career of the altruistically-minded seeker of enlightenment, these teachings provided a philosophical foundation for many of the emerging Mahayana traditions.

In addition to outlining the bodhisattva's compassionate way of life, these sutras also expand the scope and depth of Buddha's teachings on wisdom. Before this discourse, the insight of selflessness (see Chapters 2 and 13 for more on what it means to be without a self) was generally applied only to your ego-identity, or personality. If you wanted to achieve liberation, you had to penetrate this ignorant notion of self-identity to discover the selflessness at your core. The *Perfection of Wisdom Sutras* (*Prajna-paramita*) expand — or, perhaps more accurately, transform — this insight into the truth of universal emptiness (*shunyata*), teaching that you can't find even one atom of concrete, self-existent reality anywhere in the world. (For more on emptiness, see Chapter 14.)

This profound view — so contrary to the ordinary notion that things exist as separately and individually as they appear — was expounded in great detail by Nagarjuna, the founder of the Madhyamika ("Middle Doctrine") school of Mahayana Buddhism. (Some scholars even claim that the *Perfection of Wisdom Sutras* don't record the original teachings of Shakyamuni Buddha at all. Instead, they claim, Nagarjuna actually composed them.)

Descent into Lanka Sutra

Besides Nagarjuna's Madhyamika school, the other major philosophical school of Mahayana Buddhism is Asanga's Yogachara, which emphasizes the role of the mind in shaping and creating experience. Madhyamika points to the inherent emptiness of phenomena by demonstrating that every concept and assertion you may have about reality is untrue, but Yogachara teaches that this inherent emptiness is actually the nature of consciousness itself, which underlies all phenomena as a deeper, abiding truth. In other words, instead of saying, "There is only emptiness," Yogachara says, "There is only consciousness" — or Mind with a capital *m*. (Despite the apparent disagreement, many Buddhist masters have taught that *consciousness* and *emptiness* are merely indicators of the same indivisible, non-dual (that is, inseparable) reality. The Zen tradition, for example, derives from both Madhyamika and Yogachara sources. For a more detailed comparison of Yogachara and Madhyamika, see Chapter 10.)

This sutra (*Lankavatara*) is one of the main scriptural sources for the Yogachara school. Profoundly psychological in nature, it urges its practitioners to gain, through meditation, a direct and intuitive experience of consciousness itself, which is the deeper reality beyond the illusions generated by the conceptual mind.

World-Array Sutra

This beautiful scripture, which is really the last part of a vast collection of teachings known as the *Flower Ornament Sutra,* recounts the pilgrimage made by a young man named Sudhana — at the urging of Manjushri (see Figure 4-1), the bodhisattva of wisdom — to find the perfect teacher who can reveal to him the knowledge of enlightenment. This spiritual journey takes Sudhana to more than 50 teachers (each one instructs him in some aspect of the bodhisattva's path) until he finally meets Maitreya, the future Buddha, who has the knowledge he seeks. Maitreya shows Sudhana that all his teachers have revealed the same truth to him but in different guises. Under Maitreya's guidance, Sudhana realizes that no difference exists between his own mind and the minds of the infinite Buddhas throughout the universe.

Sudhana's journey represents a meditator's experiences along the path to full awakening. Its vivid imagery draws the reader into an enchanted universe that stretches imagination to the farthest limits. This sutra (*Gandavyuha*) has inspired numerous works of Buddhist art over the centuries — most notably the reliefs that decorate the gigantic monument at Borobudur in Indonesia. (Chapter 9 has info about a ton of pilgrimage sites, including Borobudur.) The predominant theme of this sutra, and of the various Mahayana traditions that derived from it, is the interpenetration of all universal phenomena. Everything that exists mirrors everything else, and the entire universe is like a vast hall of mirrors, or net of jewels, endlessly reflecting one another.

Land of Bliss Sutras

This collection of three sutras teaches the faithful how to live and die so that they can be reborn in the *Buddha field* (or pure land) of Amitabha, who (as his name expresses) is the Buddha of "Infinite Light." Described as a celestial paradise, this land is a realm or state completely outside the wheel of samsaric suffering. The compassionate Amitabha Buddha created this land while he was still a bodhisattva, and all the conditions in this pure land are right for achieving supreme enlightenment. Even the sound of the wind passing through the trees teaches the dharma.

Unlike other Buddhist approaches to enlightenment, where you rely on your own effort to propel you toward your goal, birth in this pure land (called *Sukhavati,* the "Blissful," which is also the Sanskrit name of these sutras) largely depends on your devotion to its presiding Buddha, Amitabha. He brought this realm into existence, and you can reach it simply by maintaining faith in his saving grace. (See Chapter 5 for more on the worship of Amitabha — called Amida in Japanese — in Far Eastern Pure Land Buddhism.) The worship of Amitabha represents a general move in Mahayana Buddhism away from devotion to Shakyamuni alone and toward the worship of a vast array of Buddhas and bodhisattvas.

These brief descriptions should give you a small taste of the extraordinary outburst of creative energy that produced the flowering of Mahayana over a relatively short period of time (approximately 100 BCE to 200 CE). These sutras used a form of ancient Sanskrit scholars call *Buddhist hybrid Sanskrit,* and they contain some of the most outstanding treasures of Indian literature.

Figure 4-1:
Manjushri,
the
bodhisattva
of wisdom.

Just as the reign of Ashoka saw the Theravada Buddhism of the Pali canon spread to Sri Lanka on its way to Southeast Asia (see the "Making Buddhism a Religion of the People: The Emperor Ashoka's Influence," section earlier in this chapter), the peace and prosperity of the reign of King Kanishka in North India (approximately 78 to 101 CE) enabled the Sanskrit sutras of Mahayana Buddhism to begin spreading north and east on their way to China and beyond. Mahayana monks weren't the only individuals responsible for this diffusion. Merchants and other lay practitioners also established pockets of Buddhism along the trade routes of Central Asia.

Recognizing the Major Mahayana Themes

Although the Sanskrit writings that contributed to this wave of expansion are quite diverse, you can notice certain themes in these sutras that characterize the Mahayana worldview and that reappear in the Buddhist traditions that developed in Central Asia and the Far East:

- The compassionate bodhisattva is revered as the ideal embodiment of spiritual fulfillment, replacing the arhat, who had perhaps, over time, fallen from grace in the eyes of some of the faithful.

- All beings, lay as well as ordained, have the ability to achieve the highest spiritual realization, even in the midst of "ordinary" life.

- Buddhahood is an enduring principle that exists throughout the universe. Before adopting a Mahayana worldview, the faithful focused their respect on one historical person, Shakyamuni Buddha. Now they could direct their devotion toward infinite Buddhas and transcendent bodhisattvas throughout space and time.

- The nature of all existence is essentially non-dualistic. That is, ultimate reality is beyond all divisions into "this" and "that" — beyond the reach of thoughts, words, and conceptions — but still capable of being directly realized through insight.

- Rather than moving from a lesser to a greater state of perfection, progress along the spiritual path involves recognizing the innate perfection of the present moment "just as it is."

Judging the authenticity of the teaching

Is Mahayana Buddhism an authentic expression of Buddha's original teachings?

At least 400 years separate the lifetime of Shakyamuni Buddha from the appearance of the earliest Mahayana sutras. But these sutras depict Shakyamuni and others associated with him, such as Ananda and Shariputra, as active participants. Shakyamuni is often the main speaker, telling of the innumerable Buddhas inhabiting space in the *Lotus Sutra* or describing the wonders of Amitabha's pure land in the *Land of Bliss Sutras.* But how could a monk writing in 100 CE accurately describe what supposedly took place five centuries before? Some people say that the monk must be making it up — simply writing down his own ideas and falsely crediting them to Buddha. For folks who hold this point of view — and many people do, both Buddhist and non-Buddhist — the Mahayana sutras are forgeries. Pious perhaps, but forgeries nevertheless.

The discourses recorded in the Pali canon of Theravada Buddhism must answer to the same charges. They weren't written down until many centuries after the events they describe, either. But, in this case, it's generally accepted that these *suttas* (to give these discourses their Pali spelling) were handed down orally for centuries from monks who heard them from Buddha first-hand. So, although certain changes in length and language have occurred over the ages, it's quite plausible to believe that the Theravada scriptures authentically reflect what Buddha actually said. Could the same be true of the Mahayana sutras, whose fantastic descriptions and florid style are so different from the more sober and relatively down-to-earth suttas? And, if the Mahayana sutras are accurate reflections of what Buddha taught, why don't the Theravada scriptures mention any of the same events?

These questions aren't easy to answer, and most modern readers would probably greet some of the traditional Mahayana responses with skepticism. For example, some Mahayana sources claim that while the First Council took place at Rajgir, a separate and much larger gathering was held at another site, where the great bodhisattvas in attendance recited and authenticated Buddha's Mahayana teachings. Then, because these teachings were too profound to be understood correctly by most

disciples, the bodhisattvas hid them away until the time was ripe to reveal them — as when Nagarjuna retrieved the *Perfection of Wisdom Sutras* from the land of the nagas.

Even if the details of this legend are difficult to swallow, the basic idea isn't so far-fetched. Buddha certainly could've felt that several centuries needed to pass before most people would be ready to dedicate themselves to the bodhisattva way of life, so he may have revealed the Mahayana teachings only to those folks who were ready for them, with the admonition that they pass them on only to a select few. Later, when the time was ripe, a spiritual genius like Nagarjuna or Asanga could then spread these teachings. The Dalai Lama (quite an authority, don't you think?) has even suggested that Buddha didn't have to give one of his teachings during his historical lifetime for the teaching to be authentic! The point the Dalai Lama is making is that an enlightened being never truly passes away; his inspiration is always available to those who are ready to receive it.

You can approach this question of authenticity in another way as well. The Buddha dharma isn't a static thing; like a great tree, it grows and flowers over time. What Buddha taught 2,500 years ago is like the seed of a tree, and the different traditions (including the Mahayana) are the flowers and fruit that grew from the tree. From this perspective, whether Shakyamuni actually uttered the words that a particular sutra ascribes to him isn't important. Instead, you need to investigate whether the teachings in that sutra, when put into practice, are consistent with the aims of all his other teachings. If they lead to the cessation of suffering, the opening of your heart to others, and the realization of your true nature, you can confidently consider them the teachings of the compassionate Buddha.

Bringing Up Buddhism beyond India

Buddhism ultimately came to an end in India. But the end didn't occur before Buddhism planted innumerable seeds that eventually flowered and took root in other lands, giving rise to the various Buddhist traditions recognized today.

Before its decline and demise toward the end of the first millennium CE, the Indian sangha established numerous monasteries and several major universities that nurtured, practiced, and taught Buddhist philosophy not only to Indians but also to visiting scholars and monks from Southeast Asia, Tibet, China, and possibly even Japan and Korea.

These visitors returned home with new ideas, methods, and above all realizations to inspire their own and subsequent generations of spiritual seekers. (Travel to Chapter 5 to find out more about the spread of Buddhism to the rest of Asia and ultimately the West.)

Chapter 5

Following Buddhism to the Present Day

● ●

In This Chapter:

▶ Tracing the development of Buddhism in Asia

▶ Discovering how the Way of the Elders spread

▶ Exploring the rise of the Great Vehicle

▶ Checking out the two most popular schools in the West

● ●

*N*ot long after the end of the first millennium CE, Buddhism had died out in India. But it reached its true peak in other lands as it evolved to meet the needs of new cultures that first tentatively and then wholeheartedly embraced it.

Chapter 4 traces the development of Buddhism in India (the homeland of its founder) as it diverged into two major currents and many minor schools. In this chapter, we follow this adaptable tradition as it spreads across Asia and takes various shapes by embellishing and expanding, but never abandoning, the basic teachings of the historical Buddha.

Tracing the Two Routes of Buddhism

Historians suggest that Buddhism followed two routes as it spread from India to the rest of Asia:

✔ **Southern transmission.** The first, more southern route, took the tradition known as Theravada Buddhism to Sri Lanka and then into Southeast Asia to Burma (now called Myanmar), Thailand, Laos, and Cambodia (Kampuchea).

> ✔ **Northern transmission.** The second route carried the different forms of
> Mahayana Buddhism into central Asia and across the Silk Road to China
> and, from there, to Korea, Japan, and Vietnam, as well as to Tibet and
> Mongolia (see Figure 5-1).

But this southern/northern classification does have its exceptions. Consider
Indonesia, for example. Other than in its local Chinese communities, this
Southeast Asian Muslim nation hasn't had its own living Buddhist tradition
for many centuries. But the monumental ruins at Borobudur (see Chapter 9),
which are adorned with scenes from Mahayana sutras, clearly show that
so-called northern Buddhism once thrived along the southern transmission
route. Even Sri Lanka, home to Theravada Buddhism since the earliest
times (around 250 BCE), hosted its own version of the Mahayana, and the
Theravada tradition didn't become the official form of Buddhism for this
island nation until 1160.

Figure 5-1:
The spread
of Buddhism
through
Asia.

Spreading the Way of the Elders across Southeast Asia to the West

As Buddhism established itself in the various Southeast Asian countries
along the southern transmission route, it faced different sets of challenges.

In Sri Lanka, for instance, even after it became the official form of Buddhism, Theravada (literally, "way of the elders") had to confront the threat of European colonization. Beginning in the 16th century, the Portuguese and then the Dutch gained control over much of the island. The Europeans considered it their duty to convert the people from their "pagan" beliefs, and Christianity eventually elbowed Buddhism aside. Theravada Buddhism didn't experience a return to its former prominence until the 19th century.

Both major forms of Buddhism reached Burma (now known as Myanmar) between the fifth and sixth centuries CE, but eventually the Theravada tradition prevailed. In the 11th century, the city of Pagan — adorned with thousands of Buddhist temples, of which approximately 2,000 survive today — became the capital of Burma's first unified kingdom. With the breakup of this kingdom, however, Buddhism declined and didn't return to prominence until the 19th century. Nowadays, Buddhism and other free institutions struggle to survive in the face of opposition from Myanmar's repressive regime. This nonviolent struggle is led in part by Aung San Suu Kyi, a Buddhist laywoman who gained international fame when she was awarded the Nobel Peace Prize in 1991.

Wars and government oppression have also severely weakened the various forms of Buddhism that flourished throughout Indochina in previous centuries. Although both Laos and Cambodia (Kampuchea) were once active Theravada centers, the Buddhism that remains in the wake of the communist takeovers of the 1970s has lost much of its former vitality. (The same may be true in Vietnam where Zen once prevailed.)

Theravada Buddhism takes root in Thailand

Thailand is a different story. Buddhism entered the country in about the third century CE, and in the 14th century, monks from Sri Lanka revitalized the Theravada tradition in Thailand. Today Thailand is world renowned for its opulent temples and golden statues (see Figure 5-2) and for the monks in saffron (orange-yellow) robes who walk the streets of its large cities receiving offerings from lay followers.

Buddhism permeates modern Thai culture. Consider the following examples of Buddhism's widespread presence:

✔ According to the constitution, the king must be Buddhist.

✔ Buddhist virtues like gentleness and self-restraint receive widespread observance and respect.

✔ The connection between the lay and ordained communities is particularly close, and the laity can always be counted on to provide food, clothing, and whatever other support the ordained sangha members require.

✔ Custom still dictates that every male spend at least several months of
his life wearing the robes of a monk and living according to the rules of
monastic discipline.

As in many Buddhist countries, much of what passes for Buddhist practice
today in Thailand is rather superficial, and some members of the monastic
community have responded by retreating to the solitude of the jungle to
revive the practices of the original Buddhist forest dwellers of India. Instead
of adopting the familiar priest-like role of many city-dwelling monks —
officiating at ceremonies on behalf of the laity and so on — these monks have
adopted as simple and renounced a lifestyle as possible and have returned
to the basics of their faith. Not content with treating Theravada Buddhism
simply as an institutionalized religion, they devote themselves as intensely
as possible to the practice of meditation. Their goal is nothing less than
complete emancipation from all forms of mentally created limitations — true
freedom from suffering.

The forest tradition of Thailand and neighboring Burma has had a major
impact on the Western spiritual scene. Beginning in the 1960s, a number of
westerners — at first just a few, but later a significant number — began
making their way East in search of ancient wisdom (or at least an alternative
to the materialistic culture in which they'd grown up). Although drugs and
other distractions readily available along the hippie trail to India and beyond
distracted many of these travelers, some folks actually found what they were
looking for.

Figure 5-2:
Thai
Buddha
statue.

Photo courtesy of Aruna Ratangir Buddhist Monastery.

Vipassana meditation gains popularity in the West

During the 1970s, a number of those pioneers who studied with Theravada masters in Southeast Asia returned to the West and began sharing what they'd learned with others, establishing centers that brought ancient Theravada practices and rituals right to America's doorstep (see Figure 5-3). Perhaps the best known pioneer is Jack Kornfield, a popular author and meditation teacher, who has been instrumental in introducing to the West the meditation techniques of such masters as Ajahn Chah, one of the main figures who revived the forest meditation tradition in Thailand (see Chapter 15 for more on Ajahn Chah).

Breathing it all in

The breath is a particularly good object of meditation. Unlike other objects that require considerable effort to establish and maintain — such as a visualized image of Buddha — your breath is always available right under your nose, just waiting to be observed. Also, you can find out a lot about your state of mind just by observing your breath. For example, rough, uneven breathing often reflects mental agitation, but as your mind grows calmer, your breathing follows suit. In fact, some meditators become so calm and focused that their breathing seems to stop altogether.

Experiencing this extraordinary calmness for the first time can be quite surprising; for a moment, you may even wonder whether you've died. But, of course, you haven't (at least, not as long as you're reading these words right now); your breath simply becomes far subtler than you're used to. When your mind has grown sufficiently calm and focused, you then direct your attention to the various sensations, feelings, and thoughts that continually appear and disappear in your body and mind (see Chapter 7 for more on this mindfulness meditation). Your task isn't to judge, compare, or engage these experiences, but merely to observe them.

Something arises and — without clinging to the pleasant or pushing away the unpleasant — you merely note the experience. This meditational technique is challenging because it's so simple. Instead of being distracted by the constant stream of chatter going on in your head, you directly confront your ever-changing experiences. When you become bored or frustrated (or when your mental chattering takes over), you note that as well. By becoming increasingly mindful of what's going on, moment by moment, you have the opportunity to gain an awareness of the way things actually exist, free of all mental projections.

Theravada monasteries take root in the West

Lay meditation centers are only one Western off-shoot of the Southeast Asian Theravada tradition. Followers of Ajahn Chah and other masters have established other centers in Europe, the United States, New Zealand, and elsewhere where men and women can follow the traditional lifestyle of a Theravada monk or nun without leaving their native country (refer to Figure 5-3).

For example, the earliest American follower of Ajahn Chah, Ajahn Sumedho founded the Amaravati monastery in England, and one of the monks he trained, Ajahn Amaro, is abbot of the Abhayagiri monastery in California (see Chapter 8 for a glimpse of life in this monastery). Although these centers may be small compared to their Asian counterparts, they maintain the monastic tradition with purity and authenticity, which bodes well for the future of Theravada in the West.

Figure 5-3:
Theravada monk offering flowers.

Photo courtesy of Aruna Ratangir Buddhist Monastery.

Kornfield (along with fellow pioneers Joseph Goldstein, Sharon Salzberg, and Christina Feldman) co-founded the Insight Meditation Society (IMS) in Barre, Massachusetts, in 1975. Since then, spiritual seekers have had access to instruction in Buddhist meditation without making the difficult journey to the East; they only have to make their way to the East Coast of the United States. (Years later Kornfield also co-founded Spirit Rock Meditation Center in California.)

The main practice taught at IMS and similar centers around the world is called *vipassana* (insight) meditation. These centers have adapted their practice from the Theravada teachings of Ajahn Chah and other Thai forest masters or from those of Burmese masters like Mahasi Sayadaw and U Ba Khin (and one of his primary disciples, S.N. Goenka) who spearheaded the revival of the Theravada practice tradition in their homeland. As taught in these centers, vipassana training generally begins with calming and focusing the mind by directing your attention to the rhythmic movement of the breath (see the sidebar, "Breathing it all in," for more information). When your mind is sufficiently concentrated through this or other similar techniques, the training leads you to an experience of true vipassana itself: a direct and liberating insight into the impermanent, unsatisfactory, and selfless nature of ordinary existence (see Chapters 2 and 17 for more on these three characteristics of ordinary existence). Vipassana retreats last anywhere from ten days to three months and are conducted in complete silence — except when the leader is giving instruction.

In addition to techniques for developing concentration and insight, centers like IMS offer instruction in other key Buddhist practices. *Metta* (or loving-kindness) meditation is particularly popular and widely taught, both on its own and as a part of the vipassana retreat schedule. Many of these centers also offer forms of instruction from outside the Theravada tradition and even from outside Buddhism, including courses led by Tibetan lamas, Japanese roshis, Christian priests, Native American shamans, and other spiritual teachers. As a result, an eclectic tradition seems to be emerging that draws its inspiration from a variety of sources and, in turn, can offer a variety of spiritual services to the greater community.

Driving the Great Vehicle to China and Beyond

In addition to Theravada, the other main division of Buddhism is the Mahayana, the self-styled Great Vehicle that reveres the spiritual model of the *bodhisattva* (a being who vows to help liberate all beings in addition to himself or herself). While Theravada Buddhism made its way south to Sri Lanka and other lands, the Mahayana Buddhism that survives today moved primarily north from India into Central Asia. From there, it trickled into China (in the first century CE) and then made its way to Korea (in the fourth century) and Japan (in the sixth century). From China, it also moved into Vietnam and Tibet (in the seventh century), though a later transmission brought Buddhism directly to Tibet from India.

The detailed story of Mahayana's movement across Asia is actually much more complex than that brief outline even begins to suggest, but the description provides enough detail to introduce you to the subject. While Buddhism traveled from one Asian culture to another, the tradition continued to evolve back home in India, and additional teachings (the various Sanskrit sutras we mention in Chapter 4) emerged which changed the face of Mahayana Buddhism considerably. These different scriptures eventually provided the basis for the various Mahayana traditions that sprang up across Asia.

How Chinese Buddhism evolved

To get a sense of how different Buddhist schools may have evolved in China, imagine that you live in the western part of China — the area closest to India — around the third or fourth century CE. One of your friends shows you a Chinese translation of a Buddhist scripture, and you find it fascinating but difficult to understand. (Because Chinese had yet to develop a vocabulary for Buddhist concepts, early Chinese translations from the Sanskrit were inaccurate, to say the least.) Because you're spiritually inclined and eager to discover the deeper meaning of what you've read, you undertake the long and difficult journey to India to find a teacher and a monastery where you can study.

As it turns out, the scriptures taught at the monastery you first encounter aren't the same as the ones you originally read. (Buddhism was undergoing rapid development, and new teachings were popping up everywhere.) The new scriptures appeal to you even more than the first scriptures you read because they present a much more understandable picture of Buddhist thought and practice. After years of intensive study as a monk, you master these new teachings, help translate them into Chinese, and return home to share them with others. As these teachings catch on, they may evolve into a distinct tradition or school of Chinese Mahayana Buddhism.

In ways like this, Chinese pilgrims to India brought back different versions of Buddhism and diversified the Buddhist landscape in China in the first half of the first millennium CE.

Watching Mahayana Buddhism evolve in China

Although Mahayana Buddhism was born in India, much of its later development took place in China. When it initially arrived in the first century CE, however, the Chinese didn't exactly welcome Buddhism with open arms. They were proud of their civilization (which, among other things, had produced two great philosophical traditions, Confucianism and Taoism) and looked at anything that came from foreign and "barbarian" lands with disdain. Furthermore, Buddhism's emphasis on the unsatisfactory nature of worldly life and the need to gain liberation from it didn't sit well with many Chinese. These ideas seemed to conflict with the Confucian ideal of a well-structured universe in which things worked out harmoniously if you simply carried out your proper role.

But, in the year 220 CE, the ruling Han dynasty fell. This event swept away the sense of security and stability that the Chinese had enjoyed for centuries. In the times of uncertainty that followed, many Chinese found comfort in the new faith from India, which addressed the impermanence their society was experiencing. They also began to notice certain similarities between Buddhism and Taoism and equated the *tao* (the *way*) taught by their native philosophy with the *dharma* explained in Buddhism. All the while, Buddhist teachings continued to arrive in China as merchants and monks made their way eastward from Central Asia. In addition, a number of Chinese made the long and difficult journey to India to learn more about Buddhism at its source (see the sidebar, "How Chinese Buddhism evolved," for more details). In fact, much of the knowledge historians have of the state of Buddhism in India during the first millennium CE comes from the accounts written by these early Chinese pilgrims.

Proliferation into various schools

Over the centuries, Buddhism continued to develop and evolve in China until a number of more or less distinct traditions emerged. Each tradition was mainly associated with specific teachings of Indian origin, but with their own uniquely Chinese flavor.

We say "more or less distinct" because, in the time-honored Chinese fashion, the various traditions tended to influence and borrow from one another. Even today many Chinese don't think of themselves as belonging exclusively to any one religion. They observe elements of Buddhism, Confucianism, Taoism, and even spirit worship without any sense of contradiction.

During the heyday of Buddhism in China between the sixth and ninth centuries, many Buddhist traditions (schools) flourished. The following are some of the most important of these, together with the *sutras* (discourses of Buddha) upon which they are based:

- **Tien-tai.** Based on the *Lotus Sutra* (see Chapter 4), this tradition was named after a famous mountain in China. (For more on this tradition, check out the "Examining Flower Ornament and Tien-tai: The great unifying systems" section, later in this chapter.)

- **Flower Ornament.** Based on a sutra by the same name and known as Hua-yen in Chinese, this tradition became Kegon Buddhism in Japan (see the "Examining Flower Ornament and Tien-tai: The great unifying systems" section, later in this chapter).

- **True Word.** This relatively short-lived Chinese tradition survived in Japan as Shingon Buddhism (see the "Vajrayana in India, China, Japan, and Tibet" section, toward the end of this chapter for more on the Chinese and Japanese versions of this tradition).

- **Pure Land.** Based on the *Land of Bliss* sutras (see Chapter 4), this tradition inspired the development of Jodo and Jodo Shin Buddhism in Japan (see the section, "The advent of two Pure Land schools in Japan," later in this chapter for more details).

- **Meditation.** Called Ch'an in China and Zen in Japan, the Meditation tradition claims to be based on a direct, wordless transmission of insight (as we explain in the section on Zen Buddhism later in this chapter). The *Exposition of Vimalakirti*, *Perfection of Wisdom,* and *Descent into Lanka* sutras strongly influenced the development of this tradition.

Don't be fazed by this rather long list of unusual names. We mention them simply to give you some idea of the richness and diversity of Chinese Buddhism in its prime.

Buddhism's appeal to the Chinese

Buddhism flourished in China because it offered something to almost everyone. Buddhism's sophistication impressed the intellectual elite who were even inspired to make their own contributions to Buddhist philosophy. And, although sophisticated philosophy held no interest for the uneducated masses, the promise of universal salvation certainly did. The common people were therefore drawn to more devotional Buddhist practices, calling on compassionate bodhisattvas (such as Kuanyin) for help in this life, and worshipping Buddhas (such as Amitabha) for help in the next (as we explain in the "Chronicling Pure Land and other devotional schools" section later in this chapter).

Buddhism also appealed to a number of powerful local rulers, partly because they felt that a population trained in morality and nonviolence would be easier to govern. Many of these rulers also began to believe that Buddhist monks, by virtue of their unique ordination and self-controlled way of life, possessed certain magical abilities. To protect their subjects — as well as their own positions — the local rulers tried to keep these monks on their side by promoting Buddhism as much as they could.

Despite Buddhism's appeal, opposition was strong and deeply entrenched. The conflicts that often arose between the supporters of Confucianism, Taoism, and Buddhism generally had less to do with differences in belief and more to do with groups competing for the greatest share of government support and patronage. Detractors often accused Buddhists of promoting anti-Chinese values because so many of them — especially the monks — didn't seem to be fulfilling their social and family obligations. As a result of these and other factors, the influence of the different Chinese Buddhist traditions ebbed and flowed.

In fact, Buddhism as a whole went through many ups and downs in China, sometimes enjoying the strong protection of the ruling parties, and other times experiencing bitter persecution. The last major backlash took place in 845 CE when an imperial order dismantled the Buddhist monasteries and confiscated their wealth. The emperor soon withdrew the order but not before Chinese Buddhism sank into a long, slow decline from which it never fully recovered.

After its persecution in the ninth century, Buddhism survived in China for more than 1,000 years — and even experienced some periods of brilliance — but it never again became the dynamic force it had been earlier. In the 20th century, Buddhism in China faced the additional challenges of Christianity (introduced by Western missionaries) and Communism. The so-called Cultural Revolution of the 1960s and '70s was particularly devastating; it destroyed many traditional Buddhist institutions and further weakened an already seriously diminished Buddhist community. In addition, since the mid-1950s, the Chinese government has actively suppressed Buddhism in Tibet, dismantling monasteries and persecuting many followers. Though some authentic Buddhist practice continues to take place in Taiwan, the jury is still out on whether Buddhism will ever resurface on the mainland.

Examining Flower Ornament and Tien-tai: The great unifying systems

Two schools of Chinese Buddhism — Pure Land and Meditation (*Ch'an*) — managed to survive the persecution of the ninth century relatively unscathed (see the "Chronicling Pure Land and other devotional schools" section, later in this chapter), and three others — Flower Ornament, Tien-tai, and True Word — were successfully transplanted to Japanese society before they seriously declined at home. This section takes a closer look at the Flower Ornament and Tien-tai traditions, both of which developed comprehensive philosophical systems. (For more on the True Word tradition, see the "Vajrayana in India, China, Japan, and Tibet" section, later in this chapter.)

As Mahayana Buddhism evolved in India, it gave birth to an often-bewildering array of viewpoints that caused some confusion for the early Chinese Buddhists. (For more on Mahayana in India, see Chapter 4.) The more familiar the Chinese became with the Buddhist teachings (which reached them bit by bit, not all at once), the more they wondered how the teachings fit together into a coherent whole. To make sense of this assortment of views, several Chinese schools emerged that attempted to organize these diverse Mahayana teachings according to the principles found in the particular sutra (Buddhist discourse) they cherished the most.

✔ **Flower Ornament:** The *Flower Ornament* (*Avatamsaka*) *Sutra* impressed the founders of this school so much that they revered it as the pinnacle of Buddhist thought. They claimed that Buddha proclaimed this sutra immediately after his enlightenment while he was still under the Bodhi tree. Because the sutra presented an undiluted vision of enlightenment, they argued, no one at that time could understand it. In his wisdom and compassion, Buddha then explained what the people *could* understand — the four noble truths (see Chapter 3) and the remainder of the Theravada canon. Buddha only went on to deliver his advanced Mahayana sutras after he had explained these more fundamental teachings.

No matter what else he taught, however, the massive *Flower Ornament Sutra* remained the most profound expression of Buddha's ultimate realizations — or so the masters of the Flower Ornament tradition maintained. According to their commentaries, this sutra taught the ultimate interconnectedness of everything in the universe. Although things seem to exist as separate and distinct entities — *this* table and *that* chair; ordinary beings and Buddhas — they all interpenetrate in a vast interplay of forces. By deep and repeated contemplation of this interconnectedness, they believed, the spiritual practitioner could experience ultimate peace.

✔ **Tien-tai:** The other Chinese school that attempted to arrange all Buddha's diverse teachings into a coherent whole was named after the mountain home of its founder, Chih-i (538–597). Like the Flower Ornament tradition, the Tien-tai claimed that Buddha first taught the *Flower Ornament Sutra* and afterward, realizing it was beyond the grasp of his listeners, delivered teachings that were easier to digest. But, according to Tien-tai, the final and most fully expressed version of Buddha's ultimate intention is found in the *Lotus Sutra* (which explains why the Tien-tai is also known as the White Lotus school).

According to the *Lotus Sutra,* Buddha didn't teach one doctrine to all of his disciples. He revealed different paths to suit the temperaments and abilities of his listeners. He might teach some people that the path of renunciation and morality — refraining from hurting others — leads to their happiness in future lives. He might tell others that the path of wisdom — penetrating the fiction of the self — leads to complete freedom from the cycle of rebirth. And he might teach others that the path of great compassion leads to enlightened service for others. (To find out more about these three paths, see Chapters 12, 13, and 14, respectively.) Although these paths may seem to have different goals, Tien-tai taught that Buddha's true intention was to lead everyone, in the most effective manner, to the ultimate spiritual destination — the full enlightenment of Buddhahood itself.

The White Lotus school also taught that all phenomena in the universe are fundamentally interrelated. Buddha nature pervades all reality, without exception, and you can find truth in a blade of grass just as surely as you can find it in the holiest religious texts. (For more about Buddha nature, see Chapter 2.) This integrated way of looking at things appealed to the down-to-earth Chinese who had a healthy appreciation of nature and the details of everyday life. Instead of looking for a spiritual alternative to mundane existence, Chinese Buddhists typically sought the spiritual dimension *within* the familiar, as you can sense in the lovingly depicted landscapes so typical of Chinese Buddhist art. (Many art museums have excellent examples of such Chinese landscapes. Or you can check out the images at the following Web site: www.chinapage.com/painting.)

Chronicling Pure Land and other devotional schools

So-called eclectic schools, such as the Flower Ornament and Tien-tai (or White Lotus) schools profiled in the previous section, had one major drawback. They appealed more to people who wanted to *study* Buddhism than to those who wanted to *practice* it. Fortunately, the Pure Land and Meditation schools arose and gave would-be practitioners something straightforward and relatively simple to do. Perhaps because of their simplicity and general appeal, these two schools became the predominant Buddhist traditions in China, especially after the anti-Buddhist persecution of the ninth century.

The Pure Land school derives its inspiration and direction from the Mahayana sutras that focus on Amitabha, the Buddha of Infinite Light. Unlike the historical Buddha, Shakyamuni, who walked the earth 2,500 years ago, Amitabha is a transcendental being who exists beyond the limits of ordinary time and space. (Figure 5-4 shows Amitabha, located at the top, and the other main transcendental Buddhas.) His story transports the Buddhist faithful to a mystic realm of extraordinary wonder and beauty, but paradoxically, this realm is as close as your own heart.

According to the sutras in which Shakyamuni purportedly revealed this Buddha's existence, Amitabha (Ami-to-fo in Chinese; Amida in Japanese) dwells in the western paradise of Sukhavati — the Pure Land of Bliss. This paradise came into existence as the result of a series of heartfelt vows that Amitabha (then known as the bodhisattva Dharmakara) made before his guru. In these vows, Amitabha stated that he would bring forth a sacred realm for the ultimate benefit of all beings upon his own attainment of Buddhahood. When a person is born into this realm, he or she is guaranteed to achieve full enlightenment.

Want to know the best part? To be reborn in this pure land, all you have to do is have unwavering faith in Amitabha. If you have faith, Amitabha and his entourage of bodhisattvas will appear at the time of your death and lead you directly to Sukhavati, where you'll take your seat on an open lotus flower and bathe in Amitabha's infinite light. (If your faith in Amitabha wavers, you can still be reborn in Sukhavati, but you'll have to spend some time in a closed lotus before you can experience the full blessings of Amitabha and his host of enlightened beings.)

The sutras dealing with Sukhavati describe its excellent qualities in exquisite detail. They even provide you with exact instructions for visualizing Amitabha (who is as red as the setting sun) and his gorgeous surroundings. But the main purpose of these sutras is simply to remind you of Amitabha's compassion: He already brought Sukhavati into existence for your sake. All the work has already been done; you simply have to have faith in Amitabha, and Sukhavati is yours.

Figure 5-4:
The five transcendental Buddhas.

In India, the devoted worship of Amitabha and other transcendent Buddhas and bodhisattvas formed part of Mahayana practices in general. But, in China and later Japan, Pure Land Buddhism became a tradition unto itself. You can get some idea of the hold Pure Land had — and continues to have — over people's hearts and minds by visiting almost any gallery of Far Eastern art. You're bound to see numerous depictions of Amitabha Buddha in both painting and sculpture. Sometimes he's seated and absorbed in meditation. Other times he's standing with his hands outstretched, welcoming everyone to join him in his pure land. The fondest prayer of millions of people around the world is that this figure will appear to them at the moment of death and lead them to his western paradise.

Closely associated with Amitabha is the compassionate bodhisattva Avalokiteshvara. The *Land of Bliss* sutras describe him as standing at the right side of Amitabha, helping him welcome the deceased. The object of fervent adoration in many Asian lands, Avalokiteshvara underwent an extraordinary transformation as he made his way from India to the Far East: He became a she! (See the "Kuan-yin: A transgendered divinity" sidebar for more information.) Buddhist devotees adore this transcendent bodhisattva, known as Kuan-yin in China (see Figure 5-5) and Kwannon in Japan, much like Catholics adore the Virgin Mary. And like Mary, Kuan-yin continues to intercede on behalf of the faithful. In fact, Asian newspapers still commonly report accounts of her saving the faithful from shipwrecks, fires, and other disasters.

Figure 5-5:
Kuan-yin, the compassionate bodhisattva.

Photo courtesy of Stephan Bodian.

Kuan-yin: A transgendered divinity

Many different explanations have surfaced to explain why the bodhisattva of compassion took on a female form. Some people claim that in the Far East compassion is understood to be a particularly feminine quality, so the sex change was somehow necessary. Others point out that even where this bodhisattva is depicted as male (in Tibet, for example, where he's known as Chenrezig; see Chapter 15), his features are soft and gentle (as befits his merciful qualities), so the gender change isn't as extreme as it may

first appear. Still others maintain that Kuan-yin isn't actually a form of Avalokiteshvara at all. They believe that she's a blend of Tara, the Great Mother of Indian Buddhism and local Chinese nature goddesses.

However he/she is understood, millions of Buddhists around the world call upon this compassionate bodhisattva for blessings and assistance in difficult times.

The advent of two Pure Land schools in Japan

In Japan, Pure Land Buddhism became one of the major dharma traditions and diverged into two separate schools, Jodo-shu and Jodo Shinshu.

- **Jodo-shu:** Literally translated from Japanese as the "Pure Land school," Jodo-shu was founded by Honen (1133–1212), one of the great figures of Japanese Buddhism. Honen became a monk when he was 15 and studied with teachers from various Buddhist schools, but he became increasingly disenchanted with the Buddhism of his day.

  The 12th century was a time of social and political upheaval in Japan, and Honen felt that almost no one could successfully follow the traditional practices of Buddhism in such a degenerate age. He believed that people first needed to be reborn in the Pure Land through the vow of Amitabha, and then they could achieve enlightenment. He therefore encouraged the simple practice of reciting the *nembutsu* (homage to Amitabha) together with the cultivation of strong faith in Amitabha's saving grace. In the original Sanskrit, the homage reads *Namo amitabhaya buddhaya* — literally, "Homage to Amitabha Buddha." In Japanese pronunciation, it became *namu amida butsu,* which is the chant you hear recited these days.

- **Jodo Shinshu:** A monk named Shinran (1173–1262) was one of the many disciples who received the practice of nembutsu from Honen. In his earnest quest for spiritual fulfillment, Shinran devoted many years to serious study and practice with many Buddhist teachers. But, in spite of all his hard work, he remained dissatisfied and restless. Shinran felt that he hadn't achieved anything of real value. Meeting Honen was the turning point in his life. As soon as he started reciting "Namu amida butsu," he experienced the peace that eluded him for so many years. From that moment on, he gave up his monastic vows and spent the rest of his long life wandering among the common people, many of whom became devoted to him.

In 1225, Shinran began his own tradition, which he called Jodo Shinshu (the "True Pure Land school") to differentiate it from the tradition of his deceased master. This new tradition became increasingly popular and now has more followers than any other Buddhist denomination in Japan. Shinran's approach was radical in its simplicity. He interpreted Amitabha's vow to mean that all beings are already enlightened; they just don't realize it! According to Shinran, you don't have to do anything to reach Sukhavati — not even recite the nembutsu. In fact, there's nothing you *can* do; everything has been done for you already. You still pay homage to Amitabha but not because this practice will lead you to Sukhavati. It's an expression of gratitude for having already arrived!

Currently known as the Buddhist Churches of America, Jodo Shinshu has been active in North America since Japanese immigrants first brought it with them more than 100 years ago. Still primarily popular among Japanese Americans, Jodo Shinshu has gained some non-Asian converts in recent decades and continues to be an influential force on the American Buddhist scene. (For more on the practice of Jodo Shinshu, see Chapter 8.)

The Nichiren School

A controversial figure named Nichiren (1222–1282) founded another tradition of Japanese Buddhism that deserves to be mentioned with the Pure Land schools because of some traits they have in common.

Like the Pure Land schools, Nichiren Buddhism requires little more of its followers than strong devotion and the repetition of a short phrase of homage. But, unlike the Pure Land schools, the Nichiren school isn't a Japanese version of a Chinese tradition, and it doesn't direct its devotion toward Amitabha. Instead, Nichiren is a homegrown product of Japan, and the object of its devotion isn't a Buddha or a bodhisattva; it's the *Lotus Sutra.*

Offshoots of the Nichiren school

Not long after Nichiren's passing, internal disputes among his followers led to the establishment of a splinter group that called itself Nichiren Shoshu (the "True School of Nichiren"). Although not big at first, this school survived over the centuries. Then, after World War II, one of its offshoots suddenly exploded into unexpected prominence. In 1937, a convert to Nichiren Shoshu founded a lay society known as Soka Gakkai. Within a few decades, fueled by the humiliation and hardship of the postwar years in Japan, this group grew into a powerful political, social, and economic force.

Members of Soka Gakkai follow the basic practice instituted by Nichiren — reciting "Namu myoho renge kyo" — and regard Nichiren as the Buddha of the present age. On their altar, practitioners keep a reproduction of a special diagram called the *Gohonzon* (originally drawn by Nichiren himself), which is said to embody all the teachings of the *Lotus Sutra* and is therefore given the utmost adoration. Perhaps the most distinctive characteristic of Soka Gakkai, however, is their passion for promoting their religion. Evangelism isn't a trait ordinarily associated

with Buddhism, but Soka Gakkai actively — some would say aggressively — encourages conversion. In terms of numbers, Soka Gakkai has been extraordinarily successful and boasts a worldwide membership of more than 12 million people, including a significant portion of the Japanese population and hundreds of thousands of followers in the West, including celebrities like Herbie Hancock and Tina Turner.

Another offshoot of Nichiren Buddhism is the monastic order known as Nipponzan Myohoji. The members of this order are strongly committed to world peace and have erected peace pagodas in many countries throughout the world, including Manchuria, China, Japan, England, Austria, and the United States. One of the most impressive pagodas (or stupas) is located on a hill outside Rajgir (see Chapter 9) where Buddha originally delivered the *Lotus Sutra* that's so central to the Nichiren tradition. Visitors to these pilgrimage sites see Nipponzan Myohoji followers walking in a regimented style around a beautiful pagoda and banging their racket-shaped drums in time to the chant "Namu myoho renge kyo."

The *Lotus Sutra* is a Mahayana scripture that the Tien-tai (Japanese: Tendai) tradition also reveres. As a follower of Tien-tai (see the "Examining Flower Ornament and Tien-tai: The great unifying systems" section, earlier in this chapter for more info about Tien-tai), Nichiren shared in this adoration to an extraordinary degree. He believed that the *Lotus Sutra* was so powerful that you didn't have to study or even read it to benefit from it; you merely had to recite its title with faith. Simply repeat *Namu myoho renge kyo* ("Homage to the Lotus Sutra of the Wonderful Law") and your spiritual and worldly wishes would be fulfilled. And this phrase could take care of more than just your own personal wishes: Japan was going through a tumultuous period, and Nichiren felt that only faith in the *Lotus Sutra* could save it from invasion.

Nichiren's uncompromising belief that his path was the only true path to personal and national salvation met considerable opposition. He accused the established Buddhist schools of being in cahoots with demonic forces intent on destroying Japan and made many enemies among both the Buddhist clergy and the government. He was even condemned to death, but he escaped execution — by miraculous means, according to his faithful followers. After three years in exile, he returned to Japan and lived out the rest of his life on Mount Minobu, near Mount Fuji, laying the foundation for the organization that would carry on his teachings after his death. (See the "Offshoots of the Nichiren school" sidebar to discover more about the present-day forms of Nichiren Buddhism.)

Zen: Taking root in the Far East — and the West

The Pure Land school (see the "Chronicling Pure Land and other devotional schools" section, earlier in this chapter) wasn't the only Mahayana tradition focused on giving its practitioners a direct experience of enlightenment. Another form of Mahayana Buddhism that also took root in China, moved to other Asian cultures, and eventually made its presence strongly felt in the West also offered a more practical approach. We're referring to Zen, arguably the most visible and widely recognized form of Buddhism in the West.

Zen has a reputation for being mysterious, so we begin this discussion with something simple, its name. The Japanese term *zen* (like the Chinese term that it comes from, *ch'an*) can be traced to the Sanskrit *dhyana,* meaning meditation. (Check out Chapter 14 where we discuss *dhyana,* or meditative concentration, as the fifth of the six perfections.) Because meditation has been a central practice in Buddhism from the beginning (see Chapter 7), it has never been the exclusive property of any one tradition. But, as Mahayana Buddhism began to develop in India, certain teachers emphasized meditation

more strongly than others. One of these teachers, a monk named
Bodhidharma, traveled to China in the sixth century and brought with him
his particular meditative approach. He started off his time in China, quite
appropriately, by spending nine years sitting in meditation facing a wall.
(For more on Bodhidharma, see the "Bodhidharma: A legendary Zen master"
sidebar.)

Understanding the non-dual nature of Zen

For the followers of Bodhidharma's tradition, which became known as Ch'an
(and later Zen), meditation is a direct confrontation with the present moment
and is capable of bringing about a penetrating insight into the true nature of
reality (see Chapter 10 for more on Zen enlightenment). Experiencing this
moment of spiritual awakening depends not only on the meditator's own
efforts, but also on the transformative influence of the master, who offers his
students a special transmission outside the scriptures.

Zen traces its beginnings to just such a "special transmission" between
Shakyamuni Buddha and one of his main disciples. While seated among a
group of his followers, Buddha silently picked up a flower and showed it
to the group. Sitting nearby, one of his most accomplished disciples,
Mahakashyapa, smiled. Out of all the disciples, only he experienced the
wordless transmission of insight that Buddha had offered. Buddha then said,
"I have the treasury of the true dharma eye, the ineffable mind of nirvana.
Reality is formless; the subtle teaching doesn't depend on written words
but is separately transmitted apart from doctrines. This I entrust to
Mahakashyapa."

Bodhidharma: A legendary Zen master

Although he may or may not have actually
existed, Bodhidharma is the epitome of the
tough and enigmatic Zen master whose dedication to meditation is unshakable and who
teaches by direct example rather than scripture.
Usually depicted with a shaved head, scruffy
beard, and earring (the prototypical Gen-Xer?),
the wide-eyed and concentrating Bodhidharma
became a popular subject of Zen ink drawings
in both China and Japan.

The instructive stories about this figure are legendary. In one, he supposedly cut off his eyelids
so he could meditate day and night without
falling asleep (hence the wide-eyed figure in the
ink drawings). Clearly, this tale is meant to
inspire future generations of Zen students to be
diligent and focused in their practice. In another
story, he sits impassively in the snow while a
young seeker begs him for instruction. Finally,
the young man cuts off his arm and hands
it to Bodhidharma to show his devotion
and sincerity — and Bodhidharma finally
agrees to teach him. Another cautionary tale,
though it's certainly not intended to encourage
self-mutilation!

What does this event mean? It demonstrates that ultimate reality can be clearly and directly expressed without words. In fact, words and concepts, though they may point to the truth (like a "finger pointing to the moon," as the famous Buddhist saying goes), are inadequate to express the truth fully because they're inherently *dualistic*. Words and concepts refer to a world of apparently separate, solid things and apparently separate selves that experience them. But, when an awakened being looks at a flower and sees it just as it is, clearly and without conceptual overlays (that is, beyond all limited notions of *this* and *that*), no words can convey the experience. Why? Because there's no experiencer and nothing experienced. All that's there is just pure, *non-dual* experience itself. By picking up the flower, Buddha invites others to share in this non-conceptual knowing — and Mahakashyapa expresses his comprehension with a silent smile.

Awakening to this non-conceptual, non-dual insight is the heart of Zen Buddhism. As Bodhidharma's tradition developed in China (influenced strongly by Taoism) and then entered Korea, Japan, and later Vietnam, different methods for training disciples to discover their true nature gradually evolved. Some of these different methods are found in the two schools of Zen Buddhism, Rinzai and Soto, active in Japan and around the world today.

Profiling Rinzai and Soto: Two different Zen styles

Rinzai Zen, brought to Japan from China by the monk Eisai in 1191, favors the use of *koans* (loosely translated as teaching stories) to confound the mind and arouse direct insight (for more on koans, see Chapter 8). Of the many hundreds of these often elusive and paradoxical questions and anecdotes, perhaps the koans best known in the West are "What is the sound of one hand [clapping]?" and "What was your original face before your parents were born?" Students focus their undivided attention on the koan they've been given and try to reveal its secret meaning, its living essence. Although no correct answers exist, constant confrontation with the koan — under the watchful eye of a skillful teacher — brings the Zen trainee to the very limit of conceptual thought — and eventually beyond.

The training offered by Soto Zen, introduced to Japan by Dogen in 1227, focuses on *zazen* (sitting meditation, which is also practiced in Rinzai). Zazen is formal and demanding. It emphasizes maintaining a correct, upright posture through-out each meditation session while remaining uninterruptedly aware of the pre-sent moment. (To help energize students who are tiring, the Zen master may strike them sharply with a stick carried specifically for that purpose. Though it may look frightening, the blow is stimulating rather than painful.) Teachers in this tradition often point out that you're not meditating to *become* a Buddha; instead, sitting in upright awareness is the way to express the Buddha nature you've always possessed.

In addition to zazen, both Rinzai and Soto Zen offer students the opportunity to have a regular personal interview with the master (known as *dokusan* in Soto and *sanzen* in Rinzai). In Rinzai, these interviews often take the form of spirited encounters in which the student attempts to present a worthy response to a koan and the master either accepts or rejects it. During retreats, participants may line up for hours to see the master and be dismissed in the first minute of the interview with instructions to return to their cushion to mull over the koan once again. In Soto, dokusan tends to occur less frequently and to be more focused on questions about posture, attitude, or everyday life practice — though certain teachers do use koans when they seem appropriate or useful.

Bringing Zen into your everyday life

Because Zen places a great emphasis on maintaining clear awareness of the present moment, training isn't limited only to meditation sessions or koan practice. You have to bring the same clearly focused attention to the tasks of everyday life that you bring to your more formal practice. The Soto tradition in particular emphasizes that every activity provides an opportunity to express your true nature through wholehearted care and attention. You can find many stories of Zen masters who experienced enlightenment while doing mundane household chores like raking leaves or hanging out the laundry!

The Zen focus on the practical and immediate is reflected in its austere yet highly refined aesthetic sense, which has become an integral part of traditional Japanese culture. Practitioners lovingly apply the same clear awareness and attention to detail that they cultivate in meditation to a wide range of activities such as preparing and serving tea, practicing archery, arranging flowers, and creating fine calligraphy. This ability to turn almost any activity into both an artistic and a spiritual experience has made Zen particularly attractive to Western artists and poets. (Did you know that Vincent Van Gogh, who owned an extensive collection of Japanese prints, once painted a portrait of himself as a Zen monk?)

Recognizing Zen's appeal for the West

Of all the Buddhist traditions, Zen has perhaps the longest history of direct contact with the West — contact that its simplicity and aesthetic appeal fostered. Believe it or not, the first recorded visit of a Zen master to North America occurred in 1893, when Soyen Shaku attended the World Parliament of Religions in Chicago. Soyen returned in 1905 to travel and teach. His disciple, Nyogen Senzaki, accompanied him and eventually stayed in America. Though Senzaki, who died in 1958, gained few serious students, he wrote several influential books (with an American friend, Ruth McCandless) and inspired a number of Americans who went on to train in Japan and help plant the Zen seed deep in American soil. Japanese scholar D.T. Suzuki (another disciple of Soyen Shaku) was also extremely influential. He taught at several American universities, published a series of books explaining Zen to a lay audience, and translated key Zen texts into English.

Following in Senzaki's footsteps, the next wave of Zen teachers began arriving in North America from Japan and Korea in the 1950s and '60s. The peaceful postwar atmosphere and the growing Western interest in Zen encouraged these teachers. (The Beat poetry of Allen Ginsberg, Gary Snyder, Jack Kerouac, and others, and the interest of well-known psychologists like Erich Fromm, demonstrated this growing Zen awareness.) By 1970, several large cities, such as New York, Los Angeles, and San Francisco, boasted burgeoning Zen centers — places where motivated students could gather to learn and practice meditation, listen to dharma talks, and attend longer retreats (see Figure 5-6).

Figure 5-6:
Westerners
practicing
zazen.

Courtesy of the San Francisco Zen Center.

The San Francisco Zen Center was probably the best-known of these centers. It now includes Tassajara Zen Mountain Center, the oldest Zen monastery in America (located in the wilderness near Big Sur), and Green Gulch Farm, an organic farm and practice center in nearby Marin County. The Zen Center's late founder, Shunryu Suzuki Roshi (1905–1971), wrote the classic, best-selling book *Zen Mind, Beginner's Mind* (Weatherhill). Other influential Zen masters in North America include Joshu Sasaki Roshi of Mount Baldy Zen Center in southern California; Eido Shimano Roshi of the New York Zen Studies Society; Taizan Maezumi Roshi (1931–1996) of the Zen Center of Los Angeles; and the Korean master Seung Sahn of the Kwan Um Zen School based in Providence, Rhode Island, author of several popular books, including *Dropping Ashes on the Buddha* (Grove Press).

Nowadays most major metropolitan areas and even many smaller cities have their Zen centers or sitting groups, many of them directed and led by a new generation of Zen teachers — westerners trained by Korean or Japanese teachers and fully authorized to train others. Because of its simplicity, its practicality, and its emphasis on direct experience, Zen has enormous appeal to westerners. They can practice it without accepting any new belief systems — or, as Zen puts it, without putting another head on top of their own.

Checking out Zen in China, Korea, and Vietnam

Most people associate Zen with Japan. But the tradition also flourished in China, Korea, and Vietnam, and masters from these countries have independently come to the West to teach. After its heyday in China, Ch'an (the Chinese name for Zen) gradually lost its exclusive emphasis on meditation and became more eclectic, picking up elements of Pure Land, Tien-tai, and several other Buddhist schools. Although Buddhism was first introduced to the United States by Chinese immigrants in the 1850s and '60s, Ch'an didn't make much headway outside the Chinese community until Zen Master Hsuan Hua founded Gold Mountain Monastery in San Francisco in 1970 and began teaching westerners his intensive approach, including the full range of Ch'an practices. Since his death in 1995, Hsuan Hua's successors have continued to spread his teachings in the West.

In Korea, Zen practice had become firmly established by the sixth century CE, even before it made its way to Japan, and reigned as the main form of Buddhism there for many centuries. Though suppressed during the Yi Dynasty (1392–1910), Zen (Korean: Son) managed to survive and has become a vital Buddhist school in the West, alongside Japanese Zen. In addition to Zen Master Seung Sahn, whose Kwan Um Zen School has affiliate centers throughout the Western world, several other Korean teachers have developed large followings. Though meditation has always been the primary method, Korean Zen also emphasizes the practices of chanting and bowing.

Because Vietnam, like Korea, borders China, Buddhism put down roots there in the early centuries of the first millennium CE, and over time Zen became the predominant school. Perhaps the best-known Vietnamese Zen master to teach in the West is Thich Nhat Hanh (see Chapter 15), but Buddhist monk and scholar Dr. Thich Thien-an preceded him. Thien-an arrived in Los Angeles in 1966 as a visiting professor at UCLA and stayed to teach eager Western students until his death in 1980.

From Tibet to the West: Charting the movement of the Diamond Vehicle

In the past 30 years or so another outgrowth of Mahayana Buddhism, called the Vajrayana (or Diamond Vehicle), has grown to rival Zen Buddhism's popularity in the West. Vajrayana is known by a number of names (including Tantra and the mysterious-sounding Esoteric Vehicle), but most people simply refer to it as Tibetan Buddhism after the country with which it's now most closely identified. However, Vajrayana isn't a Tibetan invention, as some influential writers once thought; it's a product of the same Buddhist developments in India that were responsible for other Mahayana traditions mentioned earlier in this chapter.

Like all the other forms of Buddhism, Vajrayana claims to transmit the authentic teachings of Buddha — even though the texts (known as *tantras*) of this approach didn't appear until long after Shakyamuni Buddha's passing. Although historians (and even other Buddhists) may have trouble accepting these late-emerging teachings as the true word of Buddha, the Vajrayana faithful claim (like followers of some other Mahayana traditions) that Buddha gave many teachings during his lifetime that were too advanced to be disseminated widely. Tantra was the most powerful of these advanced teachings, and therefore, it was most open to abuse. Tantric practitioners purportedly kept these powerful teachings hidden from general view and only passed them on to the select few who could benefit from them. Later practitioners transmitted these teachings more widely, though still with a certain air of secrecy to prevent their misuse and degeneration.

Vajrayana in India, China, Japan, and Tibet

Though hidden, Vajrayana Buddhism was practiced in India in one form or another by the fifth century CE. It then became established in China in the eighth century as the True Word (*Mi-tsung*) school. Although this school lasted only a century in China, Kukai (774–836) carried it to Japan and built a temple in 816 on Mount Koya that remains the center of what became known as the Shingon tradition.

Although people still practice Shingon Buddhism in Japan today, this tradition is not as fully developed or complete as the Vajrayana Buddhism that continued to evolve in India from the eighth century on. Maintained by master meditators known as *mahasiddhas* (greatly accomplished ones), the Vajrayana tradition thrived and eventually became a major part of the training at the famous monastic universities in northern India, such as Vikramashila and Nalanda (see Chapter 9). The destruction of Nalanda by invaders in 1199 marked the demise of the Vajrayana tradition and Buddhism as a whole in India. By the beginning of the 13th century, Buddhism was no longer a viable religion in the land of its birth, even though it left a lasting imprint on the culture of the vast subcontinent.

Fortunately, by the time of Buddhism's destruction, the mature Vajrayana tradition of India was already firmly established in Tibet and the surrounding Himalayan regions thanks to the efforts of such mahasiddhas as Padmasambhava and Atisha. Although the tradition reached Mongolia and Siberia (and even made its way back into China), Tibet remained the center of the Vajrayana world for centuries, preserving the tantric teachings as a vital, effective tradition until the brutal invasion of Tibet by the Chinese communists in the 1950s. Yet Tibet's loss has been the world's gain. With the escape of the Dalai Lama in 1959 and his forced exile in India — along with the escape of a relatively small but significant number of other great teachers — Vajrayana Buddhism has become available to the West as never before.

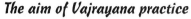

The aim of Vajrayana practice

Like other Buddhist traditions, Vajrayana practice aims at enlightenment. This tradition is distinctive, however, because of the wealth of different methods it employs to bring enlightenment about as quickly as possible. Some of these methods involve complex rituals that feature music, chanting, symbolic implements, stylized gestures (called *mudras*), mystic diagrams (*mandalas*), and words of power (*mantras*). Other methods are hidden from external view and take place solely within the Vajrayana meditator's body and mind. Whether external or internal, these various methods are ultimately directed at accomplishing the radical transformation of Buddhahood.

According to Vajrayana, you already have everything you need to experience the full and complete enlightenment of Buddhahood. For this enlightenment to become a living experience (and not remain just untapped potential), you must overcome some powerful habits, the chief of which is the tendency to identify yourself, consciously or not, as a "limited" being. That is, you're used to seeing yourself as a separate, fragmented self or ego, flawed by the delusions of hatred, greed, and ignorance (see Chapter 2), and therefore severely limited in your ability to act, speak, and think in a way that brings happiness to yourself or others.

The practice of "deity yoga"

The distinctive tantric solution to the problems arising from holding onto a limited self-identity is the practice known as *deity yoga.* Deity yoga has nothing to do with the "gods" and "goddesses" enjoying the celestial realms mentioned in Chapter 13. Instead, the practice enables you to dissolve your false, limiting ego-identity and replace it with something far better. By means of this profound practice you train to see yourself as an enlightened being, a fully evolved Buddha, free from all limitations, with a radiantly pure and blissful body, speech, and mind through which you can bring infinite benefit to others. The particular enlightened being you identify with is known in Tibetan as your *yidam,* or *meditational deity.* (See Figure 5-7 for one such meditational deity in female form; flip over to Chapter 4 for an image of a male deity, Manjushri. Aside from their outward appearance, the two deities are exactly the same; they're both manifestations of enlightenment.)

If done incorrectly, without the proper understanding, the practice of deity yoga can easily degenerate into a form of make-believe in which you're merely pretending to be something you're not. To avoid this pitfall, you must build your practice on a firm foundation. To start with, you should be well versed in the fundamentals of the Mahayana path in general, particularly the generation of universal compassion, or *bodhichitta.* (For more on bodhichitta, see Chapter 14.) Then you have to complete certain ritual practices, called *preliminaries* (Tibetan: *ngon-dro*), which are designed to prepare you for your main practices by letting you collect a powerful reserve of positive energy and cleanse yourself of certain inner obstacles. (An example of these collecting-and-cleansing practices is offering full-length prostrations; see Chapter 8.)

Figure 5-7:
Tara, the
female
deity of
compassion.

The most important foundation for practice is your reliance on a fully qualified tantric master, or guru. (The guru, or *lama* in Tibetan, is so central to Vajrayana that some early Western commentators referred to the Buddhism of Tibet as *Lamaism* — a misleading phrase that has fortunately gone out of fashion.) The guru is indispensable because he or she introduces you to the meditational deity (such as Tara in Figure 5-7) that will act as the focal point of your practice.

At the *empowerment ceremony* (Tibetan: *wang*), during which you're initiated into the practice, you need to remain undistracted by the ordinary appearances of things — including the outward form of your guru. Instead, you visualize him or her as inseparable from the transcendent form of Shakyamuni Buddha, known as Vajradhara (see Figure 5-8). Ultimately, your practice of deity yoga is successful when you have the unshakable realization that your guru, your meditational deity, and all the Buddhas are identical with the essential nature of your own mind.

Through deity yoga, you gradually get used to being enlightened. The blessings and inspiration of your guru help empower you to view your body as the pure light body of your meditational deity (Tara in Figure 5-7, for example), radiant and blissful. In place of your ordinary speech, you recite the sound of her mantra; you practice hearing *all* sounds as indistinguishable from her mantra. At the same time, you view your environment as Tara's pure land (Buddha field) and all your activities as Tara's wise and compassionate activities in liberating others from suffering. Ultimately, you experience your own mind and Tara's enlightened mind as one.

Figure 5-8:
Vajradhara, the tantric Guru Buddha.

In the beginning stages of practice, the identification of yourself and the meditational deity as one takes place largely (if not entirely) in your imagination. But, at later stages, when you become adept at controlling and directing the subtle energies flowing through your body (see Chapter 11 for more about these subtle energies), you can actually experience the enlightened transformation you previously only imagined. Eventually, you can follow in the footsteps of Tibet's beloved yogi Milarepa (see Figure 5-9). Through his intense devotion to his guru Marpa and his unwavering practice, he achieved Buddhahood during his lifetime.

Figure 5-9:
Tibet's
great yogi
Milarepa.

Vajrayana in the West

Vajrayana Buddhism contains many more methods than we briefly allude to here, but even this short account can give you an idea why this form of practice has gained a growing number of Western followers in recent years. For individuals who like rituals, the many Tibetan-style dharma centers in the West regularly host group sessions featuring mantra recitation, chanting, and other ritualized practices (see Figure 5-10).

For folks who prefer straight meditation, Vajrayana presents a broad range of practices, from elaborate visualizations to simply resting in the mind's basic purity. The tradition also offers opportunities for academic study — as demonstrated by the rapidly increasing number of translations and commentaries rolling off the presses. But, at the end of the day, the warm and compassionate lamas who teach the Vajrayana may be the most attractive feature of this tradition.

Every center has its own unique style and emphasis, depending on the teacher and the particular sect of Vajrayana he or she teaches. (See the sidebar, "Tibetan Vajrayana schools," for further details.) The Shambhala centers, established by the late Chogyam Trungpa Rinpoche (1939–1987), may be the most widespread of all. Trungpa was a prolific author and one of the first Tibetan teachers to adopt Western dress and familiarize himself with Western psychology and customs. But numerous other approaches are now available across North America, including a new generation of centers led by fully authorized Western teachers.

Figure 5-10:
Westerners
engaging in
Vajrayana
practice.

Photo courtesy of Shambhala Sun. Copyright Shambhala Sun.

Tibetan Vajrayana schools

As Vajrayana Buddhism spread from India to Tibet, a number of different schools (or sects) emerged. Although some cross-fertilization has always occurred between these schools, each has its own distinctive character. The schools with the greatest influence on the Tibetan Buddhism practiced in the West today are

- **Nyingma** (nyeeng-mah): This tradition is the oldest school of Tibetan Buddhism (its name means the "Ancient Ones"). Padmasambhava founded this tradition and established Samye, the first monastery in Tibet, in the eighth century. Among the many lamas responsible for introducing the Nyingma lineage to the West are Dilgo Khyentze Rinpoche (1910–1991), a major teacher of lamas from all traditions; Tarthang Tulku, who established the Tibetan Nyingma Meditation Center and the Odiyan Retreat Center in California; Namkhai Norbu Rinpoche, who lives in Italy and teaches regularly in the United States; and Sogyal Rinpoche, head of the world-wide Rigpa centers and author of the popular *Tibetan Book of Living and Dying* (HarperSanFrancisco).

- **Kadam** (kah-dahm): The followers of Atisha, who came to Tibet from India in 1042, started this tradition. Although this school no longer exists as a separate entity, the following three schools absorbed and transmitted its teachings.

- **Sakya** (sah-kyah): The current head of the Sakya tradition, the Sakya Trizin, speaks fluent English and has taught and traveled widely in the West. Among the other Sakya lamas who have been active in the United States are Deshung Rinpoche (1906–1987), Jigdal Dagchen Rinpoche of the Sakya Tegchen Choling center in Seattle, and Lama Kunga of Kensington, California.

- **Kagyu** (kah-gyew): The previous head of the Kagyu tradition, the Sixteenth Karmapa (1923—1981), visited the United States on a number of occasions and dedicated his main center, Karma Triyana Dharmachakra, in Woodstock, New York. After passing away in Chicago, his incarnation was born in Tibet and escaped to India in 2000; his many centers in the West now eagerly await his return. Other Kagyu lamas who have established centers and taught extensively in the West include Kalu Rinpoche (1905–1989), widely considered one of the greatest Vajrayana meditation masters of the 20th century; Thrangu Rinpoche; and Lama Lodo of the Kagyu Droden Kunchab center in San Francisco.

- **Gelug** (gay-look): Numerous lamas have represented this school in the West, including the late tutors of the Dalai Lama. Other notable lamas from this tradition who have had a great impact on the West include Geshe Wangyal (1901–1983), who founded centers in Freewood Acres and Washington, New Jersey; Geshe Lhundrup Sopa, retired professor at the University of Wisconsin; and Lama Thubten Yeshe (1935–1984) and Thubten Zopa Rinpoche of the Foundation for the Preservation of the Mahayana Tradition.

- **Rime** (ree-may): This movement combines several important lineages of Vajrayana practice. One of the leading lights of this non-sectarian movement was Jamyang Khyentze Chokyi Lodro (1896–1969). Many of Jamyang Khyentze's disciples have been influential teachers in the West, including the above-mentioned Dezhung Rinpoche, Dilgo Khyentze Rinpoche, Kalu Rinpoche, Trungpa Rinpoche, Sogyal Rinpoche, and Tarthang Tulku.

Part III
Buddhism in Practice

The 5th Wave   By Rich Tennant

TIBETAN BUDDHIST MEDITATION

STIFF JOINTED BUDDHIST MEDITATION

In this part . . .

Here's where it gets really interesting — practical answers to your questions about Buddhism. How do you become a Buddhist? How do you meditate? What does a typical day in the life of a Buddhist look like? What's a Buddhist pilgrimage? Where can you go? The following pages contain all this information and more, so start down the path.

Chapter 6

Turning to Buddhism

. . . .

In This Chapter

▶ Checking out the dharma to see if it interests you

▶ Making your way through the initial levels of involvement

▶ Renouncing the dream of material security and satisfaction

▶ Committing yourself to Buddhism as a lifelong path

▶ Considering the wholehearted path of the monk or nun

. . . .

After you know a little something about Buddhism (conceptually at least), you may want to explore the teachings in greater detail — and perhaps even sample a Buddhist practice or two for yourself. But where do you go and what do you do to get started? "Do I need to shave my head and run off to some monastery in the forest?" you may wonder. "Or can I get a taste of Buddhism right here at home?"

Buddhism comes in many shapes, sizes, and flavors, and we're certain that a Buddhist center is located somewhere near you. (So the answer is no; you don't have to head for a monastery just yet.) But before you pick up your local phone book or check out the abbreviated list of Buddhist organizations in Appendix B, you may want to read the rest of this chapter. Why? Because we think you'll enjoy it. But also because this chapter offers guidelines for approaching Buddhism gradually and thoughtfully — from your initial contact, through progressive stages of involvement, and on to the (altogether optional) moment of formally becoming a Buddhist.

Proceeding at Your Own Pace

When you first start exploring Buddhism, remember that Buddha wasn't technically a Buddhist. In fact, he didn't consider himself a member of any religion at all, merely a guy who traveled around sharing some important truths about life. So you don't have to be a Buddhist either. Buddhists and non-Buddhists alike can enjoy and put into practice the many valuable teachings that Buddha and his disciples have provided over the centuries.

Even the best-known Buddhist in the world today, the Dalai Lama, advises that you don't have to change your religion to benefit from the teachings of Buddhism. (For more information on this inspiring individual — and others — check out Chapter 15.) In fact, the Dalai Lama generally discourages seekers from other faiths from becoming Buddhists — at least until they've thoroughly explored the tradition into which they were born. When asked to identify his own religion, the Dalai Lama frequently responds quite simply, "My religion is kindness."

The message of Buddhism is clear:

- ✔ Proceed at your own pace.
- ✔ Take what works for you and leave the rest.
- ✔ Most importantly, question what you hear, experience its truth for yourself, and make it your own.

"Ehi passiko," Buddha was fond of declaring. "Come here and see." In other words, if you feel an affinity for what Buddhism says, stay for a while and explore it. If not, feel free to leave whenever you want.

Taking responsibility for your own life

Ultimately, you're responsible for deciding how you spend your life. In Buddhism, no guru or god watches over you, prepared to hand out punishment if you stray from the path. Buddha's final words — "All conditional things are impermanent. Work out your own salvation with diligence." — set the standard for this matter.

In fact, Buddha never insisted that his followers, even those who chose to join the monastic order by becoming monks and nuns (see Chapter 8), remain physically close to him or the rest of the *sangha* (community). Instead, he encouraged them to find their own way. Many of his followers wandered from place to place, meditating and sharing their understanding with others. They gathered together just once each year during the rainy season to meet with Buddha, receive teachings, and meditate together.

At the heart of this approach is the understanding that life itself provides you with the motivation you need to turn to Buddhist practice. If and when you pay close attention to your circumstances, you gradually discover that Buddha had it right: Conventional life is marked by dissatisfaction. You suffer when you don't get what you want (or you get what you don't want). Your happiness doesn't depend on external situations; it depends on your state of mind. When you realize these simple but powerful truths, you naturally look for a way out of your suffering.

Some traditions of Buddhism encourage followers to fuel their motivation —
and, therefore, their devotion — to practice by remembering certain
fundamental truths. The Vajrayana (the "Diamond Vehicle" described in
Chapter 5) refers to these truths as the *four reminders,* which we outline
in the following list. (For further information, refer to the chapters cross-
referenced in parentheses.)

✔ **Your human rebirth is precious.** Because you now have the perfect
opportunity to do something special with your life, don't waste it on
trivial pursuits (see Chapter 11).

✔ **Death is inevitable.** Because you won't live forever, don't keep putting
off your spiritual practice (see Chapter 11).

✔ **The laws of karma can't be altered or avoided.** Because you experience
the consequences of what you think, say, and do, act in a way that brings
you happiness rather than dissatisfaction (see Chapter 12).

✔ **Suffering permeates all limited existence.** Because you can't find lasting
peace as long as ignorance veils your mind, make efforts to win true
release from suffering (see Chapter 13).

These reminders can keep you from being distracted by the many seductive
appeals to your greed, lust, and fear that this materialistic culture puts forth.
Instead, they help you stay focused on taking responsibility for your own
happiness and peace of mind. (For more on the relationship between your
happiness and the state of your mind, see Chapter 2.)

Determining your level of involvement

Given its emphasis on individual freedom and self-motivation, Buddhism
naturally opens its doors to all seekers at every level of involvement. Dharma
teachings and meditation instruction are offered freely — and generally free
of charge — to anyone who wants to receive them. (In return, offering some
form of material support, such as money, is customary.)

You can attend Sunday services at many Christian churches without becoming
a member or declaring yourself a Christian, and the same thing goes for
Buddhism. You can receive meditation instruction, listen to teachings, and
even participate in meditation retreats without officially becoming a Buddhist.
Some well-known teachers, like the Indian *Vipassana* (insight meditation)
master S.N. Goenka, even hesitate to use the term *Buddhism* because they
believe that the teachings extend well beyond the confines of any one religion
and apply universally to everyone, whatever their religious involvement.
Goenka, for example, simply calls what he teaches *dhamma* (Sanskrit:
dharma) — the truth.

Buddha is traditionally described as a great healer whose teachings have the power to eliminate suffering at its root. Like any compassionate healer, he shared his abilities with anyone who happened to approach him, regardless of their religious affiliation. But Buddha also made it clear that you can't benefit unless you take the medicine — in other words, unless you put the teachings into practice.

Getting Acquainted with the Dharma

As so often happens with any involvement, people are drawn to Buddhism for a variety of reasons. Consider, for example, your favorite sport. Perhaps you learned to play it as a child, and you've been involved with it ever since. Or maybe a good friend turned you on to the sport later in life. Possibly you were inspired to learn by a spectacular match you saw on TV — perhaps by the enjoyment of a family member. Or maybe you simply saw a flyer about a class at a local rec center and decided you needed the exercise.

Believe it or not, people turn to Buddhism for similar reasons. The following examples bear that idea out.

- ✔ Some people read a book or attend a talk by a particular teacher and get so captivated by the teachings that they decide to pursue them further. Other folks tag along with a friend, without knowing anything about Buddhism, and find themselves suddenly enthralled. Still others seek out meditation practice because they've heard that it's an effective way to reduce stress or improve their health, and as meditation begins to have its desired effect, these people read more and discover that the teachings also appeal to them.

- ✔ A few folks, like Buddha himself, have an early insight into the universal suffering of human life and feel compelled to find a solution. Even more common are the many people who experience their own deep suffering in this lifetime, try other remedies (like psychotherapy or medication, for example), and find only temporary relief. For these seekers, Buddhism offers a comprehensive approach to identifying and eliminating the fundamental cause of their suffering. (For more on the cause and end of suffering, see Chapters 3 and 13.)

- ✔ And some people, for whatever reason, believe that their purpose in this lifetime is to achieve full enlightenment and that Buddhism is the tradition they were born to study.

Whatever your particular reasons for getting acquainted with Buddhism — all are equally valid and worthwhile — this initial stage of involvement can actually last a lifetime. Some devoted, long-time meditators choose to never formally declare themselves Buddhists, even though they've studied the teachings and engaged in the practices for most of their adult lives. (Stephan's first Zen teacher cautioned him never to call himself a "Buddhist," even after he became an ordained monk.)

The following sections examine a few of the many possible ways to get acquainted with Buddhism. We present them in the order in which they often occur, but the truth is that you can begin getting to know Buddhism in any way you see fit, and you may keep returning to some if not all of these points of contact throughout your life.

Reading dharma books

Many excellent Buddhist books are currently available, which makes this entry point a readily accessible and enjoyable place to start. You may want to stick to more popular fare at first, rather than getting bogged down in the difficult language of the sutras or the riddles of the Zen masters. Check out Appendix B, where we offer a representative sample of these works.

At this stage of your involvement with Buddhism, you definitely want to keep your intellect engaged as you investigate and interpret the teachings. Does what you read make sense to you? Does it mesh with your experiences and understanding? Does it shed new light on the relationship between your thoughts, feelings, and experiences? As you read, make note of any questions you may have and make sure that they eventually get answered.

In the long run, books will not provide you with satisfying answers to all the deeper questions of life: Who am I? Why am I here? How can I realize lasting happiness? You may need to *experience* the answers directly for yourself, which is why Buddhism emphasizes putting the teachings into practice, rather than merely speculating upon them intellectually.

Choosing a tradition

As you check out different dharma books, you may find teachings and traditions that particularly appeal to you. Are you drawn to the practical, progressive approach of Vipassana, which offers a variety of accessible practices and teachings for working with your mind? Or are you taken with the more enigmatic, formal path of Zen, with its emphasis on awakening here and now to your innate Buddha nature? Or maybe you're attracted to the elaborate visualizations and *mantras* of Vajrayana, which use the power of the guru and other awakened beings to energize your journey to enlightenment. (For more on these different traditions, see Chapter 5.)

A few Buddhist traditions, such as the Pure Land schools, even de-emphasize meditation in favor of faith in the saving grace of Buddhist figures known as *bodhisattvas* (see Chapter 4). If you have a strong devotional nature, you may find one of those traditions particularly appealing.

If you came to the path through the influence of a teacher or friend, you may clearly feel that their tradition is the one you want to pursue. But, if you're still shopping around, you may find it helpful to zero in on a particular approach before you take the next step of receiving meditation instruction. We're not saying that you can't shift directions at any point along the way, or that basic Buddhist practices and meditation techniques aren't remarkably similar across traditions, because you can, and they are. But the styles of practice, which may differ only slightly at the outset, begin to diverge rapidly as you become more actively involved in a particular tradition.

Receiving meditation instruction

If you live in a large city, you may be able to locate a class on basic Buddhist meditation at your local community college or adult education center. Nowadays Buddhist meditation also comes in a package known as *mindfulness-based stress-reduction* (MBSR), a program developed by researcher and longtime Buddhist meditator Jon Kabat-Zinn at the University of Massachusetts Medical Center.

As a method for reducing stress, MBSR introduces basic Buddhist teachings about the causes of suffering (think *stress* in this case) and the path to its elimination and teaches the fundamental practice of mindfulness. (For more on Buddhist meditation, see Chapter 7.) Research has demonstrated that MBSR is effective in helping to alleviate a host of stress-related health problems.

If you can't locate a basic class in Buddhist meditation (or if you're already drawn to a particular tradition), check the yellow pages or a local newspaper for listings of Buddhist centers and churches. Then be sure to call and ask whether they provide meditation instruction to the general public. Like their Judeo-Christian counterparts, some Buddhist churches offer only weekly services, ceremonies, and community events.

If you can't find what you're looking for under the Buddhist heading, check for listings under *meditation* instead. Many Vipassana and Zen groups that meet to sit together believe that this category more accurately describes what they do. (If you can find a copy at your local bookstore, the quarterly Buddhist magazine *Tricycle* provides an excellent listing of Buddhist groups throughout North America. Or check out *Tricycle* online at www.tricycle.com.) After you make a connection, don't be afraid to ask a few questions to make sure that the organization teaches the kind of meditation you want learn. Then go ahead and take the leap!

Many centers offer an evening or one-day workshop in which you can pick up the basics of meditation in a few hours. Others offer multi-week courses, which allow you to ask questions as you experiment with the approach. In any case, make sure that you have access to ongoing support, such as phone consultations or further classes, if you need it. Though the basic techniques are generally quite simple, they can take months and even years to master, and you're almost certain to encounter a variety of obstacles and issues along the way.

Developing a meditation practice

Expect to work on and develop your meditation practice for as long as you continue to meditate. Even the most accomplished meditators are constantly refining their technique. That's one of the joys and satisfactions of meditation — it offers the opportunity for endless exploration and discovery. (For more on meditation practice, see Chapter 7.)

In the beginning months of your encounter with meditation, your focus will be on finding the time and a suitable location to practice and on familiarizing yourself with the basics, such as following your breath or generating loving-kindness. You'll almost certainly have questions like

✔ What do I do with my eyes or my hands?

✔ My breathing seems labored and tight. Is there any way to loosen it up?

✔ How can I keep from losing track of my breath entirely?

Having these kinds of questions is perfectly normal, which is why follow-up guidance is crucial. More people give up meditating because they lack proper guidance than for any other reason.

In addition to technique, the teachings of Buddhism inspire and inform the practice of Buddhist meditation. Attending dharma talks, reading dharma books, and meditating regularly work in combination with one another. As your meditation skills improve, the teachings make more sense to you — and as your understanding of dharma progresses, your meditation naturally deepens.

Finding a teacher

You may be able to meditate quite happily for months or years without feeling the need for a teacher. After all, with all the dharma books available these days, the most profound teachings are just a click away at an online bookstore (or a few miles away at an offline bookstore). Sure, you may already consult a meditation instructor every now and then or attend an occasional talk by a Buddhist teacher, but choosing someone to guide you on your spiritual journey — now that's another level of involvement entirely!

In the various Buddhist traditions, the role of teacher takes different forms.

- ✔ **Theravada:** The Theravada tradition of Southeast Asia, for example, regards the teacher as a *kalyana mitra* (spiritual friend). Essentially, he or she is a fellow traveler on the path who advises you to "go a little to the left" or "head right a bit" when you veer off course. Other than this type of input, a teacher has no special spiritual authority, aside from the fact that he or she may be more experienced than you. The words *preceptor* or *mentor* may be the best everyday English equivalents to describe this teaching role.

- ✔ **Vajrayana:** In the Vajrayana, the teacher comes in several shapes and sizes, including:

  - • **Geshes:** These folks, who are usually monks, have extensive academic training and are experts in interpreting and expounding on the scriptures.

  - • **Meditation instructors:** These teachers provide expert guidance in developing and deepening your practice. They may be monks or nuns or merely experienced lay practitioners.

  - • **Gurus:** Gurus are known as lamas in Tibetan. These teachers are often, but not always, monks. Gurus, or lamas, have extensive meditation training and accomplishment and are revered by their disciples as the embodiment of the enlightened qualities of wisdom and compassion.

When you take a teacher as your guru, you're generally making a lifelong commitment. Though you can alter or terminate your involvement, developing hostility toward your guru is believed to have serious negative karmic consequences.

- ✔ **Zen:** In Zen, practitioners regard the master (Japanese: *roshi;* Korean: *sunim*) as having considerable spiritual power and authority. Like the guru, disciples deem the master to be enlightened, with the capacity to awaken similar realizations in his or her students through words, gestures, and bearing. Close personal study with a Zen master is an essential component of Zen practice and training. Zen also has its meditation instructors and junior teachers — but behind them all stands the spiritual presence of the master.

Ordinarily, the teacher you choose depends on the tradition that appeals to you. But sometimes, the process works the other way around — you're drawn to a teacher first, through his or her books or talks, and then you adopt the tradition that he or she represents. An ancient Indian saying makes the point, "When the student is ready, the teacher appears." You don't have to be in a hurry to find your teacher. As the saying suggests, finding the right teacher may depend more on the sincerity of your practice than on outer circumstances. Trust your intuition and your own sense of timing. In many traditions, establishing a relationship with a particular teacher precedes or accompanies the formal commitment to Buddhist practice.

One final word of caution: Be sure to check out a prospective teacher carefully before officially becoming his or her student (see the "Checking out the guru" sidebar in this chapter for more details). Ask questions, do some research, and spend as much time with the teacher as possible. In recent years, several Buddhist teachers in the West, both westerners and Asians, have engaged in unethical conduct that has had harmful consequences for their students and communities. As in all human interactions, don't give up your own good judgment and discernment.

Checking out the guru

A Tibetan saying points out that you shouldn't select a guru in the same indiscriminate way a hungry dog pounces on whatever piece of meat it happens to find. Entrusting your spiritual guidance to someone is serious business and demands special care. When the great Indian practitioner Atisha reached the distant land where his predicted guru lived, he didn't go to the guru immediately and request instruction. Instead he spent time living among the guru's disciples. Hanging around these folks gave Atisha a chance to check out what kind of effect the teacher had on his students (and, by implication, what kind of a person the teacher was), before making any formal commitment to him.

Another (probably mythical) story concerns a man who went up to a famous teacher and declared, "I have been observing you closely for 12 years, and I see you have all the qualities of a proper spiritual master. I am now ready to accept you as my guru." The teacher then replied, "But first I have to observe *you* for 12 years to see if you have all the qualities of a proper disciple."

When asked for guidance on this matter by Western Buddhists, His Holiness the Dalai Lama has repeatedly encouraged prospective students to take their time evaluating a teacher, using personal investigation, reason, and experience, before entrusting him or her with their spiritual welfare. In particular, he warns students against the dangers of falling prey to charisma, deceit, narrow-mindedness, or exoticism. Though 12 years may not be necessary, he advises that two or three years may be an excellent idea.

Formally Becoming a Buddhist

You don't need to declare yourself a Buddhist to enjoy and benefit from Buddhist practices and teachings. Some traditions even reserve formal initiation for individuals who choose the monastic life and simply ask lay people to observe a few basic precepts. But the step of becoming a Buddhist can have profound personal significance, solidifying your commitment to a teacher or tradition and energizing your practice. For this reason, many people consider taking this significant step at some point or another in their involvement with Buddhism.

Focusing on the importance of renunciation

Many people associate renunciation with giving up material possessions and involvements and pursuing a life of detachment and withdrawal. But true renunciation is an internal (rather than an external) movement or gesture — though it can certainly express itself in action. In many traditions, becoming a Buddhist involves the fundamental recognition that *samsaric* existence (see Chapter 13) — the world of getting and spending, striving and achieving, loving and hating — doesn't provide ultimate satisfaction or security.

In other words, when you commit yourself to Buddhism as a path, you don't renounce your family or your career; you renounce the conventional view that you can find true happiness in worldly concerns. You renounce the relentless message of the consumer society that the next car or house or vacation or accomplishment will finally relieve your dissatisfaction and bring you the contentment you so desperately seek.

Instead, you adopt the radical view that you can achieve lasting peace and happiness only by clearing your mind and heart of negative beliefs and emotions, penetrating to the truth of reality, opening yourself to your inherent wakefulness and joy, and experiencing what Buddha called the "sure heart's release."

Taking refuge in the Three Jewels

The same 180-degree turnaround in consciousness that is necessary to formally become a Buddhist lies at the heart of many of the world's great religious traditions. For example, Jesus asked his disciples to renounce worldly concerns and follow him, and many Christian churches still require their members to acknowledge Jesus as their only salvation. In Buddhism, this turning (*metanoia,* literally "change in consciousness") often takes the form of taking refuge in the Three Jewels (or Three Treasures): Buddha, dharma, and sangha.

In many traditional Asian countries, taking refuge is what defines you as a Buddhist, and lay people recite the refuge vows whenever they visit a monastery or receive dharma teachings. For Western lay practitioners, the refuge ceremony has become a kind of initiation in many traditions, with far-reaching significance. Though it may simply involve the repetition of a prayer or chant, taking refuge implies that you turn to Buddha, dharma, and sangha as your source of spiritual guidance and support. When you encounter dissatisfaction and suffering, you don't immediately assume that you can resolve it by making more money or taking the right antidepressant or getting a better job — though these can be helpful to a limited degree.

You instead reflect on the example of the enlightened teacher (Buddha who discovered the path to a life free from suffering), find wise counsel in his teachings (known as the dharma), and seek support in others who share a similar orientation (the sangha, or community). Many Buddhists repeat their refuge vows daily to remind themselves of their commitment to the Three Jewels.

When you take refuge, you may appear to be relying on forces outside of yourself for your peace of mind. But the deeper understanding provided by many great masters and teachers suggests that the Three Jewels are ultimately found inside you — in the inherent wakefulness and compassion of your own mind and heart, which are identical to Buddha's.

Receiving the precepts

In addition to taking refuge, making a commitment to abide by certain ethical *precepts,* or guidelines, signifies an important step in the life of a Buddhist. Different traditions may emphasize either refuge or the precepts, but at their core, the traditions agree that both taking refuge and committing yourself to certain precepts mark a participant's entry into the Buddhist fold.

If you're a Vajrayana practitioner, for example, you generally formalize your involvement by taking refuge — and later by taking what are called the *bodhisattva vows,* in which you vow to put the welfare of others before your own. When you take refuge, you generally receive a Buddhist name to mark your new life as a Buddhist.

In the Zen tradition, by contrast, you deepen your involvement by undergoing a ceremony in which you agree to abide by 13 precepts and (as with the Vajrayana tradition) receive a new name. (For more info on receiving precepts as a monk, see the "Entering the Monastic Way" section, later in this chapter.) The 13 Zen precepts include the 10 *grave precepts:*

Do not kill.

Do not steal.

Do not engage in sexual misconduct.

Do not lie.

Do not abuse intoxicants.

Do not speak of others' errors and faults.

Do not elevate yourself and blame others.

Do not be stingy.

Do not give vent to anger.

Do not defile the Three Jewels of Refuge.

The full Zen precepts ceremony also includes the three *pure precepts* as well as the three refuges of Buddha, dharma, and sangha. The pure precepts are

Do not create evil.

Practice good.

Actualize good for others.

Interestingly enough, the Vajrayana refuge ceremony includes a commitment to act ethically and the Zen precepts ceremony includes refuge vows. In the Theravada ceremony for becoming an *upasika* (committed lay practitioner), as practiced in certain communities in the West, participants ask to receive both the refuge vows and the precepts. Throughout Buddhism, refuge and precepts work hand in hand and reinforce each other.

In certain Buddhist traditions — including the Theravada — laypeople are expected to abide by an abbreviated list of precepts — generally the first five of the ten that we list in connection with the Zen tradition. But monks and nuns adhere to a lengthy code (the *vinaya*) that includes hundreds of regulations. (For more on following the precepts, see Chapter 12. For information on the connection between ethical behavior, meditation, and wisdom, see Chapter 13.)

Exploring further stages of practice as a layperson

Though some traditions of Buddhism believe that becoming a monk or nun tends to accelerate your spiritual progress, they all agree that you can achieve the pinnacle of Buddhist practice — enlightenment — whether or not

you become a monastic. In particular, the Mahayana tradition (see Chapter 4) offers compelling portraits of laymen and laywomen who were also great bodhisattvas, suggesting that you too can follow in their footsteps.

When you've become a Buddhist by taking refuge in the Three Jewels and receiving precepts, you devote the rest of your life to living according to these principles and teachings — not a small undertaking by any standards! In most Zen centers, everyone in the meditation hall, both monks and laypeople, chant some version of this verse at the end of meditation:

> Beings are numberless; I vow to save them.
>
> Attachments are inexhaustible; I vow to put an end to them.
>
> The dharmas [teachings] are boundless; I vow to master them.
>
> The Buddha's way is unsurpassable; I vow to attain it.

With these kinds of promises to inspire your meditation, you definitely have your life's work cut out for you. By setting your sights on lofty goals like compassion, selflessness, equanimity, and ultimately, complete enlightenment, you commit yourself to a lifetime of spiritual practice and development.

Of course, you're welcome to terminate your involvement in Buddhism at any time without karmic repercussions — other than those that may reverberate through your own mind and heart. (In the Vajrayana, after you become deeply involved with a teacher, forsaking your vows gets a bit more complicated.) In fact, in Southeast Asia, it's customary (and considered spiritually beneficial) for laymen and laywomen (and sometimes children) to shave their heads and become monks or nuns for a few days. After practicing in the monastic community briefly, they give back their robes and return to ordinary, everyday life — indelibly changed by their experience!

Entering the Monastic Way

In a number of the world's great religious traditions, the monk or nun stands as the embodiment of the spiritual ideal — the one who has given up all worldly attachments and devoted his or her life to the highest pursuits. Though Buddhism acknowledges the merit of lay practice, it too has traditionally placed the highest value on the acts of shaving the head, taking the full monastic vows, and entering a monastic community.

People are drawn to monastic practice for the same reasons they're attracted to Buddhism in the first place: the desire to eliminate suffering, benefit other beings, and achieve ultimate clarity and peace. Add to this mix a certain distaste for (or downright abhorrence of) conventional worldly life, and you have a good feel for the monastic impulse. Stephan's first Zen teacher used to say, "Monasteries are places for desperate people." Stephan knew exactly what he meant by this. (Of course, in some Asian countries, men and women become monks and nuns for other reasons as well, such as escaping worldly obligations, fulfilling parental wishes, and so on.)

Renouncing the world

In Japanese, the word for monastic ordination literally means "leaving home," perhaps because many monks and nuns traditionally entered the monastery or cloister as young people directly from their family home. (In the Theravada tradition the equivalent term is "going forth.") But the phrase *leaving home* has a deeper meaning: You leave behind the comfort and familiarity of family and friends and enter an entirely new world where the old rules no longer apply. You give external expression to your inner renunciation by cutting off your hair (a mark of personal beauty and pride), giving up your favorite clothes, and letting go of your prized possessions. (Compare these acts with Shakyamuni Buddha's own renunciation as we describe in Chapter 3.) In essence, you strip yourself of the signs of your individuality and merge with the monastic collective, where everyone wears the same robe, sports the same haircut, sleeps on the same thin mat, and eats the same rice and vegetables day after day.

In the time of Buddha (and in the traditions that continued to adhere to the full monastic code — the *vinaya*), monks and nuns were prohibited from handling or soliciting money and were allowed to own just a few simple belongings, which included items like several robes, a bowl, a razor, and an umbrella for protection from the sun. They took vows of celibacy, ate only before noon, and received their food from laypeople, either during alms rounds or through offerings brought to the monastery. The point of these regulations wasn't to cause hardship or suffering; in fact, Buddha's approach was known as the "middle way" between asceticism (severe restrictions in the comforts of life) and materialism. Rather the point was to simplify life and free the monastic to dedicate his or her life to practice and teaching.

These regulations, which the Theravada tradition of Southeast Asia still follows, have been adapted somewhat in other traditions such as Zen and Vajrayana. For example, in Japan (home to the Zen tradition), the priest, who trains for a period of months or years and then returns to his home temple to marry, raise a family, and serve the lay community, has largely replaced the monk. In Tibetan Buddhism, some lineages emphasize full monasticism (though they're not nearly as rigorous in their interpretation of the monastic code as their Theravada counterparts), but others encourage sincere seekers to combine married life and dedicated spiritual practice.

Ordaining as a monk or nun

The ceremony of ordaining as a monk or nun is a solemn and auspicious occasion marking the participant's entry into an order that dates back 2,500 years. In the West, ordination generally occurs as the culmination of years of practice as a layperson, though some people bolt from the starting gate like thoroughbred horses and head full speed for the monastery.

If you wish to receive ordination, you must first ask a senior monk — often, though not always, your current spiritual teacher — for permission. Then you obtain the required robes, shave your head (in some traditions you keep a lock to be shaved off during the ceremony itself), and set your life in order. During the ceremony, you recite the refuge vows and receive the appropriate number of precepts, depending on the level of your ordination and the tradition you follow (see Figure 6-1).

Figure 6-1: The newly ordained in the Theravada tradition.

Photo courtesy of Aruna Ratangir Buddhist Monastery.

For example, there are 16 precepts (including the three refuges) in the Zen tradition (listed in the "Receiving the precepts" section, earlier in the chapter), 36 vows for the novice nun in the Vajrayana tradition, and 227 vows for the fully ordained monk in the Theravada tradition, just to name a few. After taking refuge and receiving precepts, you assume a new name (which, when translated into English, often expresses some aspect of the Buddhist path such as "stainless love," "pure mind of patience," "holder of the teachings," and so on). At that point, you've crossed from one world into another, and your life as a monastic begins.

The significance of the Buddhist robe

Perhaps the most distinctive mark of the Buddhist monk is the cloth that's traditionally draped over the left shoulder. In Buddha's time, monks wore it over a simple waistcloth (or sarong) — not luxurious apparel by any means, but not insignificant either, especially in a country where ascetics still wander around naked. The monks were permitted to have three robes, which they often pieced together from bits of rag and dyed a uniform color, generally saffron (light orange).

When Buddhism made the journey over the silk route to Tibet and China, the robe went with it. But, in these colder climes, monks required additional layers of clothing, which they adapted from traditional styles. The colors of the robes changed too — from the saffron of India to the maroon of Tibet and the dark browns and blacks of China and Japan. But the traditional practice of draping a separate piece of cloth over the left shoulder (leaving the right arm free)

has remained consistent across most Buddhist traditions. In some countries, monks replace the full cloth on informal occasions with a smaller version that they wear around their neck and over their chest like a bib.

In addition to being practical (in some countries, the robe doubles as a blanket, ground cloth, head covering, and windbreaker), the robe has profound spiritual significance. It represents the act of renouncing the world and dedicating one's life to the dharma. Some traditions regard the robe as an object of reflection and even veneration, as the following Zen verse, which monks chant in the morning as they put on their robe, reveals:

Vast is the robe of liberation,

A formless field of benefaction.

I wear the Tathagata's [Buddha's] teachings,

Saving all sentient [conscious] beings.

Dedicating your life to the dharma

If you enter a Buddhist monastery, you do so because you're eager to devote all your time and energy to the practice, teaching, and realization of the dharma. To accomplish your goals, you rise early, day after day, and follow a routine consisting exclusively of meditation, chanting, ritual, study, teaching, and work. You may have limited contact with the outside world (generally monasteries are more open to lay practitioners at certain times of the year than at others), but for the most part, you turn your attention inward, toward spiritual matters. (For a detailed description of life in a Western Theravada monastery, see Chapter 8.)

In both their structure and purpose, Buddhist monasteries resemble their Christian counterparts. Western Buddhist monks have even become interested in the Rule of Saint Benedict, the official code that has governed Catholic and Anglican monasteries for centuries. And a Carmelite (Catholic) monk and Zen practitioner Stephan knows said that he felt right at home in a Zen monastery. Whether the goal is to get closer to God or experience enlightenment, monasteries throughout the world have a remarkably similar role to play — they're places where men and women get to dedicate themselves wholeheartedly to truth.

Women in Buddhism

Like many religions, both Eastern and Western, Buddhism has traditionally failed to give women equal status with men. Though Buddha was explicit in treating men and women equally, making it clear that women had the same capacity for enlightenment as men and creating a female monastic order equivalent to the male order, his followers over the centuries haven't always been so open-minded. Instead they've more or less mimicked the attitudes of their respective cultures where women have traditionally been regarded as inferior and subservient.

The full monastic (Pali: *bhikkuni*) ordination for women died out in India and Sri Lanka about 1,000 years ago and was never transported to Southeast Asia. Though it has survived in certain Mahayana countries (most notably China), full ordination has yet to be revived in the West. Instead, women in the Theravada tradition who seek to practice as nuns receive ten precepts, as well as numerous other more informal regulations. Other Buddhist traditions, including Zen and Vajrayana, also have their nuns, but they too are subservient to the monks. (The historical record does show that certain women, despite the rampant sexism of the times, emerged as accomplished yogis and masters.)

In recent decades, however, Western women Buddhists of every persuasion have strongly criticized this institutional sexism and required their teachers and communities to recognize their full equality. The result has been the rapid emergence of women as powerful practitioners, scholars, and teachers. In the Zen tradition, women in the West have generally been given the same ordination as men (as Zen "priests"), and it appears that just as many women as men are Western Vajrayana lamas these days. Clearly, Western Buddhists, like their Eastern ancestors, are adapting to the culture of their times. (See Appendix B for a list of books that deal with the topic of women in Buddhism.)

Chapter 7

Meditation: The Central Practice of Buddhism

As part of their religious training, Buddhists around the world engage in a variety of different activities — from reciting prayers and studying religious texts to performing such household tasks as tending the garden, serving tea, and making beautiful flower arrangements. In fact, from a Buddhist point of view, virtually any activity — even cleaning toilets — can become a religious practice. You simply have to approach the task with the proper attitude and motivation.

But of all the different activities you can think of, most people identify one in particular as typically Buddhist, and that activity is meditation. Although not all people who call themselves Buddhists meditate — or make it part of the everyday routine that we describe in Chapter 8 — meditation is still the hallmark of Buddhism.

But what exactly is meditation, and what can you accomplish with it? Well, we're glad you asked. In this chapter, we look into this practice more closely and try to show you why and how meditation plays such a central role in Buddhism.

Dispelling Some Meditation Myths

Because people have a lot of mistaken ideas about what it means to meditate, we want to deal with some of them right off the bat. Consider the following:

✔ **Meditation doesn't mean spacing out.** Many people — including quite a few Buddhists, we're afraid to say — think that meditation is some kind of vacation from reality. All you have to do is sit back, close your eyes, and let your mind drift away to some never-never land. But, if meditation consisted of simply letting your mind roam freely, this world would be home to a lot more highly accomplished meditators than currently occupy it. Allowing your mind to drift this way and that doesn't do anything but further ingrain whatever bad mental habits you already have.

✔ **The goal of meditation isn't to have your mind go completely blank, to stop thinking entirely.** Although you do eventually want to identify and eliminate certain types of distorted thinking (if you want to alleviate your suffering), as a beginner you can't hope to simply switch off your mind like you turn off a light switch. Any attempt to do this is bound to leave you feeling frustrated.

✔ **Meditation isn't something you can do only while sitting down.** Although certain practices (which we describe in Chapter 8) are best done in a seated position, you can do others while standing, walking, or even lying down. (You need to be careful about using this last posture, however. What starts out as meditation can easily turn into sleep.)

Defining Meditation

Webster's New World Dictionary (Wiley) defines *meditation* as "deep, continued thought; solemn reflection on sacred matters as a devotional act."

This definition isn't too bad in a general sense, but it doesn't really get to the heart of the matter. We prefer the following definition: A method for transforming your view of reality or for getting in touch with parts of yourself that you didn't know about before.

Performing a balancing act

Buddha once compared meditation to playing a stringed instrument. (You can think of a guitar, though Buddha used an Indian lute, a *vina,* in his analogy.) If the strings are too loose, you can't get them to make any sound at all. And, if they're too tight, they may break when you play them.

In the same way, the mind in meditation shouldn't be too relaxed, which can lead to sleepiness, or too tight, which can make the body tense and uncomfortable and the mind itself more agitated. Instead, find a natural balance between alertness and relaxation. Then meditation will proceed easily and gracefully.

So many different types of meditation exist that coming up with one defini-tion that covers them all is difficult. But if we had to pick one word to explain meditation, we might try something like *familiarization.* The term may be a bit awkward, but it does convey much of what meditation is all about. Allow us to explain.

Meditation is a way of becoming so familiar with yourself — with your thoughts, sensations, feelings, behavior patterns, and attitudes — that you get to know yourself more intimately than you ever thought possible. Some teachers describe meditation as the process of *making friends with yourself.* Instead of turning your attention outward, to other people or the external world, you turn it inward, back on yourself. As a result, parts of your heart and mind that may have been underdeveloped or even unknown to you beforehand, gradually — through this process of repeated familiarization — become a natural part of who you are and how you relate to the world.

For example, you may think that the only way you can possibly relate to those annoying neighbors of yours is as you've always done: with anger, bit-terness, and frustration. But through the practice of meditation you can tap inner reserves of tolerance, understanding, and even compassion that you never knew you had. Although you may not end up *loving* your neighbors, don't be surprised if you become more friendly with them than you ever imagined you could.

Despite the popular association of meditation with religious cults and obses-sive navel-gazing, it has nothing in common with that other well-known process for changing how you think and feel — brainwashing. Brainwashing is something that one person or group does to another, generally without the target's consent or full awareness. With meditation, even though others may help you become familiar with the techniques, you're the one applying these techniques, and you only make use of them after you determine that they're worthwhile. No one's forcing you to do anything.

Meditation is something that you engage in voluntarily because you have good reason to believe it will benefit you. If you ever find yourself in a situa-tion where someone is forcing you to think a certain way against your will or better judgment, head for the exit as soon as you can. That person is *not* teaching meditation.

Exploring the Benefits of Meditation

Meditation is a method for getting to know your own mind. But why do it? "Wouldn't it be easier," you may think, "just to leave my mind alone? I've man-aged to muddle my way through to this point by simply letting what happens happen, so why interfere now?"

Buddha addressed these doubts by comparing the ordinary mind — that is, the mind of ordinary, unenlightened beings — with a mad elephant. In ancient times, when wild elephants were common in India, this image made perfect sense to Buddha's disciples, and even today, many villagers have firsthand experience of the extensive destruction an enraged elephant can cause. But the mind that operates under the influence of poisons like hatred and greed is even more destructive than a whole herd of temperamental elephants. It not only can trample the happiness of your present life, but it also can destroy your happiness in countless future lives. The solution to this problem? You need to do something to tame the mad-elephant mind, and that something is meditation.

Recognizing the condition you're in

To appreciate the value of meditation, you must check to see how your mind is operating right now. A lengthy investigation shouldn't be necessary for you to realize that your mind has been subjected to some pretty heavy influences in the past. These influences have shaped your attitude, conditioning you to react to the events in your life in certain set ways. Unless you've already attained a high degree of spiritual realization, this conditioning — much of it negative — is still affecting you. (By *spiritual realization,* we mean the freedom that comes from penetrating through your conditioning to the peace and clarity that lie beneath.)

For example, just think about the way your surroundings constantly bombard you with gross and subliminal messages about how you should think and behave. You walk into a store, and some super-new-and-improved-electro-thingamajig seems to jump off the shelf and demand that you buy it. Suddenly you feel that if you don't purchase that product right away, your life will be incomplete. Where did that "got to have it" impulse come from? Would you say that this kind of reaction is a spontaneous expression of your basic makeup? Is it a natural expression of your mind's fundamental purity? Or is it a habitual response conditioned by the hours of advertising you've been exposed to?

Here's a completely different example. You see a stranger in the distance, and even though you know nothing about him and he's done nothing to you, you instantly dislike him. You may feel so uncomfortable just looking at him that your muscles begin to tense up, as if you were preparing for a fight. Again, ask yourself where that aggressive impulse comes from. Is it a natural, freely arising response to some objectively real threat the stranger poses? Or does his complexion and overall appearance just happen to fit the profile of some ethnic group that you've learned to fear or identify as a potential enemy?

Some forms of conditioning, such as advertising and political propaganda, are relatively easy to identify. Other forms, such as those you were subjected to in early childhood ("You're a terrible child; you can't do anything right!"), are more difficult to recognize. Still other forms of conditioning — those that may have left their imprint on your mind in a previous lifetime — may be completely beyond your ability to recall them, at least for the moment. But all these forms of conditioning shape your mind in one way or another. They all exert a long-lasting influence on what you do, say, and think.

Meditation is a method for "deprogramming" the effects of conditioning. After you recognize that you tend to react to certain situations in a way that only increases your anxiety and discomfort, you'll be motivated to neutralize as many of these damaging influences as you can. In place of the greed, hatred, ignorance, and other delusions that have shaped your responses in the past, you can choose to familiarize yourself with positive, productive states of mind like contentment, patience, loving-compassion, and wisdom.

Buddhist masters are fond of reminding their students that the mind can be either their worst enemy or their best friend. When you allow it to run wild, like a mad elephant, goaded on by ignorant conditioning and distorted thinking, your mind is your worst enemy. But, when you tame your mind and work to get past negative patterns to reach the more beneficial states of mind beneath — that is, by meditating — your mind becomes your best friend.

Getting an attitude adjustment

One of the first things that you can find out from meditation is how to keep yourself from responding to situations in a knee-jerk fashion. This accomplishment may not seem earth shattering, but in fact, it's enormously valuable.

Maybe you have an annoying person in your life, someone you have to encounter over and over again. (We'll call him Pat. If you find it more helpful to think of this annoying person as a woman, just switch the following pronouns from masculine to feminine.) Pat may be a family member, neighbor, co-worker, or just someone you run into on the street every day. But, whoever he is, he generally rubs you the wrong way. It may be something he does or says, his tone of voice, or simply the way he looks. Or maybe he once said or did something so gross and disgusting that you can't think of him without being reminded of it. Or maybe you don't have the slightest idea why you find Pat so annoying; you just do.

The first order of business is to be clear about whether the way you react to Pat is creating a problem for you. After all, if nothing's wrong, you have nothing to fix. Simply being annoyed isn't much of a problem; after all, life is full of petty annoyances. But, if you feel the uncontrollable urge to kick Pat in the shins every time you see him, you probably agree that there's a problem that needs fixing. Simple annoyance has escalated to anger, and even to hatred. Even if you manage to keep your hostility under wraps, you're still seething with anger and resentment on the inside, and you still have a problem that you definitely have to take care of before it eats you alive.

So how do you take care of hostility? Not by acting out — that only makes matters worse. If you're committed to the Buddhist approach, you've realized that the only effective way to change any situation for the better is by working first and foremost on yourself. As long as your own attitude remains unchanged, whatever you do about the target of your negativity won't solve the underlying problem.

Turning an old phrase upside down: Don't do something — just sit there

When you're trying to work on your own mind so that you can handle difficult situations more effectively, one of the hardest things to figure out is when to respond to these situations and when to do nothing. To return to good ol' annoying Pat: When he's pushing all your buttons, you have to decide whether you're going to confront him directly and try to resolve the conflict between the two of you, or whether you're going to refrain from responding to him at all. Each situation you face is unique and there are no pat answers as to which choice is best. But to have any chance of making a wise choice, you can't simply follow your old habits blindly. After you give in to your accustomed frustration and anger, the opportunity to respond with clarity and wisdom is lost.

Meditation gives you a way to sidestep your old destructive habits. As you discover how to tame your mind through mediation, a time will come when you can deal peacefully with difficult situations *as they unfold*. In the beginning, however, this feat is virtually impossible to accomplish. You get too caught up in what's happening to act objectively or skillfully. So, what's the best strategy, at least at first, to deal with difficult and stressful situations? Do nothing. If you can avoid encountering Pat, that's great. But, if meeting him is inevitable, try to put up with the annoyance as best you can, without reacting to it.

Preparing the groundwork

Although not reacting to a difficult situation may offer a short-term solution to your problem, the only truly effective, long-lasting solution begins *before* you run into the problem. That's the best time to work on your attitude and prepare yourself for dealing skillfully with whatever you might encounter. Enter meditation.

Before you leave your room in the morning, spend a few minutes sitting quietly by yourself, allowing your mind to settle down. (See Figure 7-1 for an example of a comfortable meditation posture.) When you're ready, imagine that you're encountering the anger-provoking situation (your good buddy, annoying Pat, for example) later that day. Picture the encounter as vividly as you can in your mind's eye. Imagine him doing whatever he generally does to set you off. Then — this part requires quite a bit of practice at first — step back from the situation and simply observe what's going on. Look at the annoying person as if you were seeing him for the first time, almost as if you were watching a documentary about someone you never met. Notice the expressions on his face, the words and phrases he uses, his actions, and so on. Think of this process as taking an inventory, noting what you find without making any judgments.

Figure 7-1:
Sitting
meditation
posture.

Then, in a similarly objective manner, take a look at your own reactions as if observing them from the outside — as if someone else had taken your place in the encounter. Check out how you're feeling, what you're thinking, how you're responding. Be as objective as possible, like a scientist who sets up an experiment and then steps back to observe what happens.

This type of observation requires a real balancing act. You have to figure out how to alternate between two different states of mind. To begin with, you have to imagine your annoying encounter vividly enough so that you can react realistically within it, with feeling, as if the scene were actually happening. You're not pretending to react; you're actually recreating your typical reactions but on a reduced scale. Because these reactions arise in a safe, controlled environment — inside your own meditation — you're protected from creating the kind of negativity that confronting Pat in the flesh usually brings.

But, as the encounter plays out in your meditation, find a corner of your mind that's not caught up in the reactions stemming from the encounter. Use this calm vantage point to observe, as dispassionately as you can, what's happening. Jon's meditation teachers compare this corner of the mind to a spy in wartime. (Some Buddhist traditions call it the *witness,* the *observer,* or simply *mindful awareness.*) The spy isn't involved in the conflict; he or she inconspicuously stays on the sidelines and simply observes what's happening on the battlefield. You may be surprised to discover that you have the capacity to observe what's happening to you without getting caught up in the action — but you do. And the more you use this capacity, the stronger it becomes — kind of like a muscle.

Changing your perspective

When you discover how to switch comfortably between the main part of your mind that recreates the experience — in this case, the experience of an annoying encounter with the tiresome Pat — and the corner of your mind that merely observes your reactions, you can proceed in a number of different ways.

- ✔ **Experiment with different ways of viewing the situation.** Instead of only seeing Pat from your own limited perspective, try to see him through another's eyes. Someone probably thinks that Pat is a pretty good guy. Try observing *that* Pat for a while and see how your reactions to him begin to change. You may even have liked Pat in the past; if so, try to recall a time when you felt friendly toward him.

  By focusing on this kinder and friendlier version of Pat, you can start to discover positive traits in your adversary that you either forgot about or never noticed. With this discovery, your vision of Pat will start to lighten up a bit, your concrete view of him as nothing but an annoying person will begin to dissolve, and you'll notice that your own negative reactions to him will become less intense. This accomplishment opens up the possibility that your relationship with Pat may evolve over time. The two of you may even become best friends (but don't hold your breath waiting for *that* to happen). Yet, even if you and Pat don't become bosom buddies overnight, at least you won't have as serious a problem with him anymore.

- ✔ **Focus less of your attention on the problem and more of your attention on your reactions to it.** Pat annoys you. That's a problem. And this annoyance probably feels quite concrete — like a lump in your chest. But, as you observe this feeling more closely, you may notice that the annoyance isn't nearly as substantial as it first appeared. Like all feelings, it arises in your mind, stays there for a short time, and then subsides. There's nothing solid or concrete about it. If you don't remind yourself how much you dislike Pat, that annoying feeling will fade away by itself. Experiencing the insubstantial, fleeting nature of your feelings will keep you from buying into them as strongly as you once did. This recognition alone will alleviate much of the difficulty in your relationship.

Did you notice that neither of these two approaches attempts to change Pat in any way? Instead, they change *your* own attitudes, viewpoints, and reactions. You don't have to completely forget about Pat. If he's doing something harmful and you know a skillful, effective way to help him change his behavior, go for it. But you can't count on that. The only thing you definitely have power over is your own attitude, so that's what meditation seeks to work on.

Buddha's teachings are filled with many different methods for changing the way you look at things so that you can reduce your discomfort, develop skillful ways to deal with difficult situations, open your heart to others, and sharpen your wisdom. We share some of these meditation techniques at various places throughout this book, where they're appropriate. But all these techniques have certain qualities in common. They help you to

 ✔ Be more flexible and creative in the way that you handle potentially difficult situations

 ✔ Let go of old habit patterns that keep you trapped in dissatisfaction and frustration

Appreciating your life

Meditation has numerous other benefits. Many of these benefits involve showing up for your life with greater awareness and presence, which lets you find more enjoyment and develop a greater appreciation for other people and circumstances.

The following list details a few of these additional benefits. For more about the benefits and practice of meditation, check out *Meditation For Dummies* (Stephan Bodian, Wiley), from which we adapted this list.

 ✔ **Awakening to the present moment:** Meditation teaches you to slow down and meet each moment as it comes.

 ✔ **Making friends with yourself:** When you meditate, you find out how to welcome every experience and facet of your being without judgment or denial.

 ✔ **Connecting more deeply with others:** As you awaken to the present moment and open your heart and mind to your own experience, you naturally extend this quality of awareness and presence to family and friends.

 ✔ **Relaxing the body and calming the mind:** As the mind settles and relaxes during meditation, the body follows suit. And the more regularly you meditate, the more this peace and relaxation ripples out to every area of your life.

> ✓ **Lightening up:** Meditation enables you to find an open space in your mind in which difficulties and concerns no longer seem so threatening and constructive solutions naturally arise.

> ✓ **Experiencing focus and flow:** Through meditation, you can discover how to give every activity the same enjoyable, focused attention that you currently give only to peak moments like playing a sport or making love.

> ✓ **Feeling more centered, grounded, and balanced:** To counter the fears and insecurities of life, meditation offers a sense of inner stability and balance that external circumstances can't destroy.

> ✓ **Enhancing performance at work and play:** Studies have shown that basic meditation practice can enhance perception, creativity, self-expression, and many of the other factors that contribute to superior performance.

> ✓ **Increasing appreciation, gratitude, and love:** As you discover how to welcome your experience without judgment or aversion, your heart gradually opens as well — to yourself and others.

> ✓ **Aligning with a deeper sense of purpose:** When you welcome your experience in meditation, you may find yourself connecting with a deeper current of meaning and belonging.

> ✓ **Awakening to a spiritual dimension of being:** As your meditation opens you to the richness of each fleeting moment, you naturally begin to see through the veil of distorted perceptions and beliefs to the deeper reality that lies beneath.

Understanding the Threefold Nature of Buddhist Meditation

The example we use earlier in this chapter of how to manage your feelings when confronted by a difficult situation emphasized letting go of old habits and viewing the situation in a new way. The example also involved, as a starting point at least, not buying into your accustomed reactions and, instead, sitting back and "doing nothing" (that is, not reacting).

But the teachings of Buddha contain many other methods besides simply doing nothing. In Buddhism, the practice of meditation basically involves three separate but interrelated aspects or skills: mindful awareness, concentration, and insight. Though the various traditions differ somewhat in the techniques they use to develop these skills, they generally agree that mindful awareness, concentration, and insight work hand in hand and that all three are essential if you want to attain the goal of *spiritual realization* (see the "Recognizing the condition you're in" section, earlier in this chapter).

Distinguishing between analytical and intuitive meditation

The great Tibetan Buddhist master Kalu Rinpoche makes a useful distinction between two types of meditation — analytical and intuitive. In *analytical meditation,* you use your conceptual mind to examine and validate the teachings you receive. You can think of this approach as preparing your mind for the deeper levels of meditation by eliminating any doubts you may have and clarifying your intellectual understanding. Analytical meditation may also take the form of exploring your habitual patterns of behavior and reactivity and finding more beneficial alternatives. (Check out the "Changing your perspective" section in this chapter for more info on this type of meditation.) But, to experience the truth about reality directly, you need to advance to the second kind of meditation.

In *intuitive meditation,* you stop searching and exploring with your conceptual mind and open your awareness so that reality can reveal its nature to you. The experience is immediate in the sense that the mind doesn't mediate your contact with reality. Instead, you have a direct insight into the way things are that can't be reduced to conceptual terms. Mindfulness meditation (see the "Developing mindful awareness" section in this chapter), Zen meditation (*zazen*), and the blend of "calm abiding" and insight practiced in the Tibetan tradition are, for the most part, forms of intuitive meditation.

Developing mindful awareness

Before you can penetrate through the layers of conditioning and see clearly and deeply into the nature of existence, your mind needs to settle down enough to make such insight possible. This part of the process is where two of the three key components of Buddhist meditation come in handy — mindful awareness and concentration.

To get a better idea of how mindful awareness (often called simply mindfulness) operates, consider the popular Buddhist metaphor of the forest pool. If wind and rain constantly batter the pool, the water will tend to be agitated and cloudy with sediment and organic debris, and you won't be able to see all the way down to the bottom. But you can't calm the pool by manipulating the water. Any attempts to do so will merely cause more agitation and add to the problem. The only way to clear the water is to sit patiently, watching the pool, and wait for the sediment to settle by itself.

This patient, diligent attention is known as *mindful awareness,* one of the cornerstones of Buddhist meditation. Buddha taught four foundations of mindfulness:

- Mindfulness of the body
- Mindfulness of feelings

> ✔ Mindfulness of the mind
>
> ✔ Mindfulness of mental states

When you're mindful, you're simply paying "bare attention" to whatever you're experiencing right now — thoughts, feelings, sensations, images, fleeting fantasies, passing moods — without judgment, interpretation, or analysis.

Most of the time, you edit and comment on your experience: "I don't like what I'm hearing." "I wish she would act differently." "I must be a horrible person to have such negative thoughts." But mindfulness meditation invites you to welcome your experience just the way it is — and if you do resist, judge, or attach meaning to your experience, you can be mindfully aware of that as well!

Beginning practitioners of mindfulness meditation generally start by paying attention to the coming and going of their breath (see the "Mindfulness of the breath: A basic Buddhist meditation" sidebar in this chapter for more details). Over time you gradually expand your awareness, first to your physical sensations, then to your feelings, and finally to the contents of your mind. Eventually you may graduate to "just sitting," also known as *choiceless awareness,* in which your mind is open and expansive and you welcome whatever arises without selectively picking and choosing certain experiences to focus on.

Buddhists are generally encouraged to practice mindfulness throughout their day, in every activity (although mindfulness is especially cultivated on the meditation cushion or chair). Whether driving your car in traffic, waiting in line at the bank, picking up your kids at school, talking with a friend, or washing the dishes, you can be mindful of your feelings, sensations, and thoughts wherever you are and within whatever situation you find yourself. Mindful awareness has the added benefit of making life more enjoyable — the more you show up for your life, the more you appreciate it.

Deepening concentration

The more mindful you are, the more your concentration naturally strengthens and deepens, an additional benefit of mindfulness. If ordinary, everyday awareness resembles a 100-watt light bulb, concentration is like a floodlight or, if you finely hone and focus it, a laser beam. You may already be aware of moments in your daily life when your concentration naturally focuses and deepens — like when you're playing a sport, making love, or watching a riveting movie on TV. When you concentrate, you tend to become absorbed in what you're doing — so much so, in fact, that you may lose all self-consciousness and merge with the activity itself.

Mindfulness of the breath: A basic Buddhist meditation

Begin by finding a quiet place where you won't be disturbed by interruptions or loud noises for 20 minutes or longer.

Set aside your preoccupations and concerns for the moment and sit down in a position that's comfortable for you. You may choose to sit cross-legged on a cushion in traditional Asian fashion or on a straight-backed or ergonomic chair. Whatever position you choose, be sure to keep your spine relatively erect (yet relaxed) so you can breathe easily and freely.

Now gently rest your attention on the coming and going of your breath. Some traditions recommend focusing on the sensation of the breath as it enters and leaves your nostrils; others prefer to focus on the rising and falling of your belly as you breathe. Whatever you choose to concentrate on, stick with it for the full meditation period. Be aware of the subtle changes and shifts in your sensations as you breathe in and out. When your mind wanders off (daydreaming or fixated thinking), gently bring your awareness back to your breath.

Don't try to stop thinking — thoughts and feelings will naturally come and go as you meditate. But remain uninvolved with them as much as possible. Enjoy the simple experience of breathing in and breathing out.

After 15 or 20 minutes, slowly move your body, stand up, and resume your everyday activities.

Many traditions of Buddhism encourage the development of focused concentration because it gives the mind the power to penetrate deeply into the object of meditation. Buddha described nine levels of increasing meditative absorption, called the *jhanas*. In the Theravada tradition of South and Southeast Asia, monks and nuns are sometimes taught to advance through the jhanas until their concentration is so powerful (and their minds so calm) that they can use it to peer deeply into the waters of reality. (For more on the forest pool metaphor, see the "Developing mindful awareness" section earlier in the chapter.)

The Theravada tradition as it's practiced in the West (where it's often referred to as Vipassana) doesn't generally emphasize the jhanas, perhaps because most teachers never learned the method from their Asian teachers. The mind states encountered in the jhanas (including bliss, joy, and delight) can be so enjoyable and seductive that meditators sometimes get stuck at that level and lose interest in developing insight. Also, some teachers, both Western and Asian, believe that the jhanas aren't necessary for insight or may be too difficult for most meditators to cultivate.

Whether or not you practice the absorptions, concentration can lend power to whatever meditative technique you're practicing. In the Zen tradition, for example, focused concentration (called *joriki*) is highly prized for its ability to help unlock the secrets of the spiritual riddles known as *koans.* (See Chapter 5 for more about koan practice.) In the Vajrayana tradition, meditators learn the concentration practice known as *calm abiding,* which helps make the mind peaceful and clear (like a calm pool of water) and allows deeper penetration, or insight, to take place. Ultimately, the Vajrayana practitioners consider true meditation to be the union of this calm abiding and insight.

Developing penetrating insight

After you develop your mindfulness and deepen your concentration, you can turn your attention to reality itself. The earliest stages of meditation have definite benefits (as the "Exploring the Benefits of Meditation" section earlier in this chapter explains), but this final stage — insight, or wisdom — lies at the heart of all Buddhist traditions.

After all, Buddha didn't teach stress-reduction or performance-enhancement techniques. Instead, he taught a complete path leading to unsurpassable happiness and peace. To reach this noble goal, you need to experience a life-changing insight into the fundamental nature of who you are and how life functions. (Needless to say, stress reduction and performance enhancements have their own considerable relative value.) For a more detailed treatment of this life-changing insight, see Chapter 13.

Resting in the nature of mind

After you become adept at mindfulness and have some insight into the way things are, you can practice the approach known as "just sitting" in Zen or as "resting in the nature of mind" in the Vajrayana tradition. Paradoxically, this technique involves the absence of all technique and mind manipulation of any kind. The Tibetans use terms like *nonmeditation* and *non-contrivance.* It's actually an advanced technique generally reserved for experienced meditators, but some teachers in the West teach it primarily, and many westerners with some spiritual sophistication seem eager to learn it.

To rest in the nature of mind, you must have direct experience of this mind-nature, which is usually transmitted from teacher to student. In Zen, just sitting (*shikantaza*) is often described as expressing your innate Buddha nature without trying to achieve or understand anything at all. Because this approach requires the guidance of a teacher, we refer to it but don't attempt to teach it in this book.

At this point, we simply want to point out that the various Buddhist traditions differ in the methods they recommend for achieving this insight and even in the contents of the insight itself.

- ✔ In the Theravada (or Vipassana) tradition, you discover that reality (you included) is marked by impermanence, dissatisfaction, and the absence of an abiding, substantial self.

- ✔ In the Vajrayana tradition, you recognize the vast, open, and luminous quality of the entire phenomenal world.

- ✔ In Zen, you awaken to your true nature, which is variously described as *true self, no self, suchness,* and *the unborn.*

In reality, these differences may be more a matter of words and concepts than of actual experience. The important point, however you describe the insight, is that it liberates you from the suffering caused by your distorted views and habitual patterns and brings with it unprecedented levels of peace, contentment, and joy.

Developing the Three Wisdoms as the Foundation for Insight

To prepare the groundwork for gaining insight, developing the following three wisdoms (drawn from the Vajrayana tradition) can be helpful. These wisdoms involve different forms of analytical meditation. (For more on analytical meditation, see the "Distinguishing between analytical and intuitive meditation" sidebar in this chapter.)

- ✔ The wisdom gained from listening
- ✔ The wisdom gained from reflection
- ✔ The wisdom gained from meditation

The next few sections take a closer look at each of these wisdoms.

Cultivating wisdom from listening to the teachings

When you first become acquainted with the teachings of Buddha, you rely mostly on the first of the three wisdoms: the wisdom gained from listening to (or reading about) his teachings, the dharma. You can think of this wisdom as the most basic level of understanding available to you.

For example, you may want to check out what Buddhism is like or how it addresses some of the issues you're dealing with in your life. So, when you find out that someone is giving a lecture on Buddhism, you decide to attend. Or maybe you go to a library or bookstore and happen to spot a book on Buddhism (like this little black and yellow number in your hands right now) and decide to pick it up and see what it has to say. At this point, of course, you've made no commitment to the Buddhist path; you're just browsing. But, as you listen to the lecture or read the book (preferably *this* book), you begin to collect information that can form the foundation of your future understanding.

But the wisdom gained from listening isn't always wise, is it? You can hear or read something for the first time and come away from it with a completely mistaken idea of what it really means. For example, according to the teachings of Buddha, the ultimate level of truth is *shunyata,* a Sanskrit word often translated as "emptiness." (We discuss this very important topic in some detail in Chapter 14.) Based on the way you ordinarily use the word *emptiness,* you could easily misinterpret Buddha's statement to mean that nothing really exists. But this notion is emphatically *not* what emptiness means here at all. In fact, such a misinterpretation can lead to some serious mistakes.

The more you listen or read, however, the less likely you are to make this mistake and similar mistakes. If your sources are reliable, this first wisdom becomes sharper as your collection of information grows. You begin to get a better idea of just what the Buddhist teachings are about, even though you may still not understand them in any great detail. At the very least, you're becoming somewhat familiar with certain words and phrases that appear over and over again in the teachings, and this familiarity helps point your mind in the right direction.

Cultivating wisdom from reflecting on what you heard

By itself, the wisdom gained from listening won't take you very far. If you want to progress spiritually, you have to understand the meaning of what you hear or read. You accomplish this understanding by cultivating the second wisdom: the wisdom gained from reflection.

Reflection means that you wrestle with the teachings you've heard (or read) until you extract their intended meaning. You perform this deed by engaging all your mental faculties in as close an examination and as precise an investigation as you can. These actions recall Buddha's advice (mentioned in Chapter 1) not to accept his teachings at face value but to test them for yourself to see if they're true or not.

To start this process off, you may want to check to be sure that the teachings you've heard are logically consistent. If Buddha seems to be saying one thing in one place and something completely different someplace else, you should consider two possible explanations: Either Buddha doesn't know what he's talking about (we wouldn't bet on this choice) or the contradiction you've spotted is only apparent and not actual.

Buddha taught people who differed greatly from each other in many respects — their intellectual capacities, their backgrounds, the problems they faced, and so on — so he didn't say exactly the same thing to everyone. He may have told one person to do something that he told another to avoid if it was necessary to bring each of them along the path. But even so, when you look at Buddha's teachings as a whole, you should be able to discover an overall consistency. If you can't, something is wrong with the teachings themselves, or you haven't fully understood yet how they fit together.

Buddha meant for people to take his teachings as personal advice on how to be truly happy and fulfilled. So, when you examine the teachings — cultivating the wisdom that comes from reflecting on what you have heard or read — ask yourself how you can put these teachings into practice in your life. Are they applicable? Do they throw light on your experience? And finally, do they work?

Cultivating wisdom from meditating on what you understand

The kind of intelligent examination we mention in the previous section is itself one form of meditation, but the third wisdom refers to something beyond that practice. Perhaps we can explain it best by using an analogy.

To flavor your favorite food, you can marinate it. The marinade you use probably consists of a special mixture of spices, oils, herbs, or wine. You may have first found out about this marinade recipe by reading it in a cookbook; this is similar to gaining the first wisdom. But reading the recipe isn't enough; you still have to figure out how to put all the ingredients together properly, which is like applying the second wisdom. If you stop here, however, all your culinary efforts will be wasted. To get the taste you want, you have to place the food into the marinade and actually let it soak up the flavor. Performing this step is like applying the third wisdom.

If you want your mind to receive the full benefit of a particular teaching, you can't simply read it and think about it intellectually. You have to apply it so thoroughly that you absorb its full flavor. In other words, you have to cultivate the wisdom of single-minded meditation, the third wisdom. In this way, you can achieve true transformation of your mind.

Two examples should make this concept clear. Impermanence, or change, is a major theme in Buddhism (see Chapters 3 and 11). Things don't stay the same, not even you; whether you're prepared for it or not, each passing second brings you that much closer to the end of your life.

Reading these words is one thing, and it's another thing to examine their meaning intellectually. But, for this teaching to take such deep root in your mind that it transforms your life and gives you a new perspective on your mortality, you need to go beyond the first two wisdoms. You have to reach the unshakable conclusion that you yourself will die someday and that the only thing that will count then will be how well you have taken care of your mind.

When this realization occurs, put it at the focal point of your awareness and unwaveringly place your attention on it. You're no longer simply "thinking about" your mortality, investigating to see if the claim is true or not. You've done that. Now you're allowing the conclusion that you've reached — "I myself am going to die, and nothing but dharma training can help me when I do" — to permeate your mind; you're marinating in it. Over time, you repeat this process, examining the teachings on impermanence and death and then single-pointedly meditating on the personal conclusions that you draw. Eventually this idea will soak into your mind, transforming your attitude toward life and death from the inside out.

A second example concerns the cultivation of love, another topic of immense importance in Buddhism. Although you may have started out disliking a guy named Pat (see the "Getting an attitude adjustment" section, earlier in this chapter, for more on Pat), after being exposed to the teachings on love, you decide to give them a try. You find out how not to buy into your limited view of this fellow and begin seeing him in a new light. You discover that your attitude toward him softens, and instead of wishing him ill, you want him to be happy.

At first your desire for his happiness may be rather feeble. But, when you place your mind on this wish in meditation, its flavor soaks into your consciousness, transforming it. Afterward, even if Pat continues to behave annoyingly, the whole way you view him and react to him will be different. Then, because something in you has changed so radically, perhaps something in Pat will open up as well. At the very least, by softening your own attitude, you give him the space to change.

Chapter 8

A Day in the Life of a Buddhist

*T*he earlier chapters of this book explain how Buddhism evolved in Asia, grew into various, different traditions, and made its way to the West. But how do you actually practice the Buddhist methods and teachings? Sure, most Buddhists meditate, but how exactly do they meditate? What else do they do? How do they spend their time? How do their daily lives differ from yours?

In this chapter, we answer these questions by giving you a firsthand look at Buddhist practice through detailed day-in-the-life accounts of practitioners from four different traditions practiced today in the West. Buddhism comes in many different shapes and sizes, but the one thing that all these traditions have in common — and that makes them quintessentially Buddhist — is the importance they place on basic dharma teachings. Examples of these teachings include the four noble truths and the eight-fold path (see Chapter 3), the three marks of existence (impermanence, no-self, and dissatisfaction; see Chapters 2 and 17), and the cultivation of core spiritual qualities such as patience, generosity, loving-kindness, compassion, devotion, penetrating insight, and wisdom.

We think that this chapter will bring the religion to life for you and make it more down to earth and immediate than any other chapter in this book.

Surveying the Role of Monasteries in Buddhism

Buddhist monks and nuns have traditionally relinquished their worldly attachments in favor of a simple life devoted to the three trainings of Buddhism (see Chapter 13 for more on the three trainings):

  ✔ **Precepts:** Ethical conduct

  ✔ **Concentration:** Meditation practice

  ✔ **Wisdom:** Dharma study and direct spiritual insight

To support these endeavors, monasteries are generally set apart from the usual commotion of ordinary life. Some monasteries are located in relatively secluded natural settings like forests and mountains; others are situated near or even in villages, towns, and large cities where they manage to thrive by serving the needs of their inhabitants for quiet contemplation *and* the needs of lay supporters for spiritual enrichment.

Wherever they're located, monasteries have traditionally maintained an interdependent relationship with the surrounding lay community. For example, in the Theravada tradition, monks and nuns rely exclusively on lay supporters for their food and financial support (for more on this, see Chapter 4). The tradition prohibits monastics (a catch-all term for monks and nuns) from growing or buying food or earning or even carrying money. So monks and nuns often make regular alms rounds to local villages and towns (during which they receive food from their supporters) and open their doors to the laity to receive contributions of money, food, and work.

Likewise, Tibetan Buddhist monasteries are often situated near towns or villages. The monasteries draw their members as well as their material support from these nearby communities. The exchange works both ways. The laity in both Tibet and Southeast Asia traditionally benefits from the dharma teachings and wise counsel offered by the monks and nuns.

In China, the monastic rules changed to permit monks and nuns to grow their own food and manage their own financial affairs, which allowed them to become more independent of lay supporters. As a result, many monasteries in China, Japan, and Korea became worlds unto themselves where hundreds or even thousands of monks gathered to study with prominent teachers. Here the eccentric behavior, mysterious teaching stories (Japanese *koan;* see the sidebar, "Entering the gateless gate: Koan practice in Zen," in this chapter for more information), and unique lingo of Zen flourished. (See the "Growing a Lotus in the Mud: A Day in the Life of a Zen Practitioner" section, later in the chapter for more details.)

Despite their doctrinal, architectural, and cultural differences, Buddhist monasteries are remarkably alike in the daily practice they foster. Generally, monks and nuns rise early for a day of meditation, chanting, ritual, study, teaching, and work.

Renouncing Worldly Attachments: A Day in the Life of a Western Buddhist Monk

An excellent model of Buddhist monasticism in the West is Abhayagiri, a Theravada Buddhist monastery situated in the woods of northern California, about a three-hour drive north of San Francisco.

Scattered around Abhayagiri's 280 forested acres are little cabins that house the monastery's five fully ordained monks, two nuns, and four *novices* (monastics in training). As in the forest tradition of tropical Buddhist countries like Thailand, where Abhayagiri's two resident teachers (who are included among the five monks in residence) began their training, each practitioner has his or her own sparsely furnished cabin for individual meditation and study.

The monastics at Abhayagiri didn't choose their strict lifestyle on a whim. The five fully ordained monks began as novices by adhering to first eight and then ten precepts before they committed to the full *vinaya* (ethical code) consisting of 227 main precepts. (For more on precepts, check out Chapter 12.) That's no small task, as you can imagine: Just memorizing and keeping track of all those rules can be a major undertaking!

The nuns are committed to following a training developed especially for women of the Theravada tradition in the West. The full ordination procedure for Theravada nuns fell into disuse in Southeast Asia about 1,000 years ago (possibly due to the effects of war and famine and the inferior status of women in traditional Asian societies). This new training for nuns is based on the ten-precept ordination and embodies some 120 rules and observances that reflect and somewhat condense the original vinaya for nuns that consisted of 311 rules.

Among other restrictions, monks and nuns abstain from sexual activity of any kind and refrain from physical contact with the opposite sex. They can't eat solid foods after midday, sell anything, ask for or handle money, or go into debt.

Needless to say, these regulations shape monastic life in significant ways. For example, monks and nuns must rely on lay people to deal with monastery finances, and they can't engage in any project unless the monastery has money on hand to fund it. No movies, no TV, no music, no midnight snacks. Most lay people can't even begin to imagine a life of such utter simplicity and discipline! Yet Abhayagiri merely follows the time-honored model for Buddhist monastic life that's been passed down for thousands of years.

Though Abhayagiri is a monastery devoted to the spiritual pursuits of its monks and nuns, lay people come and go regularly to offer food, participate in practice, renew their precepts and refuge vows, and receive teachings from the resident instructors.

Lay men and women visiting for the first time can also arrange to stay at the monastery for up to one week, as long as they agree to follow the schedule and participate in practice. For people who've stayed at the monastery before, longer visits are possible. Because the monastery isn't very old (it was founded in 1996), accommodations are quite limited, and most visitors bring their own tents.

Following a day in the life

As a monastic at Abhayagiri, you follow a schedule that's typical of Buddhist monasteries the world over. You rise at 4:00 a.m. — well before the sun — shower, dress, and walk the half mile from your cabin to gather with your colleagues at the main building for chanting and meditation that begins at 5:00. For the first 20 minutes you chant various scriptures that express your devotion to practice (see Figure 8-1) and touch on familiar dharma themes, such as renunciation, frugality, loving-kindness, old age, sickness, and death. After taking refuge in the Three Jewels (Buddha, dharma, and sangha), you meditate silently with the other monastics for an hour and then participate in more chanting. (For more on meditation in the Theravada tradition, see Chapter 5.)

Figure 8-1: Western Theravada monks chanting together.

Photo courtesy of Aruna Ratangir Buddhist Monastery.

Following chores from 6:30 to 7:00 a.m., you meet to discuss the morning work assignments over a light breakfast of cereal and tea. After you determine your responsibilities, you work diligently and mindfully until 10:45 a.m. and then don your robes for the main meal of the day, a formal affair offered to you by lay members. After you and the other monastics help yourselves, the laity take their share and eat with you in silence. Everyone helps wash up and put things away. You then spend the afternoon meditating, studying, hiking, or resting on your own. Remember, you've seen the last of solid food until 7:00 a.m. tomorrow morning — and private stashes are definitely not allowed!

Tea and fruit juice are served in the main hall at 5:30 p.m., followed by a dharma reading and discussion at 6:30 and meditation and chanting at 7:30. Sometime between 9:00 and 10:00 p.m. you're off to your cabin to continue your meditation or to rest in preparation for yet another long day that begins at 4:00 a.m.

Though fixating on the rigors and relative strictness of such a routine is easy, we want to emphasize the joy and fulfillment that accompanies a life of such purity, awareness, and devotion to truth. Without the many distractions of postmodern lay life, the subtle insights and revelations of the spiritual life come more quickly and easily into focus. That's why Buddha recommended the monastic life and why so many devoted practitioners have followed his example.

Punctuating the calendar with special events

In addition to the regular daily schedule we outline in the previous section, the lunar quarters (that is, the days corresponding to the quarter, half, and full phases of the moon) and the three-month rainy-season retreat punctuate the monastic calendar.

Vipassana centers for lay people

In addition to monasteries, the Theravada tradition in the West supports lay practice centers much like Zen centers (see the "Growing a Lotus in the Mud: A Day in the Life of a Zen Practitioner" section later in the chapter). At these practice centers, lay people can gather to learn how to meditate, listen to dharma talks, attend workshops on Buddhist themes, and participate in retreats of varying lengths (from one day to three months). Frequently using the term *vipassana* (insight) rather than Theravada, Western teachers (some of whom have trained in Asia) staff these centers, which may be closely affiliated with nearby monasteries.

On the lunar quarters (roughly every week), you observe a kind of Sabbath: You get up when you want, set aside the usual program of meditation and work, and refrain from touching computers or phones. Instead, you go on alms rounds with the other monastics — you walk the streets of the local town in your robes, begging bowl in hand, receiving food from anyone who wishes to offer it (see Figure 8-2). Then you devote the rest of the day to personal practice.

Figure 8-2:
Theravada monks receiving alms from lay supporters.

Photo courtesy of Aruna Ratangir Buddhist Monastery.

In the evening, one of the resident teachers offers a dharma talk that's open to the lay community. Lay members who attend and stay the night take the three refuges (Buddha, dharma, and sangha) and commit to following eight precepts for the duration of their stay — the usual five precepts for lay people (with monastic celibacy in place of the customary precept governing lay sexual behavior) plus three precepts with a "twist" of renunciation: no eating in the afternoon, no entertainment or self-adornment, and no lying on a luxurious bed (also understood as no overindulging in sleep). (For more on the five basic precepts, see Chapter 12.) Both laity and monastics practice meditation together until 3:00 a.m., followed by morning chanting. The rest of the day is completely unstructured, and monastics often use it to catch up on their sleep.

On Saturday nights the monastery hosts a regular dharma talk that draws even more of an outside audience than the lunar gatherings.

The high point of the year at Abhayagiri comes at the beginning of January when the three-month rains retreat begins. Fashioned after the traditional monsoon assembly in India, when the wandering monks gathered to practice together, the retreat coincides with the rainiest time of the year in northern

California. It gives the monks and nuns an opportunity to observe noble silence, turn their attention inward, and intensify their practice. Overnight guests and outside teaching engagements are prohibited, and the schedule becomes more rigorous with many more group practice sessions scheduled throughout the day. In addition, monastics take turns retiring to their individual cabins during this period for solitary retreats.

Taking a bow

Stephan's first Zen teacher used to say, "Buddhism is a religion of bowing." By this he meant two things:

✔ Bowing expresses the surrender of self-centered preoccupation, which is one of the core teachings of Buddhism.

✔ Buddhists bow a great deal.

Both statements, in fact, are true. In every tradition of Buddhism, bowing plays an important role. Buddhists bow to their altars, their teachers, their robes, their sitting cushions, and to one another. As a traditional expression of gratitude, respect, veneration, acknowledgement, and surrender, bowing occurs both spontaneously and in prescribed situations and contexts. In other words, sometimes you bow because you feel like it, and sometimes you bow because you're expected to.

Bowing is also a common practice in traditional Asian societies. Did Asians bow before Buddhism? The religion began in India 2,500 years ago, made its way to Southeast Asia several hundred years later, and has had a foothold in Tibet, China, Korea, and Japan since the middle of the first millennium. For this reason, Buddhism, bowing, and Asian culture are inextricably entwined.

Bowing in Buddhism takes different forms, depending on the culture and circumstance.

✔ In Southeast Asia, for example, you show respect by holding your hands in prayer position to your slightly lowered forehead.

For a full bow, kneel in that position (sitting on your buttocks), lay your palms on the ground about four inches apart, and touch your forehead to the ground between your hands.

✔ In Japanese Zen, execute a half bow by holding your hands together at chest level and then bowing from the waist. For a full bow, start off with the half bow and then continue with the Southeast Asia style of bow, except with palms up rather than down.

✔ In Tibetan Buddhism, show respect by touching your joined hands to your forehead, throat, and heart (indicating the dedication of body, speech, and mind) and executing a full prostration by (more or less) extending the full bow of Zen until you're lying face down on the ground.

Though bowing may lapse into mere formality, the deeper intention is to express heartfelt respect and devotion. The regular practice of bowing in Buddhist monasteries and communities contributes to an atmosphere of harmony, loving-kindness, and peace. As a westerner taught to "bow down to no one," you may find yourself resistant to the practice at first. But you may soon discover that it encourages a flexibility and openness of mind and heart that feels good inside — and it's Buddhist to the core! In any case, just remember, as Stephan's first teacher often told him: "Wherever you turn, you're simply bowing to yourself."

Growing a Lotus in the Mud: A Day in the Life of a Zen Practitioner

Zen first gained a foothold in North America around the turn of the last century, but it didn't achieve widespread popularity until the '60s and '70s when Zen teachers began arriving in larger numbers and young people (discontented with the religion in which they were raised) began seeking alternatives. (Check out Chapter 5 for more details about Zen itself.)

Since that time, the uniquely Western expression of Buddhist practice known as the *Zen center* has appeared in cities and towns across the North American continent. Like monasteries, Zen centers offer a daily schedule of meditation, ritual, and work combined with regular lectures and study groups. But, unlike their monastic counterparts, the centers adapt their approach to the needs of busy lay practitioners who must balance the demands of family life, career, and other worldly obligations with their spiritual involvement.

Though Zen temples in Japan and Korea have lay meditation groups, nothing quite like the Zen center has ever emerged in Asia. The reason is quite simple: Lay practitioners who fervently commit themselves to Buddhist practice are far more common in the West than in Asia, where serious practitioners generally take monastic or priestly vows. Maybe this phenomenon is the result of the Western belief that we can have it all: spiritual enlightenment and worldly accomplishment. (The Judeo-Christian ethic so prominent in North America teaches that daily life is inseparable from spiritual practice.) Or perhaps westerners simply have no choice: In a culture where the monastic style of practice isn't widely acknowledged or supported, practitioners have to make a living while studying the dharma.

In any case, Buddhism has its own strong precedents for this approach: The Mahayana tradition, of which Zen is a part, views lay and monastic members as equal in their capacity to achieve enlightenment, and the Zen tradition in particular has always emphasized the importance of practicing in the midst of the most mundane activities, such as washing the dishes, driving a car, and taking care of the kids. The Mahayana tradition expresses the idea in this way:

> Just as the most beautiful flower, the lotus, grows in muddy water, so the lay practitioner can find clarity and compassion in the turmoil of daily life.

Though Zen centers form the spiritual hub of their respective communities, members continue their practice throughout the day by applying meditative awareness to every activity.

Following a day in the life

At the heart of Zen practice is *zazen* (literally, "sitting meditation"), a form of silent meditation understood to be both a method for achieving enlightenment and an expression of your already enlightened Buddha nature. In other words, you can *be* the truth and seek it too! How's that for a two-for-one deal?

As a Zen practitioner, you're encouraged to practice zazen on your own, but sitting with other members of the *sangha* (community) is considered particularly effective and favorable. (Sangha is regarded as one of the Three Jewels of Buddhism, along with Buddha and dharma.) So most Zen centers offer daily group meditations — usually in the early morning before work and in the evening after work (see Figure 8-3). Depending on how much time you have to spare and the schedule at your local center, you can spend from one to three hours practicing Zen with others.

Figure 8-3: Lay westerners practicing zazen.

Courtesy of the San Francisco Zen Center.

At *zendos* (meditation halls connected with Zen centers) across the country, meditators repeat the familiar ritual of gathering in the predawn dark to practice together. (Though Zen is best known in the West in its Japanese form, and we use Japanese terms throughout this section, remember that Zen began in China and has been introduced to the West by Korean and Vietnamese teachers as well.)

After entering the zendo, you bow respectfully to your cushion or chair and then position yourself in preparation for zazen. Even in its Western incarnation, Zen is notorious for its careful attention to traditional formalities. Meditation begins with the sounding of a bell or gong and generally continues in silence for 30 to 40 minutes. Depending on the school of Zen to which you belong (for more on Zen schools, see Chapter 5) and the maturity of your practice, you may spend your time following your breaths, *just sitting* (a more advanced technique involving mindful attention in the present without a particular object of focus), or attempting to solve a *koan* (an enigmatic teaching story; see the sidebar, "Entering the gateless gate: Koan practice in Zen," for more details). Whatever your technique, you're encouraged to sit with an erect spine and wholehearted attention.

Between meditation periods, you may form a line with other practitioners and meditate while walking mindfully around the hall together. Following a period or two of sitting, everyone generally chants some version of the four *bodhisattva vows:*

- ✔ Sentient (conscious) beings are numberless; I vow to save them.
- ✔ Attachments (or delusions) are inexhaustible; I vow to put an end to them.
- ✔ The dharmas (truths) are boundless; I vow to master them.
- ✔ The Buddha way is unsurpassable; I vow to attain it.

During the service that follows meditation, you bow deeply three or nine times to the altar (which usually features a statue of Shakyamuni Buddha or Manjushri Bodhisattva, flowers, candles, and incense) and chant one or more important wisdom texts, which generally include the *Heart Sutra*. These texts offer concise reminders of the core teachings of Zen, and the altar represents the Three Jewels of Buddhism, the ultimate objects of reverence and refuge: Buddha, dharma, and sangha.

When you finish your morning meditation, your Zen practice has just begun. Throughout the day, you have constant opportunities to be mindful — not only of what you're doing or what's happening around you, but also of the thoughts, emotions, and reactive patterns that get triggered by life events. Whether on the cushion or on the go, this steady, inclusive, mindful awareness lies at the heart of Buddhist practice in every tradition.

In particular, the Zen tradition emphasizes taking mindful care of every aspect of your life because the deeper truth is that you're not separate from the tools you use, the car you drive, the dishes you wash, and the people you meet. The world is your very own body!

When you get behind the wheel of your car, for example, you can stop to sense the contact of your back against the seat, listen to the sound of the engine as it starts, pay attention to the condition of the road, and notice the state of your mind and heart as you head down the street. When you stop at a traffic light, you can be aware of the impatience you feel as you wait for the light to change, the sounds of the traffic around you, the warmth of the sun through the window, and so on. As you can see, every moment from morning to night provides an opportunity to practice.

In addition to meditation and service, most Zen centers offer weekly dharma talks by the resident teacher and regular opportunities for private interviews with the teacher to discuss your practice. These face-to-face encounters may touch on any area of practice, including work, relationships, sitting meditation, and formal koan study. The Zen master isn't a guru endowed with special powers. Practitioners regard him or her as a skilled guide and an exemplar of the enlightened way of life.

Entering the gateless gate: Koan practice in Zen

When you think of Zen, what image comes to mind? Perhaps it's the shaven-headed monks in black robes sitting silently facing the wall. Or maybe it's the Zen master making some enigmatic statement or engaging in some unusual behavior designed to rouse his students from their spiritual slumber.

This last image figures prominently in the Zen teaching stories known as *koans,* which teachers have used for centuries (especially in the Rinzai Zen tradition) to serve as a catalyst for awakening their students. Rather than an intellectual exercise, koan study is a process of spiritual reflection designed to confound the conceptual mind, bypass the intellect, and elicit a direct insight (*kensho*) into the non-dual nature of reality — that is, our inherent oneness with all of life.

Some masters, especially those in the early years of Zen in China, didn't need such stories. In direct contact with their disciples during day-to-day monastic life, they had ample opportunity to transmit the dharma through their spoken words, gestures, behaviors, and above all, their silent presence. But, as monasteries grew and teachers became less accessible, the teaching encounter became increasingly confined to public dialogues and the interview room, where masters would challenge and encourage their disciples and test their understanding.

In this context, Zen masters began using traditional questions and true stories of classic teacher-student encounters, initially to provoke kensho and then to teach different aspects of the multifaceted jewel of *prajna* (enlightened wisdom). Over the centuries, these stories and questions were collected and systematized into a kind of graduate program in living from the enlightened perspective. With Zen's emphasis on "direct transmission outside the scriptures," koans, along with the transmission stories and poems of the great masters, became the focal point of study for serious Zen practitioners, and they're still widely used today in Asia and now in the West. Among the best-known koans are "What is the sound of one hand?" "What was my original face before my parents were born?" and "Who am I?"

If you're a serious Zen student but can't practice at the center, either because you're sick, you live too far away, or you can't arrange your calendar to include it, you can generally follow some version of this daily schedule on your own by sitting in the morning and again, if possible, in the evening. Then, to energize and deepen your practice, you can make it a point to attend one or more intensive retreats each year.

Attending silent retreats

Most Zen centers in the West offer regular one- to seven-day retreats (Japanese: *sesshin*) featuring as many as a dozen periods of meditation each day, morning and evening services, daily dharma talks, and interviews. (Korean Zen also offers retreats devoted primarily to chanting and bowing.) As a rule, these rigorous retreats are held in silence and offer an opportunity to hone your concentration, deepen your insight into the fundamental truths of Buddhism, and possibly catch a glimpse of your essential Buddha nature (an experience of awakening known in Japanese as *kensho* or *satori*). Retreats of more than one or two days are generally residential, though some centers allow you to attend part time while continuing your everyday life.

In keeping with the Mahayana spirit of general equality among monastic and lay practitioners, larger Zen centers often have country retreat centers that provide monastic accommodations and training for both ordained monks and nuns and lay practitioners. For example, the Zen Center of San Francisco — which describes itself as one of the largest Buddhist sanghas outside of Asia, a diverse community of priests, lay people, teachers, and students — includes three separate facilities:

- ✔ **City Center:** This facility serves urban members.
- ✔ **Green Gulch Farm:** The farm combines a suburban practice center and a working organic farm.
- ✔ **Tassajara Zen Mountain Center:** Situated in the heart of a wilderness area and isolated from the outside world during the winter months, this facility offers two three-month residential training periods each year that are inspired by the traditional monastic trainings of Japan.

All three facilities offer regular residential retreats, but the program at Tassajara is particularly intense.

Gathering for special events

Every Zen center has its own calendar of special ceremonies and events that punctuate the year. At the Zen Center of San Francisco, for example, these events include

- ✔ Memorial ceremonies honoring the founder, Suzuki Roshi
- ✔ Full-moon bodhisattva ceremonies
- ✔ Winter solstice events
- ✔ New Year's Eve celebrations
- ✔ Martin Luther King, Jr., ceremony
- ✔ Spring equinox events
- ✔ Buddha's birthday and enlightenment day
- ✔ Annual ceremonies honoring the founder of Zen in China, Bodhidharma, and the founder of Zen in Japan, Ehei Dogen

Many centers also offer weekly study groups focusing on Buddhist scriptures and the teachings of the great Zen masters. And Zen communities, like churches of other denominations, sponsor social gatherings where members get to mingle and enjoy one another's company!

Devoting Yourself to the Three Jewels: A Day in the Life of a Vajrayana Practitioner

In addition to North American converts to Buddhism, the continent has many thousands of ethnic practitioners who carried their Buddhist practice with them from Asia or learned it from their Asian parents or grandparents.

Some of these Asian American Buddhists are monks and nuns (many come from Southeast Asia) who have transplanted traditional forms and practices to Western soil. But most folks are lay men and women for whom Buddhism is often more a matter of devotion and ritual than meditation and study.

For these Asian Americans, being a Buddhist may involve

- ✔ Going to the temple on the weekend to listen to a sermon
- ✔ Chanting sutras in the language of their homeland
- ✔ Participating in the special ceremonies that mark the changing of the seasons and the turning of the year
- ✔ Sharing food at temple gatherings
- ✔ Helping fellow temple members in times of need

Though they may not practice formal meditation, ethnic Buddhists are often equally devoted to embodying such Buddhist values as loving-kindness, compassion, and equanimity in their work and family lives.

Of course, many traditional lay practitioners do practice meditation, and some of them have studied with accomplished teachers and devoted their lives to deepening their dharma wisdom. As an ethnic lay practitioner of Tibetan Vajrayana Buddhism now living in the West, for example, you may engage in some or all of the following daily practices (for more info on the Vajrayana Buddhism of Tibet, see Chapter 5):

- You rise early, between 5:00 and 6:00 a.m., to begin your day with meditation.

- You walk around (circumambulate) your house, which holds a sacred shrine containing statues, scrolls, and other ritual objects.

- As you walk, you finger your *mala* (Buddhist rosary) while chanting a sacred mantra such as *Om mani padme hum* (the famous mantra of Chenrezig, the bodhisattva of compassion) or the longer mantra of Vajrasattva, the bodhisattva of clarity and purification.

- After cleaning your shrine, you offer 108 prostrations (see Figure 8-4 to get a glimpse how they're done) as an expression of your devotion to and refuge in the Three Jewels (Buddha, dharma, and sangha).

- You engage in a particular practice your teacher has given you, often a visualization of a particular deity accompanied by chanting, prayer, and prostrations.

- As you go about your day, you constantly chant *Om mani padme hum*, either aloud or silently to yourself, while cultivating the qualities of compassion and loving-kindness for all beings.

- You spend an hour or two in the evening studying certain special teachings recommended by your teacher.

- Before you go to sleep, you make offerings of incense and candles at your altar, meditate, do additional prostrations, and recite long-life prayers for your teacher and for His Holiness the Dalai Lama.

As you can see, the life of a traditional Vajrayana lay practitioner is permeated by spiritual practice. Of course, some people are more devoted than others, and young people are more inclined to diverge from the traditional ways of their parents. But in general Tibetan culture, even in exile, is filled with strong Buddhist values that often express themselves in dedicated practice.

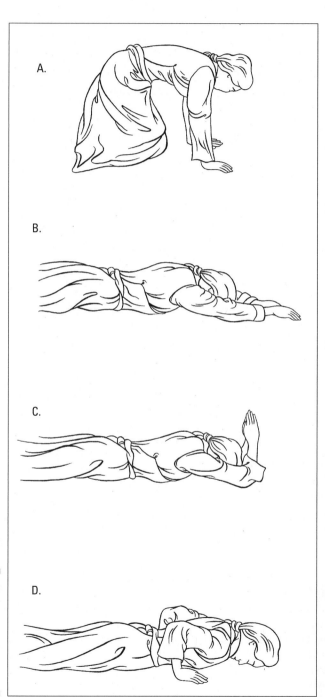

A.

B.

C.

Figure 8-4:
Performing
full
prostrations
in the
Tibetan
style.

D.

Trusting the Mind of Amida: A Day in the Life of a Pure Land Buddhist

Unlike most other forms of Buddhism that recommend spiritual practices (particularly meditation) as the means to enlightenment, Jodo Shinshu (a popular form of Japanese Pure Land Buddhism whose name means "true essence of the Pure Land way") teaches its followers not to rely on their own personal practice. Instead, Jodo Shinshu instructs practitioners to rely on the "great practice" of Amida Buddha himself, who took a vow to lead all beings to enlightenment. (Check out Chapter 5 for a more in-depth discussion of many facets of Pure Land Buddhism.)

As a Jodo Shinshu follower, you're taught that entry to the Pure Land (which is more a state of mind than a future realm) occurs through *other power* (that is, the power of what Amida Buddha has already accomplished) rather than through whatever you yourself may try to do. Jodo Shinshu understands Amida (or Amitabha in Sanskrit) to be an expression of the infinite, formless, life-giving Oneness that, out of deep compassion, took form to establish the Pure Land and lead beings to Buddhahood.

Shinran (the 13th-century Japanese founder of this tradition) did recommend certain practices, such as "hearing the dharma" (listening to sermons), reading scriptures and contemporary commentaries, internalizing basic Buddhist principles, and "learning to entrust yourself to the mind of Amida" rather than to your own limited effort and point of view. But the point of these practices is not to eliminate negativity and purify your mind, as in other Buddhist traditions. You practice to realize that you're already swimming in an ocean of purity and compassion right now.

Shinran himself left the monastic life to marry and raise a family because he felt that making the Buddhist teachings more accessible to lay people was extremely important. In this spirit, Jodo Shinshu emphasizes that everyday life in the context of family and friends is the perfect setting for spiritual practice. As a result, Jodo Shinshu followers lead ordinary lives that differ little from those of their non-Buddhist counterparts, except that they attempt to put basic Buddhist principles like patience, generosity, kindness, and equanimity into practice. They get up and go to work, make dinner, and help their kids with their homework just like everyone else.

Without prescribed techniques, practice becomes a matter of attitude, rather than activity. At the same time, followers of Jodo Shinshu can engage in any traditional Buddhist practice, such as meditation or *nembutsu* (chanting the mantra *Namu amida butsu* — "Homage to Amida Buddha"), as long as they do it as an expression of their gratitude for the gift of Amida's grace (not as a means to enlightenment).

On Sunday mornings, followers generally gather at their local temple to listen to a dharma talk while their children attend the Buddhist version of Sunday school — a short sermon followed by an hour-long class about Buddhist values. If they're strongly motivated, adult members may join a discussion or study group focusing on Jodo Shinshu themes.

Seasonal holidays also bring the community together to celebrate special occasions like Buddha's birth, enlightenment days, the vernal and autumnal equinoxes, and a summer ceremony honoring the spirits of departed ancestors. For many practitioners, the temple (like the local church or synagogue) is the focal point of social and community life. Temples often offer classes in martial arts, flower arranging, taiko drumming, and Japanese language that instill Buddhist principles and Japanese culture and values.

Chapter 9

Walking in Buddha's Footsteps

*T*wo thousand five hundred years ago, Shakyamuni Buddha inspired his original disciples and their daily spiritual practice by delivering his teachings. His enlightened presence profoundly affected most of the people he met. Even when people came to Buddha in an agitated state of mind, they often discovered that his peaceful demeanor automatically calmed them.

But what about future generations of Buddhists who don't have the opportunity of meeting Shakyamuni in person? Well, Buddha suggested that they could receive inspiration for their practice by visiting the places where he stayed during his lifetime. This recommendation is the basis for the custom of making a pilgrimage to the places he blessed by his presence. This custom continues today, and in this chapter, we talk about these blessed places and some of the practices that Buddhists perform while visiting them.

Visiting the Primary Places of Pilgrimage

Pilgrimage is the practice of visiting a site of religious significance to fulfill a spiritual longing or duty or to receive blessings or inspiration. One of the most universal of religious practices, pilgrimage is performed by hundreds of millions of people around the world. Muslims consider it their duty to make a pilgrimage to the holy city of Mecca at least once during their lifetime. Many Jews journey to Jerusalem to pray at the Western Wall and view the great biblical battle sites. Christians may trace the footsteps of Jesus from Bethlehem to Golgotha or visit the sacred places where great saints performed miracles.

Buddha specified four pilgrimage sites of major significance for his followers:

- ✔ **Lumbini:** Site of his birth
- ✔ **Bodh Gaya:** Site where he attained full enlightenment under the Bodhi tree
- ✔ **Sarnath:** Site of his first dharma discourse
- ✔ **Kushinagar:** Site where he passed away

According to some traditions, Buddha claimed that visiting these and other important sites (while thinking about the events that had occurred there) permits an individual of faith to purify negative karma accumulated in past lives (see Chapter 12 for more on the accumulation and purification of negative karma).

After Buddha's passing, his teachings flourished in India for more than a thousand years, and these pilgrimage sites grew to be important Buddhist centers (see Figure 9-1 for a map of these sites). But eventually Buddhism began to die out in India. By the 13th century, it had virtually disappeared from the subcontinent, and many of the sites suffered from neglect and fell into ruin.

Figure 9-1:
Major
Buddhist
pilgrimage
sites in
northern
India.

Fortunately, by the time Buddhism disappeared in the country of its birth, it had already taken root in other Asian cultures (see Chapter 5 for more on the spread of Buddhism). So, when the job of re-establishing these sacred Indian sites kicked into high gear in the 19th century, many Buddhists — and Western archeologists — were up to the task. As a result of their ongoing efforts, present-day pilgrims can once again visit these sites and receive a blast of inspiration for themselves.

The next few sections take a closer look at each of the four sites.

Lumbini: A visit to Buddha's birthplace

A good place to begin a Buddhist pilgrimage is Lumbini, which is now in Nepal near the border with India. You can get to it relatively easily by catching a train to the North Indian city of Gorakhpur and then switching to a bus that'll take you across the border. (Gorakhpur is also the jumping off point on your way to Kushinagar, site of Buddha's passing, described later in the chapter.)

The area north of modern Gorakhpur was once part of the kingdom of the Shakyas, the clan into which Buddha was born, and Lumbini itself was his actual birthplace (see Chapter 3 for more about Buddha's life story). Buddhist pilgrims from all over the world visit Lumbini to honor Shakyamuni, the founder of Buddhism, and express their devotion and gratitude to him for entering this world and blazing the path leading to lasting peace, happiness, and spiritual fulfillment.

When Buddhists visit Lumbini (and the other major pilgrimage sites), they express their devotion in a number of different ways. In the case of Lumbini, they head to the modest shrine purporting to mark the exact spot where Shakyamuni was born, and leave offerings there as a sign of their respect. These offerings typically consist of flowers, candles, incense, and anything else considered pleasant and attractive. (You don't have to worry about finding the items you want to offer; Buddhist and Hindu pilgrimage sites throughout India and the surrounding area are filled with small outdoor shops selling everything you may need.)

These pilgrimage sites are also excellent places to engage in whatever formal practices you're accustomed to performing (see Chapter 8 for some of the practices Buddhists from different traditions commonly engage in). For example, many people report that their meditations are more powerful at sites like Lumbini than they are at home, as if the place itself, blessed by Buddha and other great practitioners of the past, gives added strength to their spiritual endeavors.

You may wonder how people know that this small village is really the site of Buddha's birth. Even though it fell into disrepair a long time ago, experts have been reasonably certain about the location of Lumbini since the end of the 19th century. At that time archeologists uncovered an important piece of evidence — an inscribed pillar — left behind more than 2,000 years earlier by one of the most influential of all Buddhist pilgrims: the great Emperor Ashoka. (For more about Ashoka, one of the most important figures in Buddhist history, see Chapter 4.)

Except for remnants of the Ashoka pillar, however, very little survives at Lumbini from the early years of Buddhism. When Jon visited Lumbini in 1973, a rather nondescript shrine and a nearby bathing pool set in an open field were about the only items of interest. But things have changed in Lumbini since that visit. U Thant, the late secretary general of the United Nations, wanted to restore the area to its former glory, and UNESCO (the United Nations Educational, Scientific, and Cultural Organization, in case you were curious) has been helping to develop the site.

Even when a pilgrimage site is in a rundown condition, you can benefit from visiting it — provided you have the proper attitude and understanding. For one thing, visiting the ruins of historically important sites gives you the opportunity of coming face to face with impermanence. To the conscientious Buddhist pilgrim, such ruins serve as a powerful reminder that even the most impressive monuments will one day crumble into dust. If you want to find true lasting value in this ever-changing world, you have to discover for your-self the eternal spiritual truths that enlightened beings like Shakyamuni were born to reveal. If you can keep thoughts about impermanence in mind, you will take away more from your visit to Lumbini than a handful of souvenirs and some snapshots.

Bodh Gaya: Place of enlightenment

If Buddhists have a Mecca, it's Bodh Gaya, the site of the magnificent Mahabodhi temple (see Figure 9-2), which stands just east of the famous Bodhi tree (for more on the Bodhi tree, see Chapters 3 and 4). This temple (which is actually a large *stupa,* a monument housing relics of Buddha) marks the single most important spot in the entire Buddhist world: the so-called "diamond seat" upon which Buddha attained full enlightenment more than 2,500 years ago. (Incidentally, *mahabodhi* means "great enlightenment" in Sanskrit.)

Most pilgrims reach the town of Bodh Gaya by first taking a train to the city of Gaya (where you can find one of Hinduism's most holy shrines) and then continuing south 13 kilometers by taxi, auto-rickshaw, or — if you're fond of crowded conditions — bus. The road between Gaya and Bodh Gaya runs alongside a riverbed that's dry for much of the year — especially in winter. Winter is the height of the pilgrimage season here, and with good reason. Even though many Buddhists celebrate the anniversary of Buddha's enlightenment in May or June, you may not be comfortable visiting Bodh Gaya at that time of year — unless you're a big fan of temperatures that regularly reach 120 degrees Fahrenheit and more.

Hindu pilgrims and Bodh Gaya

Buddhists aren't the only pilgrims who flock to Bodh Gaya. Like all Buddhist shrines, the Mahabodhi temple attracts Hindu pilgrims as well. Many Hindus consider Buddha to be one of the manifestations of their god Vishnu, the Preserver. They believe that whenever sufficient need arises, Vishnu descends to Earth in the appropriate form as an *avatar* (literally: "one who descends") to provide divine assistance. Buddha is widely regarded as the ninth major avatar of Vishnu, and many Hindus feel that his special mission was to stop the custom of animal sacrifice.

Well before you enter the village of Bodh Gaya, you can see the top of the "Great Stupa" (as the Mahabodhi temple is often called) towering 55 meters above the surrounding plain. No one knows the age of the structure for certain, but accounts of Chinese pilgrims date its existence to no later than the seventh century (and possibly quite a few centuries earlier).

TIP

Taking a sacred walk

One of the most widely observed practices at shrines like the Mahabodhi temple is *circumambulation,* a Latin mouthful that just means walking around.

Figure 9-2: The Mahabodhi temple in Bodh Gaya, site of Buddha's enlightenment.

Photo © Claire Pullinger/Nomad Pictures.

ANECDOTE

"Practicing dharma is even better"

Buddhist teachers never get tired of reminding their students that the value of their actions depends mostly on their mind and motivation. This idea is also true of the practice of *circumambulating* (walking around) holy sites, as you can see in the following story.

Dromtonpa (or more simply Lama Drom) was an 11th-century Tibetan master who founded the famous monastery of Radreng and is considered to be a predecessor of the line of Dalai Lamas. One day he saw an old man circumambulating the monastery and told him, "What you're doing is good, but practicing dharma is even better." Thinking that he should be doing something else, the old man stopped circumambulating and

began reading a dharma text. But soon Lama Drom came over to him again and said, "Studying texts is good, but practicing dharma is even better." "Maybe he means meditation," the old man thought, so he stopped reading and sat down to meditate. But, when Lama Drom saw him again, he told the old man (you guessed it), "Meditating is good, but practicing dharma is even better."

Well, at this point, the old man was pretty confused. He asked Lama Drom, "What should I do to practice dharma?" The Lama answered, "Give up attachment to the worldly concerns of this life. Until you change your attitude, nothing you do will be a real dharma practice."

Just before sitting down on the eve of his enlightenment, Buddha demonstrated his great respect for the Bodhi tree by walking around it clockwise seven times. Since then, the circumambulation of sacred objects has become a revered practice in certain Buddhist traditions. Buddhists come from all over the world to circumambulate the Mahabodhi temple and pay their respects at the site of one of the defining moments of Buddhist history. At the height of the pilgrimage season, you can see Buddhists performing circumambulations at every hour of the day and night. And, if you happen to be there on an evening of a full moon — when the power of such practices is thought to be much greater — you can easily be swept up in the swirling mass of humanity that seems to flood the area.

Feeling Buddha's influence

The area around the Mahabodhi temple contains many smaller stupas and shrines, some of which mark places where Buddha stayed during the seven weeks immediately after he attained enlightenment. Many pilgrims make circle upon circle as they walk from one of these sacred structures to the other. Throughout the extensive grounds, pilgrims take part in other religious practices as well, such as reciting prayers, making offerings, or simply sitting in quiet meditation. A favorite place for this last activity is a small room on the ground floor of the Mahabodhi temple that's dominated by an ancient and particularly beautiful statue of Buddha. Sitting there in front of this blessed image in the very heart of the Great Stupa gives you the feeling of being in the presence of Buddha himself.

In fact, throughout much of Bodh Gaya, Buddha's influence is still very much alive. One of Jon's teachers told him that he loved Bodh Gaya because you don't have to try to meditate there; meditation comes automatically. Buddhists from around the world have taken advantage of this special place by building temples in the area surrounding the Mahabodhi grounds. The number of temples has grown significantly in recent years. In fact, certain portions of Bodh Gaya now look like a Buddhist theme park, filled with examples of the most diverse religious architecture Asia has to offer.

Venturing to other notable sites

Not far from Bodh Gaya are other pilgrimage sites that, although not nearly as built up as those within Bodh Gaya itself, are still of great interest. For example, on the other side of the dry riverbed are the spots where Buddha spent six years fasting before his enlightenment and where he broke his fast by accepting Sujata's offering (see Chapter 3). You can also find caves used by some of the great meditators of the past in the surrounding hills.

Zen and the question of merit

Of all the schools of Buddhism, Zen (one of the first to gain popularity in the West) has a reputation for questioning traditional religious assumptions — and for good reason. (For more on Zen, check out Chapters 5, 7, and 8.) When the subject is accumulating spiritual merit through pilgrimage or other good works, Zen goes against the traditional grain by teaching that anything short of full enlightenment has only limited value. The following exchange between Bodhidharma, the legendary monk who brought Zen from India to China, and the Chinese emperor is a case in point.

Shortly after arriving in China in the sixth century CE, Bodhidharma met with the Chinese emperor, Wu, who was a devoted follower of Buddhism. Wu had built many temples, translated scriptures, and even taught Buddhism himself. He undoubtedly expected Bodhidharma to confirm the value of his good works. "I have built so many temples and performed so many services," said the emperor. "How much merit do you think I have accumulated?"

"No merit whatsoever," Bodhidharma replied, to the emperor's surprise. "These are just minor effects on the relative level." By contrast, he added, "The ultimate wisdom is unspeakably perfect, inherently empty, and silent beyond words. Such merit can't be earned through worldly actions of any kind."

Bodhidharma is urging the emperor to set his sights on enlightenment, rather than taking pride in the merit he has achieved. Kind and compassionate actions, such as service to others, do have relative value, of course, but by themselves they don't bring about spiritual awakening, which is the ultimate aim of the Buddhist spiritual journey.

Sarnath: The first teaching

When Buddha decided the time was ripe to share the fruits of the enlightenment he'd achieved under the Bodhi tree, he traveled to the Deer Park in Sarnath to teach his former companions. Sarnath is on the outskirts of Varanasi (or Benares, as it's widely known in the West). Even in the time of Buddha, Benares was already an ancient holy site. Benares is probably most famous as the place where Hindus come to cleanse themselves of impurities by bathing in the sacred waters of the Ganges River and to cremate the bodies of their loved ones.

But Buddhist pilgrims turn their attention a little to the north of Benares to Sarnath, where Buddha first turned the wheel of dharma by teaching the four noble truths that form the basis of all his subsequent teachings (as we explain in Chapter 3). Buddhists around the world commemorate this event because the dharma he taught is considered Buddha's true legacy.

You can find all the sites associated with Buddha's first teaching within a relatively new park in Sarnath. Two stupas once stood on this site. The one built by King Ashoka was destroyed in the 18th century, but the Dhamekha stupa of the 6th century still remains (see Figure 9-3). During the period when Buddhism declined in India, many precious works of art were lost. But, fortunately, a number of these items have since been unearthed and are currently on exhibit in Sarnath's small but excellent museum. Among the items on display is the famous lion capital from the pillar Ashoka erected here. This image is now used as the symbol of modern India and appears on its currency, and the wheel design also located on the capital is reproduced on India's flag.

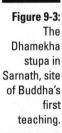

Figure 9-3:
The Dhamekha stupa in Sarnath, site of Buddha's first teaching.

Photo © Ian Cumming/Tibet Images.

Buddhists from various Asian countries have built temples in Sarnath as they've done in Bodh Gaya (check out the "Bodh Gaya: Place of enlightenment" section, earlier in this chapter). The tradition of learning that flourished in Sarnath during the early years of Buddhism has also been reintroduced. The Institute of Higher Tibetan Studies, libraries, and a publishing venture are all relatively new expressions of this tradition. In these and other ways, concerned individuals and groups have rekindled the dharma flame originally lit at Sarnath.

Kushinagar: Buddha's passing

The least developed of the four major pilgrimage sites is Kushinagar, where Buddha passed away at the age of 80. Because he was a fully enlightened being who no longer suffered from the illusion of being a separate self, Buddha didn't fear death or think of it as a dreaded event. For Buddha, death was *parinirvana,* or final liberation.

Sometime before he passed away, Buddha announced to his closest attendant, Ananda, that the time for him to enter parinirvana was approaching and that he wished to journey back to the country of his birth to pass away. The two men walked northward, and when they reached a pleasant grove not far from their destination, Buddha decided that it would be his final resting place. He walked into a clearing between two large trees, lay down on his right side in what's known as the *lion posture,* entered progressively deeper states of meditation, and then passed away. Afterward his body was cremated.

Although archeological evidence proves that numerous Buddhist monasteries once stood in Kushinagar and that King Ashoka built several stupas there, very little remains today. However, an ancient statue of Buddha reclining in the lion posture has been restored. This statue, along with a few other monuments to mark Buddha's final resting place and cremation, is all that's left to see. Many pilgrims report, however, that Kushinagar possesses an extraordinarily calm atmosphere, making it a perfect site for peaceful meditation.

Seeing Other Important Pilgrimage Sites

Four other places of Buddhist pilgrimage in northern India deserve at least a brief mention:

- **Rajgir:** The capital city of the kingdom of Magadha, whose king, Bimbisara, was a disciple of Buddha
- **Shravasti:** The area in which Buddha spent 25 rainy seasons

✔ **Sankashya:** The place where Buddha returned to Earth after teaching his mother

✔ **Nalanda:** The site of a world-renowned monastic university

The next few sections take a closer look at each of these sites.

Rajgir

When Buddha left his father's palace at the age of 29 in search of an end to all suffering (see Chapter 3 for more details), he passed through the kingdom of Magadha where he caught the eye of King Bimbisara. Buddha promised the king that, if his search was successful, he would return to Rajgir and teach him.

As a result of this promise, Rajgir became one of the most important places where Buddha turned the wheel of dharma. On a hill called Vulture's Peak, just beyond the city, Buddha delivered some of his most important teachings such as the *Heart Sutra* (see Figure 9-4).

Figure 9-4:
Teaching the *Heart Sutra* at Rajgir.

Rajgir is an ancient city, and visitors can still see and use the baths where Buddha refreshed himself. They can also view the remains of the parks given to Buddha by his first patrons for the sangha community to use. Many important events in Buddhism's early history took place in Rajgir, including the gathering of the First Council where 500 monks collected and compiled Shakyamuni's teachings. (To find out more about the historical development of Buddhism, including the meeting of the First Council, check out Chapter 4.)

For many of today's visitors to Rajgir, the most impressive sight is a large stupa, visible for many miles around, that Japanese Buddhists constructed on the top of the hill above Vulture's Peak. This stupa, radiantly white in the glare of the sun, is adorned on four sides with gold images illustrating the four major events in Buddha's life mentioned throughout this chapter: his birth, enlightenment, first turning of the wheel of dharma, and entrance into parinirvana.

Shravasti

Even today, the monsoon season in India (which lasts from about June to September in northern India) makes travel difficult. During the time of Buddha, before paved roads existed, getting around must've been close to impossible. So Buddha remained in retreat with his disciples during this time, and he spent his first rainy season in Rajgir. But, for 25 rainy seasons after that, he and his followers gathered at Shravasti, where a wealthy merchant had invited them to stay. The area became known as the Jetavana Grove, an often-mentioned site of Buddha's teachings.

Many events in early Buddhist history are associated with Shravasti, but the one that catches the imagination is Buddha's display of miraculous powers, as recorded in the Vajrayana tradition. Generally speaking, Buddhists tend to downplay the importance of the extraordinary powers that sometimes result from deep meditation. They're generally ignored or kept hidden unless an overwhelming purpose for displaying them arises. These powers aren't troublesome, but they can distract the practitioner from the true aim of meditation — spiritual realization.

According to the Tibetan tradition, Buddha had a good reason to display his miraculous abilities in Shravasti. During the years that he traveled across India giving teachings, gurus from opposing philosophical schools often challenged him to debate points of doctrine and to engage in contests of miraculous abilities. For the first couple of decades after his enlightenment, Buddha consistently declined to take up these challenges. But, when he was 57, he chose to accept the challenge because he realized that it would enable him to bring a large number of people into the dharma fold. So he announced that he would meet with six other spiritual teachers and engage in the contests they desired with the understanding that whoever lost, along with his followers, become the disciple of the winner.

You can probably guess how this contest turned out. Buddha overwhelmed the crowds who'd gathered with a pyrotechnical display of his magical abilities — from flying through the air to producing countless manifestations of himself so that the sky was filled with Buddhas! The defeated rivals and their followers developed great faith in Buddha, who then gave them dharma teachings. The whole event lasted 15 days and is still commemorated in various Buddhist lands. In Tibet, for example, Lama Tsongkhapa (whom we mention in Chapters 3 and 15 as the guru of the First Dalai Lama) instituted a 15-day prayer festival in Lhasa to mark the New Year and recall the events at Shravasti.

Sankashya

Perhaps the most obscure major pilgrimage site is Sankashya, where according to Tibetan tradition, Buddha descended after visiting his mother in the celestial realm where she had taken rebirth. (Remember that not every Buddhist tradition shares this mythic view of Buddha.) As we explain in Chapter 3, Buddha's mother, Queen Maya, died within a week of giving birth to him, and she was reborn in another realm as a glorious *deva* (god). To repay her kindness, Buddha ascended to the realm she inhabited when he was 41 years old and gave her teachings on the topic of higher knowledge (see Chapter 4 for more about this topic). Sankashya is the spot where Buddha, flanked by the great gods of ancient India, returned to Earth after this special teaching.

Nalanda

Last on the list of pilgrimage sites is Nalanda, which is located near Rajgir. At one time, Nalanda was the site of a mango grove where Buddha often stayed. But it became famous several centuries after the time of Buddha when an influential monastic university grew up there. This university shaped the development of Buddhist thought and practice in India and around the world. Nalanda was one of the major seats of learning in Asia, attracting Buddhists and non-Buddhists alike, and it remained influential until its destruction at the end of the 12th century.

Even though it now lies in ruins, the extensive excavations at Nalanda give visitors an idea of the huge size of this and other Buddhist monasteries of the time and the enormous impact they must have had on Indian culture. The list of individuals who studied and taught at Nalanda includes the names of many of the most revered Indian Buddhist masters, many of whose works are still studied today. Jon recalls sitting in the grounds there, reading the dedication chapter from the work of one of these masters — Shantideva's *Guide to the Bodhisattva Way of Life* — trying to imagine what it must have been like when Nalanda was alive and flourishing. When Jon thinks back to that afternoon, he can still contact the inspiration that he received then. This, for him, is one of the greatest blessings of pilgrimage.

Going on Pilgrimage Today

Although Shakyamuni Buddha spent his entire life in the northern portion of the Indian subcontinent, this is not the only part of the world where a person can go on Buddhist pilgrimage. As Buddhism spread throughout India and beyond (see Chapters 4 and 5), many different places became associated with important teachers and famous meditators, and these, too, became destinations of the devout (or merely curious) Buddhist pilgrim.

We can't possibly do justice to the large number of Buddhist holy places that are still visited by pilgrims to this day. Even in a relatively small area like the Kathmandu valley of Nepal, you could spend months going from one sacred spot to another and still not see them all. The following short list, therefore, is just a sampling of the rich treasure of sites you may consider visiting some day:

- **Temple of the Sacred Tooth,** in Kandy, Sri Lanka (formerly Ceylon). A tooth said to belong to Shakyamuni Buddha is enshrined here. On the full moon of August every year, a magnificent festival is held — complete with elephants — in its honor.

- **Shwedagon Pagoda,** in Rangoon, Myanmar (formerly Burma). This world-famous golden monument, housing eight of Buddha's hairs, rises over 320 feet and is the most venerated of all Burmese Buddhist shrines.

- **Mount Kailash,** in western Tibet. This remote, pyramid-shaped snow mountain is reputed to be the focal point of profound spiritual energies and the home of both Hindu and Buddhist deities. Those hardy enough to make the rugged journey here and complete the circuit around this sacred mountain report this pilgrimage to be a high point (literally as well as figuratively) of their lives.

- **Borobudur,** in Java, Indonesia. This enormous structure of many terraces — built in the shape of a sacred *mandala* (or circular diagram symbolizing the inner and outer universe) — is filled with hundreds of Buddha statues and stupas. Carved along its walls are exquisitely rendered scenes depicting the spiritual journey; these are arranged in such a way that as you make your way around and up the various terraces, you are presented with increasingly elevated states of enlightened experience.

- ✔ **The 88 Sacred Places** of Shikoku, Japan. The great Japanese Buddhist master Kukai (774–835 CE) established a pilgrimage route around the beautiful and mountainous island of Shikoku, and people of all ages and nationalities come to complete all or part of the circuit.

- ✔ **Almost anywhere.** Inspired by Kukai's example, a number of modern-day Buddhists have established pilgrimage routes through scenic areas of their own countries. Some of the Beat poets associated with California, for example, made a practice of walking around Mount Tamalpais, a mountain north of San Francisco sacred to Native Americans. This practice continues today, and with the founding of an ever-growing number of monasteries, retreat centers, and temples in the West, trails linking them to Buddhist pilgrimage routes are bound to grow.

Part IV
Traveling the Buddhist Path

The 5th Wave   By Rich Tennant

"I'm thinking of taking a spiritual journey, but I want to make sure I look right for the trip."

In this part . . .

You can think of this part as a handy foldout map. Here we lay out the entire Buddhist path — with the goal of enlightenment right in front of you from the beginning. Now, all you have to do is get there — and with our guidance you'll have a head start! This part lights up the important landmarks on your journey and shows you how to advance into new and inspiring terrain.

Chapter 10

What Is Enlightenment Anyway?

A pioneering book detailing the sudden awakening experiences of ten meditators drew Stephan to the practice of Buddhism in the late 1960s. Presented in the form of letters and journal entries, these dramatic accounts chronicled years of intensive meditation practice and the powerful, life-changing breakthroughs that ultimately (though not immediately) followed. Men and women wept and laughed with joy as they finally penetrated through years of conditioning and once and for all realized who they really were.

As a young college student, Stephan had experienced his share of suffering and had searched Western philosophy looking for solutions, so he was enthralled by what he read. He immediately became hooked on meditation. If those ordinary folks could wake up, he thought he could too.

In those days, few people had even heard the word *enlightenment* used in the Buddhist context, and the available books on Buddhism for a general audience may have filled half a bookshelf at best. Things have really changed in the past 30 years! Today, Buddhist books regularly make the *New York Times* bestseller lists, and everyone seems to be seeking enlightenment in one form or another. You can read popular manuals for "awakening the Buddha within" or achieving "enlightenment on the run," and you can take "enlightenment intensives" at your local yoga studio. One perfume company even produces a scent they call Satori, the Japanese word for enlightenment.

But what does enlightenment really mean? Though the current quick-fix culture has trivialized it, *enlightenment* is actually the deepest of all realizations in Buddhism, the culmination of the spiritual path, which may take a lifetime of practice and inquiry to achieve. In this chapter, we describe (as much as words possibly can) what enlightenment is — and is not — and explain how it changed shape as Buddhism evolved and adapted to different cultures.

As you read this chapter, please keep in mind that words can only point to dimensions of experience that simply can't be contained in words. To use a traditional Buddhist analogy, words are like fingers pointing at the full moon. If you get caught up in the fingers, you may never get to appreciate the magnificent sight of the moon in the sky.

Considering the Many Faces of Spiritual Realization

If you read the stories of the world's great mystics and sages, you find that spiritual experiences come in a dazzling array of shapes and sizes. For example:

- Some Native American *shamans* enter altered states in which they journey to other dimensions to find allies and other healing resources for their tribe members.

- Some Hindus experience powerful jolts of energy known as *kundalini,* enter blissful states that last for hours, or merge in union with divinities like Shiva or Kali.

- Christian saints and mystics have encountered transformative visions of Jesus, received visitations from angels, and manifested the *stigmata* (marks resembling the crucifixion wounds of Christ) in their hands and feet.

- The Hebrew Bible is filled with tales of prophets and patriarchs who meet Jehovah in one form or another — the fire in the burning bush, the voice in the whirlwind, and so on.

Though such dramatic experiences can have a transformative spiritual impact on an individual, they may or may not be enlightening, as Buddhism understands this term. In fact, most traditions of Buddhism downplay the importance of visions, voices, powers, energies, and altered states, claiming that they distract practitioners from the true purpose of the spiritual endeavor — a direct, liberating insight into the essential nature of reality.

The basic Buddhist teaching of impermanence (Pali: *anicca*) suggests that even the most powerful spiritual experiences come and go like clouds in the sky. The point of practice is to realize a truth so deep and fundamental that it doesn't change because it's not an experience at all; it's the nature of reality itself. This undeniable, unalterable realization is known as *enlightenment.*

One of Buddha's core teachings was the *four noble truths* (see Chapter 3 for more information), in which he explained the nature and cause of suffering and pointed to an "eight-fold path" for its elimination. This path culminates in enlightenment, also known as the "sure heart's release," in which all sense of separation dissolves — and with it the negative emotions and mind-states based on the illusion of separation such as greed, anger, jealousy, longing, and fear. (Buddhists have some disagreements over what's revealed when this sense of separation disappears; we explain more about this in just a moment.)

Buddha also taught that all beings have the same potential for enlightenment as he had. Instead of regarding himself as some exalted, special case, Buddha emphasized that he was just a human being with the same inner tendencies and temptations as other people. One of the truths to which he awakened under the Bodhi tree was this essential spiritual equality. The only thing distinguishing ordinary beings from a Buddha, he taught, are the distorted views, attachments, and aversive emotions that block the truth from our eyes.

All traditions of Buddhism would undoubtedly agree on the fundamental teachings about enlightenment that we outline in the two previous paragraphs — after all, these teachings come from the earliest and most universally accepted of the Buddha's discourses. The traditions differ, however, over the contents of enlightenment and the precise means for achieving it. What is the actual goal of the spiritual life? What do you awaken to — and how do you get there? Believe it or not, the answers to these questions actually changed over the centuries as Buddhism evolved.

Most traditions believe that their version of enlightenment is exactly the same as Buddha's version. Some even claim that theirs is the only true version — the deeper, secret realization that Buddha never dared reveal during his lifetime. Other commentators insist that the realization of later Buddhist masters carried both practice and enlightenment to dimensions that Buddha himself had never anticipated. Whatever the truth may be, the traditions clearly differ in significant ways.

In the rest of this chapter, we offer you a glimpse of enlightenment from three different points of view: Theravada, Vajrayana, and Zen. Though this brief tour certainly can't cover every conception of enlightenment (even within Buddhism), it does cover the basics — at least, as much as words can. Ultimately, as all traditions agree, enlightenment surpasses even the most refined intellectual understanding and simply can't be contained in our usual conceptual frameworks.

As you read the following sections, keep this old Buddhist adage in mind: Painted cakes can't satisfy hunger. You can look at pictures of pastries all day long, but you won't feel fulfilled until you taste the real thing for yourself. In the same way, you can read dozens of books about enlightenment, but you won't really understand what they're talking about until you catch a glimpse of the actual experience. Does that sound like an invitation to practice Buddhism? Well, you're right — it is!

Reviewing the Theravada Tradition's Take on Nirvana

The Theravada tradition bases its teachings and practices on the *Pali Canon,* a collection of Buddha's discourses (Pali: *suttas*) that were preserved through memorization (by monks actually in attendance), passed along orally for many generations, and ultimately written down more than four centuries after Buddha's death. (For someone like Stephan who has a hard enough time remembering a few phone numbers, such memorization skills boggle the mind.) Because these teachings can be directly traced to the words of the historical Buddha, some proponents of the Theravada tradition claim that it represents original Buddhism — that is, Buddhism as the Enlightened One actually taught it and intended it to be practiced and realized — and many traditions refer back to the Pali Canon as a reliable source of Buddha's earliest insights.

The Theravada tradition elaborates a detailed, progressive path of practice and realization that leads the student through four stages of enlightenment, culminating in *nirvana* (Pali: *nibbana*) — the complete liberation from suffering. The path itself consists of three aspects or *trainings:* ethical behavior, meditation, and insight. (For more on the three trainings, see Chapter 13. For more on the Theravada tradition, check out Chapter 5.)

Defining nirvana

Because Buddha considered craving and attachment to be two of the root causes of all suffering, he often defines *nirvana* as the extinction of craving or the absence of desire.

The term *nirvana* literally means "blowing out," referring to the flame of desire that keeps us unenlightened beings cycling endlessly from one rebirth to the next. When you attain nirvana, you blow out this flame and completely free yourself of all negativity — not only do craving and attachment come to an end, but hatred, anger, and ignorance also disappear as the sense of a separate self dissolves. Just because the terms used to refer to nirvana emphasize the absence of certain undesirable qualities, don't mistakenly assume that nirvana itself is negative. These seemingly negative terms point to an unconditional truth that lies beyond language and thus can't be accurately described in words. In his wisdom, Buddha realized that positive terms, which appear to describe a limited state, may be more misleading than helpful because nirvana isn't a state and has no limitations.

In the Theravada tradition, nirvana is considered the absolute truth, the complete realization of things as they are: Everything constantly changes and lacks a permanent, everlasting essence or self. When the illusion of a separate self totally dissolves, only nirvana remains. There's no longer any tendency to refer to or protect a separate me, because it's clearly seen that such a me has never existed, except as a collection of passing thoughts and feelings. Nor is there the slightest dissatisfaction because all traces of craving have disappeared. If nirvana has a particular feeling or tone, it's generally characterized as unshakable tranquility, contentment, and bliss (see Figure 10-1). Sound appealing?

Figure 10-1:
Shakyamuni
Buddha, the
classic
embodiment
of clarity
and peace.

Photo courtesy of Aruna Ratangir Buddhist Monastery.

Revealing the four stages on the path to nirvana

As he guided his followers over the 45 years that he taught, Buddha recognized four distinct levels or stages of realization, each one marked by a deep and unmistakable experience of selflessness followed by certain changes in outlook and behavior. The experience generally occurs during intensive meditation, when the attention has become one-pointed, and follows extensive study and understanding of the basic truths of Buddhism (especially the three marks of existence: selflessness, impermanence, and dissatisfaction).

The following list explains the four distinct stages on the path to nirvana.

✔ **Stream-enterer:** The first direct insight into selflessness is often the most powerful because it's unlike anything you've ever experienced before. For a timeless moment (which may last just an instant), no one is there — that is, there's no trace of a separate self anywhere. A feeling of tremendous relief, often accompanied by joy and bliss, generally follows the experience: At last, you've had the insight you've been seeking for so long. At last, you've "entered the stream" of realization.

When you become a stream-enterer, you can never again believe that you're really a separate self that lives inside your head and looks through your eyes. Your experience forever eliminates this illusion. When you look within, you can't find a self anywhere. In everyday life, however, you may still feel like a separate somebody and may still get caught up by greed, anger, ignorance, and various other negative feelings and patterns. Fortunately, the stage of stream-enterer also brings an unshakable confidence and dedication to the Buddhist spiritual path, so you're motivated to keep deepening and refining your realization.

✔ **Once-returner:** After you become a stream-enterer, your practice includes reminding yourself of your new realization of "no-self," as well as paying attention to the ways that you're still attached and your resistance to life as it unfolds. After a period of time (generally years of devoted practice) in which your concentration gets even stronger and your mind becomes even more tranquil, you have another direct insight into no-self. (Remember, knowing this truth as a concept or memory is one thing, but experiencing it directly, beyond the conceptual mind, is something else entirely.)

This insight (essentially the same as the first but even stronger and clearer) brings a significant reduction in attachment and aversion and the suffering that accompanies these states of mind. For example, occasional irritation and preference replace hatred and greed, which no longer have any hold over the once-returner. Someone who reaches this stage has only one more rebirth before becoming completely enlightened — hence the name *once-returner*.

✔ **Never-returner:** After the experience that signals entry to this stage, all of the worst hindrances, such as hatred, greed, jealousy, and ignorance, completely drop away, but a hint of a self-sense (a "me") still remains — and with it, the slightest trace of restlessness and dissatisfaction sticks around as well. The experience itself is rarely accompanied by any emotion or excitement, just a clearer recognition of what has already been seen twice before. These people appear to be extremely content, peaceful, and without desire, but the subtlest preference for positive rather than negative experiences remains.

✔ **Arhat:** At this stage, the path bears ultimate fruit in nirvana — any residual trace of a separate self falls away for good. The experience, frequently accompanied by unimaginable bliss, has been compared to falling into the depths of a cloud and disappearing. At this point, the circumstances of life no longer have the slightest hold over you; positive or

negative experiences no longer stir even the slightest craving or dissatisfaction. As Buddha said, all that needed to be done has been done.
There's nothing further to realize. The path is complete, and no further
rebirths are necessary.

Getting a Handle on Two Traditions of Wisdom

As Buddhism developed over the centuries, various schools emerged that differed in how they framed the path to enlightenment and how they understood the ultimate goal of this path. (For more on these developments, see
Chapters 4 and 5.) The Mahayana ("Great Vehicle") tradition — which gave
rise to various schools still popular today — shifted the emphasis from the
experience of *no-self* to the experience of *emptiness*. The idea of emptiness is
a bit more elusive than the concept of no-self and more difficult to put into
words. But stick with us — you should have a pretty good notion what emptiness means before we're through!

The two main branches of the Mahayana tradition understood emptiness (or
ultimate reality) in two quite different ways. The Madhyamika (Sanskrit for
"middle doctrine") school refused to assert anything at all about ultimate
reality. Instead, these folks chose to refute and discredit any positive asser-
tions that other schools made. The end result left practitioners without any
belief or point of view to hold onto, which effectively pulled the rug out from
under their conceptual minds and forced them to, in the words of the great
Mahayana text the *Diamond Sutra,* "cultivate the mind that dwells nowhere" —
the spacious, expansive, unattached mind of enlightenment.

By contrast, the Yogachara (Sanskrit for "path of yoga") school said that everything is only mind, or *consciousness.* (This view gave rise to the other name for
this school, Chittamatra or "consciousness".) The great masters of Yogachara
taught that consciousness is the essence or spirit that infuses and animates the
material world, and that it can be directly experienced in deep meditation.
Ultimately, in fact, no separation exists between the mind of the practitioner
and the external world — inside and outside are one and inseparable.

From the union of Madhyamika and Yogachara arose the two major represen-
tatives of the Mahayana ("Great Vehicle") tradition, Vajrayana and Zen. Over
the centuries many Zen and Vajrayana masters realized and taught that "consciousness only" and "emptiness" are merely different words for the same
indivisible, non-dual (that is, inseparable) reality. (By the way, if some of
these concepts seem elusive right now, don't worry — they should become
clearer in the sections that follow. You may also find it helpful to remember
that an understanding of emptiness is the culmination of the Mahayana path
and can take many years to accomplish!)

Realizing the Mind's Essential Purity in the Vajrayana Tradition

The Vajrayana (or tantric) tradition of Buddhism, which began in India and flowered in Tibet, retains the basic understanding of no-self and expands on it. After you look deeply into your heart and mind (using techniques adapted from the Madhyamika tradition; see the previous section for more info) and discover the truth of no-self, you naturally open to a deeper realization of the nature of mind (or consciousness), which is pure, vast, luminous, clear, non-locatable, ungraspable, aware, and essentially non-dual.

"Non-dual" simply means that subject and object, matter and spirit are "not two" — that is, they're different on an everyday level, but one and inseparable at the level of essence. For example, you and the book you see in front of you are different in obvious ways, but you're essentially expressions of an inseparable whole. Now don't expect us to put this oneness into words the mind can understand, though mystics and poets have been trying their best for thousands of years. If you want to know more, you just may have to check it out for yourself.

Not only is the nature of mind innately pure, radiant, and aware, but it also spontaneously manifests itself in each moment as compassionate activity for the benefit of all beings. Though conceptual thought can't grasp the nature of mind, this mind-nature (like no-self) can be realized through meditation in a series of ever-deepening experiences culminating in complete realization, or Buddhahood.

In Vajrayana, the path to complete enlightenment begins with the extensive cultivation of positive qualities like loving-kindness and compassion and then progresses to the development of various levels of insight into the nature of mind. Practitioners are taught to visualize themselves as the embodiment of enlightenment itself and then to meditate upon their inherent awakeness, or Buddha nature. (For more on the Vajrayana path, see Chapter 5.)

Generally, navigating the path from beginning to end requires a qualified teacher, diligent practice, wholehearted dedication, and numerous intensive retreats.

Taking the direct approach to realization

In addition to visualization practices, the Vajrayana offers a more direct route to enlightenment known as *Dzogchen-Mahamudra,* considered the highest teaching of the Tibetan tradition. *Dzogchen* means "great perfection" in Tibetan, and *Mahamudra* is Sanskrit for "great seal." Both terms refer to the insight that everything is perfect just the way it is.

These two approaches evolved separately through two distinct schools, but they're generally considered to be slightly different expressions of the same non-dual realization. (For a complete explanation of non-dualism, see the second paragraph earlier in this section.) Traditionally, only practitioners who completed years of preliminary practice qualified to learn about Dzogchen-Mahamudra, but today in the West, anyone sincere and motivated enough to attend a retreat can explore this approach to enlightenment.

In Dzogchen, teachers provide their students with a direct introduction to the nature of mind, known as *pointing-out instructions.* The students then try to stabilize this realization in their meditations and ordinary lives. The goal is to embody this realization without interruption until the separation between meditation and non-meditation drops away and the mind is continuously awake to its own inherent nature in every situation. In Mahamudra, practitioners first learn to calm the mind and then use this calmness as a foundation for inquiring deeply into its nature. When the mind recognizes its own nature, practitioners rest in this mind-nature as much as possible. (Now don't ask us to explain what this "resting" involves — like so much else in this chapter, it eludes words.) Though the approach of Dzogchen-Mahamudra may be considered direct, mastering it is extremely difficult and may take a lifetime — at least.

Understanding the complete enlightenment of a Buddha

The Theravada tradition considers the final goal of spiritual practice, exemplified by the arhat (see the section, "Reviewing the Theravada Tradition's Take on Nirvana," earlier in the chapter for a reminder of what arhat means), to be eminently attainable in this lifetime by any sincere practitioner. In the time of the historical Buddha, numerous disciples achieved complete realization and were acknowledged as arhats, which meant that their realization of no-self was essentially the same as Buddha's.

In the Vajrayana tradition, by contrast, the realization of Buddhahood appears to be a loftier ideal. The completely enlightened experience the end of all craving and other negative emotions, but these folks also exhibit "ten million" beneficial qualities, including boundless love and compassion, infinite, all-seeing wisdom, ceaseless enlightened activity for the welfare of all beings, and the capacity to speed others on their path to enlightenment. And the bodies of the completely enlightened display the 32 major and 80 minor marks of the Buddha, characteristics that are recognized throughout Buddhist Asia.

Needless to say, many of the faithful (especially at the beginning levels of practice) may see such an advanced stage of realization as a distant and unattainable dream. This feeling may be compounded by the many inspiring stories of exceptional sages who meditate for years in mountain caves and achieve not only a diamond-like clarity of mind and inexhaustible compassion, but also numerous superhuman powers.

Yet dedicated Vajrayana practitioners do gradually see their efforts lead to greater compassion, clarity, tranquility, and fearlessness and a deeper and more abiding recognition of the nature of mind. Indeed, Vajrayana promises that everyone has the potential to achieve Buddhahood in this lifetime by using the powerful methods it provides. (For more on Vajrayana practices, see Chapter 5.)

Standing Nirvana on Its Head with Zen

Zen takes a different approach to enlightenment than the Theravada and Vajrayana traditions. Rather than emphasizing a progressive path to an exalted spiritual ideal, the great Zen masters teach that complete enlightenment is always available right here and now — in this very moment — and can be experienced directly in a sudden burst of insight known in Japanese as *kensho* or *satori*. In fact, some Zen schools even de-emphasize the enlightenment experience altogether, teaching that the wholehearted practice of sitting meditation (Japanese: *zazen*) — or wholehearted practice in any situation — is enlightenment itself.

Zen is filled with stories of great masters who compare their enlightenment with Shakyamuni's enlightenment and speak of him as if he were an old friend and colleague. At the same time, enlightenment (though elusive) is regarded as the most ordinary realization of what has always been so. For this reason, the monks in many Zen stories break into laughter when they finally "get it." Awakened Zen practitioners are known for their down-to-earth involvement in every activity and for not displaying any trace of some special state called "realization."

Tuning into the direct transmission from master to disciple

The clearest account of the Zen attitude toward enlightenment may be found in this famous verse by the Chinese master Linji (Japanese: *Rinzai*):

A special transmission outside the scriptures,

No dependence on words and letters.

Directly pointing to the human mind,

See true nature, become Buddha.

Pure as the driven snow

Generation after generation has told and retold the following Zen story, recorded in the Platform Sutra of the Sixth Patriarch, to illustrate the distinction between a partial, progressive view of realization and the more complete view of the great Zen masters, who understand the mind to be intrinsically pure — and, therefore, in no need of purification through various methods and practices. The Fifth Patriarch of Zen in China, Hung-jen, gathered his monks together and asked each of them to write a verse that expressed their grasp of *true nature* (also known as *Buddha nature*). If he found one among them whose wisdom was clear, he promised to pass on his dharma lineage to him and make him the Sixth Patriarch, his successor.

That night, the head monk came forward and wrote the following verse on the monastery wall:

> The body is the Bodhi tree,
>
> The mind is a clear mirror.
>
> We must strive to polish it constantly
>
> And not allow any dust to collect.

When the Fifth Patriarch read the verse, he knew that it showed some relative appreciation of the value of practice, but it also clearly revealed that the person who wrote it had not entered the gate of realization — and he told this to the head monk. In public, however, he praised the verse as worthy of study. Several days later, a young, illiterate novice who worked in the kitchen threshing rice heard someone reciting the verse and asked to be taken to the wall where it was written. There he had someone inscribe the following verse:

> Bodhi [awakening] has no tree,
>
> The mirror has no stand.
>
> Buddha nature is originally clear and pure.
>
> Where is there room for dust to collect?

In other words, your fundamental nature needs no polishing through spiritual practice because it's never been stained — even for an instant. When the Fifth Patriarch saw this verse, he knew that he had found his successor. Even though the young novice couldn't read or write, Hung-jen acknowledged his enlightenment and made him the Sixth Patriarch of Chinese Zen.

The verse makes several important points, which the following list expands on:

- ✔ **Special transmission outside the scriptures:** Zen traces its lineage back to Mahakashyapa, one of Buddha's foremost disciples who apparently received the direct transmission of his teacher's "mind essence" by accepting a flower with a wordless smile (see Chapter 5 for more info). Since then, masters have directly "transmitted" their enlightened mind to their disciples, not through written texts, but through secret teachings passed on from mind to mind (or, as Stephan's first Zen teacher liked to say, "from one warm hand to another"). But the truth is that enlightenment itself isn't transmitted; it has to burst into flame anew in each generation. The teacher merely acknowledges and certifies the awakening.

✔ **Directly pointing to the human mind:** The master doesn't explain abstract truth intellectually. Instead, he points his disciples' attention directly back to their innate true nature, which is ever-present but generally unrecognized. With the master's guidance, the disciple wakes up and realizes that she isn't this limited separate self, but rather pure, vast, mysterious, ungraspable consciousness itself — also known as Buddha nature or big mind.

✔ **See true nature, become Buddha:** Having realized true nature, the disciple now sees with the eyes of Buddha and walks in Buddha's shoes. No distance in space and time separates Shakyamuni's mind and the disciple's mind. Illustrating this point, some version of the following passage appears again and again in the old teaching tales: "There is no Buddha but Mind, and no Mind but Buddha."

The great Zen masters inevitably teach that Mind includes all of reality, with nothing left out. This very body is Buddha's body, this very mind is Buddha's mind, and this very moment is inherently complete and perfect just the way it is — a truth known as *suchness* or *thusness.* Nothing needs to be changed or added to make this body, mind, and moment more spiritual or holy than it already is — you merely need to awaken to the nondual nature of reality for yourself. (Turn your attention to the sidebar, "Pure as the driven snow," for some more info.)

Checking out ten ox-herding pictures

Since the ten ox-herding pictures were first developed more than eight centuries ago in China, Zen students have consulted them as a reliable map to the stages of enlightenment, and Zen masters have used them to instruct and inspire their students. (Check out www.buddhanet.net to see traditional line drawings of these pictures.)

The images chronicle the progressive stages of the path, beginning with the search for the ox (that is, true nature) and culminating with the complete liberation, exemplified by the bodhisattva (shown in Figure 10-2).

Though the first direct insight, or *kensho,* occurs in the third picture, numerous additional kenshos reveal themselves along the way until kensho itself becomes the clear, unobstructed eyes with which you see reality at all times.

The following list offers a brief description of each picture followed by an explanation of its meaning.

Figure 10-2:
The
bodhisattva
joyfully
entering the
world.

Photo courtesy of Stephan Bodian.

- ✔ **Seeking the ox: Figure wanders through the forest, rope in hand.** You seek true satisfaction in life but can't find it in the usual mundane places — career, relationships, family, and material objects. Because you haven't yet been introduced to the possibility of awakening to your true nature, you don't really know where to look.

- ✔ **Finding the tracks: Figure follows the footprints of the ox.** You've been introduced to the teachings of Zen, and you at least know where to look to find your true nature. You're on the trail through the practice of meditation but haven't seen the ox with your own eyes.

- ✔ **Glimpsing the ox: Figure glimpses the rear of the ox.** You have your first direct insight, or kensho, at last! Now you're sure that the ox of true nature is everywhere and expresses itself as everything. But this realization quickly slips into the background, and you're still a long way from making it your constant companion.

- ✔ **Catching the ox: Figure holds the resistant ox by a rope.** You're aware of your true nature in every moment and situation; you're never apart from it — even for an instant. But your mind continues to be turbulent and unruly, and you need to concentrate to keep from getting distracted.

- ✔ **Taming the ox: Figure leads the docile ox by a rope.** Finally the mind settles down as every trace of doubt disappears. You're so firmly established in your experience of true nature that even thoughts no longer distract you because you realize that, like everything else in the universe, they're just an expression of who you fundamentally are.

- ✔ **Riding the ox home: Figure, playing a flute, sits atop the ox.** Now you and your true nature are in total harmony, like a horse and its rider. You no longer have to struggle to resist temptation or distraction because you're completely at peace, inextricably connected with your essential source.

✔ **Forgetting the ox: Figure sits in a thatched hut at sunrise.** At last the ox of true nature has disappeared because you completely embody it without separation. The ox was a convenient metaphor to lead you home. Ultimately, however, you and the ox are one! With nothing left to seek, you're thoroughly at ease, meeting life as it unfolds.

✔ **Forgetting both self and ox: An empty circle.** The last traces of a separate self have dropped away, and with them, the last vestiges of realization have vanished. Even the thought "I am enlightened" or "I am the embodiment of Buddha nature" can no longer occur. You're at the same time completely ordinary and completely free of any attachment or identification.

✔ **Returning to the source: Nature in full bloom without an observer.** After you've merged with your source, you see everything in all its diversity (painful and pleasurable, beautiful and ugly) as the perfect expression of this source. You don't need to resist or change anything; you're completely one with the *suchness* of life.

✔ **Entering the world with helping hands: Happy, big-bellied bodhisattva with a sack over his back (see Figure 10-2).** With no trace of a separate self to be enlightened or deluded, the distinction between the two dissolves in spontaneous, compassionate activity. Now you move freely through the world like water through water, without the slightest resistance, joyfully responding to situations as they arise, helping where appropriate and naturally kindling awakening in others.

Finding the Common Threads in Buddhist Enlightenment

The experience of enlightenment, though described slightly differently and approached by somewhat different means, bears notable similarities from tradition to tradition.

✔ **Enlightenment consistently signals the end of the illusion of separation.** (Notice we said *illusion* because Buddhism teaches that, rather than doing away with separation, you awaken to the fact that it never existed to begin with.) When you're enlightened, you no longer identify yourself as a distinct, isolated somebody inside your body or head confronted by a world of separate objects and others. Instead, you view reality as one continuous and interdependent whole — whether this reality consists of no-self, emptiness, true nature, mind, consciousness, or the ever-changing flux of phenomena. At a relative level, of course, you still know the difference between your body and your neighbor's body, lock your keys in your car at the worst possible time, pay the bills (or forget to pay them), and kiss your children (not someone else's) good night.

✔ **In all traditions, enlightenment also inevitably brings the end of all greed, anger, ignorance, and fear and the birth of unshakable, indescribable peace, joy, loving-kindness, and compassion for others.** Though these positive heart qualities may seem to get more press in the Mahayana tradition (whereas the Theravada seems to emphasize the elimination of negative qualities), they're definitely the natural expressions of the enlightened vision that dawns at the moment of complete realization — whether it's the tenth ox-herding picture of Zen, the full Buddhahood of the Vajrayana, or the nirvana of the Theravada. (Of course, both Theravada and Mahayana actively encourage the cultivation of compassion and other loving qualities; see Chapter 14.)

✔ **Enlightenment in every tradition involves being fully in the world but not of it.** (Please note that some enlightened people, like forest-dwelling monks, are less "in the world" than others.) Never again can you take the game of life seriously. You've seen through the apparent solidity and importance of material existence and its concerns, and you're no longer caught up in them because you clearly comprehend the empty — or insubstantial, impermanent, or innately perfect — nature of everything that occurs. Like the bodhisattva in the tenth ox-herding picture (see Figure 10-2 earlier in the chapter), you move through life with a smile on your face and a heart filled with love, offering help when it's needed and inspiring happiness and freedom wherever you go.

Chapter 11

A Matter of Life and Death

Shortly before the start of the third game of the 1989 World Series between the Oakland Athletics and the San Francisco Giants, a strong earthquake hit the greater Bay Area. Jon was living just north of Santa Cruz at the time, about ten miles from the epicenter, and witnessed the damage the quake caused firsthand. Fortunately, considering the large population of the area, relatively few lives were lost. But, within 15 seconds, the event brought millions of people face to face with the fragility of their lives, and the resulting emotional upheaval lingered for a long time.

The event caused many people to question some of their basic assumptions about what was really important in life. Conversations, even between strangers, quickly turned to spiritual matters. Attendance at meditation courses in the area increased dramatically and stayed high for many months after the earthquake. The event seemed to shake people up in more ways than one.

A close confrontation with death — whether through natural disaster, severe illness, or some other life-threatening event — often leads people to reevaluate and ultimately change their lives. The founder of Buddhism, Shakyamuni Buddha, began his spiritual journey when he encountered a corpse for the first time while venturing into the world outside his pleasure palaces (see Chapter 3). The path he discovered as a result of his journey is the subject of Chapters 12, 13, and 14. In this chapter, we focus on Buddha's teachings on death, but don't be concerned if the subject matter sounds depressing. Our intention is to show how a deep appreciation of your own mortality can motivate you to become spiritually involved and how death itself can be a powerful teacher.

Taking Death Personally

You need a number of things to stay alive, such as a regular supply of food and drink, appropriate clothing and shelter, and medical care when you get sick. But, as Buddhist masters like to say, dying doesn't take much at all — you merely need to breathe out and not breathe back in again.

If you stop breathing for just a few minutes, you'll soon be knocking on death's door. Death isn't remote or unusual — it's the one thing that's definitely going to happen to you (see "The story of the mustard seed" sidebar). As the old saying goes, you can rely on two things in life — death and taxes.

But there's a big difference between a mere intellectual understanding that death is inevitable and a heartfelt appreciation that this reality applies to you personally. For example, if you polled a number of teenagers and asked them, "Do you think you're going to die someday?" they'd all answer yes. But, if you examined the way many of them live, you'd probably conclude that teenagers think that they're immortal. Think of the risks some (notice we say *some*) teenagers routinely take: binge drinking, reckless driving, extreme sports, and unprotected sex, just to name a few. Despite what they may say, some teenagers seem to believe that death only happens to other people.

We're not picking on teenagers; we're just using them as a rather obvious example. The fact is that *most* people live their lives as if they're never going to die. They only confront the inevitability of their own mortality when they're faced with the death of a loved one or a life-threatening illness of their own. And, when the event has passed, the window on reality that so suddenly opened quickly closes, and they forget about death — at least for the time being.

Buddhism has always considered death to be one of the most powerful teachers, but this doesn't make it a joyless or life-denying religion. Buddhism simply acknowledges that death has an unparalleled capacity to force you to look deeply into your own heart and mind and recognize what really matters. This profound contemplation of death actually fuels your vibrant aliveness and self-awareness and motivates you to change your life in significant ways.

You may want to stop reading for a few minutes and consider your own attitude toward death. Do you ever give death much thought? Sure, you're uncomfortable with the idea of dying; most people are. You may even feel a certain anxiety as you move through life's inevitable transitions, knowing that they're bringing you closer and closer to your ultimate demise. But do you ever consciously contemplate your own mortality and its implications for how you lead your life? That's exactly what Buddhism encourages you to do.

The story of the mustard seed

The following true story is commonly told as a reminder that death awaits everyone, and you can't avoid it. Needless to say, the death of a child is one of the most poignant losses of all — and one of the most powerful reminders of impermanence.

A woman named Kisa Gotami lived in Buddha's time. The death of her young son upset her so much that she went mad with grief. Clutching onto his lifeless form, she wandered from place to place looking for some medicine to cure her beloved child. Her friends felt sorry for her and said, "Gotami, why don't you approach Buddha? Perhaps he can help you."

With infinite compassion, Buddha told Gotami, "Go to town and bring me one tiny mustard seed. However, make certain that this seed comes from a house where no one has ever died."

The distraught mother immediately began searching from house to house for the seed. Although everyone was eager to help her, they all had the same story to tell. "Last year my husband died," said one. "Three years ago I lost my daughter," said another. "My brother died here yesterday," said a third. Everywhere she went, Gotami heard the same thing.

At the end of the day, Kisa Gotami returned to Buddha empty-handed. "What have you found, Gotami?" he asked gently. "Where is your mustard seed? And where is your son? You're not carrying him any longer."

"Oh Buddha," she answered, "today I have discovered that I'm not the only one who has lost a loved one. Everywhere, people have died; all things must pass away. I realize how mistaken I was to think that I could have my son back. I've accepted his death, and this afternoon, I had his body cremated. Now I've returned to you."

Buddha then accepted Kisa Gotami as his disciple and ordained her as a nun in his order. Her understanding of reality deepened with her practice of dharma, and she soon achieved *nirvana* — complete liberation from suffering.

Recognizing Your Life as a Rare and Precious Opportunity

To contemplate death — or any other dharma topic — start right where you are at this moment. Take a close look at your present situation. We probably don't need to point out that you're a human being (unless, of course, you're reading this sentence in a bookstore on Mars).

Although your humanness may be obvious, you can take it for granted or simply dismiss it as insignificant. What's the problem with these options? From a Buddhist point of view, as a human being, you're uniquely positioned to accomplish the primary goal of spiritual training — complete liberation from suffering and dissatisfaction, resulting in a life of lasting happiness and boundless compassion for others (see Chapter 14 for a description of this fully compassionate way of life).

As a human being with the interest and ability to turn your mind to *dharma practice* (spiritual training), you have the capacity to achieve this goal. But here's the question: Will you choose this life direction? Your brief existence is going to come to an end all too quickly and, if you don't choose wisely, you may be throwing away a rare and precious opportunity to do something valuable with the time you have left.

Why do we call your existence "a rare and precious opportunity?" With six billion people living on this planet and more being born every minute, you may not think that being human is particularly rare. But stop and consider the number of creatures in a small garden or a local pond — or a rainforest clearing. For every human being, millions of other creatures of every description inhabit the Earth. And, among all of these different kinds of life forms, how many species actually have the self-awareness necessary to do anything truly significant with their lives?

Even among your two-legged brothers and sisters, not too many folks have the life circumstances, interests, motivation, or the innate potential to support inner growth, or spiritual awakening (see Chapter 10 for more on what it means to awaken spiritually). Many people grow up in environments so unsettled, impoverished, or violent that anything beyond mere survival is an unaffordable luxury. Others live in such remote areas or under such repressive regimes that they have no opportunity to hear valid spiritual teachings, much less practice them. And some folks simply lack the intelligence or the inclination to get the spiritual ball rolling.

By contrast, you have the time, energy, interest, and freedom to pick up this book and read about Buddhism. You probably even have life circumstances that would allow you to study and practice the dharma in your spare time. Compared with billions of other beings, you have a unique opportunity. You might even consider it to be "a rare and precious opportunity." Now you have to decide what to do with it.

The turtle and the golden yoke

Drawn from traditional Buddhist sources, the following analogy graphically illustrates how unusual it is to find yourself with both the inner and outer necessities for spiritual development.

Imagine that a golden yoke is floating on the surface of the vast ocean. The winds and currents blow the yoke here and there. Deep in the ocean lives a blind turtle that, once every 100 years, swims up and briefly lifts his head above the surface. The odds are very slim that the turtle will surface at the precise point where his head will poke through the hole in the ever-wandering golden yoke.

Buddhism teaches that if you don't take advantage of the opportunities that you now enjoy, your chances of finding an optimal situation again are even less than the blind turtle's chances of being in the right place at the right time.

"If you do not extract the meaning of your precious existence now," wrote the great eighth-century Indian master Shantideva (see Chapter 18), "when can you ever hope to encounter it again?"

Facing Reality: The Nine-Part Death Meditation

Buddhism teaches that, if you're going to take full advantage of this precious opportunity to do something significant with your existence, you should keep the reality of death uppermost in your mind as a constant reminder and motivator. Otherwise, when you eventually do come to the end of your life, you may regret having wasted your time on trivial pursuits.

The following nine-part meditation on death, adapted from the Vajrayana tradition (see Chapter 5), is designed to help practitioners make the most of their lives and to avoid the regret and panic that can arise if they die without properly preparing themselves for the inevitable. The meditation is written for dedicated students of dharma, but you may want to read it over to get a general idea of what the approach involves. Then, if you want to continue, you can thoroughly examine each section, comparing it with your own experience and deeply contemplating the truths within.

As you examine the different points of the meditation, try to keep them in mind even when you're not meditating and see if they make sense in your everyday life. Then, as you become more familiar with each point, you can see if your attitude and conviction begin to develop in the manner that the meditation describes.

If you decide to pursue the meditation further, you can place your new understanding and conviction at the focus of your single-pointed attention (as explained in Chapter 7) and integrate this deeper understanding into your life. Then the meditation practice won't remain a mere intellectual exercise but will actually affect the way you both live and die.

We don't intend this meditation — or the rest of the material in this chapter, for that matter — to depress or demoralize you. Its ultimate purpose is actually quite the opposite. You can use it to wake up from your illusion of immortality and set yourself firmly on the path to spiritual development. You may find it disturbing, but we really hope you'll also find it thought-provoking and even inspiring.

If you had a year to live . . .

The following is a meditation on life in the face of death, adapted from the work of Stephen Levine, a Buddhist teacher who has worked extensively with the dying.

1. **Sit quietly and comfortably for five minutes or so drawing your awareness inward toward the coming and going of your breath.**

2. **Now imagine that you just got a phone call from your doctor telling you that she has discovered widespread cancer in your x-ray results and she estimates you have about a year to live.** Take a deep breath and let it out — a year to live! Of course, you could dispute this prognosis, seek out other opinions, and battle aggressively to eliminate the cancer. But, for now, just take in the news.

3. **Notice the feelings that arise — perhaps sadness, anger, fear, or regret.** Where does your mind take you: to the tragic image of leaving your loved ones behind; the frightening thought of dying alone; the many mistakes and unkindnesses for which you'd like to apologize; all the places you'd like to visit and people you'd like to see before you die?

4. **Consider what really matters most to you** *right now.* What would you need to do and say to feel complete before you die, to feel that you weren't leaving any loose ends behind and that you were dying in peace? If you really had a year to live, how would you change your life, beginning right now?

Spend at least ten minutes recording your thoughts and impressions.

Understanding that your death is definite

You first have to face the cold, hard facts: Your death is a certainty. You can't get around it. You're definitely going to die. To reinforce this realization, consider the following:

- **You can't do anything to prevent the inevitable.** Nothing that you or anyone else does can keep death from occurring eventually. How well you take care of yourself, how famous you become, or where you decide to travel doesn't make any difference in the end: Death will find you. Think of the millions and millions of people who were alive a mere 120 years ago. Not one of them is still living; why shouldn't death pay you a visit too?

- **Your life span is always shrinking.** With each tick of the clock and beat of your heart, the time you have left to live is growing that much shorter. When a condemned man is led to his execution, each step he takes brings him closer to his end; time is taking you steadily in the same direction.

✔ **You will die whether or not you've done anything worthwhile in this life.** Even if you do practice the dharma taught by Shakyamuni Buddha, you get no assurance that you'll get very far in your practice before you punch that big time clock in the sky. Death doesn't say, "Oh, okay, I'll just wait until you're finished doing what you're doing. No, don't worry; I'll come back later." Likewise, you can't send death away from your doorstep or turn the lights off and pretend you're not home if you're not quite ready for it (of course, it would be nice if you could).

After you consider all the ways in which your death is certain — providing further insight from your own experience and understanding — put your foot down and decide that you *definitely* must do something to protect yourself from suffering both now and in the future. This "something" is the practice of dharma, or following the spiritual path.

This death meditation, though it may seem grim, isn't designed to depress you. Its purpose is to mobilize and motivate you to seek liberation from suffering now, rather than at some random point in the future. In other words, you could say that the death meditation is intended to sober you up (without the cold shower and strong, black coffee) and open your eyes to the simple truth: Nothing lasts, everything changes, and this body also will turn to dust one day.

Realizing that the time of your death is uncertain

When you fully appreciate that your death is definite, you can turn to the second of the three major considerations in the death-awareness meditation: The exact *time* of your death is most uncertain:

✔ **The human lifespan isn't fixed.** Although statisticians can calculate the average lifespan for a man or woman living in a particular country, you have no guarantee that you'll live to be that age (and some people may not even want to). Young people can die before their elders, and healthy people can die before people who are ill. It happens all the time. You can make a delicious meal, but you may not live to finish it; you can set out on an interesting journey, but you may not live to complete it.

✔ **Many factors can contribute to your death.** Open a medical textbook and read the long list of fatal diseases. Open a newspaper and read all the ways people lose their lives. Many real threats to your life exist, but you have relatively few ways to protect yourself. Even some of the things that are supposed to enhance your life can close the curtain on the final act. You need food to stay healthy, but thousands of people choke to death each year while eating. Taking a vacation is supposed to provide rest and relaxation, but thousands of people die each year in accidents while on holiday.

- **Your body is fragile.** Just because you're strong and healthy doesn't mean that it'll take a lot kill you. Something as small as a pinprick can lead to infection, disease, and death — all in a very short time. Newspapers are full of stories about people who were apparently healthy one day and dead the next.

When you fully appreciate that the time of your death is uncertain, you may naturally conclude that you can't afford to postpone your practice of dharma any longer — you must practice *right now,* from this moment on. The point isn't to be uptight and afraid of enjoying yourself; rather, staying alert to the reality of every passing moment, being as clear and present as you can, is the key.

Using death awareness as your spiritual ally

Finally, consider what you could use at the time of your inevitable death:

- **Wealth can't help you.** Many people spend nearly all their time and energy trying to accumulate as much money and as many possessions as they can. But all the wealth in the world can't buy your way out of death. ("Um, Death, why don't you take my credit card and go buy yourself something nice?" doesn't work. Sorry.) Rich or poor, everyone must face it. Also, no matter how many material possessions you've acquired, you can't take even the smallest particle with you. In fact, attachment to your belongings only makes letting go at the time of death more difficult.

- **Friends and relatives can't help you.** You may be the most famous or popular person in the world. An army of your supporters may surround your deathbed. But not one of them can protect you from death or accompany you on your ultimate journey. Your attachment to your friends (like your material possessions) may only make letting go and dying with a peaceful mind more difficult.

- **Even your body can't help you.** All your life you've pampered your body, clothing it and feeding it and taking care of it in every way possible. But as death approaches, your body, instead of being helpful to you, can easily prove to be your adversary. Even if you have a spiritual practice, the pain your dying body subjects you to can make it extremely difficult for you to focus your mind on what you have to do.

All these considerations point to the inevitable conclusion that only your practice of dharma (whatever that may mean to you) can support you at the time of your death. (See Chapters 1 and 2 for a general understanding of Buddhism and dharma practice and Chapters 12 to 14 for more specific suggestions.) Death is generally regarded as a time to practice the dharma as single-pointedly and continuously as possible, without distraction.

Reaping the Result of the Death Meditation

In the beginning, when you're first getting used to the death-awareness meditation, you may find the whole subject distasteful and rather morbid. But the further into it you go, the more you can benefit (yep, we said benefit).

If you practice the meditation wholeheartedly, your life may begin to take on a direction and a purpose that it lacked before. And your spiritual practice, whatever form it happens to take, may grow in strength. If you're a practicing Buddhist and you genuinely take death awareness to heart, you may find that your attitude as you approach death is transformed as well:

- ✔ As a beginning practitioner, you may still be afraid to die, but at least you don't have any regrets, knowing that you've done everything you could and didn't waste your life.

- ✔ As an intermediate practitioner, you may not be happy about dying, but you have no fear, convinced that you can handle death and whatever comes next.

- ✔ As an experienced practitioner, you may actually welcome death because you know that it will be the gateway to awakening.

Surveying Different Buddhist Attitudes toward Death

In this chapter, we mention that we're discussing death from a Buddhist point of view. But the truth is that all Buddhists don't share a single view of death. As with so many dharma topics, each Buddhist tradition has its own distinct way of relating to death and the process of dying.

All traditions would agree that death is a powerful motivator, that the truth of who you are doesn't die (only your body and personality), and that the moment of death can be an especially opportune time to awaken to this higher truth of who you really are. But, even though different traditions share the same or similar attitudes, they often emphasize different aspects of the death experience.

The following sections comprise a brief guided tour of the various ways that the major Buddhist traditions understand death. Although this quick survey can't be exhaustive, it's broad enough to give you an idea of the wealth of Buddhist approaches to this important topic.

Theravada: Getting off the wheel of existence

The theme of Buddha's first teaching (as recorded in the Pali canon of the Theravada tradition) was how to gain release from the cycle of existence, known as samsara. (See Chapter 3 for more about Buddha's first teachings, and Chapter 4 for more about the Theravada tradition.) *Samsara* is sometimes called a vicious circle because it consists of an endlessly repeating pattern of births, deaths, and rebirths in which no lasting satisfaction can be found. The ultimate goal of the Theravada teachings is to find a way out of this vicious circle and experience the inexpressible peace of *nirvana* — complete freedom from all suffering and dissatisfaction.

Because death is simply the boundary between the end of one life and the beginning of the next, your suffering doesn't end when you die. Death merely accelerates your next rebirth. The only real solution is to stop being reborn. How can you do this? Intriguingly enough, by realizing that there's no one who dies and no one who is reborn!

"That's ridiculous," you may object. "Clearly, *I'm* the one who is going to die and — assuming rebirth is true (which I'm not at all sure about) — *I'm* the one who's going to be reborn." But who or what is this "I" that you're talking about? By searching for an answer to this important question, you can solve the riddle of birth, death, and rebirth. So put your tray tables up and return your seats to their full, upright position; you're about to embark on an explanatory ride that may get a little bumpy.

As we discuss in more detail in Chapter 13, "I" is just a convenient way of talking or thinking about the nonstop series of events arising in your body and mind: I have a headache; I don't like the pain; I'll take an aspirin; I wonder if it'll help; I feel a little better; and so on. All of these sensations, thoughts, memories, feelings, likes, dislikes, and so forth are continuously bubbling up in your experience, lasting for a brief moment, and then subsiding again — only to be replaced by others. They appear to refer back to some permanent, enduring "me," but where exactly is this "me" or "I"? In your brain? Your body? Your heart?

When you closely analyze your experiences, all you find are these ever-changing mental and physical events. Other than these momentary events, there's nothing else you can discover.

No matter how exhaustively you may search, you won't find a separate, unchanging, self-contained "I" at the core of your being who's having these experiences; you'll merely find these momentary experiences, themselves, giving rise to one another.

Death and rebirth work the same way: There's no solid, unchanging "I" that dies and then is reborn; there's only the pattern of the ever-changing momentary events perpetuating themselves. To interrupt this pattern and break free from cyclic existence (samsara), you need to give up your inborn belief in a concrete "I" (or self). This mistaken belief in a concrete "I" feeds the desires and attachments that bind you to the wheel of samsara; the insight of *no-self* — that is, the wisdom of selflessness, which helps you overcome your belief in a concrete "I" — enables you to break free from this wheel. (See Chapters 13 and 14 for more about the wheel of samsara and how to overcome false views about the "I" or "self.") The aim of Theravada practice is to develop such a degree of penetrating insight into the true nature of your existence that the causes for being reborn in samsara vanish, or dry up, and you experience the release of nirvana.

Vajrayana: Turning death itself into the path

In the Vajrayana traditions practiced in Tibet and the surrounding regions, death is more than an unpleasant reality to be endured; it's an opportunity that a properly trained practitioner can use as a pathway to enlightenment itself.

To transform death into a spiritual path, you need to become well-versed in the details of the dying process. You have to have a good conceptual understanding of the stages you go through as you die, and you must be able to rehearse them in your daily meditation practice (and even in your dreams) as if they were actually happening to you. In fact, by the time *tantric yogis* (expert Vajrayana practitioners) come to the end of their lives, they've already "died" numerous times and know exactly what to expect.

According to the Vajrayana teachings, your physical form isn't the only body you possess. Underneath this physical form is a subtler "body." All the energies that support your physical and mental functions (including the way your senses operate, how your digestive system works, and even the way your mind processes thoughts and emotions) flow through this underlying body. If you're familiar with Chinese acupuncture and how it manipulates the force it calls *chi* or the way Hindu yoga directs the subtle breath, or *prana,* then you have some idea of the type of energy we're talking about.

The main aim of Vajrayana practice is to awaken an energy far more refined than any of the other energies flowing through you. When you can do this, you have access to what's known as the *mind of clear light,* which is the priceless treasure of the tantric yogi. When this penetrating awareness is coupled with insightful wisdom, it can burn away all obstructions from your mind, allowing you to experience the purity of full enlightenment within this short life. (That's the theory at least.)

Achieving enlightenment in this way is an extraordinary accomplishment, and even skillful Vajrayana practitioners may not be entirely successful during their lives. But every human being, whether or not he or she has practiced these advanced meditation techniques, naturally experiences the clear light at the time of death, at least for a moment.

The more prepared you are, the better you'll be able to remain fully conscious during this clear light of death experience and use it as your spiritual path to awakening. Even if you fail to awaken completely, you may still be able to direct your mind (through a forceful technique the Tibetans call *po-wa,* or the transference of consciousness) so you can consciously take rebirth in a pure realm of existence (a so-called Buddha field or pure land) where everything is conducive to achieving full awakening. But, if you don't reach a Buddha field, your preparation is still valuable. It provides you with a head start of sorts in your next life.

By remaining as fully conscious as possible during the death process and controlling your rebirth, you can bring increased benefit to others in your future lives. This approach agrees with the compassionate vow to dedicate your practice to the liberation of others rather than to your own release from samsara. The Tibetans have a unique tradition in which highly skilled lamas who can direct their rebirth are discovered and then brought up in a way that enables them to continue their spiritual practices from one life to the next. For example, the 14th Dalai Lama was discovered as a child to be the reincarnation, or *tulku,* of the 13th Dalai Lama. Check out Chapter 15 for more about the way the Dalai Lama was discovered.

The Vajrayana isn't the only Buddhist tradition that uses the death experience as a pathway to enlightenment. For centuries, followers of the Chinese and Japanese schools of Pure Land Buddhism have used their devotion to Amitabha Buddha as a way of gaining access to his Buddha field at their death (see Chapters 4 and 5 for more information on Pure Land Buddhism). In all these cases — whether you're practicing a highly technical yogic method or relying on your faith, devotion, and altruistic intentions — death ceases to be an obstacle to your spiritual development and becomes an opportunity to carry your development forward.

Zen: Dying the "great death" before you die

In the Zen Buddhist tradition, fearlessness in the face of death is one of the hallmarks of the truly enlightened. (For more on enlightenment, see Chapter 10; for more on Zen, see Chapter 5.) When you realize that you are the vast ocean of existence itself, life and death at the relative level become mere waves rising and falling on the surface of who you are. Your physical body may die, and this particular existence in space and time may come to an end, but you remain the unborn, the deathless, the eternal, the abiding reality — known as *big mind, great way,* or *true self* — that underlies both life and death.

There's a famous Zen story that illustrates this realization quite well. A notoriously cruel and ferocious samurai is looting and pillaging a particular village with his band of henchmen when he sees the local Zen master sitting quietly in meditation. The samurai walks up behind the master, applies the sharp blade of his sword to the master's neck, and arrogantly announces, "You know, I am someone who could cut off your head without batting an eye." To this, the master replies calmly, "And I am someone who could have his head cut off without batting an eye." Stunned to the core by the master's response and realizing that he has met his superior, the samurai immediately bows before the master and becomes his disciple.

The realization that you are the deathless, which occurs at the moment of full enlightenment (Japanese: *daikensho*), is known paradoxically as the "great death" because it signals the end of the illusion of being a separate self. For this reason, Zen urges you to "die before you die" (as the master in the previous story has already done), meaning that you put an end to separation (the idea of a separate "I") and awaken to your oneness with all of life. Only then does death lose its grip on you.

On a more everyday level, Zen emphasizes giving yourself so diligently to each activity that you completely lose yourself and leave no trace of a separate self behind. So Zen actually encourages you to die in each moment before you actually die — to let go of attachment and control with every action and every breath, just as you'll need to let go at the moment of death.

Dealing with the Death of a Loved One

Buddhism offers various practices for transcending the fear of death by realizing that there's no separate self that can die, but it also acknowledges that most people don't have such a profound understanding and will naturally be afraid of death and grieve when they lose someone they love. Buddhism considers this pain completely normal and understandable and welcomes it with compassion as a natural expression of the human condition. After all, if your heart is truly open to others and you wish the very best for them, watching them die can be extremely sad.

At the same time, even a preliminary grasp of concepts such as impermanence, selflessness, and emptiness, coupled with some appreciation of the nature of attachment and the suffering it can cause, can help ease your pain of loss. Buddhist meditation, the simple practice of being with your experience just the way it is, can be a powerful support by allowing the pain to surface and eventually release. If you don't block out your deep pain or grief or let it turn into anger or bitterness, grief can actually foster the precious spiritual quality of compassion for the suffering of others — compassion for the many millions of people throughout the world who experience similar separation and pain.

Whatever your response to the death of a loved one, the most important point, from a Buddhist perspective, is to be kind and compassionate toward yourself. Instead of using Buddhist philosophy in an attempt to talk yourself out of your grief, you can tenderly allow your experience to be exactly the way it is, which can be a tremendous relief. This unconditional acceptance of the way things are lies at the very heart of Buddhism.

Chapter 12

Getting Your Karmic Act Together

• •

In This Chapter

▶ Laying down the law — what goes around comes around

▶ Checking out ten actions you want to avoid

▶ Making up for your mistakes

• •

*O*ne of Jon's closest friends has been deeply involved in Buddhist studies for more than 30 years now, but you could say that his first encounter with Buddhism was almost an accident. He was a chemistry major in college when he decided that test tubes and Bunsen burners were no longer his thing. Unsure of his future career path, he opened the school's catalogue of classes to try to fill his class schedule, and listed right there after chemistry was Chinese studies. The title intrigued him, so he decided to give it a shot. One thing led to another, and today, he's a widely published authority on Buddhism.

Most people who become interested in Buddhism don't approach it in such a roundabout fashion as this person did. And of those folks who do show some curiosity, only a relatively small number take their interest to the point of adopting Buddhism as their way of life (see Chapter 6 for the different ways you can approach Buddhism). But even if you have only a casual interest in Buddhism, you probably want to understand something about its basic principles. In this chapter, we discuss one of the most fundamental principles of Buddhist practice — being careful about your actions, words, and thoughts. Or, to put it another way, minding your karma.

Appreciating the Law of Karmic Cause and Effect

Buddhism teaches that you're responsible for your own life — whether you're happy or sad, whether you find yourself in a pleasant or a painful situation, and so on. It's all basically up to you. You can discover how to regulate your life experience, and your behavior today can actually shape your future life circumstances.

Buddhists believe that when you behave in a certain way and with a certain intention, certain results follow. Specifically, if you act compassionately, in a beneficial way driven by positive motivations, the results you experience will be pleasurable. But, if your behavior is harmful or downright destructive, harm will come back to you in the future. This pattern is called the *karmic law of cause and effect.*

Karma is similar to other types of cause-and-effect relationships, such as the relationship between a seed and a sprout. As a song from the long-running musical *The Fantasticks* says, if you plant a carrot, you'll get a carrot, not a Brussels sprout. Buddhist teachers even talk about planting the seeds of karma and experiencing the future results (or effects) in terms of these karmic seeds ripening.

But, according to Buddhism, the intentions that drive the actions are more important than the actions themselves. If you accidentally squash a bug, you bring minimal or no karmic consequences to yourself because you didn't see it and, therefore, didn't mean to hurt it. But, if you crush an insect deliberately, especially out of anger or malice, you'll experience your karmic just desserts.

We're not talking about rewards and punishments here when we talk about karma. You're not a bad boy if you cheat on your taxes or a good girl if you help the old lady across the street. The law of karma doesn't carry that kind of judgmental baggage; it's much more practical and down to earth. The point is simple: If you act with ill will, you'll experience ill will in the future. If you act with love, you'll experience love in return. Or to continue the metaphor of the seeds: As you sow, so shall you reap.

Experiencing Karmic Consequences

Although the basic idea of karma is simple — positive causes lead to positive effects; negative causes lead to negative effects — karma itself is quite complex.

For one thing, karma can develop (or ripen) in a number of different ways. For example, take an extremely negative action like brutally and angrily murdering someone. If you don't cleanse yourself of this powerful negativity — in other words, if you don't purify this karma (see the "Purifying negative karma" section at the end of this chapter — you can experience its results in any or all of the following ways:

✔ In this lifetime, you may experience painful, turbulent emotions such as guilt, terror, and more rage. And, because of the negativity you project, you're more likely to be the victim of a violent act yourself.

✔ After this life, you may be reborn in a realm filled with extreme suffering. (See Chapter 13 for more about such a "hell" realm.)

✔ When you're born as a human again, you may have a short life filled with sickness and other difficulties.

✔ In your future life as a human, your surroundings won't be conducive to good health. For example, food will lack nutrition, and medicines will lack the power to cure disease.

✔ Even as a young child in a future life, you may display a sadistic nature — taking delight in killing small animals, for example. With this kind of negative predisposition to harm others, you continue to plant the seeds for even more suffering in the future. Of all the results of negative karma, this outcome is the worst because it just perpetuates misery for yourself and others.

Another reason karma can be difficult to understand is the time lag between the cause and its effect. This delay is the reason that cruel, corrupt people may thrive (at least temporarily) while compassionate, ethical people may suffer. A tremendous amount of time may pass between your action (cheating someone) and the reaction you experience (someone cheating you).

The same idea is also true for positive actions; the results may take a long time to show up. Even though some karmic effects ripen rather quickly, you don't experience most of the outcomes for one or more lifetimes! Talk about waiting (and waiting) for the other shoe to drop. As one Buddhist teacher is fond of saying, if your own back began to break just as you started to crush a bug, no one would have to warn you to stop. The connection between cause and effect would be obvious to you, and you'd naturally change your behavior. Unfortunately, the law of karma doesn't necessarily provide such immediate feedback.

Following Buddha's Ethical Guidance

As Shakyamuni Buddha sat under the Bodhi tree on the night of his enlightenment (see Chapter 3), his mind achieved an extraordinary level of clarity. Among other things, he saw the pattern of cause and effect in his previous lives. He saw how his actions in earlier lifetimes led to results he experienced in later ones. This understanding wasn't theoretical; Buddhists believe that he was able to perceive this pattern as clearly and directly with his mind as you can perceive colors and shapes with your eyes.

When the time came for him to provide spiritual guidance, Buddha was able to see how the law of karmic cause and effect also shaped the lives of others. He could see the exact historical causes of their current problems and understand the reasons behind their good fortune. Because he understood their past so well, he intuitively knew the most effective way for each of them to progress spiritually. You could say that because Buddha saw how each person tied his or her own karmic knots, he could give precise advice on the best way to untie them.

You can read more of Buddha's insights into the workings of karma in the collection of teachings known as *vinaya* (ethical discipline). (See Chapter 4 for more on the different divisions of Buddha's teachings.) Until you've achieved the level of mental clarity that enables you to see the pattern of your own karma as directly as Buddha did, you can rely on his guidance to tell the difference between actions that lead to desirable results and actions that lead to suffering.

The Buddhist system of ethical discipline didn't emerge as an absolute set of regulations. It began instead as a series of rulings that Buddha made in response to certain specific situations (see Chapter 4 for an example). Subsequently, his disciples wrote down and codified these injunctions, and eventually, they came together as the various codes of conduct that have been followed in Buddhist monasteries for 2,500 years.

Shortly before his death, Buddha told his attendant, Ananda, that the *sangha* (monastic community) could nullify individual minor rules after his passing. In his customary fashion, the Enlightened One was attempting to simplify the teachings and emphasize their essence or spirit. But Ananda forgot to ask which rules were minor, and none of the monastic councils over the centuries could agree on the issue. So the entire vinaya, with its more than 200 rules, has remained intact — though it applies only to fully ordained monks and nuns; lay practitioners generally follow 5, 8, 10, or 16 ethical guidelines, or precepts, as listed in the next section.

Exploring the Buddhist Precepts

Buddha's teachings on karma are vast and would take an extremely long time to read in their entirety. Fortunately, various traditions have summarized the advice in various ways over the centuries, such as in the following lists of precepts. The five basic precepts recited by lay people throughout the Buddhist world are probably the simplest and most universal place to start:

- ✔ Do not kill.
- ✔ Do not steal.
- ✔ Do not engage in sexual misconduct.
- ✔ Do not lie.
- ✔ Do not use intoxicants.

Different traditions have embellished these five precepts in their own unique ways. For example, in the Theravada tradition, novices in a monastery first take eight precepts (with the lay vow not to engage in sexual misconduct changing to the monastic vow of celibacy), and later, they take ten precepts, adding the following to the initial five:

✔ Do not eat after midday.

✔ Do not engage in singing, dancing, music, or any other kind of entertainment.

✔ Do not use garlands, perfumes, or adornments.

✔ Do not sit on a luxurious seat or sleep on a luxurious bed.

✔ Do not accept or hold money.

In Zen and certain other East Asian Buddhist traditions, the ten *grave precepts,* which are followed by both monks and nuns and lay people, consist of the universal first five plus the following:

✔ Do not speak of others' errors and faults.

✔ Do not elevate yourself and blame others.

✔ Do not be stingy.

✔ Do not give vent to anger.

✔ Do not defile the Three Jewels of Refuge (Buddha, dharma, and sangha).

The full precepts ceremony, a kind of initiation into the Buddhist fold, includes the three *pure precepts* (do not create evil; practice good; and actualize good for others) as well as the three refuges of Buddha, dharma, and sangha.

Arranging the precepts behind three doors

In the Vajrayana tradition, the ten primary precepts, which are quite similar to Zen's precepts, are described as the ten non-virtuous actions to avoid if you want to stop suffering. (The ten virtuous actions are simply the opposite of these non-virtuous actions.) The Vajrayana tradition arranges these actions according to the three doors through which you make contact with your world:

✔ **Door number one.** The three actions of your body:

- Killing

- Stealing

- Sexual misconduct

✔ **Door number two.** The four actions of your speech:

- Lying

- Divisive speech

- Harsh speech

- Idle gossip

> ✔ **Door number three.** The three actions of your mind:
>
> • Coveting what belongs to others
>
> • Ill will
>
> • Wrong views

Taking a deeper look at the ten non-virtuous actions

The following sections take a closer look at each of the ten non-virtuous actions in turn. The explanation we give is broadly applicable to all Buddhist traditions.

Killing

Taking another person's life bears the most karmic weight of any physical action. In the "Experiencing Karmic Consequences" section earlier in the chapter, we list some of the suffering that can result from killing — especially if it's carried out in a brutal manner while under the influence of a strong delusion like anger. Though relatively rare, such violent activity is far more common than most people would like to admit. Picking up your daily newspaper makes this point all too clear.

Although killing is listed as a physical action — something you do with your body — you can create the negative karma of taking life without lifting a finger. For example, if you order someone else to do the killing for you, you incur the full karmic consequences of the action. The amount of karma the person who actually carries out the order creates depends on several factors, including how willingly he or she participates in the deed.

Even when the killing is intentional, the heaviness of the karma you create — and, therefore, the heaviness of the karmic consequences you experience later — greatly depends on your state of mind. The stronger the delusion that motivates you — such as anger, jealousy, and the like — the heavier the karma you collect. Taking someone's life with great reluctance while wishing that you didn't have to is one thing, but killing someone out of hatred and rejoicing in the misery you cause is far more serious.

Who or what you kill also helps determine the strength of the karma that you create. For example, killing one of your parents is far more serious than killing an ordinary stranger. One person isn't inherently more valuable than another, but in relation to you and your particular karmic history, your parents occupy a uniquely important place because they've shown you special kindness by providing you with life. Similarly, killing a highly evolved spiritual practitioner, someone who can provide great benefit to others, is far more serious than snuffing out the life of an insect.

Don't get the idea that Buddhism condones certain types of killings because the karmic weight of killing can vary depending upon the circumstances. Not so! Buddha taught love and compassion for all. The ethical system he voiced is based on causing others as little harm as possible.

Stealing

Although hatred often motivates killing, desire generally motivates people to steal — or take what's not given to them. To be guilty of stealing, you must take an object of value that belongs to someone else. Taking something that belongs to no one and then making use of it isn't considered stealing because no one is harmed.

Stealing can occur in many different ways: You can sneak into a house, rob a person at gunpoint, or rip people off over the phone or on the Internet. All these types of stealing have one thing in common: They bring harm to others and yourself. The people you steal from lose their wealth or possessions, and you face the karmic consequences of your actions. For example, if you cheat someone in a business deal, you may experience great difficulty finding and accumulating the material necessities of life in the future. Just as wealth is the result of practicing generosity (see Chapter 14), poverty is the karmic result of stealing from others in the past — even if the past happens to be a previous life.

As with killing (and all the other non-virtuous actions), stealing ultimately depends on your mind. Here's an illustration: Suppose you visit your friends' house and accidentally take their umbrella home with you. This isn't stealing. Your friends don't realize that their umbrella is missing, and you don't notice your mistake, so the umbrella sits in your closet for weeks. Although you have the umbrella in your home, you still haven't stolen it. One day you look in the closet and realize that you have an umbrella that isn't yours. You figure out that it belongs to your friends and decide to return it to them, but you don't get around to it. This is *still* not stealing (though it *is* procrastination). Then one day, perhaps months later, you think to yourself, "I've had this umbrella for a long time, and my friends haven't mentioned it. They obviously don't need it, so I'll just keep it." The moment you make this decision to keep what doesn't belong to you, you've taken what was not given, and that's when you accumulate the karma of stealing.

Sexual misconduct

Sexual misconduct is the last of the three negative actions of body (check out the "Arranging the precepts behind three doors" section earlier in this chapter for an overview of the categories), and it refers primarily to rape and adultery. But, from a broader perspective, it can also refer to any irresponsible use of sexuality (like promiscuity or sexual addiction, for example). Rape and other forms of sexual abuse clearly inflict great harm on the victims — a harm that they sometimes feel for the rest of their lives. Sexual addictions are perhaps less destructive, but they often inflict emotional pain on the parties involved and rob the addict of precious time and energy that could be spent on more constructive life pursuits.

Interpreting the precepts

Though every Buddhist tradition agrees on five fundamental precepts (and the various Mahayana schools agree on five more), the traditions interpret these ethical guidelines differently. For example, Theravada tends to read them quite literally and require strict adherence to the letter of the rule; Mahayana tends to take a more situational slant, with some latitude for interpretation based on the circumstances; and the Vajrayana and Zen traditions take a more comprehensive, multidimensional approach.

As a case in point, consider the Zen tradition, which relates to the precepts on a number of levels. On the relative, mundane level, they serve as helpful guidelines for action — rules that support you in your pursuit of the enlightened way of life. On a deeper level, they refer to the contents of your mind as well as your physical actions. If you desire someone else's possessions, you're stealing; if you lust after a person's body, you're engaging in sexual misconduct. At the deepest (or ultimate) level, Zen understands the precepts as a spontaneous expression of true nature — and an accurate description of how an enlightened person naturally behaves without attempting to follow any particular rules.

For example, the enlightened person can't kill because she doesn't see other people as separate from herself; she can't steal because there's nothing that doesn't belong to her; and she doesn't lie because she has no self to defend. At this level, the precepts provide an ideal standard against which you get to view your own tendencies and behaviors and assess the clarity of your own understanding.

Recent studies show that perpetrators of sexual abuse were often childhood victims of abuse. Sexual abuse is truly an evil that tends to perpetuate itself, and you don't need to have the clear understanding of a Buddha to recognize this point. But Buddha added something about this vicious circle that's not as obvious to ordinary understanding: The karmic results of committing sexual violence include having to experience it yourself in the future. In other words, although a victim of abuse may or may not grow up to be a perpetrator — and most do not — the perpetrator will definitely be a victim sometime in the future because of his or her transgressions (unless he or she manages to remove this karmic stain; see the "Purifying negative karma" section at the end of this chapter).

Adultery also causes a great deal of grief for individuals, families, and society as a whole. Although cultural standards vary greatly from country to country (what's acceptable in some places is strictly forbidden in others), sexual behavior between two people becomes misconduct when it amounts to taking what's not given freely. If you're unfaithful to your spouse, or if you're responsible for weakening or breaking up another couple's marriage, you may experience disharmony and sexual infidelity in your own marital relationships in the future — in this life or future lives — as a karmic consequence of this illicit behavior.

Lying

Lying means that you purposely mislead someone by saying something that you know isn't true. Simply making an untrue statement isn't lying; you have to intend to mislead someone into believing that you're telling the truth. Lies range from the mass deceptions often attempted by political propaganda to the small fibs and little white lies you may tell to get out of uncomfortable social situations. You don't even have to say anything to engage in this negative action; a nod of the head or a gesture can be as misleading as false words.

One of the main problems with lying is that it often forces you to cover your tracks with even more lies. You soon find that you've assembled so many lies that you can't keep your story straight anymore and must suffer the embarrassment of being found out. (You may recognize this as the plot line behind many television sitcoms.)

The results of lying can be even worse than momentary embarrassment. For some people, lying becomes a habitual way of life, and they can no longer tell the difference between what's true and what's false. It's as if they're taken in by their own deceit. From a karmic perspective, Buddha said that, as a consequence of lying, you won't be believed even when you speak the truth.

Sometimes, however, you may find yourself in a situation where telling the unvarnished truth isn't a good idea. For example, if you know that an angry man with a gun wants to kill the person hiding behind the curtain, should you answer him truthfully when he asks you if you know where the person is? Of course not. You know that a completely truthful answer will result in murder — which is far more serious than merely veiling the truth — so you can mislead him without accruing the karmic consequences of lying. If you're devoted to the practice of compassion, you must do all you can to prevent the murder from taking place, but you need to be sure that your motive for not telling the truth is compassion for everyone involved — the would-be murderer as well as the intended victim. You not only want to save a life now, but you also want to prevent the gunman from collecting any more negative karma for the future.

Divisive speech

Divisive speech refers to the kinds of things you may say to break up a friendship between other people or to prevent people from getting back together after they've broken up. People can have many different motives for behaving in such a disruptive way. For example, if you're jealous of a close relationship, you may try to sabotage it for your own personal gain.

Your speech can be divisive whether the statements you make are true or false. If your intent is to split people up or prevent a reconciliation, your statements fall under the divisive category — even if they're true. One result of this negative action is that you'll have a hard time finding friends and companions in the future.

One obvious case does exist in which causing disharmony between others is considered appropriate — when they're plotting to commit a crime or perform some other harmful action. If you can break up their conspiracy and prevent them from creating problems for themselves and others, you're acting with kindness. But you have to be very clear about your intentions.

Harsh speech

Harsh speech refers to the kinds of things you say when you want to hurt someone else's feelings. As with divisive speech, these insults can be true or false; your intention to belittle, embarrass, or upset someone else makes them harsh. The karmic consequences of this kind of speech — as you may guess — are that you'll be subjected to verbal abuse in the future.

In America and perhaps elsewhere, an entire tradition of humor seems to be based on insulting others. The idea of a celebrity roast, for example, is to hurl as many clever insults at the guest of honor as you can in as short a time as possible. No one is supposed to get hurt at these affairs, and the guest is expected to laugh louder than everyone else as the skewering proceeds. But, occasionally, he or she *does* take something personally, and then things can quickly turn ugly.

Because words often carry more weight than you intend and can be more damaging than you imagine, be careful about what you say. After you develop the habit of insulting others, controlling your speech becomes more difficult. You may not be aware of the aggression inside you, but it nevertheless gives unexpected power to the words you utter "just in fun."

Idle gossip

Idle gossip is the last of the negative actions of speech. By its very nature, idle gossip is less serious than any of the other actions of body or speech mentioned in this section. The problem, however, is that it's by far the biggest waste of time.

Idle gossip includes all types of frivolous speech and can be about anything. Some people refer to it as "diarrhea of the mouth," and like harsh speech, it's a habit that's easy to fall into and difficult to break. If you spend your time and energy chattering about things that have no consequence, people eventually discount what you say as unimportant and stop taking you seriously.

Covetousness

Now come the three negative actions of the mind itself, beginning with coveting, or desiring to possess, what you don't have. Even if you don't act on this impulse, the fact that you look at others' possessions in this greedy way creates difficulties for your mind, which begin with restlessness. Then, when your desire to possess a particular item becomes strong enough, even greater problems arise. For example, if you want something badly enough, you may be tempted to steal it, which creates even worse karmic consequences.

Crazy wisdom: The "virtue" of breaking the precepts

Although Buddhism in general has consistently upheld the highest ethical standards, especially for members of the monastic community, certain traditions also celebrate their share of holy rebels and fools who break the conventional precepts in order to teach people through their exploits. This unconventional approach has become known in the West as *crazy wisdom*.

For example, the adventures of the vagabond yogi Drukpa Kunley, who taught dharma while drinking beer with peasants and sleeping with prostitutes, are legendary in Tibet. And in Japan, the equally outrageous exploits of Zen Master Ikkyu, who also headed one of the most prominent monasteries of the day, have achieved similar notoriety.

Usually, these *bodhisattvas* (enlightenment-bound people dedicated to enlightening others) have awakened to the most profound, non-dual view, which sees everything as sacred, including activities — like drinking and engaging in sexual intercourse — that traditional religious standards often consider objectionable. By breaking the precepts with this vaster perspective in mind, they're actually adhering to the higher spirit of the precepts, whose primary purpose is to facilitate awakening, not lay down some absolute standard of right and wrong.

Unfortunately, the crazy-wisdom tradition has been misunderstood, even among Western-based teachers of Buddhism, and several of these teachers have been involved in scandals in which their grossly unethical behavior has caused harm to their students and the larger community. Their cautionary tales offer ample evidence that only the most enlightened bodhisattvas dare venture into the territory of crazy wisdom. Otherwise, it just degenerates into harmful, self-serving misconduct.

 Covetousness is a discontented, dissatisfied state of mind. Energizing that state of mind is the expectation (often not clearly expressed, even to yourself) that if you just possessed that one attractive item, you'd finally be happy. But, as the Buddhist teachings repeatedly point out, you can't gain satisfaction by running after the various objects of the senses, no matter how attractive they may appear (see Chapter 2).

If you fail in your attempt to acquire the desired object, you're going to feel dissatisfied. But, even if you're successful and get it, the object inevitably fails to live up to your exaggerated expectations. Then, like salt water, instead of satisfying your thirst, the object only makes you thirstier. In this way, you only bring yourself more and more discontent.

 Because covetousness is a purely mental activity, it's harder to control than the physical and verbal actions that arise from it. To counter this disruptive mental attitude, you have to familiarize yourself with a different way of looking at things: You have to learn how to meditate (as we discuss in Chapter 7). You have to train yourself to recognize that the things you desire aren't as permanent or as inherently attractive as you imagine them to be.

Ill will

This powerful mental attitude is behind many of the things that you may do or say to harm others. In this destructive state of mind, you take delight in the misfortune of others, actively wanting them to suffer. Ill will is the exact opposite of love, which is the wish for others to be happy.

As with covetousness, controlling this kind of harmful intention is more diffi-cult than controlling the more obvious verbal and physical actions that arise from it. To successfully keep this attitude in check, you have to train yourself to see others as deserving of your respect, care, and love. Instead of focusing on traits that feed your ill will, familiarize yourself with others' good qualities until your heart opens toward them with compassion.

Realistically speaking, however, sometimes your negative feelings toward someone are simply too raw and powerful for you to transform by the method we just suggested — at least for the time being. In this case, your best bet may simply be to forget about the person you're angry with and turn your attention to the feeling of ill will itself. Like a scientist examining a poiso-nous snake, observe this destructive emotion as carefully and objectively as you can. Don't buy into it (don't follow its demands and start shouting or fighting), but don't try to suppress it either. Simply observe it.

As you watch your ill will dispassionately, you'll discover that, like all feelings, this negative emotion is not as solid as it first appears. Like a wave that rises from the ocean one minute and sinks back into it the next, the ill will rises in your heart, lasts for a short while, and then disappears again. A similar wave may rise up and take its place, but it too will inevitably subside. If you can stand back and simply observe this process (which is similar to the breath-awareness technique that we explain in Chapter 7), your negative feelings will eventually exhaust themselves.

Wrong views

Although you may have many different types of erroneous ideas about things, the wrong views we're talking about here have a rather specific meaning. You hold a wrong view when you actively deny the reality or existence of things that are true.

For example, according to Buddhism, the Three Jewels of Buddha, dharma, and sangha are reliable guides in which you can place your faith and trust. Also, the karmic law of cause and effect that we outline earlier in this chapter is true: Your actions *do* have consequences not only in this life, but in future lives as well. To deny these things is an indication that you've fallen under the influence of wrong views. In this context, having a wrong view doesn't mean doubting the Buddhist teachings on karma and so forth or simply being unfamiliar with them. It means actively claiming that they're false.

For example, if you really wanted to commit a certain non-virtuous action, such as adultery, you may try to convince yourself (and the other person) that nothing is wrong with what you intend to do. Besides, you may add, nobody will find out or get hurt. In this example, what you're really trying to do is excuse your misbehavior by advocating a view that flies in the face of Buddha's teachings on cause and effect. Promoting wrong views leads to serious mistakes; that's why this non-virtuous action of mind is so dangerous.

Dealing with Transgressions

Buddha didn't reveal the workings of cause and effect or identify actions to be avoided to scare his disciples. His goal was to protect them from unwanted suffering. After all, he isn't called the Compassionate Buddha for nothing. But what is his advice for those folks who, despite these teachings (or without knowing about them), make mistakes anyway?

The different Buddhist traditions have different ways of addressing this question, and we consider some of these in the following sections — atoning for mistakes and purifying negative karma.

Atoning for mistakes

During the early years of Buddha's ministry, one of his main disciples, Shariputra, asked Buddha to formulate a code of rules for the sangha community of monks to follow. (We mention only monks here because this particular incident occurred before women were admitted to the sangha.) Buddha replied that the sangha didn't need such a code at that time because even the least-advanced monks had their feet firmly planted on the path to spiritual awakening.

But, as the sangha grew larger, conditions changed, and a code of conduct gradually emerged for a number of reasons:

- To help safeguard the monks from the influence of attachment, hatred, and ignorance
- To ensure harmony within the sangha itself
- To preserve good relations between the sangha and the wider lay community

These monastic training rules (which make up the *vinaya,* as explained earlier in the section, "Following Buddha's Ethical Guidance") didn't spring into being all at once. They developed over time as Buddha offered guidance in individual cases (a lot like civil laws develop as a series of precedents in court cases). More than 200 rules were eventually formulated, and the custom arose of holding a meeting every two weeks (on new-moon and full-moon days) during which these rules were recited aloud and individual monks stepped forward to acknowledge their transgressions.

In the Theravada tradition, a monk can also make such an acknowledgement to one other monk as a daily practice of confession. As for lay followers of this tradition, when they realize that they have transgressed their precepts, they can revive them — retaking them either from a monk, or by themselves in front of a Buddha image, or by simply creating the intention in their own mind to renew and retake the practices of virtuous living.

The rules of conduct for monks and nuns list four grave offenses that lead to automatic expulsion from the sangha:

- ✔ Engaging in sexual intercourse
- ✔ Stealing
- ✔ Killing a human being
- ✔ Lying about one's spiritual attainments

But most of the rules covered in the monastic code deal with far less serious offenses, and the offenders can generally atone for them by honestly admitting their transgressions. As practiced in the Theravada tradition, such a declaration of wrongdoing doesn't erase the negative karma from breaking the rule, but it does strengthen the individual's determination to avoid breaking the same rule again. Also, it lets the fellow sangha members know that the person is still intent on following the monastic way of life as purely as he or she can.

Purifying negative karma

From the perspective of certain Mahayana (or Great Vehicle) traditions, you can purify your negative karma no matter how heavy it is — though if you are a monk or nun, committing any one of the four grave offenses mentioned in the "Atoning for mistakes" section of this chapter will still get you expelled from the sangha community. (For more on the Mahayana, see Chapters 4 and 5.)

As far as purifying negative karma in the Theravada tradition is concerned, practicing virtuous living and cultivating insight are the general means for protecting yourself from experiencing the consequences of harmful actions. However, some actions are so heavy — such as killing your parents — that you may not be able to purify them completely. Even Maudgalyayana — a foremost disciple of Buddha noted for his supernormal powers — met a grisly demise as the karmic result of having killed his mother in a past life.

In Zen, purification takes place through a process of atonement that differs significantly from the Theravada version. In addition to the admission of wrongdoing and determination not to act that way again, Zen atonement is understood as an opportunity to wipe the karmic slate clean and return to the primordial purity of your original nature.

Zen practitioners use the following verse (in one translation or another) in the atonement ceremony itself and also as a preamble to other important ceremonies to ensure that they're based in the purity of true nature:

All the evil karma ever committed by me since of old,

Because of my beginningless greed, anger, and ignorance,

Born of my body, mouth, and thought,

Now I atone for it all.

In some other traditions, such as the Vajrayana, practitioners accomplish this purification by conscientiously applying the *four opponent powers* (the four R's):

- ✔ **Regret: Feeling remorse for the harm you've done; recognizing and admitting your mistakes.** Don't confuse this open and honest declaration or admission of your mistakes with guilt, which is counterproductive. Guilt traps you in the past, solidifying your identity as a "bad" person and making it more difficult to move on to more constructive behaviors.

  Regret involves acknowledging that you've made a mistake, which is the first step to undoing it. Instead of trapping you in the past, sincere regret motivates you to take care of yourself and others by changing your behaviors — both now and in the future.

- ✔ **Resolve: Determining not to repeat that destructive action again.** Admitting you've made a mistake isn't enough; you need to exert effort to keep from repeating it. The best thing would be to vow never to commit that particular harmful action again for the rest of your life.

  But you have to be realistic. If you think that keeping a lifelong vow would be impossible, you can try your best not to act that way again for a specific amount of time (several months, perhaps, or even the next few days). By training yourself in this way, you eventually build enough strength and confidence to stop the activity entirely.

- ✔ **Reliance: Depending upon your refuge in the Three Jewels and your dedication to others to eliminate negativity.** Whenever you commit a non-virtuous action, you direct it against another being or against the Buddha, dharma, and sangha. By relying on the very same objects, you can help purify whatever negativity you engaged in.

  If your action is directed against the Three Jewels, such as by showing them disrespect (treating dharma texts carelessly, for example), you can begin to rectify your mistake by reminding yourself of their excellent qualities and reasserting the refuge you take in them. And, if you've harmed other beings, remind yourself of your compassionate intention to win enlightenment for their sake.

  These two reliances — taking refuge and developing the compassionate *bodhichitta* motivation (which we talk more about in Chapter 14) — are embodied in the following popular prayer:

> I go for refuge, until I'm enlightened,
>
> To Buddha, the dharma, and the highest assembly.
>
> By the virtuous merit that I collect.
>
> By practicing giving and other perfections,
>
> May I attain the state of a Buddha in order to benefit all sentient beings.

✔ **Remedy: Taking specific positive actions to counterbalance whatever negativity you created.** Specific virtuous actions directly oppose the ten non-virtuous actions listed in the "Taking a deeper look at the ten non-virtuous actions" section earlier in this chapter. For example, saving and protecting the lives of others is the opposite of the first harmful action — killing. A powerful way to neutralize harm you may have committed is to do something completely contrary to the negativity you want to purify — acting out of love rather than hate, generosity rather than miserliness, compassion rather than ill will, and so on.

Some of the generally recommended activities to counterbalance negativity include

- Serving the poor and needy

- Visiting people in the hospital

- Saving the lives of animals (even bait worms) about to be killed

- Making offerings to monasteries and other religious organizations

- Reciting passages from traditional dharma texts (and, better still, meditating on their meaning and putting them into practice)

- Drawing holy images

By following Buddha's advice, you can save yourself from experiencing some of the most serious consequences of your negative actions — for the time being at least. But, to rid yourself of these consequences entirely, you must go deeper, as we describe in Chapter 13, which deals with breaking free of the cycle of dissatisfaction altogether.

A powerful remedy

The Oscar-winning film *Gandhi* had a notable impact on millions of people. One scene in particular deserves mention here because it clearly illustrates the power of a correctly applied remedy to defuse even the heaviest negative karma.

Gandhi had gone to Calcutta in response to the violence that had broken out in that Indian city between the Hindu and Muslim communities. Engaged in a prolonged fast that he vowed to continue until the violence stopped, the great leader was close to death, and a large crowd gathered around him. Suddenly a Hindu rushed up to the bed and thrust a piece of bread toward him. Obviously distraught, the man cried, "Eat this! I won't have your blood on my conscience, too."

The man then revealed that in the fighting he'd killed a young Muslim boy and now fully expected to go to hell for his evil deed. Despite his weakened condition, Gandhi looked intently at the poor man and told him, "I know a way out of hell for you." He explained that the man should go through the city and find a young Muslim boy whose parents had been killed in the violence. He should take that orphan home and raise him as his own child. "But remember," Gandhi added, "you must bring him up as a Muslim!"

Chapter 13

Breaking Free of the Cycle of Dissatisfaction

*Y*ou may not know very much about Buddhism (until you finish reading this book), but we bet you've heard about nirvana (and not just the rock band). This term even pops up in casual conversation. For example, people say things like, "Relaxing in a warm bath at the end of a hard day: Now that's my idea of nirvana!"

But what does *nirvana* actually mean? Is it a blissful feeling you can experience when you kick your meditation practice into high gear? Or is it a kind of Buddhist heaven, like a reward waiting for good Buddhists when they die?

Neither of these notions is actually correct, but at least they both convey the sense that nirvana is truly wonderful, the highest form of good, and something definitely worth reaching. Nirvana (often translated as "enlightenment" or "liberation") isn't a place for you to go. It's a state of extraordinary clarity, peace, and joy that you can attain as a result of practicing the Buddhist spiritual path. (For more on enlightenment, travel over to Chapter 10.)

Nirvana is what you achieve when you free yourself from the underlying cause of all suffering — the illusion of being a separate self. Strictly speaking, nirvana isn't even a state. It's your natural condition hidden under layers of distorted ideas and habitual patterns. (Some traditions prefer other words than nirvana to describe this natural condition. To discover what they are, check out Chapter 10.)

One way to get a handle on the rather elusive concept of nirvana is to recognize what prevents you from experiencing it. So, in this chapter, we present the Buddhist explanation of the mechanism (known as the 12 links) that perpetuates dissatisfaction and the practices that you need to undertake to break free from suffering and achieve lasting peace and happiness.

Feeling like Life's a Big Rat Race

If you read the first two chapters of this book, you already have some idea of how negative states of mind — so-called delusions, or *kleshas,* such as hatred, jealousy, and so on — cause problems for you as soon as they arise. But they do more than simply cause problems. They force you to go from one unsatisfactory situation in life to another, searching for happiness and peace, but ultimately finding only disappointment and frustration.

The Sanskrit term for this pattern of recurring frustration is *samsara* (cyclic existence). This term conveys the ideas of uncontrollable wandering and restless motion that leads nowhere. If you've ever thought of your life as a rat race — your efforts to get somewhere just lead you around in circles — you've tasted the frustrating nature of samsara. Pretty bitter, huh?

Is the picture really as bleak as we've just painted it? Doesn't your life contain pleasurable aspects, moments of happiness to be enjoyed? Of course it does. But the point we want to make is that as long as your mind is under the influence of the delusions, the negative states of mind, these moments won't last. You'll inevitably experience frustration, dissatisfaction, and outright misery. That's why the Buddhist teachings say that the nature of samsara is suffering.

Remember that samsara doesn't describe reality itself, but your distorted experience of reality based on your negative mind-states. The rat race, in other words, exists in your mind, and the way out doesn't require changing your life — it requires changing your mind. In fact, some traditions of Buddhism teach that samsara *is* nirvana, meaning that this life is perfect the way it is, you just have to wake up to this perfection by transforming your mind. (For more on waking up to this perfection, see Chapter 10!)

Spinning the Wheel of Life: The Meaning of Wandering in Samsara

You can easily see how patterns of frustration and dissatisfaction repeat themselves in your daily life. For example, if you're a short-tempered person who always gets angry with others, you inevitably find yourself in hostile situations where you have to confront people who dislike you. These confrontations just cause you to get even angrier. If you go to sleep in an angry state of mind, your dreams may also be disturbing. Then, when you wake up the next morning, you may discover that you're already in quite a foul mood. And so it goes.

The Buddhist teachings claim that the pattern of suffering repeats itself on a much larger scale than simply waking up angry because you were upset when you went to bed. The delusions don't merely force you from one unsatisfactory experience to the next or from one unsatisfactory day to the next. They also force you to wander uncontrollably from one unsatisfactory lifetime to the next!

Buddha explained how deluded states of mind keep you trapped in these recurring patterns of dissatisfaction by teaching about what he called *dependent arising* or *interdependent origination*. (If you think these terms are obscure, take a look at the Sanskrit for them: *pratitya-samutpada*.) All these fancy words merely point to the same truth: Things happen to you for a reason.

From the Buddhist point of view, your life experiences, both good and bad, aren't random, meaningless events. Nor are they rewards or punishments handed out to you by some controlling force outside yourself, so blaming God or fate doesn't work. Your experiences result from a series of causes and effects that begin in your own mind. (For more about karmic cause and effect, see Chapter 12.)

Buddha illustrated this mechanism of cause and effect in a diagram popularly known as the *wheel of life*. (Check out Figure 13-1 for a representation of this wheel and Figure 13-2 for a diagram of its different parts.) Perhaps the best place to begin a summary of these important teachings is at the hub of this wheel.

Figure 13-1:
The wheel
of life.

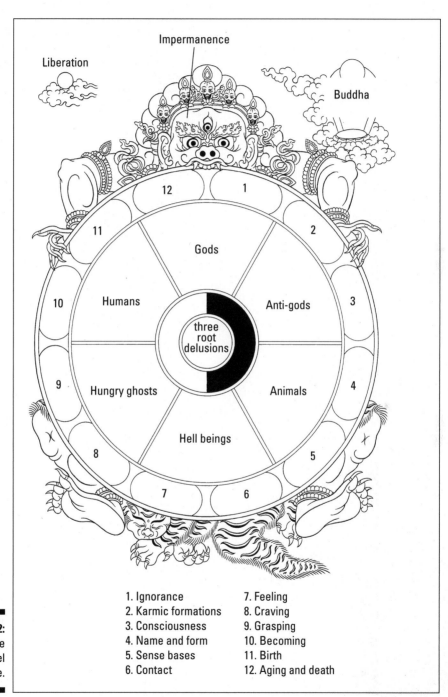

Impermanence

Liberation

Buddha

12 1

11 2

Gods

10 Humans Anti-gods 3

three
root
delusions

9 Hungry ghosts Animals 4

Hell beings

8 5

7 6

Figure 13-2:
A guide
to the wheel
of life.

1. Ignorance
2. Karmic formations
3. Consciousness
4. Name and form
5. Sense bases
6. Contact

7. Feeling
8. Craving
9. Grasping
10. Becoming
11. Birth
12. Aging and death

Identifying the root delusions

If you look at the center of the wheel of life (shown in Figure 13-3), you see three animals, which represent the three root delusions:

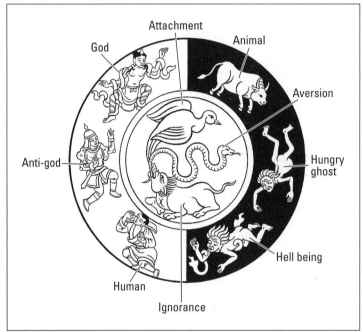

Figure 13-3:
The three
root
delusions.

- ✔ **Pig:** Represents ignorance, even though the pig is a relatively intelligent animal.

- ✔ **Rooster:** Represents desire or attachment. In some versions of the wheel, other birds take the rooster's place.

- ✔ **Snake:** Represents hatred.

If you've read Chapters 1 and 2, you're already somewhat familiar with these delusions. But now we want to explore a bit more closely how they're related to one another.

Grasping at a solid self

In this illustration of the wheel of life, the bird and snake emerge from the pig's mouth to indicate that ignorance is the source of all the other delusions. This version of ignorance doesn't simply mean to not know something. Instead, this type of ignorance holds on tightly to a mistaken idea of how things exist. You could say that it actively promotes a distorted picture of reality (see Chapter 2 for more about ignorance).

You can get an idea of how this ignorance works by performing the following exercise to discover how you ordinarily think of yourself.

1. **Use the word "I" in a sentence or two and see what you find.** For example, if you describe what you're doing right now, you may come up with something like this: "I'm sitting here reading this explanation and trying to figure out what it means."

   Notice that as soon as you talk about yourself, you automatically mention something that's going on with either your body (sitting) or your mind (trying to figure out the explanation) or both (reading). Try this little experiment several times until you clearly see that each time you use the word "I," you're referring to some aspect of your body, your mind, or both.

2. **Take a closer look at your body and mind.** Some Buddhist philosophical texts call this body-mind combination the *basis of imputation of the I,* which is just a fancy way of stating what you've already discovered: You use the term "I" or "me" (or your name) to refer to something going on in your mental and physical makeup. Now it's time to delve a little deeper.

   When you slowly and carefully examine what you consist of, you discover that all the elements that make up your body and mind (the five aggregates, or *skandhas,* mentioned in the *Heart Sutra*) are in a constant state of flux. Your physical sensations and your thoughts, feelings, and emotions are constantly changing — often at a very rapid rate. And you can't really point to anything within this constant flux and say, "This is something solid and permanent." (You only experience the full force of this type of examination meditation if you do it repeatedly over a period of time. Right now we're just presenting an abbreviated explanation to give you a general idea how to proceed.)

3. **Instead of coming up with an emotionally neutral statement about yourself as you did in Step 1, bring to mind a moment of great stress or excitement.** This point is where the exercise really gets interesting. Perhaps someone insults or embarrasses you in front of a crowd, and you become uncomfortable, self-conscious, and resentful. (You can also use the example of being praised in front of others and feeling proud or getting a big head as a result, but we'll stick to just one example here.) At times like this, you probably don't think, "That person just insulted some momentary aspect of my body or mind." Instead, popping up in the center of your chest is a solid, permanent, almost tangible, sense of self, and you feel like *that* is what has just been attacked: "How dare he say that about *me* in front of all these people!"

The concrete, self-existent "I" or "me" that appears to you *at that moment* has nothing whatsoever to do with your reality. You'll never find anything either inside or outside of your body-mind combination that corresponds to such an apparently concrete sense of self. This apparently concrete self is solely the creation of ignorance — a bad habit of the mind. And this ignorance — sometimes called *I-grasping* or *self-clinging* because of the unrealistic way it holds onto a false image of yourself — is the root of all suffering, without exception.

The snake and the rope

The Buddhist teachings offer the following famous analogy to help you better understand how belief in the false self leads to suffering and how wisdom can eliminate that suffering. Imagine that it's nighttime and you're out walking. On the path, you see what appears to be a snake, coiled and ready to strike. Fear and panic immediately grip your heart. But, when you shine a light on your would-be assailant, all you find is a piece of rope. To be on the safe side, you shine your light all around you, but no matter where you look, you can't find a snake. With the realization that a snake was never there to begin with — that it was just a figment of your imagination — you finally relax and continue on your way unafraid.

The false "I" is like the falsely imagined snake. As long as you believe that it's real — as long as you hold onto it as true — you experience fear, frustration, disappointment, and all the other forms of suffering and dissatisfaction. But when you use the light of wisdom to search long and hard enough, both inside and outside your body and mind, you discover that you can't find a solid and separate "I" anywhere. When you become convinced — not just intellectually but in the depths of your heart — that this falsely imagined "I" never existed at all, you'll stop believing in it, and all the suffering generated by this mistaken belief will evaporate.

Be careful when you do this kind of examination. You don't want to arrive at the mistaken conclusion that you don't exist at all. You *do* exist; after all, isn't someone reading these words? What *doesn't* exist — what has *never* existed and *never will* exist — is this falsely imagined, apparently separate and concrete self that you've always believed in so strongly. Breaking this habit isn't easy, but it's definitely possible.

Watching the growth of hatred and attachment

As long as you hold on tightly to this false image of a separate self — believing it to be the "real you" — you continue to imprison yourself. When you think this supposedly concrete "I" is being attacked, you immediately feel defensive. You strongly dislike what's happening to you, and hatred begins to grow in your heart. You may even begin plotting revenge against your tormentor, thereby ensuring that the pattern of attacks and counterattacks continues. And so the cycle of suffering keeps on spinning.

Hatred isn't the only negative state of mind that pops up. Attachment and all the rest of the delusions arise automatically as you try to maintain or defend this ignorantly conceived self. You become furious if you feel that this self is under attack, but you also *crave* anything that you feel would support or enhance it. This delusion is responsible for the compulsive got-to-have-it mentality. As long as you're under the influence of this I-grasping ignorance, you're feeding a desire that can never be satisfied.

You use all your energy trying to make this false "I" secure, but your efforts are doomed to fail. How can you provide security for something that never really existed in the first place? You just end up wearing yourself out and hurting others along the way.

When you're able to see that the concrete self that you've been clinging to all this time is just an illusion (generally after extensive training in meditation), you can begin to let go of this creation of ignorance. Letting go feels like having a heavy, unnecessary burden lifted from your shoulders. No longer neurotically compelled to defend or promote this phantom-like self, you're free to experience a deep sense of contentment and peace. To put it in more mundane terms: Because you're no longer so full of yourself, you can finally chill out.

Surveying the six realms of existence

Surrounding the hub of the wheel of life (Figure 13-1) are two semicircles (which you can also see in Figure 13-3), one light and the other dark, representing the two major types of action (or *karma*) that you can create — positive and negative. (Chapter 12 has a bunch of additional information on karma.) The three beings located in the left semicircle have accumulated positive karma that is leading them upward to the three "higher" realms of gods, anti-gods, and humans (check out Figure 13-2 for a roadmap to all the realms), while the burden of negative karma is dragging the three beings in the right semicircle down to the "lower" realms of the animals, hungry ghosts, and hell beings. (Don't worry, we explain these six realms in more detail later in this section.)

Don't take the terms *higher* and *lower* too literally. You won't find the gods up in the clouds or the hell beings deep underground, even if some traditional explanations may give you that impression. Your mind creates karma and experiences its results, no matter where you may be dwelling. A particular realm, or state of existence (or, better yet, state of mind), is called "higher" or "lower" depending on the amount of obvious suffering it contains. Beings in the higher realms experience less suffering and more pleasure when compared to the beings in the three lower realms. But, whether they're higher or lower, all six realms lie within the bounds of cyclic existence, and all the beings currently trapped there by ignorance carry the burden of dissatisfaction.

Here are the six realms listed in order from highest to lowest:

✔ **Gods:** (See Figure 13-4, top portion.) Also called *devas* (celestial beings), gods occupy the highest position within cyclic existence and are usually depicted as living in the most sumptuous surroundings. Depending on the specific type of karma they created to be reborn here, these long-lived beings spend their lives either intoxicated by pleasure or absorbed in some form of deep concentration. Some gods mistake their realm for nirvana, but unlike true liberation, this realm (like the other five) is only temporary. When a god's powerful positive karma is exhausted — karma doesn't last forever; you use it up as you experience its results — he or she has no choice but to fall back to one of the lower, far less enjoyable realms. So you can't even find security in the god realm. Although humans are not gods, those people who live the lifestyle of the rich and famous can be said to experience a god-*like* existence, both in terms of the extraordinary pleasures available to them and the constant threat that these pleasures may be snatched from them at any moment.

✔ **Anti-gods:** (See Figure 13-4, bottom portion.) Also called *asuras* (demigods), these beings experience an existence similar to the one in the realm just above them (the god realm), but they can't fully enjoy the pleasures of their realm. Because their enjoyments, like their positive karma, are inferior to those of the more fortunate gods, the anti-gods are plagued by tremendous jealousy, the predominant delusion of this realm. This jealousy provokes them to war against their more powerful neighbors (you can see them fighting in Figure 13-4) thereby repeatedly subjecting themselves to the agony of defeat (without the corresponding thrill of victory, no less). In the human realm (which we discuss in just a second), some of the not-as rich and famous experience problems of jealousy and competitiveness similar to those of the anti-gods.

Figure 13-4:
The god and anti-god realms.

✔ **Humans:** (See Figure 13-5, left.) The third realm of the three higher realms is the one you're experiencing now. As Buddha noted at the beginning of his own spiritual journey (which we catalogue in Chapter 3), this realm is filled with the suffering of sickness, old age, and death — not to mention the frustration of not getting what you want and the anguish of being separated from what you like. While living in this realm, you can experience something quite similar to the pleasures and pains of the other states of existence. In fact, that's why birth in this realm can be so fortunate: You have enough suffering to be motivated to break free from cyclic existence and enough leisure to do something about it.

✔ **Animals:** (See Figure 13-5, right.) This realm, the highest of the three lower realms, is the one with which humans have the closest connection. Although a wide range of experiences exists within this realm, the vast majority of animals lead lives of constant struggle, searching for food while trying to avoid being eaten themselves. This rough existence, driven by instincts they can't control, is a reflection of the type of behavior that's largely responsible for their birth as an animal in the first place. In addition to hunger and fear, animals also suffer from heat and cold and (in the case of many domesticated animals) the pain of performing forced, heavy labor. Unfortunately, desperate circumstances or limited intelligence forces many humans to live an existence not much different from their animal neighbors.

✔ **Hungry ghosts:** (See Figure 13-6, left.) This realm is one of continual frustration, thwarted desire, and unsatisfied craving. The predominant suffering of these unfortunate beings (called *pretas* in Sanskrit and sometimes referred to as *wandering spirits*) is unrelieved hunger and thirst, and the main cause for being reborn here is miserliness. Often depicted as having narrow necks and cavernous stomachs, these beings have great difficulty finding and consuming food and drink. Most people haven't encountered *pretas* directly — though Jon has met a few folks who claim to have made contact with them — but you may know of Scrooges who hold onto their possessions in such a miserly fashion that, like a *preta,* they've completely banished joy from their lives.

✔ **Hell-beings:** (See Figure 13-6, right.) This realm is the lowest of all the realms within cyclic existence, and it's filled with the most intense suffering. The main cause for experiencing this kind of a painful rebirth is committing extremely harmful actions, such as murder, while under the influence of powerful delusions — especially hatred. Within the human realm, people who endure particularly intense forms of physical or mental agony beyond the range of ordinary experience are said to lead a hell-like existence.

Figure 13-5:
The human and animal realms.

Figure 13-6:
The hungry-ghost and hell realms.

Though Buddhist mythology depicts these realms as having an objective existence, they're just as often used to refer to human beings who are stuck in a particular mind-state. For example, someone who never gets enough — someone who's never satisfied with the amount of material possessions he or she has — is often called a hungry ghost, and someone who's consumed with hatred is generally regarded as inhabiting the hell realm. By contrast, people may refer to someone who lives a life of wealth and ease but has little concern for spiritual matters as being stuck in the god realm.

As if the miseries depicted in this list weren't enough, a major defect of life within cyclic existence is that you can't find rest or certainty anywhere. One minute you're sipping the nectar of the gods, and the next minute you're wandering about looking for anything to quench your unbearable thirst. Even as a human being, you can be buffeted up and down and around the various realms in a matter of minutes. The entire wheel of life is in the grip of impermanence (which is represented by the monster in Figures 13-1 and 13-2). As your mind changes, so do your experiences.

These various realms of experience, or states of existence, aren't places waiting for your visit. They're not preexisting destinations to which you're sent as a reward or punishment. You create the causes for experiencing the pleasures and pains of these realms by what you do, say, and think.

Understanding the twelve links

In teachings known as the *twelve links of dependent arising,* Buddha described the mechanism that drives you from realm to realm within cyclic existence and keeps you trapped in suffering and dissatisfaction. In the depiction of the wheel of life (check out Figure 13-1), these twelve links are located around the outer rim. The following list explains their symbolism.

- ✔ **Ignorance: A blind man hobbling along.** (See Figure 13-7, left.) Here, once again, ladies and gentlemen, is the root delusion ignorance, direct from the hub of the wheel (see the "Identifying the root delusions" section earlier in this chapter). But here ignorance isn't a pig; it's a feeble blind man stumbling from one difficulty to another. He can't see where he's going because he's blinded by his own ignorance, completely mistaken about the way things (including the self) actually exist. He's feeble because, even though ignorance is powerful in the sense that it's the source of all suffering, it has no firm support and, therefore, can be overcome by wisdom.

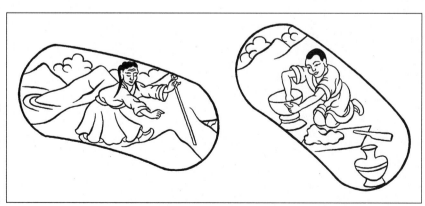

Figure 13-7:
The ignorance and karma links.

✔ **Karmic formations: A potter at his wheel.** (See Figure 13-7, right.) This link is also known as *compositional actions,* or more simply as just plain *action.* In ignorance, you engage in actions of body, speech, and mind; these actions — or karma — shape a new life, just like the potter takes a lump of clay and shapes a new pot. (Keep in mind that as long as you continue to grasp onto a mistaken view of yourself — that's the first link: ignorance — even your positive actions will shape a new life within cyclic existence for you. Of course, this new life will be much more pleasant than one shaped by negative actions. See the explanation of the differences between the "higher" and "lower" realms of samsara in the earlier section, "Surveying the six realms of existence.")

✔ **Consciousness: A monkey scampering up and down a tree.** (See Figure 13-8, left.) The actions of the previous link leave impressions on your consciousness that carry over into your future lives; the monkey climbing up and down a tree symbolized this movement from one life to the next.

✔ **Name and form: Two people carried in a boat.** (See Figure 13-8, right). If you're going to be reborn as a human again, your consciousness (carrying its impressions from the past) eventually enters the womb of your future mother where it joins with the united sperm and egg of your parents. *Name,* symbolized here by one of the two travelers, refers to the mental consciousness that joins the united sperm and egg. *Form,* symbolized by the other traveler, refers to the tiny embryo that will grow into the new body for this consciousness.

In some illustrations of the wheel of life, only one person is shown in the boat. In that case, the person stands for *name,* the mental consciousness coming from a previous life, and the boat symbolizes *form,* the fertilized egg into which this consciousness enters.

Simply put, name and form refer to the newly conceived being's embryonic mind and body.

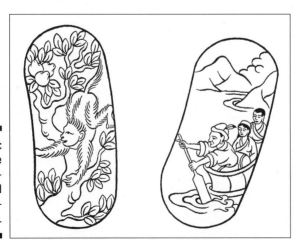

Figure 13-8: The consciousness and name-and-form links.

✔ **Six sense bases: An empty house.** (See Figure 13-9, left.) As the fetus develops in the womb, the bases for the six senses (see Chapter 2) begin to develop. At this point, however, the senses aren't functioning yet. Therefore, their bases are symbolized by a house that, although complete on the outside, is empty inside.

✔ **Contact: A man and woman embracing.** (See Figure 13-9, right.) As fetal development continues, the senses eventually develop to the point where they make contact with their respective objects. This initial contact — which occurs at different times for the different sense organs — is symbolized by two people touching or kissing.

✔ **Feeling: A person with an arrow in his eye.** (See Figure 13-10, left.) As a result of this sensory contact, feelings of pleasure, pain, or neutrality are experienced, beginning in the womb and continuing throughout life. Through this link of feeling (sometimes called *response*), you reap the results of your past karma, experiencing pleasure as the result of virtuous actions and pain as the result of non-virtuous or harmful actions (plus neutral feelings as the result of actions that are neither virtuous nor non-virtuous). An arrow sticking in a person's eye graphically illustrates the immediacy and intensity of feeling.

✔ **Craving: A person drinking alcohol.** (See Figure 13-10, right.) The eighth link, *craving* (or *attachment*), is the desire that arises from the feelings of the previous link. When you experience pleasure, you want it to continue; when you experience pain, you want it to stop. Your wish to repeat what feels good and to separate yourself from what feels bad is like a powerful addiction, and that's why a person drinking alcohol symbolizes this link. Like feeling, craving occurs throughout your life, but this link becomes crucial at the time of your death when you develop an especially strong desire to continue living.

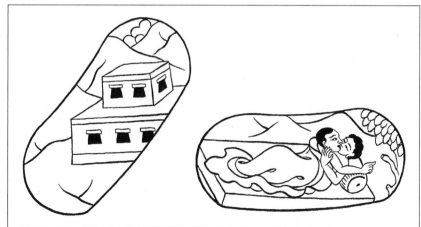

Figure 13-9:
The sense bases and contact links.

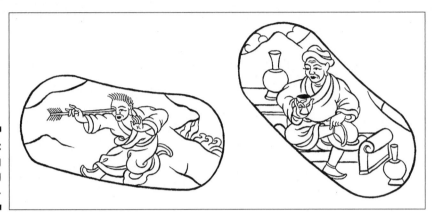

Figure 13-10:
The feeling
and craving
links.

- **Grasping: A monkey snatching fruit.** (See Figure 13-11, left.) This link represents a more intense form of craving. As your desire grows, you tend to grasp at pleasurable objects the way a monkey snatches at fruit. As you approach death, you tend to grasp at a new body to replace the one you're about to lose. This action isn't a conscious, thought-out decision on your part; it's the automatic consequence of the craving and grasping that you've become accustomed to throughout your life.

  Now that your old body is dying, your deeply engrained habit of I-grasping (see the "Grasping at a solid self" section earlier in this chapter) compels you to seek a replacement. As someone once jokingly put it, "In such a state of panic, you'll probably jump into the first friendly womb that comes along."

- **Becoming: A pregnant woman.** (See Figure 13-11, right.) As the links of craving and grasping increase in strength at the time of death, they begin to ripen one of the many karmic seeds already planted on your consciousness. The potential for this seed, or *karmic impression,* to lead directly to a new life is now activated, as symbolized by the pregnant woman ready to give birth. Rebirth is assured. (This link is called *becoming,* or sometimes *existence,* because it leads to your next life coming into existence.)

- **Birth: A woman giving birth.** (See Figure 13-12, left.) The seed activated during the previous link finally ripens fully, and your dying consciousness is propelled ("blown by the winds of karma," if you want to be poetic about it) toward the circumstances of its next rebirth. A woman giving birth symbolizes this link (even though you actually first make contact with your next rebirth realm at your conception).

- **Aging and death: A person carrying a corpse.** (See Figure 13-12, right.) From the moment of your conception, the process that inevitably leads to your development, deterioration, and death begins. Along the way, you'll be forced to carry the burden of unwanted suffering, which the person carrying the corpse symbolizes.

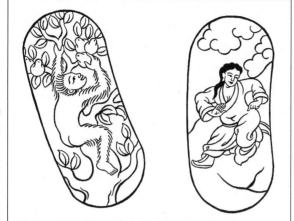

Figure 13-11:
The grasping and becoming links.

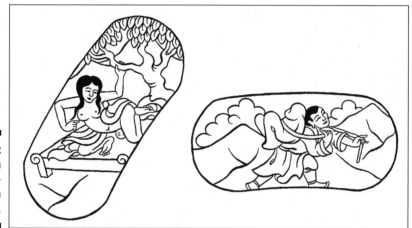

Figure 13-12:
The birth and aging-and-death links.

Buddha's purpose for teaching the twelve links — beginning with ignorance and ending with a corpse — wasn't to bum you out or depress you. Quite the opposite! His intention was to make you acutely aware of the way your ignorantly motivated actions inevitably lead to recurring suffering so that you'll be motivated to find a way out. The Buddha, depicted standing outside the wheel of life (look back at Figures 13-1 and 13-2) and pointing to the moon of liberation, or nirvana, represents this way out.

Cutting through Suffering: The Three Trainings

The question the spiritual traveler seeking liberation must ask is, "How can I cut through this 12-linked chain of dependent arising, gain release from the realms of suffering, and achieve lasting happiness and peace?" To answer this question, you have to determine which of the 12 is the weakest link!

When, prior to his enlightenment, Buddha spent six years engaging in austere practices of self-denial (such as standing on one leg for hours at a time and eating just one grain of rice a day; see Chapter 3), he was in effect trying to break the sixth and seventh links — contact and feeling. He thought that if he could win sufficient control over his senses and find out how to endure even the most painful feelings, he could conquer suffering completely. But at the end of six years, he discovered that he wasn't any closer to his goal; he was just weak and exhausted. Trying to starve your senses into submission doesn't work because it addresses only the outward symptoms of suffering, not its actual causes.

Some people seem to think that they can find lasting happiness by attacking the twelfth link — aging and death. They avoid fattening foods, exercise regularly, apply special creams at the first sign of wrinkles, take their vitamins, receive hair-replacement therapy, and so on — all in the hopes that this behavior will somehow prevent them from growing old. (Some people even plan to freeze their body because they hope that doctors in the future will be able to cure them of the illnesses responsible for their deaths.) Taking care of your health is certainly worthwhile, but no matter what you do for your body, you won't be able to put off aging and death forever.

The weakest of the twelve links are the ones that seem to be the strongest at first. Ignorance, craving, and grasping — the first, eighth, and ninth links — are responsible for first creating and then perpetuating the cycle of recurring suffering and dissatisfaction. Ignorance motivates the karmic actions that plant seeds of suffering in your mind; craving and grasping ripen these seeds at the time of death, sending you to a rebirth in which further suffering and dissatisfaction are inevitable.

These three links are powerful, but they're all based on a fundamental misconception — a distorted view, a lie. They all hold onto an idea about the nature of the self or "I" that conflicts with reality. In this respect, they're weak. If you can develop the wisdom that sees things the way they actually exist, you can cut through these links and win complete freedom from cyclic existence (samsara). We're not talking about a detached, unfeeling withdrawal from life. Instead, we're referring to freedom from the suffering that occurs when you're caught on the wheel of life.

Buddha taught that the way to achieve this freedom is by engaging in what he called the *three trainings,* which form a tripod on which the entire structure of Buddhist practice rests. These three trainings are

- **Moral discipline:** The strength
- **Concentration:** The sharp aim
- **Wisdom:** The tool

The following is a traditional analogy to explain these three trainings. Imagine that you have a tree in your backyard producing poisonous fruit. Of course, you want to protect yourself and others from this dangerous situation, so you decide to get rid of the fruit. But how do you do that? You may try pruning back the branches of the tree, but this tactic helps only for a little while. Sooner or later, the branches will grow back and start producing more poison.

The poisonous fruit in this analogy stands for all deluded thoughts and actions that keep you trapped in cyclic existence, forcing you to experience suffering and disappointment over and over again. Pruning back the branches is like applying a temporary antidote to these delusions — like countering hatred by practicing patience (see Chapter 14). These measures help in the short run, but as long as the source of these delusions (the tree itself) remains standing, the delusions will reappear sooner or later.

The only way to be sure that you remain completely safe from danger is to chop through the trunk of the tree so nothing ever grows from it again. The trunk of the tree is ignorance — the mistaken view of the way you and all other things exist.

Just as you need three different things to chop down a tree (a sharp ax, a steady aim, and a strong arm), you also need the three trainings to free yourself from samsara. These three trainings work together as follows:

- **A sharp ax:** Without a sharp ax, you won't be able to cut anything down. In this case, your ax is the wisdom you develop by hearing about, examining, and finally meditating deeply on the Buddha's teachings. Specifically, you have to develop the penetrating wisdom to directly see that the solid, concrete sense of self you've been grasping is a fiction — a false projection of your mind.

- **A steady aim:** Having a sharp ax isn't enough. To cut through the trunk of the tree, you need a steady aim that gives you the ability to hit the same spot again and again. If you just flail around, even the sharpest ax won't help. Only a perfectly concentrated mind — which you can develop by bringing your awareness back again and again to a chosen object of meditation (see the breath-awareness technique in Chapter 7, for example) — can give you the steady aim needed to effectively wield the ax of wisdom. If your attention is lax or distracted, your aim will be untrue, and your wisdom will never penetrate.

✔ **Strength:** You're not done yet. If you lack the necessary physical strength, you won't be able to swing the ax with precision and power. The same idea is true for your spiritual practices. You need the strength that comes from observing a regimen of moral discipline. You can't lead an unethical life, causing harm to yourself and others, and hope to gain the degree of concentration and insight needed to eliminate ignorance from your mind.

If you practice the three trainings in combination with one another, Buddha has said that you can definitely bring cyclic existence to an end and experience the inexpressible peace of liberation. You don't have to die to reach nirvana, but you do have to tame your mind. To put it another way, you need to follow the training first outlined in the eight-fold path revealed in Buddha's first discourse (which we discuss in Chapter 3). With moral self-discipline as your base and heightened concentration giving you focus, your wisdom can cut through ignorance and help you free yourself from the cycle of recurring misery in this very life.

Chapter 14

Fulfilling Your Highest Potential

· ·

· ·

Someone always seems ready to urge you to make the most of your life. Your parents encouraged you to do your best. And your teachers probably nagged you to live up to your potential. Even television advertisements often harp on the same theme: Wear a particular brand of athletic shoes and then just do it. Join the army so you can be all that you can be!

Buddhism gives similar encouragement to its practitioners — though its scope and focus are quite different from those of the advertising industry and your friends, teachers, and parents. According to Buddhism, you have the power to make a success not only of this life, but also of your future lives. You can purify your negative karma, achieve happiness and peace of mind, and eventually attain *nirvana,* which is complete liberation from the cycle of suffering and dissatisfaction (see Chapter 13). The best part is that you can do all these things regardless of your life circumstances.

Of course, such lofty goals may be the work of a lifetime, but it's good to know that you have the potential — what Buddhism calls your *innate Buddha nature.* This Buddha nature is your birthright, and it's inside you right now waiting for you to recognize it and unleash its capacity. That's what Buddhist practice is all about!

In this chapter, we present an overview of the path that leads to the *actualization,* or fulfillment, of your highest potential. But first you need to be as clear about exactly *why* you want to follow such a path. In other words, what's your underlying motivation? For your practice to be complete, your motivation should go beyond your merely personal satisfaction to include the happiness and fulfillment of others. This deep wish for the benefit of *all* beings (not just your friends, and not just other humans either) lies at the heart of Buddhism. In the Great Vehicle (Mahayana) tradition (of which Zen and Vajrayana, among others, are a part), this wish is known as the *bodhisattva vow.* In the Theravada tradition, it takes the form of the *four immeasurables.*

Ordering a Round of Happiness for Everyone and Everything

Consider the following hypothetical situation. (If you think that another Buddhist analogy is coming, you're right.)

You and your entire family are at home when suddenly you smell smoke. The smoke quickly thickens, and you realize that your large two-story house is on fire. You pass a staircase leading up, but realizing that the fire will soon engulf the upper floors as well, you search for another escape route. Groping your way through the heavy smoke, you finally make it to the front door. Breaking free, you reach the yard outside. There, finally out of danger, you lie down to catch your breath.

The question is, "How do you feel now that you've reached safety? Are you content? Have you done everything you had to do?" Despite the fact that you're safe, the answer has to be no. Why? Because your family may still be trapped inside. As long as your loved ones are in danger, how could you possibly be content with just your own escape?

This analogy clearly demonstrates how incomplete focusing exclusively on your own liberation from suffering ultimately feels. Such self-centered preoccupation ignores the welfare of the countless other beings — human and otherwise — currently stuck in pain and dissatisfaction. Buddhism teaches that we're all interconnected and interdependent. At the deepest level, we're all one. With this larger picture in mind, fulfilling your highest potential must inevitably include providing for others' happiness and fulfillment as well.

The determination to benefit all beings as well as (or sometimes even before) yourself is known as the *vow of the bodhisattva.* The *bodhisattva* is the being whose enlightenment isn't complete until every living thing is enlightened too! Although the Mahayana tradition regards the bodhisattva as the ultimate role model, the bodhisattva spirit is just as pervasive in the Theravada tradition (see Chapter 4 for more on the Theravada and Mahayana traditions).

Dedicating Your Heart to Others

In Buddhism, the path that leads you to the greatest fulfillment must inevitably be based on the most all-encompassing motivation. In the Mahayana tradition, this compassionate motivation is known by its Sanskrit name, *bodhichitta.* Breaking the word into two parts makes it easier to understand:

- ✔ *Chitta* is mind, attitude, or heart. (We also discuss *chitta* in Chapter 2.)
- ✔ *Bodhi* stands for the supreme goal of enlightenment, or Buddhahood.

Putting the two words together, you get bodhichitta, the compassionate state of mind that wishes to attain enlightenment for the benefit of others. Some commentators call it simply the *awakened heart* or, as a translator we know likes to say, the *dedicated heart.* By cultivating bodhichitta, you awaken compassion in your heart for the suffering of others and dedicate your efforts to their benefit as well as your own.

No matter how much you've suffered or been hurt, compassion definitely exists in your heart right now, though it may be buried beneath layers of grief, anger, and self-protectiveness. (On the other hand, instead of hiding your compassion, suffering often evokes strong compassion as a response.) The problem is that your compassion may be conditional and limited in its scope. For example, you probably find it easy to feel compassion for a suffering family member, close friend, or small child, but your compassion for some others may not arise so spontaneously.

In Buddhism, the goal is to develop an unconditional compassion that extends to *all* beings, regardless of whether they've helped or harmed you in the past. This brand of compassion helps you break through your prejudices, stereotypes, and other forms of limited, judgmental thinking that prevent you from embracing all beings as your brothers and sisters. To aid in your cultivation of such all-encompassing "great" compassion, the Vajrayana tradition recommends two related approaches:

✔ Recognizing that everyone is a member of one family

✔ Realizing the basic equality of yourself and others

Keeping it all in the family

If you already believe in reincarnation (see Chapter 13), then seeing how you're related to everyone else isn't that big of a stretch. Your past lives (as explained in certain Buddhist traditions, at least) have been infinite, so you've had more than enough time to have been born as every other being's son, daughter, sister, brother, or any other family member. Take that annoying person who just cut you off on the highway or the mosquito who just left a painful bite on your arm: Why couldn't each of these beings have been your adored and adoring mother sometime in the past?

Calling on Mommie Dearest — or not

One traditional method for developing great compassion and the dedicated heart begins by recognizing that, at one time, all beings have been your mother. As your mom, they've loved, protected, and cared for you in all the ways that the typical Mother's Day card mentions. You can experience an immediate change in attitude (even toward an annoying person) if, for a moment, you can relate to that person as your loving mother.

These meditations for developing a compassionate, dedicated heart are part of the Buddhist mind-training tradition particularly favored by the Tibetans and must be used wisely to have the desired effect. In dealing with an annoying person, for example, the point is to shift your attitude from resentment or dislike to something positive. Therefore, when you practice visualizing him or her as being someone near and dear to you, make certain that you choose your role model wisely.

Traditionally, as we mention earlier, the model you first select is your own mother because she carried you in her womb, gave birth to you, and did the 1,001 things necessary to keep you alive and healthy. But, when some people think about their mother, they find it difficult to remember such kindnesses. They can recall only problems — some very severe — that they've had with a rather difficult woman. In this case, don't think of others as having been your mother because doing so may only increase your resentment toward them. Choose someone you remember as selfless and nurturing, no matter who he or she may be. Eventually, as your love, understanding, and forgiveness grow, you can also open your heart to your mother and perhaps rediscover a bond you'd forgotten.

Getting connected to the world — through eating

Fortunately, you don't *have* to believe in reincarnation to appreciate that all beings are part of one large family. As nature shows us every day, the lives of all beings on this planet are interconnected, and seeing how everyone is related to everyone else makes good sense. It has become a matter of survival.

You can use this interconnectedness to improve your meditation on great compassion. Start by thinking of anything you do on a daily basis that helps sustain or enhance your life. A good activity to begin with is eating. Imagine that you're just about to put some food into your mouth. When you can almost taste it, press your mental pause button and think about how this piece of food got to where it is now. (You can also do this meditation at the dinner table, but if you're eating with others, be prepared for some funny looks as you suddenly freeze in mid-bite.)

Say you're about to eat a spoonful of rice. Ask yourself where the grain came from. It may have grown in a paddy field many miles away, perhaps even on another continent. Think of the many people involved in the difficult task of planting this rice. Then think about all the work it took to harvest this grain and thresh it and to bring it to market and sell it. All these tasks required the strenuous effort of hundreds upon hundreds of people, most of whom received shockingly small pay for their backbreaking labor. But the rice hasn't yet reached your mouth: It still has to be transported, perhaps repackaged, and then sold again. Finally it has to be prepared and served, and in many cases, you may not be involved in even these last two relatively simple procedures.

You can analyze whatever you eat in pretty much the same way. In each case, you'll realize that your enjoyment of even one small bite of food is totally dependent upon a countless number of others. Even though they didn't purposely intend to benefit you, the fact remains: Without their effort, you wouldn't have the food to eat. Your enjoyment depends completely upon their kindness.

You can apply this way of thinking to other aspects of your living situation. Ask yourself who's responsible for the house you live in, the clothes you wear, and even the language and ideas you use. In each case, the answer remains the same — other people. The more you look at things in this way, the more you can develop an appreciation of the infinite kindness you've received from others. As your heart opens to them, you'll naturally wish to return this kindness in the best way possible.

Figuring out what all beings desire

A person who translated extensively for the Dalai Lama (see Chapter 15) once remarked, "I never attended a teaching by His Holiness where he didn't mention that all beings are alike in their desire to be happy and free from suffering." The translator then went on to add that you can draw one of two conclusions from this observation: Either the Dalai Lama doesn't have much to say, or this point is extremely important. You can safely opt for the second choice.

Agreeing that all beings want to be happy and to avoid unhappiness isn't difficult. In fact, thinking of any behavior *not* motivated by these twin desires is the difficult thing. People may define happiness quite differently from one another (the music that some people like to listen to may make you cringe), but however they define it, happiness is what they want and unhappiness is what they definitely want to avoid. Even when people harm themselves in some way — by committing suicide, for example — it's generally in a misguided attempt to get rid of pain.

Even though recognizing how universal these twin desires are isn't difficult, the implications of this apparently simple fact are profound. When a person harms you, for example, you usually take it quite personally. "He attacked me on purpose," you may think, and then you may look for ways to hurt him back. But your attitude will change quite significantly when you realize that your attacker is motivated by the same desire for happiness that motivates you. This fact doesn't mean that you have to sit back passively and let someone abuse you. What purpose would that serve? But it does mean that whatever action you do decide to take — even if you decide to defend yourself forcefully — becomes motivated more by concern and understanding and less by the malicious desire to retaliate. Acting with this motivation in mind automatically improves the odds that your actions will be skillful and effective.

Looking at others as equal to yourself also helps reduce your selfishness, the cause of most (if not all) of your problems. Instead of constantly being involved with the tired refrain "Me, me, me," you may find yourself developing a genuine interest in the welfare of others. When you're in a group of people, for example, you may no longer feel such a terrible urge to put your wants and needs first. Instead, realizing that every person in that group also wants to be happy, you may open your heart and mind to *their* wants and needs.

Becoming a child of Buddha

The more you dedicate your heart to the welfare of others, the more you begin to realize that most people, though they claim to want happiness, engage in behaviors that only destroy their chances to find real peace and happiness. If you're honest, you'll undoubtedly find that you're making the same mistakes — and this situation doesn't change the moment you pick up a book (preferably *this* book) about Buddhism or one of the other great spiritual traditions of the world. (If it did, the publisher would definitely raise the cover price.) But at least it's a start; you're beginning to look in the right direction for true peace of mind and fulfillment.

As your understanding and sympathy for others deepen — in part as a result of dedicating your heart to their welfare — a sense of responsibility for all your sisters and brothers begins to grow in your heart as well. You begin to recognize that, in a certain sense, all beings are blind and stumbling toward the edge of a steep cliff. Who has more reason to help them than you? This train of thought may eventually result in a powerful resolve to free yourself from destructive habits and misguided points of view and to develop all the positive qualities necessary to effectively guide your family along the path to true happiness.

The moment you develop this pure, spontaneous wish in the depths of your heart and dedicate yourself to serving others in this way, you've given birth to the precious *bodhichitta* motivation. In that moment, you've become a *bodhisattva* — a son or daughter of Buddha — and entered the path that leads eventually to full enlightenment.

Nurturing the Four Heavenly Abodes

Just as Buddhism offers numerous meditation techniques for quieting and clearing the mind and gaining insight into the deeper truths of life, it also offers methods for cultivating the four core qualities known as the *heavenly abodes* or *immeasurables:*

- Compassion
- Loving-kindness

> ✔ Sympathetic joy
>
> ✔ Equanimity (peace of mind)

In Pali, these heavenly abodes are referred to as *brahmavihara*. The term literally means "dwelling of the gods," denoting qualities that are especially sublime.

Wisdom (or insight; see the "Cultivating the ultimate perfection: Insightful wisdom" section later this chapter) and compassion (or loving-kindness) are considered to be flip sides of the same coin. When you see deeply into the impermanent, selfless, suffering nature of reality, you naturally experience love for others, compassion for their suffering, and a passionate wish to help free them from their pain. At the same time, the more open your heart and the greater the love and compassion you feel, the more your limiting viewpoints fall away to reveal the essentially empty, insubstantial nature of reality.

For this reason, the development of insight and the cultivation of the four brahmaviharas go hand in hand in Buddhism. (If the brahmaviharas seem to overlap the bodhichitta motivation we discuss in the "Dedicating Your Heart to Others" section earlier in this chapter, it's because they're the Theravada equivalents. We expand on them here because they offer another powerful way of describing the fulfillment of your highest potential.) Buddha himself described the spiritual path as the "liberation of the heart which is love" and the culmination of the path as the "sure heart's release." No matter how much insight you have, unless your heart is brimming over with love and compassion, you haven't achieved full liberation.

Although we outline the four heavenly abodes in separate bullets, these four qualities aren't really separate. They're four aspects or facets of the precious jewel that is the fully awakened heart. Though Buddha and other great masters and teachers exemplify this heart, don't forget that it's also alive inside you right now as your own Buddha nature; layers of accumulated hurt, resentment, and fear merely hid it from your view. When you practice the four brahmaviharas, you provide fuel for this heart, which, like a powerful sun, gradually burns away the clouds of negative emotions, distorted beliefs, and habitual patterns.

One cautionary note: The cultivation of loving-kindness and compassion doesn't involve meddling in other people's affairs or taking the morally superior attitude that declares, "I'm a bodhisattva with pure motivation who has something important to offer to you, you lowly suffering being!" Quite the contrary: The qualities of love, compassion, equanimity, and joy in the happiness of others, when practiced correctly, break down the barriers of apparent separation between yourself and others and reveal the inherent oneness of all life. They show you the ways in which you yourself are suffering, closed-hearted, and otherwise stuck or misguided. Whenever you find yourself pointing a finger at others, even if it's in apparent compassion, remember to turn that finger around and point it back at yourself.

Meditating on the four heavenly abodes

In the Theravada tradition, meditations designed to cultivate love, compassion, joy, and equanimity have a similar structure:

1. Connect with your own essential goodness — or, if that's not handy, your own innate wish for happiness and well-being.

2. Spend some time imagining a person who easily and naturally brings the quality in question to mind. In the case of loving-kindness, this person may be your mother or someone else who has loved and cared for you unconditionally. With compassion, you may think of someone you love who's experiencing great pain or suffering right now.

3. When you're in touch with the quality, direct it outward, toward yourself (quite difficult for some people), then toward those who have benefited you in the past, loved ones, friends, neutral parties, and then (believe it or not) toward people who irritate or anger you.

4. Extend the quality to all beings everywhere.

Traditionally, certain prescribed phrases are used to generate these qualities, such as "May you be happy" (for loving-kindness), "May you be free of your pain and sorrow" (for compassion), "May your good fortune continue" (for sympathetic joy), and "May we all accept things as they are" (for equanimity). But you can feel free to experiment with different wordings until you find phrases that are most meaningful for you. At first contacting these qualities may be difficult, but don't worry (and certainly don't get upset with yourself): they're down there somewhere. When they start flowing, the practice of the brahmaviharas gets easier, and the qualities begin to arise more naturally and spontaneously in everyday life.

Extending loving-kindness

In Buddhism, especially the Theravada tradition, the quality known as loving-kindness (Pali: *metta*) is considered on a par with insight in its power to awaken and transform. In *loving-kindness,* you value and cherish others as if they were your very own children, and you wish for them the same good fortune, health, happiness, and peace of mind that you wish for your dearest friends and family members.

By extending love to others, you reflect back to them their inherent loveliness, their innate Buddha nature, and thereby encourage them to open their hearts and grow both personally and spiritually. At the same time, you gradually loosen the hold that negative emotions like resentment and disappointment have over your own heart.

But Buddha, in his wisdom, realized that you can't love others fully until you learn to love yourself. "If you search throughout the entire universe," he often said, "you won't find anyone more deserving of love and affection than yourself." So begin the practice of metta by first extending it to yourself.

Developing compassion

As we explain in the "Dedicating Your Heart to Others" section earlier in the chapter, compassion lies at the heart of the exalted motivation known as bodhichitta. But what exactly is compassion? Often people confuse it with the tendency to overburden themselves with the suffering of others and to harm themselves in the process of trying to help others. As one of my teachers used to say, this habit isn't true compassion, but rather idiot compassion (or, as self-help books like to call it these days, codependency).

Genuine *compassion* (*karuna* in both Pali and Sanskrit) involves first acknowledging the suffering of others, which is common in the world, and then gradually learning to open your heart to feel it deeply without letting it overwhelm you.

If you're like most people, you understandably try to avoid feeling suffering — not only others' suffering but also your own. After all, suffering is generally painful; besides, you may feel helpless because you can't do anything about it. And suffering often brings out other unpleasant feelings like anger (at the cause of suffering), fear (of suffering yourself), and grief.

But genuine compassion is actually empowering because a clear perception of the way things are usually accompanies it. The truth is that millions of people are suffering, and you can only do so much about it. From these clear perceptions and the compassionate feelings arise the strength and skill to do whatever you can to alleviate suffering, along with the acceptance that you can only do so much. The serenity prayer expresses this spirit quite beautifully: "God, grant me the serenity to accept the things I cannot change, the courage to change the things I can, and the wisdom to know the difference."

Nurturing sympathetic joy

Strangely enough, many people find sympathizing with the suffering of others easier than rejoicing in their happiness or success. Perhaps this trait is the result of the Western "no pain, no gain" work ethic, which emphasizes struggle and hardship while being suspicious of more expansive feelings like rapture and elation. After all, how many people genuinely rejoice in even their own well-being? Or perhaps you feel jealousy rather than joy because of the tendency, especially in the West, to compete with others, to judge, compare, and demean rather than approve and appreciate. Because of these tendencies, which were apparently common in Buddha's time as well, sympathetic joy (Pali: *mudita*) is generally considered the most difficult of the four brahmaviharas to develop.

The practice of loving-kindness

The following steps are a traditional exercise for connecting with the unconditional love in your heart and directing it to others. Don't hurry. Take as much time as you can; feel the love in addition to imagining it. Begin by closing your eyes, taking a few deep breaths, and relaxing your body a little each time you exhale. Then continue with the following steps:

1. When you feel relaxed, imagine the face of someone who loved you very much as a child and whose love moved you deeply.

2. Remember a time when this person showed his or her love for you and you really took it in.

3. Notice the gratitude and love that this memory stirs in your heart. Allow these feelings to well up and fill your heart.

4. Gently extend these feelings to this loved one. You may even experience a circulation of love between the two of you as you give and receive love freely.

5. Allow these loving feelings to overflow and gradually spread throughout your whole being.

6. Now consciously direct this love to yourself. You may want to use some traditional Buddhist phrases: "May I be happy. May I be peaceful. May I be free from suffering." Or you may want to choose other words and phrases that appeal to you. Just be sure to keep them general, simple, and emotionally evocative. As the recipient, be sure to take in the love as well as extending it.

7. When you feel complete with yourself for now, imagine someone for whom you feel gratitude and respect. Take some time (at least a few minutes) to direct the flow of love to this person using similar words to express your intentions.

8. Now take some time to direct this loving-kindness to a loved one or dear friend in a similar way.

9. Direct this flow of love to someone for whom you feel neutral — perhaps someone you see from time to time but toward whom you have neither positive nor negative feelings.

10. Now for the hardest part of this exercise: Direct your loving-kindness to someone toward whom you feel mildly negative feelings like irritation or hurt. By extending love to this person, even just a little at first, you begin to develop the capacity to keep your heart open even under challenging circumstances. Eventually, you can extend love to people toward whom you experience stronger emotions like anger, fear, or pain.

Like any meditation, loving-kindness benefits from extended practice. Instead of a few minutes for each step, try spending five or even ten minutes. The more time and attention you give it, the more you'll begin to notice subtle (or not so subtle) changes in the way you feel from moment to moment. Eventually the loving-kindness you generate in this exercise will begin to extend to every area of your life.

Sympathetic joy cuts through the comparing, judging mind to embrace the happiness of others on their terms. Usually you view other people through the lens of your own prejudices, ideas, and expectations and judge their efforts and accomplishments accordingly. When you cultivate sympathetic joy, however, you develop the capacity to see others clearly, just the way they are, and share in their happiness and success as if you're on the inside, feeling what they feel. By doing so, you not only enrich their experience, you increase your own store of happiness and joy as well. In addition, you break down the barriers that separate you from others and establish the possibility of ongoing mutual love and support.

Establishing equanimity

Considered the culmination of the brahmaviharas (and the one that protects the other three), *equanimity* (Pali: *upekkha*) is the spacious, balanced peace of mind that embraces life just the way it is.

This quality emerges when you meditate upon and deeply realize the essential Buddhist truth of *impermanence* (everything is constantly changing) and let go of trying to control what you simply can't control. You just let things be. In the formulation used by the great Christian mystics: "Not my will, but Thy will be done, O Lord!"

Equanimity doesn't mean passivity or indifference. You can take action to make important changes in your life with the same balance and peace of mind that you bring to sitting quietly in meditation. In equanimity, as in the other brahmaviharas, you're completely open to life as it presents itself. You don't shut down your heart or deny what's happening, but you have a deeper trust that life unfolds in its own meaningful and mysterious way, and you can only do so much to make a difference.

You may prefer certain life circumstances over others, but you have faith in the larger cycles, the bigger picture. Just as loving-kindness is compared to the love of a mother for her child, equanimity is compared to the love parents feel when their children become adults — providing warm support coupled with ample space and letting go.

From equanimity arises fearlessness in the face of life's ups and downs — a quality that can be just as contagious as panic or rage. In the movie *Fearless*, Jeff Bridges plays a man whose equanimity during and after a plane crash radiates peace and reassurance to the other passengers. (As we describe in the "Practicing open-hearted generosity" section later in this chapter, giving the gift of fearlessness is one of the four primary forms of generosity.)

Cultivating the Six Perfections of a Bodhisattva

As you may guess, simply wanting to become enlightened so you can help others most effectively isn't enough. You must actually follow the path that leads to this achievement.

In Buddhism, this path is outlined in numerous ways, often involving lists of one kind or another: the eight-fold path (see Chapter 3), the three trainings (see Chapter 13), the ten ox-herding pictures (see Chapter 10), and so on. Another helpful framework for understanding the path — one that emphasizes the cultivation of positive qualities and is used extensively throughout Buddhism for guiding students in their practice — is the six perfections.

Perfection is the commonly accepted translation of the original Sanskrit term *paramita,* which literally means "to carry across." The poetic image suggested here is a vast ocean of suffering, on the other side of which lies the far shore of enlightenment. By relying on these six practices, or perfections, the compassionate bodhisattva can ferry beings across — including herself!

The bodhisattva path (to switch from the ocean back to dry land) is a union of compassion (often called *method* because it's the means for benefiting others) and insightful wisdom into the true nature of reality. The first five perfections make up the compassionate method aspect of the path:

- ✔ Generosity
- ✔ Ethical behavior
- ✔ Patience
- ✔ Effort
- ✔ Concentration

And just as the eyes lead the body along a path, the sixth perfection gives guidance and direction to the rest:

- ✔ Wisdom

In the following sections, we largely adhere to the Vajrayana approach to interpreting the perfections. But they have broad application in Buddhism and are generally understood in more or less the same way. (In some traditions, ten perfections are listed instead of six. In those cases, concentration is omitted, and renunciation, truthfulness, resolve, equanimity, and loving-kindness are added.)

Generally regarded as qualities to be cultivated and perfected, the paramitas can also be understood from another perspective (see, for example, the discussion in Chapter 10 of the Zen and Tibetan *Dzogchen,* understanding of enlightenment) as essential aspects of your inherent and always available Buddha nature. In this view, instead of striving to achieve the perfections, you need merely awaken to and express your Buddha nature (also known as true self or the nature of mind). When you do so, the perfections naturally flower by themselves.

Practicing open-hearted generosity

Generosity is first on the list because it's considered the easiest of the six perfections to practice. Also called giving, or even charity, *generosity* refers to the openhearted attitude that allows you to give others whatever they need without stinginess or regret.

This perfection is traditionally divided into four types:

- ✔ **Bestowing dharma:** You don't have to be a fully qualified Buddhist master to give others *dharma* (spiritual guidance that leads beings out of suffering), though the greater your dharma understanding and realization, the more effectively you can guide them. But you do have to have the proper motivation: truly wishing to benefit others and not simply looking to impress them with your knowledge.

- ✔ **Bestowing protection:** Humans and animals constantly face danger, even of losing their lives. Protecting them from danger — by scooping a bug out of a swimming pool, for example — characterizes this second form of generosity. This powerful practice not only directly benefits the beings you rescue, but it also increases your respect for the sanctity of all life. In addition, the positive karma you generate by protecting and saving the lives of others can serve to lengthen your own life span (see Chapter 12 for more on karma).

- ✔ **Bestowing material aid:** Most people think of this type of generosity when they consider the practice of giving. Because human beings need so many different things to survive and prosper, such as food, clothing, shelter, and gainful employment, you have countless opportunities to practice material giving. Sharing spare change with the homeless person on the street, donating money to your favorite charity, and buying food for a sick friend are common examples of this form of giving. Just be sure to use your discriminating wisdom when you provide material aid to someone. Giving a bottle of wine to an alcoholic, for example, may not be the wisest form of generosity.

✔ **Bestowing fearlessness:** Above all, you offer this precious gift to others when you display it in your own behavior — and you can't manifest fearlessness unless you cultivate it in your heart by practicing meditation and working with the distorted beliefs that cause inappropriate or excessive fear. Classical statues of Buddha often show him in the gesture of bestowing fearlessness with one arm raised and palm facing forward (see Figure 14-1). (Interestingly enough, another gesture often accompanies this raised hand. The other arm directed down with palm facing forward denotes giving.) Because the Buddha's teachings help reduce fear and other forms of suffering, the first form of giving implicitly includes fearlessness, as does the second, which provides beings with the fearlessness that comes with physical safety.

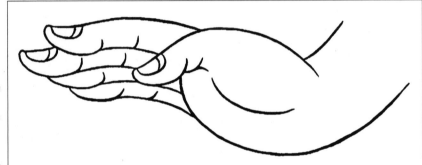

Figure 14-1: Gesture of bestowing fearlessness.

Keep in mind that the practice of generosity doesn't depend as much on *what* you give as on your *attitude* toward giving. You perfect this practice in your mind as you overcome all reluctance to help others and learn to let go of your attachments — to material possessions, time, energy, and even points of view. In this way, generosity fuels your own liberation because it gradually frees you from grasping and greed.

You don't need to give anything tangible to practice generosity; even cultivating the *wish* to give counts a great deal, especially when it weakens your self-clinging. Ultimately, the deepest expression of this paramita involves the recognition that the giver, gift, and receiver are inherently one and inseparable.

Following the self-discipline of ethical behavior

This perfection is also called morality, but we're a bit cautious about using that term because it smacks too much of a puritanical attitude toward pleasure that's foreign to much of Buddhism. The underlying meaning of *ethical behavior* in Buddhism is the avoidance of giving harm to others. You could simply call it goodness or virtue. As with generosity, the perfection of goodness (or ethical behavior) is traditionally divided into several types:

- **Restraint:** Your attempts to not commit negative actions while following the traditional ethical precepts fall into this category. For example, when you formally take refuge in the Three Jewels of Buddha, dharma, and sangha (in Theravada and Vajrayana) or receive the precepts (in Zen), you vow to refrain from telling lies. (For the scoop on taking refuge and receiving the precepts, see Chapter 6.) Every effort you make to live up to this vow expresses the discipline of self-restraint. The same holds true for any other vows you take as you progress along the spiritual path.

- **Accumulating virtue:** Progress along the spiritual path requires you to store up positive energy, especially when you've dedicated yourself to benefiting others. Accumulating virtue, therefore, is like charging your spiritual batteries. Throughout this book, we describe many such virtuous activities — such as making offerings to the Three Jewels, performing prostrations (see Chapter 8), praying for the welfare of others, studying the dharma, and adhering to the precepts — all of which contribute to this form of ethical discipline.

- **Benefiting others:** Benefiting others is the whole purpose of developing bodhichitta. In daily life, you have so many opportunities to help people around you that listing them all here is simply impossible. In brief, they include everything you do with your body, speech, and mind that's directed toward the welfare of others. Even the tiny act of lighting one candle on your altar, if done with the wish of purifying the darkness of another person's mind, is an example of this form of ethical discipline.

Developing patience

Patience is the direct opposite of anger and irritation, so it's one of the main practices of a compassionate bodhisattva. In addition to harming others, your anger and irritation have a disastrous effect on your own spiritual development. Therefore, keeping your mind as free as possible from this type of negative energy is extremely important.

Anger often arises when you feel like you're under attack, when you're not getting what you want when you want it, or when some situation or person frustrates you. But face it: The world is full of people and things that can upset you, so what are you going to do, get angry with each and every one of them? Anger does unleash powerful energy, but trying to use this energy to solve your problems only creates more problems. As soon as you steamroll your way over one obstacle, two more obstacles inevitably spring up in its place.

A famous Buddhist analogy states that if you want to protect your feet from thorns, covering the entire surface of the Earth with leather is a wasteful, inefficient way of going about it. Simply cover the soles of your feet with leather, and the thorns can't harm you. In a similar fashion, you can't protect yourself from life's difficulties by trying to overwhelm them with anger. By practicing patience, however, you can keep your mind free from anger, and as a result, your "problems" will no longer be able to bother you. Like wearing shoes, this approach is a much more effective way of protecting yourself.

The practice of patience is traditionally divided into three parts:

✔ **Remaining calm:** If you can refrain from retaliating with anger when someone or something harms or frustrates you, you're practicing this form of patience. One way to accomplish this feat is to think of how much worse you'll make the situation if you retaliate. Another way is to analyze the situation carefully and realize that the other person is ultimately attempting to find happiness, just as you are, but in an annoying and misguided way. Often the only way to improve a difficult situation is to simply refuse to engage with anger. If you do decide to confront the person, you can then do so with compassion and wisdom, which makes all the difference in the world.

✔ **Accepting suffering:** Even when someone or something isn't attacking or irritating you, you'll still continue to experience suffering in life as long as you haven't uprooted its causes within your own mind and behavior (see Chapter 13). In other words, as long as you're prey to the twin delusions of greed and aversion (wanting what you don't have and wanting to destroy what's bothering you), you're definitely going to suffer. And, until you succeed in achieving full enlightenment, at which point anger disappears from your heart forever, you need to find a way to relate to this suffering that doesn't involve losing your temper.

One way is to motivate yourself by viewing patient self-control as an opportunity to exhaust your negative karma (see Chapter 12). Another is to cultivate equanimity (one of the four immeasurables we discuss in the "Establishing equanimity" section earlier in this chapter), which allows you to accept your experience, no matter how painful. Finally, at the deepest level, anger dissolves and patience naturally arises when you view other people, including those that disturb you, as no different from yourself.

✔ **Developing certainty in the dharma:** Throughout this book, we talk about the practice of dharma — basically, training your mind — as being the only reliable way of protecting yourself and fulfilling your highest potential. But old habits are hard to break, so when difficulties arise, your tendency is to react to them in the same unskillful and destructive ways you've always used. In other words, when push comes to shove, you tend to forget all the dharma you've ever heard and shove back. This third aspect of patience involves searching for the appropriate dharma solution to each problem you face, and then making the concerted effort to apply this solution directly to your present situation, no matter how hard it may be.

The empty boat

A traditional story illustrates the foolishness of anger in light of the core Buddhist teaching of no-self, or selflessness. In the middle of a thick fog, a man is out fishing in his little boat when another boat slices through the mist and crashes into his. At first the man curses and yells at the person piloting the other craft, calling him names and demanding that he back off and give him space. When he looks more closely, however, he discovers that the other boat is empty — no one is manning the rudder. Suddenly his anger disappears and he realizes the pointlessness of his rage.

In the same way, the people who seem to keep deliberately attacking you are actually empty of a separate, independent self. Rather than

exerting conscious control over their actions, they're acting automatically, under the influence of unconscious conditioning and habit patterns over which they have no control — just as the boat was carried along by the waves in the fog. Because there's no one to blame, anger can be seen as a ridiculous waste of time.

This story isn't intended to imply that you're not responsible for your actions. Quite the contrary: Buddhism is rigorous in requiring that practitioners recognize how they create the problems that plague them. But it also acknowledges that until you become aware of what you're doing and start taking steps to change your behavior, you're as out of control as the boat without a pilot.

Practicing with enthusiastic effort

In its most positive sense, *effort* (which you can think of as perseverance or commitment) is the delight you feel when doing what you know is the right thing, which in the Buddhist context generally means practicing dharma. Instead of resisting, you dig in with gusto knowing that you're on the right track. Some texts even claim that perseverance or enthusiastic effort is the most important paramita because it gives energy to the other five.

One of the main obstacles to progressing in dharma practice, as in any area of life, is laziness — also known as resistance. The fourth perfection is divided into three parts because each of them counters a specific form of laziness:

- ✔ **Overcoming sloth:** *Sloth* here refers to what most people mean by laziness. It includes procrastination and any of the other bad habits that may keep you from practicing dharma right now. If you recognize what a rare and precious opportunity you have to make this life meaningful, and how easily this opportunity can be lost (see the discussion of death in Chapter 11), you'll find the energy and determination to put whatever dharma you've learned into practice right away.

- ✔ **Overcoming attraction to trivial pursuits:** As uncomfortable as admitting it may be, most people fill their days with unimportant distractions that aren't genuinely relaxing or fulfilling but merely occupy their time and keep them from doing what really matters in life. Watching TV, listening to talk shows, playing video games, filling out crossword puzzles — how many hours do you spend each day engaging in activities that have no deeper meaning? When you recognize how much time you waste in such trivial pursuits (and we don't mean the board game), you can deal with your addictive behavior and free up more time for dharma practice.

✔ **Overcoming defeatism:** This final form of enthusiastic effort counters whatever delusions of inadequacy or incompetence you may have. You may think that your negative mind is so strong and your practice of dharma so weak that you have no hope of making progress on the spiritual path.

To weaken the hold of such defeatist ideas and eventually eliminate them from your mind altogether, you can use what are called *affirmations* (for example, "I am a loving person, and I have the power to help others") to remind yourself that you too have the innate Buddha nature and, despite your busy mind and unskillful behavior, possess the same inherent virtues as everyone else. Reading dharma books can reduce your self-doubt and fuel your perseverance. Remember that all the realized beings of the past, including Shakyamuni Buddha, were at one time even more deluded than you are now. If they could generate the effort to complete their path, what's preventing you from doing the same?

Sharpening your concentration

The basic Buddhist technique for developing *concentration* is simply to chose a particular object of meditation, place your attention on it, and then keep it there without wavering. You can choose from a wide range of objects, including your breath (see Chapter 7), a patch of color, the visualized image of Shakyamuni Buddha, or even your own mind, just to name a few.

Different traditions have their own favorite practices, and some measure of concentration is important for all of them. For example, followers of certain devotional Pure Land schools of Buddhism focus their energy on gaining rebirth in the western paradise of Amitabha Buddha. As part of their training, they may practice visualizing this Buddha and his surroundings in as much detail as possible, until the image appears with utter clarity to their mind's eye. Followers of the Rinzai Zen tradition focus much of their attention on resolving *koans* (enigmatic teaching stories) — such as the famous "What is the sound of one hand?" or "What is your original face before your parents were born?" — until they break through the limitations of ordinary, conceptual thought. (See Chapter 5 for more on these two traditions.) Without strong and continuous concentration, neither the Pure Land follower nor the Zen practitioner is likely to achieve great success — and the same holds true for serious practitioners of other traditions as well.

Strong powers of concentration take time to develop, though occasionally a novice meditator may make surprisingly rapid advances (see the story of

Dipa Ma in Chapter 15). Even though you try to focus on one specific object (your breath, for example), any number of attention grabbers can easily distract you, including

- Sounds (of traffic, birds, and so on)
- Physical sensations (pain in your knees or itching)
- Memories (for example, what you had for breakfast)
- Anticipations and expectations for the future (maybe what you want for lunch)
- Almost any other experience that you can name

Many of these experiences are distracting because they stimulate strong desire, attachment, irritation, or frustration. (Check out the account in Chapter 3 of Mara's attempt to interfere with Buddha's concentration under the Bodhi tree by conjuring up images of his wife and child.) For this reason, meditators trying to develop powerful, single-pointed concentration also generally practice letting go of their strong attachments and aversions by recognizing how fleeting and unsatisfactory they are (see Chapter 2). Deep concentration can only grow in a contented mind.

In the early stages of your practice, you have to be patient and persistent, firmly (but gently) placing your attention back on the meditation object every time it wanders away, which will probably happen quite a bit. But, if you practice diligently enough, your attention will begin to gravitate naturally toward the meditation object (instead of the distractions) and eventually come to rest there on its own. Instead of being at the mercy of your fickle mind, you gradually become adept at controlling it.

As your concentration deepens, you naturally progress through a number of well-defined stages of meditation. Although you can read about these stages in various meditation manuals, practicing under the guidance of a competent teacher is important — at least until you're well established in the practice. Otherwise, you can get sidetracked in numerous ways. You can even practice what you think is meditation for many years, when in reality, you're only building up habits of mental dullness.

If your practice is diligent enough, you can reach a level of concentration far beyond what you normally experience. For example,

- You can develop the capacity to direct your attention to your chosen object of meditation and have it remain there with little or no effort, undisturbed by distractions or dullness.

  This level of concentration not only deepens your meditation practice, but it also has beneficial effects on your life in general. Disturbances like anger, greed, and jealousy can't easily arise in a calmly focused mind; when they do, they don't remain there for long.

✔ Deep concentration also brings the body and mind into balance, resulting in the disappearance of even chronic ailments.

✔ Deep concentration allows you to focus unwaveringly on any task, enabling you to function far more effectively at work and play.

Ultimately, however, the purpose of developing the power of deep concentration is to enable you to investigate the nature of reality. Only in this way can you develop the penetrating insight that eliminates ignorance, the root cause of all suffering and dissatisfaction. This insight, also known as wisdom, is the subject of the last of the six perfections.

Cultivating the ultimate perfection: Insightful wisdom

Buddhism encourages you to develop many different kinds of wisdom, including the ability to discriminate properly between actions that are destructive and actions that are beneficial to both yourself and others.

However, the perfection of wisdom (*prajna-paramita* in Sanskrit) refers to something deeper: The perfection of *wisdom* is insight into the way things actually exist, no longer misled by the false way they *appear* to exist. This wisdom reveals that the true nature of all things (you included) is marked by emptiness (*shunyata* in Sanskrit). (According to some schools of Buddhism, this wisdom reveals *anatma:* the *selflessness* of all things, which is another way of saying more or less the same thing.) Without this penetrating wisdom, the first five perfections are blind; and without the first five, your development of the perfection of wisdom will be weak. But, when they're cultivated together, in a union of compassionate method and wisdom, they give you the strength and vision to make it all the way to enlightenment.

Emptiness isn't the easiest reality to comprehend. Even the different Buddhist schools have different ways of understanding it. When the Buddhist wisdom teachings state, "All phenomena are empty" or "The self is empty," what exactly do they mean? Right off the bat you have to understand that these profound teachings are *not* saying that all these things are totally non-existent. Such things (or phenomena) as people, mountains, clouds, and so on do exist. They're just "empty," meaning they lack something. Practicing the perfection of wisdom means examining exactly what they're lacking as precisely as you can.

At this point you may scratch your head and wonder, "What's all the fuss about understanding that things lack something they never had?" The answer is that, according to the insights of the great masters and sages of Buddhism, all suffering and dissatisfaction, without exception, are rooted in your mistaken views of how things exist. Under the influence of these mistaken views, you superimpose qualities onto reality that reality doesn't possess. So if you want to eliminate suffering (and who doesn't?), you have to identify and eliminate all these mistaken views.

If you haven't directly perceived the truth, you mistakenly believe that things have a concreteness and a separateness — sometimes called an abiding, substantial self-nature (*atman* in Sanskrit) — that they don't really possess. To eliminate your suffering once and for all, you need to deeply realize that phenomena are totally empty of this substantial, abiding self-nature — they're empty of all the false views you mistakenly project onto them. One translator likes to call *shunyata,* or *emptiness,* "the absence of the fantasized," meaning that phenomena are empty of your fantasies and false projections about them.

So how do you meditate on emptiness? One way is to start by identifying the habitual views you have about people and things and then recognize how limiting and badly informed these views are and how they lead inevitably to suffering and dissatisfaction (see Chapter 13). In particular, investigate your concrete views of yourself — your habit of thinking that you're this or that kind of person with particular, fixed characteristics, independent of all the moment-by-moment changes going on in your body and mind. In other words, take a long, close look at how you perpetuate a particular image of yourself — your supposed identity, what you imagine to be an abiding, substantial self.

Explaining emptiness

Contrast the way you ordinarily use the term emptiness with the way it's used in Buddha's *Perfection of Wisdom Sutras.* For example, after a fire has destroyed a neighbor's house, you may point to the "empty" lot, indicating the absence or lack of the house that used to be there. Or you may point to a bottle that has only a little liquid left in it and say, "That bottle is almost empty."

In both these examples, you're talking about the absence of something that was once there, something that once existed. But, when the wisdom teachings say that all things are empty, they don't mean that phenomena lack something that once existed. Quite the opposite! The whole point behind the Buddhist teachings on emptiness is that all phenomena, you included, are empty of something that *never* existed in the first place — a solid, permanent, substantial self or essence. (For more on emptiness, see Chapter 10.)

The more you look for this solid sense of self inside you, the more elusive and ungraspable it becomes. Eventually, if you've prepared yourself well enough and your concentration is firm enough, you can experience a breakthrough to an awareness of reality "just as it is." All conceptions of *this* and *that* fall away in an experience completely beyond words or concepts. As you grow more and more accustomed to this penetrating wisdom — this direct experience of reality itself, free of distorted views — your realization, or enlightenment, deepens and stabilizes. Motivated by your compassionate wish to free others from their ignorantly created prisons, you can then lead them wisely and skillfully to enlightenment as well. (For more on enlightenment, see Chapter 10.)

Chapter 15

Four Modern Buddhist Masters

*T*he other chapters in Part IV give you an idea of how a follower of Buddhism can develop his or her mind and awaken spiritually. This information is interesting and helpful (at least we hope it is), but you may be left with a nagging question, "How can I be sure that this stuff really works?"

You may want to know for yourself whether the claims made on behalf of the Buddhist path are believable — that the path really does lead to the type of self-transformation illustrated in the stories about Buddha and later masters (see Chapter 3). The only way to find out for certain that the claims are true is to test out the Buddhist teachings for yourself and see what happens. But not everyone feels motivated to make a serious commitment to practice without a source of inspiration who can demonstrate that the spiritual path is really worth following. Your personal *guru,* or spiritual mentor, traditionally plays this role. (Check out Chapter 6 for more information about the different types of spiritual teachers.)

Because you probably haven't found a teacher or guru yet, we provide you with the next best thing in this chapter: a detailed look at four modern-day Buddhist masters whom Buddhists and non-Buddhists alike admire as inspiring examples of what the spiritual life can produce. Although all four of these folks were born in Asia — and the first two passed away toward the end of the 20th century — their influence is still very much alive in the West today.

Dipa Ma (1911–1989)

Even though Buddha's teachings are open to everyone, men — and especially monks — have dominated the history of Buddhism from its beginnings until today. This situation is regretful but not really surprising. For several thousand years now, all of the world's major cultures have been organized along patri-archal (male-dominated) lines, and Buddhist organizations simply reflect this cultural bias.

Fortunately, this unbalanced situation is beginning to change, especially in the West, where a growing number of women practitioners and teachers have achieved prominence in Buddhist circles. But, whether you're a man or a woman, you can find inspiration in the life of Dipa Ma, a Bengali housewife who overcame extremely challenging life circumstances to become one of the most accomplished Buddhist masters of her day. A generation of Vipassana teachers in the West revere her.

Spending her early years as a wife and mother

Dipa Ma, whose original name was Nani, was born in 1911 to a Buddhist family in a small village in what's now Bangladesh. The oldest of seven chil-dren, Nani displayed an unusually strong interest in Buddhism at an early age. Instead of pretending to cook and keep house like the other little girls, she loved to spend time with Buddhist monks and make flower offerings to images of the Buddha. She also expressed keen interest in her studies, but her formal education came to an end at the age of 12, when, as custom dic-tated, her family gave her away in marriage to a man more than twice her age.

Fortunately, her husband, Rajani, was a kind man who soon took a job as an engineer in Rangoon, Burma (now Myanmar), where the couple became actively involved in the Buddhist community. Although Nani and Rajani grew to love one another, their marriage had one major flaw from the traditional point of view: It produced no children. For more than 20 years, the couple remained childless until Nani surprisingly found herself pregnant at last. But her joy didn't last long because her long-awaited daughter died when she was only three months old. Nani almost passed away from grief, but four years later, she was pregnant again. This time her daughter, whom the couple named Dipa, survived. Nani was so happy that from then on she became known as Dipa Ma — Dipa's mother.

Overcoming physical ailments through meditation

During their marriage, Dipa Ma frequently asked her husband for permission to meditate, but he consistently refused, suggesting that she follow the Indian custom of waiting until she was older before pursuing a spiritual life.

Throughout a life of tragedy and sorrow, Dipa Ma kept her wish to learn meditation alive. She experienced heart disease, the death of an infant son, illnesses
that kept her perpetually bedridden, and finally, the heart attack and sudden
death of her husband. A widow and invalid at the age of 44, Dipa Ma found
herself in the depths of despair with nothing left to do but face the prospect
of death. At this point, her doctor recommended meditation as the only hope
for her survival. Dipa Ma realized, more clearly than ever before, that only
the practice of meditation would relieve her suffering and offer her true
peace. Entrusting her daughter to the care of a neighbor, she headed to the
Kamayut Meditation Center in Rangoon.

Amazingly, after only one brief period of instruction, Dipa Ma managed to
attain the state of deep meditative concentration known as *samadhi.*
Returning to her daughter, she continued her meditation practice at home for
several years before meeting with the Bengali meditation teacher Munindra
and his esteemed Burmese master Mahasi Sayadaw — both of whom were
instrumental in bringing the living practice of Buddhist meditation to the
West. During a retreat at Mahasi Sayadaw's center, she quickly progressed
through deeper experiences of *samadhi* until she eventually experienced the
first stage of enlightenment, a moment of inexpressible stillness that changed
her life forever.

At each successive stage of her inner journey, Dipa Ma broke through thicker
barriers of torment and pain and let go of deeper levels of attachment. With
these experiences, her health returned: Her blood pressure returned to
normal, her heart palpitations all but disappeared, and she regained her
physical stamina after years of illness and physical torment. Gradually, she
progressed through the stages of enlightenment (see Chapter 10), relinquish-
ing all traces of grief, anger, and fear and achieving an unflappable peace and
composure until her realization was complete. Within little more than a year,
the debilitated mother and housewife had been transformed into a living
embodiment of the Buddhist teachings.

Sharing her story with others

Astounded and inspired by her example, the friends and neighbors who had
all but given up hope for her survival just a few years before began to practice meditation themselves. Dipa Ma eventually began accepting students,
teaching them how to make every moment of their lives into a meditation.
For example, she taught mothers and housewives how to be steadfastly
mindful whenever they washed the dishes, did the laundry, or nursed their
babies. "You can't separate meditation from life," she often advised. "The
whole path of mindfulness is whatever you're doing. Be aware of it." Later,
when she left Myamar and moved to a small apartment outside Calcutta, she
attracted a steady stream of housewives who wanted to engage in her practical approach to mindfulness training.

Shortly after her spiritual awakening, under the guidance of Munindra, Dipa Ma developed many of the seemingly miraculous powers that you only read about in the legends of ancient meditation masters — appearing in two places at the same time, walking through walls, and traveling in time. But she soon stopped demonstrating these *siddhis* (the name for these extraordinary powers) because, by themselves, these powers don't lead to release from suffering — the one true goal of practice. Instead, she instructed her students to observe the precepts of pure moral behavior and dedicate themselves to the welfare of others, practices that she followed for the remainder of her life.

Though she treated each person who came to her like her own son or daughter and showered everyone she met with her love and blessings, Dipa Ma could also be fierce in encouraging her students to extend themselves further, practice more diligently, and use each moment as if it were their last. In a culture that still considered women inferior, Dipa Ma told her female students that they could actually go deeper in practice than men because their minds were softer and their emotions more accessible. Among the people who came to receive instruction, encouragement, and inspiration from Dipa Ma were westerners like Joseph Goldstein, Sharon Salzberg, and Jack Kornfield. These individuals went on to become some of the most influential meditation teachers in North America (see Chapter 5 for more on the spread of Buddhist meditation to the West). In the 1980s, Dipa Ma twice accepted their invitation to visit their Insight Meditation Society in Massachusetts to help lead retreats. She died quietly in her small apartment in Calcutta in 1989, with her daughter and a devoted student at her side, as she bowed toward Buddha with her hands pressed together in prayer.

Ajahn Chah (1918–1992)

The Theravada ("Way of the Elders") is the oldest continually existing Buddhist tradition in the world (see Chapter 4 for more on Theravada history), and its presence in the West owes a great deal to the work of modern-day elders like the Venerable Ajahn Chah (see Figure 15-1).

Finding his way in the forest of life

Born in 1918 in a small village in northeast Thailand, Ajahn Chah spent several years as a novice monk as a young man and then returned to his family to help out on their farm. At the age of 20, he resumed the monastic life, taking full ordination in 1939 and devoting his first years as a monk to learning Pali (the language of the Theravada scriptures) and studying the traditional Buddhist texts — the typical training in most Thai monasteries of the day.

Figure 15-1:
Ajahn Chah.

*Photo courtesy of DTOH Sambhantaraksa.
Copyright Abhayagiri Buddhist Monastery.*

But the death of his father led Ajahn Chah to seek more than intellectual understanding. He began a quest to discover the essential meaning of Buddha's teachings. He'd read a lot about the *three trainings* of morality, meditation, and wisdom, but he still couldn't understand how to put the teachings into practice. His burning question eventually led him to Ajahn Mun (1870–1949), the leading force in Thailand for the revival of the ancient forest-dwelling tradition of Buddhist meditation. (*Ajahn* — also spelled *Achaan* — is a term of respect given to senior monks who've begun to teach.) Ajahn Mun taught him that, though the written teachings are extensive, the central practice, mindfulness, is actually quite simple. (For more on mindfulness, see Chapter 7.)

With the way of practice clarified, Ajahn Chah spent several years traveling around Thailand and living in cobra-infested jungles and cremation grounds — traditional places for deepening meditation practice and confronting the fear of death. After years of wandering, during which his own awakening deepened and clarified, Ajahn Chah was invited back to his home village. Disciples began to gather around him, despite the poor shelter, sparse food, and malarial mosquitoes in the area. The purity and sincerity of his practice attracted these people in the face of these difficult conditions. Ajahn Chah founded the monastery now known as Wat Pah Pong, and branch monasteries gradually sprang up in the surrounding area.

Ajahn Chah became known for his great ability to tailor his explanations of dharma to each particular group of listeners. Arising from the depths of his own meditative experience, his talks were always clear, often humorous, and inevitably profound. Soon monks and lay people from all over Thailand found their way to his monastery (*wat*) in the forest to share in his wisdom.

Blazing the monastic trail

In 1966, the newly ordained American monk Venerable Sumedho, who began training at a monastery near the Laotian border, came to stay at Wat Pah Pong. The community accepted him as a disciple as long as he was willing to eat the same food and undergo the same austere practice as the other monks. By the time Venerable Sumedho had spent five rainy-season retreats at Wat Pah Pong, Ajahn Chah considered him qualified to teach. Together they started the International Forest Monastery. Venerable Sumedho became the abbot of the first monastery in Thailand run by and for English-speaking monks.

Other westerners came and went during the '60s and '70s, including Jack Kornfield — one of the pioneers of Vipassana in the United States and one of the founders of the Insight Meditation Society in Massachusetts and the Spirit Rock Center in California. After a stint in the Peace Corps in Thailand, Kornfield spent several years as a monk at Wat Pah Pong under Ajahn Chah's guidance before returning to the West and beginning to teach in 1975.

When Ajahn Chah was invited to teach in Great Britain in 1977, he brought Venerable Sumedho and several other monks with him. Seeing the Western interest in dharma, Ajahn Chah allowed Sumedho and other monks to stay behind at the headquarters of the English Sangha Trust in London to teach. The following year, the Chithurst Buddhist Monastery was established in Sussex, England. This event marked the first time that highly trained western-ers brought the living Theravada monastic tradition to the West. (In 1983, the monastery moved to Hemel Hempstead, England, and was renamed Amaravati.) Eventually Western disciples, through Ajahn Chah's guidance and inspiration, established additional centers in Europe, Australia, New Zealand, and elsewhere.

After several more visits to the West, Ajahn Chah's diabetes began to worsen, and his health began to deteriorate. Like a true master, he used his worsening condition to teach his disciples about impermanence and the necessity to follow the spiritual path diligently. Even when he became bedridden and could no longer speak, his presence attracted numerous monks and lay people to his monastery to practice. Finally, in 1992, Venerable Ajahn Chah passed away after bringing untold benefit to spiritual seekers around the world.

Thich Nhat Hanh (born 1926)

The last half-century has seen the growth of a movement known as *Engaged Buddhism,* which combines traditional Buddhist principles with nonviolent social action inspired by modern teachers like Gandhi and Martin Luther King, Jr.

One of the founders of and most influential figures in this movement is the Vietnamese Zen monk Venerable Thich Nhat Hanh (see Figure 15-2), who has worked tirelessly and extensively on behalf of poor and oppressed people around the world.

Figure 15-2:
Thich Nhat
Hanh.

*Reprinted with permission of Parallax Press,
Berkeley, CA. Photo by Nang Sao.*

Working for peace in times of war

Born in central Vietnam in 1926, Thay (as his students call him) became a Buddhist monk in 1942. He was a founding member of a center of Buddhist studies in South Vietnam by the time he was 24. After spending two years studying and teaching comparative religion in the United States, Thay returned to Vietnam, where he helped lead a resistance movement, based on Gandhi's principles of nonviolence, against the forces destroying his country during the Indochinese Wars.

Thich Nhat Hanh also founded Youth for Social Service, an organization that sent more than 10,000 monks, nuns, and young social workers into the countryside to establish health clinics and schools and help rebuild villages that had been bombed during the wars in Indochina. In a pattern that repeated itself many times, Thay's calls for reconciliation between the warring parties got him into trouble with both sides in the ongoing Vietnamese conflicts.

In 1966, shortly after the start of armed U.S. intervention in Vietnam, Thich Nhat Hanh traveled to the United States without official sponsorship or sanction of any kind. His mission was to describe to the American people the suffering of their Vietnamese brothers and sisters and to appeal to both military leaders and social activists for a cease-fire and a negotiated settlement. Martin Luther King, Jr., also a proponent of Gandhi's brand of nonviolence, was so moved by Thich Nhat Hanh and his proposals that he publicly came out against the Vietnam War and, in 1967, nominated Thay for the Nobel Peace Prize. During that same visit, Thich Nhat Hanh met Thomas Merton, a well-known Catholic monk and author, who reportedly told his students, "Just the way he opens the door and enters a room demonstrates his understanding. He is a true monk."

Continuing his quest, Thich Nhat Hanh traveled to Europe where he twice met Pope Paul VI to urge Catholic and Buddhist cooperation in helping bring peace to Vietnam. At the request of the Unified Buddhist Church of Vietnam, Thay led the Buddhist delegation to the Paris Peace talks in 1969. But, in 1973, when the peace settlement turned South Vietnam over to the Communists, the government refused to let him reenter his homeland. Since then, Thay has lived in France, leading meditation retreats, writing, and continuing his work on behalf of peace and reconciliation.

Forging new beginnings from classic ideals

In 1982, Thay established Plum Village, a large retreat center and meditation community near Bordeaux where people from around the world gather to practice mindfulness. Plum Village also serves as a refuge where activists involved in the work of peace and social justice can come for rest and spiritual nourishment and a place where Vietnamese expatriates can find a home away from home. Using Plum Village as his home base, Thay continues his frequent travels, leading retreats and giving workshops on mindfulness and social action around the world. His gentle teachings are firmly based on classical Buddhist themes, such as mindfulness, insight, and compassion. These teachings emphasize that, in order to achieve peace in the world, we need to be at peace ourselves. His more than 75 books of prose, poetry, and prayers have established Thay as an internationally recognized author.

In recent years, Thich Nhat Hanh has established a new Buddhist lineage (or school) that he calls the Order of Interbeing. This order is based on a reworking of the traditional Buddhist precepts (see Chapter 12 for more information on the precepts) known as the 14 "mindfulness trainings." Each mindfulness training begins with an awareness, either of certain Buddhist truths or of certain widespread inequities and injustices. The awareness is then followed by a commitment to behave in a more compassionate, mindful, spiritually-informed way.

Here, for example, are two of Thich Nhat Hanh's 14 mindfulness trainings, from his book *Interbeing* (Parallax Press):

Aware of the suffering caused by exploitation, social injustice, stealing, and oppression, we are committed to cultivating loving kindness and learning ways to work for the wellbeing of people, animals, plants, and minerals. We will practice generosity by sharing our time, energy, and material resources with those who are in need. We are determined not to steal and not to possess anything that should belong to others. We will respect the property of others, but will try to prevent others from profiting from human suffering or the suffering of other beings.

Aware of the suffering created by fanaticism and intolerance, we are determined not to be idolatrous about or bound to any doctrine, theory, or ideology, even Buddhist ones. Buddhist teachings are guiding means to help us learn to look deeply and to develop our understanding and compassion. They are not doctrines to fight, kill, or die for.

Thay has made the precepts more relevant to contemporary concerns, including the growing threat to the environment, the exploitation of developing nations by multinational corporations, and the conflict and terrorism caused by religious fanaticism. Through his worldwide influence on people who work for peace, this gentle monk, who practices the slow walking and mindful awareness that he teaches, has helped further the cause of peace and justice by embodying peace and justice himself.

The Dalai Lama (born 1935)

The world's most famous Buddhist leader is the monk Tenzin Gyatso, more popularly known as the Fourteenth Dalai Lama of Tibet. (The title *Dalai,* Mongolian for "ocean," was bestowed upon an outstanding Tibetan *lama* — that is, a *guru,* or spiritual teacher — more than 400 years ago by a Mongolian king. This king was so impressed by the lama's spiritual presence that he considered him to be an "ocean of wisdom." Each successive Dalai Lama has had *Gyatso,* which is Tibetan for "ocean," as part of his official name. By the way, the word *Tenzin* in the present Dalai Lama's name means "holder of the teachings.") Because this revered spiritual teacher and political leader is so widely known, we offer a somewhat more extensive account of his life and work than that of the three teachers we discuss earlier in this chapter.

Understanding the legacy of reincarnation

The present Dalai Lama is the 14th in a line of Tibetan spiritual masters that stretches back more than 500 years. Included in this lineage are some of the most accomplished meditators, teachers, authors, and poets in Tibetan history. Since the time of the Fifth Dalai Lama, Lobzang Gyatso (1617–1682) — known to all Tibetans as the Great Fifth — the successors of this line have also been the spiritual and secular leaders of the Tibetan nation. (This setup is like one person holding the position of pope and king at the same time.) During the reign of the Great Fifth, the Potala Palace, the residence of the Dalai Lamas, was built in Lhasa. Other than the Dalai Lama himself, this imposing structure remains the single most-recognizable symbol of Tibet today.

One of the unique aspects of Tibetan culture is the way in which the position of spiritual and secular leader passes from one generation to the next. A person doesn't become the Dalai Lama by inheriting the throne from a deceased relative, nor does he receive this position as the result of an election. Instead, when each Dalai Lama dies, his successor is *discovered* and then installed in his place.

This system is based on the principle of *reincarnation* (see Chapter 13 for more on this process). According to Buddhist teachings, when well-trained meditators have gained sufficient control over their mind through spiritual practice, they can remain conscious while dying and actually choose where they'll be reborn and to which parents. Selecting where they'll be reborn increases the chances that they'll be discovered at an early age (often by one or more of their former disciples). These young children (called *tulkus,* or incarnate lamas) are then educated in the same spiritual disciplines their predecessors mastered. Teachings they had given to others are now given back to them. Because they're already familiar with these teachings from past lives, their education generally proceeds quite rapidly, allowing them to quickly resume the function for which their spiritual career has prepared them: being of maximum benefit to others.

Many incarnate lamas lived in Tibet. And, according to some accounts, 200 (out of approximately 1,000) managed to escape when the Chinese took Tibet in the 1950s. The most important of these *tulkus* to escape is the Dalai Lama, who is revered as the human embodiment of the bodhisattva of compassion, *Chenrezig* in Tibetan. Considered the protector of the Land of Snows (Tibet), Chenrezig (see Figure 15-3) is the patron deity of the Tibetan people.

Reviewing the early life of the present Dalai Lama

By the time of the Great Fifth, the Dalai Lama had become the supreme secular and spiritual leader of the Tibetan people. Like the Fifth Dalai Lama, the Thirteenth was also called the *Great,* and when he passed away in 1933, numerous signs indicated that his reincarnation would be born somewhere northeast of Lhasa, the capital of Tibet. The *state oracle* — a clairvoyant monk whom the government always consulted on important matters — confirmed that the search for the new Dalai Lama should concentrate on the far northeastern province of Amdo, not far from the border with China.

Figure 15-3:
Chenrezig,
the bod-
hisattva of
compassion.

To narrow down the search, the *regent,* a lama acting as temporary ruler, decided to visit a holy site known as Oracle Lake to see if he could receive a vision of the new Dalai Lama's birthplace. At the lake, he received several visions consisting of a series of letters, an image of a three-storied monastery with a turquoise and gold roof, and a nearby house with unusual gutters and surrounded by miniature juniper trees.

The committee in charge of deciphering these clues determined that the monastery must be Kumbum, a sacred site in Amdo and the birthplace of the great master Tsongkhapa, the main *guru* (teacher) of the First Dalai Lama. A group of high lamas, led by Keusang Rinpoche, a close friend of the Great Thirteenth, headed for Kumbum monastery to look for children in the area who showed promise of being the next Dalai Lama. When they reached the small village of Taktser, which contained a house that matched the Oracle Lake image, they felt their search was coming to an end. In this house, they discovered two-and-a-half-year-old Lhamo Thondup — born on July 6, 1935. Keusang Rinpoche soon became convinced that this was the child.

When he returned to Taktser several weeks later, Keusang Rinpoche brought two canes with him. One of the canes had belonged to the Great Thirteenth. Young Lhamo grabbed that cane and declared, "This is mine! What are you doing with it?" Lhamo also took the rosary that Rinpoche was wearing around his neck — the rosary that the Thirteenth Dalai Lama had given him — and claimed it as his own. Later that evening, Keusang Rinpoche placed a number of ritual objects on a table in front of Lhamo, and the boy immediately picked up the items that had belonged to his predecessor and ignored the rest. By this time, Keusang Rinpoche knew that they had found the reincarnation of the Dalai Lama. But negotiations with the local warlord took more than a year, and the three-month journey to Lhasa didn't begin until July 1939 when Lhamo was four years old. The following spring, Lhamo Thondup was formally enthroned as the Fourteenth Dalai Lama and dressed in the robes of a monk. In the beginning, his tutors simply concentrated on teaching him to read. But eventually, the young boy began following the rigorous schedule of a monk. He woke up early in the morning, recited prayers, meditated, and memorized and recited texts — all before lunch! After lunch, his lessons continued with even more study of the philosophical texts that make up the most important part of a monk's education. By the time he was 12, the Dalai Lama took part in serious debate, learning how to energetically and skillfully defend and attack the different philosophical positions presented in these texts.

Dealing with the Chinese

One aspect of the Dalai Lama's training differed significantly from that of ordinary monks. In addition to his studies, he also spent part of his day attending meetings with government ministers. Although he was just a child, his presence at these decision-making meetings made him aware of the enormous responsibility that he'd be expected to assume someday. And that day came sooner than anyone imagined.

In late 1949, China began massing troops along the eastern border of Tibet. They were preparing for an invasion that would eventually engulf the whole country and bring to an end a culture and a way of life that had endured for centuries. The Chinese had wanted to incorporate Tibetan territory into China for a long time, and the Communist revolution in China (shortly after the end of World War II) gave them an opportunity to enter Tibet unopposed by the other world powers.

For the next ten years, the Dalai Lama tried to negotiate with the Chinese authorities who had assumed control of Tibet with the stated purpose of "liberating Tibet from the forces of imperialism." The only imperialist forces, however, were the invading Chinese themselves. The Dalai Lama tried to save the Tibetans from the devastation facing them, but he could do little. In 1954, China's top leaders invited the Dalai Lama to meet with them in Beijing. The officials tried to get him to see the benefits of Communism. But, when he complained to Chairman Mao that Chinese soldiers were attacking and destroying Tibetan religious institutions, the core of the Tibetan cultural identity, he received a callous reply. "Religion is poison," the Chinese leader told him. At this point, the Dalai Lama realized just how terrible the situation had become.

In 1956, the 2,500th anniversary of Buddha's passing, the Dalai Lama accepted Indian Prime Minister Nehru's invitation to travel to India to celebrate this important occasion. In India, he informed Nehru of the dangers facing Tibet and received the prime minister's assurance that if war broke out with the Chinese, the Tibetans would be welcome to seek asylum in India.

Despite the deteriorating situation, his mounting responsibilities, and the many distractions he faced, the Dalai Lama continued with his monastic studies and, in early March 1959, completed his *geshe* degree (roughly equivalent to a doctoral degree in philosophy and divinity). Just a few days later, the steadily worsening situation in Tibet came to a head. On March 10 (commemorated every year since then as National Uprising Day), tens of thousands of Tibetans surrounded the Dalai Lama's summer residence, the Norbu Lingka, to protect him from the Chinese forces that were about to kidnap him.

The state oracle declared that the Dalai Lama's only option was to leave for India immediately and continue the campaign to save Tibet from there. So, on March 17, disguised as a soldier, the Fourteenth Dalai Lama slipped out of the Norbu Lingka and began his journey into exile. Two weeks later, after passing over some of Tibet's roughest snow-covered terrain, he reached India to begin a new life. (For a dramatic and generally accurate version of this story, check out Martin Scorsese's film *Kundun.*)

Finding freedom in exile

Nearly a million Tibetans, accounting for one-sixth of the total population, attempted to flee with the Dalai Lama in 1959 and shortly thereafter. But fewer than 100,000 actually made it safely to India and neighboring countries. In Tibet, the death toll from the brutal Chinese takeover was staggering. Many people who managed to evade the Chinese forces didn't fare much better. Disease, malnutrition, the extreme climatic differences, and the hardship of the journey killed tens of thousands.

For the young Dalai Lama, life in India was very different than life in his homeland. He soon settled into a modest residence in the North Indian town of Dharamsala, a far cry from the forbidding Potala Palace in Lhasa. In Tibet, he had lived as a virtual prisoner — both the Chinese and ancient Tibetan religious customs and institutions restricted his activities. Now he was much freer to take charge of his life and create policies more in line with his personal principles and his interest in scientific and democratic methods.

Shortly after arriving in India, the Dalai Lama set up Tibet's government-in-exile in Dharamsala and began instituting democratic reforms in the exile community, all the while continuing to monitor events inside Tibet itself.

With the help of the Indian government, the Dalai Lama has opened settlement communities and reestablished monasteries. Under his guidance, children's schools, medical facilities, handicraft centers, and other cultural organizations have been established in India (and in other countries as well). In these and countless other ways, the Dalai Lama, through his promotion, support, and encouragement, has managed to preserve the Tibetan cultural identity despite the devastating destruction and genocide.

Embracing the role of Buddhist ambassador to the world

Over the years, the Dalai Lama (who is as willing to learn as he is to respond to requests for teachings) has established warm, mutually respectful relationships with leaders and followers of many other faiths. This same spirit of mutual sharing has marked his frequent contact with scientists, political leaders, social activists, psychotherapists, artists, musicians, and countless other individuals and groups from all walks of life.

The Dalai Lama has become a major participant in attempts to find common ground among the world's religions. His commentaries on the Christian gospels, for example (collected under the title *The Good Heart: A Buddhist Perspective on the Teachings of Jesus,* published by Wisdom Publications), are considered a major contribution to interfaith dialogue. He has also shown keen interest in scientific discoveries about the workings of the brain and how they may relate to the Buddhist understanding of mind. To return the favor, he has proposed that scientific research be performed on advanced Tibetan meditators so that the West can begin to document, using its own methods, the transforming effect of spiritual practices. The Mind Science conferences that have taken place between His Holiness and leading figures in Western science and philosophy already have led to the publication of numerous books.

Just 50 years ago, the world of the Dalai Lama was still quite narrow. Few people had access to him, and he had limited access to the outside world. Now his smiling face and infectious laugh are known to millions of people around the globe (see Figure 15-4). He spends much of his time traveling, visiting Tibetan communities abroad and giving teachings attended by thousands of participants. Numerous documentaries have been made about him, as well as two major movies — *Seven Years in Tibet* and *Kundun* — to which he has given extensive support.

Since receiving the Nobel Peace Prize in 1989 for his nonviolent struggle on behalf of the Tibetan people, the Dalai Lama has become the world's most widely recognized Buddhist and a revered symbol for the Buddhist virtues of

wisdom, compassion, tolerance, and respect. Even people who have no interest in religion recognize and respond to his goodness, simple humanity, and
humor. He has truly become a Buddhist ambassador to the world.

Figure 15-4:
Tenzin
Gyatso, the
Fourteenth
Dalai Lama
of Tibet.

Photo © Brian Beresford/Nomad Pictures.

Part V
The Part of Tens

The 5th Wave   By Rich Tennant

BUDDHIST CAFE

DHARMA DAY
SPECIAL

ALL-U-CAN-ABSTAIN
BUFFET $9.00

MOHO

In this part . . .

This part is the ultimate in one-stop shopping. You can discover (and figure out how to dispel) ten common misconceptions about Buddhism and find ten ways to apply the insights of Buddhism to your everyday life. What more could you want? Grab a cart and start loading up on knowledge.

Chapter 16

Ten Common Misconceptions about Buddhism

In This Chapter

▶ Getting the story on Buddhism straight

▶ Checking out your own preconceived ideas

▶ Replacing fiction with fact

*I*f the subject of Buddhism is relatively new to you, you may believe that your mind is like a clean slate with no pre-existing ideas about Buddhism and its teachings. But, as teachers of Buddhism, we're guessing that you probably have at least a few preconceptions about Buddhists, Buddha, or the Buddhist way of life. We're not saying that someone sat you down and fed these ideas to you. You could've picked them up from a comment on the nightly news, a picture in the newspaper, or a remark you overheard while watching a documentary on Asia. Though their intentions are generally good, the mainstream media are filled with distorted ideas about Buddhism.

As someone who regularly teaches (and attends) classes in Buddhist thought and meditation practice, Jon has noticed that certain misconceptions pop up again and again in students' comments and questions. He can even remember the misconceptions that he had while studying Buddhism for the first time. For example, after reading one or two books that emphasized the importance of eliminating desire if you want to reach Buddhahood, Jon feared that a Buddha might resemble some of the statues he'd seen in Asian art galleries — serene and balanced, to be sure, but also lifeless and cold. Jon didn't find that prospect appealing at all! But he dropped this misconception as soon as he met the Tibetan lama who eventually became his main teacher. His hearty laughter and warm, affectionate nature blew the misconception right out of the water.

In this same spirit of shining light on false impressions, we present ten misconceptions in this chapter that surface more or less regularly among new (and sometimes even experienced) students of Buddhism. After explaining how these misconceptions can arise, we attempt to put them to rest. Who knows? Maybe one or two of them will be familiar to you.

Buddhism Is Only for Asians

Buddhism got its start in India, spread first to neighboring Sri Lanka, and then stretched out its arms to the rest of Asia (see Chapters 4 and 5 for more on the historical development of Buddhism). Every traditional form of Buddhism (forms like Tibetan Buddhism, Vietnamese Buddhism, and Japanese Zen) originated in Asia. If you're like most people, the mental pictures you have of Buddhist monks and nuns are decidedly Asian. Taking that line of reasoning one step further, some folks presume that there's something about Buddhism that makes it appropriate for the "eastern mentality" (whatever that means) but unsuitable for westerners.

But Buddhism belongs to no one continent, nation, or ethnic group. As long as people suffer under the burden of negative emotions, destructive habits, and distorted thinking, Buddha's teachings about mindfulness, wisdom, and compassion can offer effective methods for achieving lasting happiness and peace of mind.

In fact, millions of men and women in Europe and the Americas have adopted Buddhism as their spiritual path and started to adapt its rituals and forms to their needs. And a great many of the Buddhist teachers in the West these days were born and raised in the West, supplanting the Eastern teachers who carried the religion to foreign shores in previous generations.

Of course, in the United States, many Asian Americans still practice Buddhism — but now, many Americans of other races and ethnic groups do too. Buddhism is quickly becoming as American as hard work and apple pie.

To Buddhists, Buddha Is God

Because Western religions are God-centered, it's understandable that many people think Buddhists worship Buddha in the same way Christians or Jews worship God. Likewise, folks may think that Buddhists consider Buddha to be the creator of the world and the supreme being who judges our actions, hands out rewards and punishments, plays a major role in determining our destiny, and generally has an active hand in the way our lives unfold.

But none of these concepts apply to Buddhism. As we explain in more detail in Chapter 3, the historical Buddha was an ordinary human being like everyone else. By sitting quietly in deep meditation, he was able to penetrate through the layers of attachment, anger, ignorance, and fear in his own mind and heart and realize the truth of his essential nature. He felt moved to help lead others out of their own self-created suffering, so he then arose from his meditation and spent the next 45 years sharing his insights and methods with others.

While making this point, though, we don't want to place an unbridgeable gulf between what "God" and "Buddha" may mean to some people. Some traditions of Buddhism do revere certain Buddhas and bodhisattvas in a rather special way. Instead of thinking of them merely as individual beings who lived in a specific country during a specific century, they revere them as the embodiment of eternal spiritual qualities, like compassion and wisdom. These essential qualities aren't limited to any one time or place, but completely go beyond, or transcend, history. Although Buddhists don't worship these so-called "transcendent" Buddhas and bodhisattvas in exactly the same way that Jews and Christians worship God, they definitely treat these figures as objects of great devotion. Moreover, they believe that these transcendent beings can, on occasion, intervene in human affairs, especially by helping to empower spiritual transformation.

Also, certain Buddhist teachings say that the ability to achieve the same enlightenment that Shakyamuni Buddha achieved exists right now as a potential in each and every being. Sometimes referred to as your *Buddha nature,* this potential isn't much different from what some followers of God-centered religions call the *Divine within* or *Christ consciousness.* (We discuss Buddha nature a bit more in Chapter 2.) In this sense, God and Buddha don't seem so different after all.

Buddhists Are Idol Worshippers

If you enter a Buddhist temple, you're likely to see behavior that appears to be *idolatry* (the worship of idols). Devotees stand reverentially with their palms pressed together in front of an altar decorated with flowers, incense, and other offerings and featuring a statue of Buddha (sometimes accompanied by other strange figures). Then they suddenly bow down, in some cases stretching their body out full length on the floor in the direction of the altar.

Although this scene may look suspiciously like idol worship, which many belief systems warn against, when this practice — called *offering prostrations* — is explained in detail (see Chapter 8), quite a different picture emerges.

For the devotee, the image on the altar represents his or her own inherently pure and undefiled Buddha nature, which is fully embodied by the Buddha and the various bodhisattvas (those other "strange figures" we mention earlier; see the preceding misconception, "To Buddhists, Buddha Is God," for more about these figures). This essential nature is luminous, wise, compassionate, and filled with other transcendent qualities, such as loving-kindness, composure, and generosity. When you bow or perform prostrations conscientiously (not as an empty ritual), you humble your false pride, honor your

Buddha nature, and express the strong wish that you and all beings may real-ize and express your Buddha nature for yourselves. Clearly, this practice is a far cry from idolatry.

Because Buddhists Think Life Is Suffering, They Look Forward to Dying

This particular misconception is one of the most popular — and most persis-tent — false impressions about Buddhism. And not without reason. After all, the first of the four noble truths at the heart of Buddha's teachings is known as the truth of suffering (check out Chapter 3 for all four). Many people also have images etched into their minds of the Vietnamese monks who sat in full meditation posture, set themselves on fire in protest against war and oppres-sion, and calmly burned to death. And a related misconception is never far behind: Buddhists consider it wrong or even sinful to have fun.

The misunderstanding can be largely dispelled if, instead of interpreting the first noble truth to mean "Life is nothing but suffering," you change the trans-lation to the simpler and more accurate statement: "Life contains suffering." Isn't this statement undeniably true? Don't we all suffer, if not constantly, then certainly from time to time, for one reason or another? The truth of this formulation becomes even clearer if you change it further: "A life governed by negative emotions and destructive habit patterns inevitably fills with suf-fering and dissatisfaction."

In addition, the first and second truths of *suffering* and its *cause* don't tell you the whole story. They're completed by the third and fourth noble truths of the *cessation* of suffering and the *path* that leads to this cessation. As we explain in Part IV, understanding the truth of suffering merely informs and motivates you to follow the path that leads to the *end of suffering* — the inex-pressible joy and peace that dawns when you awaken to your essential Buddha nature. (For more on awakening, or enlightenment, see Chapter 10.)

In short, Buddhists aren't morbidly fixated on suffering. On the contrary, Buddhists are primarily concerned with achieving an enduring happiness and freedom that doesn't depend on the unpredictable circumstances of life. If you need proof, just look at the smiling face of the Dalai Lama, the most visi-ble Buddhist in the world these days.

As for suicide, Buddhism strictly forbids it unless *excellent and compelling* reasons exist — which usually consist of saving the life of someone else. Only those Vietnamese monks can know whether they had such excellent and compelling reasons. Buddhists themselves have disagreed on this issue, but one thing is certain: The monks burned themselves not because they loved death more than life, but because they felt such compassion for the suffering of their countrymen that they were willing to sacrifice their own lives in the hope that such a dramatic act could make a difference.

Buddhists Think That Everything Is an Illusion

The Buddha's teachings aim to remove all false, misleading views about reality because these views are the primary cause of suffering and dissatisfaction. To express this point, Buddhist texts compare the world of appearances (in which most people are completely caught up) to an insubstantial dream, mirage, or illusion. Unfortunately, some people mistakenly interpret this metaphor to mean that nothing actually exists, that things are just a figment of your imagination, and that what you do really doesn't matter because nothing makes sense anyway.

But Buddhism considers this excessively negative interpretation to be one of the biggest obstacles to spiritual development. People who fall under its spell are in danger of behaving recklessly and ignoring the workings of cause and effect ("After all, everything's just an illusion"), which just creates more suffering for themselves and others. After this misconception has taken root, it's one of the most difficult to eradicate.

You can go a long way toward avoiding this misunderstanding by inserting the little word *like* in the right spot. Things aren't illusions; things are *like* illusions: They appear to exist in one way but, in fact, exist in another way. For example, in an optical illusion, one line can look longer than another line but actually be shorter. In the same way, reality may appear to be a collection of solid, separate, material objects. In fact, however, it is a constantly changing flow, in which everything is interrelated and nothing is as separate or independent as it appears to be.

At the relative, everyday level, things do exist. Otherwise, how could we have written this chapter, and how could you be reading it? The point is that until you remove the veils of misconception obscuring your wisdom, you can't perceive reality directly, just the way it is. (To explore this concept further, check out Chapters 2, 13, and 14.)

Another popular (and perhaps less confusing) metaphor is the ocean and its waves. If you only look at the surface, you may mistakenly believe that the ocean consists of a series of separate waves that come and go one after another. But, if you look beneath the surface, you realize that the ocean is far vaster and more mysterious than you initially believed — just like reality.

Buddhists Don't Believe in Anything

This misconception is closely related to the one we discuss in the "Buddhists Think That Everything Is an Illusion" section. In the wisdom teachings of Buddhism, you frequently come across the term *emptiness* (Sanskrit: *shunyata*). The world of appearances that we mention in the illusion section is sometimes called *conventional* (or *relative*) truth. Buddhism gives the status of *ultimate* truth only to emptiness itself. However, if you think that this emptiness is a synonym for *nothingness,* you're making a big mistake. Buddhists believe in emptiness — or, more accurately, look to experience emptiness directly for themselves — but that doesn't mean that they believe in nothing. Falling into such an extreme rejection of everything is a major pitfall on the spiritual path.

The important thing to keep in mind when dealing with this particular misconception is that emptiness, as used here, does *not* mean nothingness. In fact, one of the core teachings of Mahayana Buddhism is that form (and everything else, for that matter) *is* emptiness; you can't separate emptiness from the more relative, superficial way in which things appear. In a famous Zen formulation, the mountains and rivers aren't really mountains and rivers, and at the same time they are. (If you think that's a paradox, you should see some of the other Zen teachings! For more on Zen, see Chapters 4 and 5. For more on emptiness, see Chapter 14.)

At the same time, the statement that Buddhists don't believe in anything does have some truth. The historical Buddha always urged his followers not to take his words as a matter of belief, but instead to put them into practice and experience their validity for themselves. In this sense, Buddhism has always encouraged healthy doubt and emphasized personal experience over established dogma.

Only Buddhists Can Practice Buddhism

Some people who encounter Buddhism through a book or a teacher find that it helps them make sense of things in this world that they didn't understand before. But they hold themselves back from practicing the teachings because they think that they have to become Buddhists first — and they don't really want to go that far. Maybe they already belong to another religious tradition and don't feel comfortable with the idea of giving it up. Or maybe they're not yet ready to identify with any particular movement or "ism."

Many Buddhist teachers, including the Dalai Lama, urge westerners not to abandon the religion in which they were raised. Listen to Buddhist teachings and follow them if you wish, they advise, but remain true to your own tradition.

After all, every religion has its own outstanding qualities and values, and you may find it easier to progress spiritually in a familiar setting and community.

But, if you find that certain Buddhist teachings appeal to you, don't worry about converting: Simply put them into practice as much as you can. The fact is that many Christians and Jews these days, including well-known ministers, rabbis, and priests, practice Buddhist forms of meditation because they find that the techniques and the teachings support and deepen their understanding and appreciation of their own tradition. Several practicing Catholics have even been recognized as Zen masters! If done correctly, Buddhist meditation can make you an even better follower of your own religion — or a better atheist if that's what you happen to be. (For more on the stages of involvement in Buddhism, make a commitment to turn to Chapter 6.)

Buddhists Are Only Interested in Contemplating Their Navels

Undoubtedly Buddhism places a great emphasis on silent introspection. Turn your attention inward and tame your wild and unruly mind, the teachings suggest. Many people, even experienced Buddhists, interpret this to mean that they have to turn their backs on the outside world and concentrate exclusively on getting their own act together.

But Buddhism teaches that the highest motivation of all is to benefit others. The problem is that you can't hope to help others in the most effective way possible if you're still trapped by your own negative emotions and habitual patterns such as ignorance, greed, jealousy, anger, and fear. So whether you want to help others or just help yourself, you need to start with the same step: Turn inward through meditation and other practices and work with your own mind and heart. Eventually, if your altruistic motivation is strong, you'll naturally share the wisdom and compassion you develop with the people around you.

At the same time, Buddhism doesn't seem to have the long, well-established traditions of charity, good works, and social action that the Judeo-Christian tradition possesses. For this reason, some Buddhist leaders have suggested that Buddhism has a lot to learn from Christianity about methods for benefiting the poor, sick, and unfortunate. In recent years, inspired in part by their Christian brothers and sisters, Buddhists have created a social action movement of their own, known as *Engaged Buddhism*.

Of course, if you want examples of prominent Buddhist teachers committed to social action, look no farther than Thich Nhat Hanh, who was nominated for the Nobel Peace Prize in 1968 for his peace activism during the Vietnam

War, and the Dalai Lama, who was awarded that prize in 1989 for his tireless work on behalf of the Tibetan people. (For more on these two important teachers, see Chapter 15; and to discover more about Engaged Buddhism, check out the reading list in Appendix B.)

Buddhists Never Get Angry

The practice of meditation can be understood from several different points of view. According to the Zen tradition, for example, the idea that you're meditating to achieve anything at all limits your practice and takes you away from the present moment. According to the point of view shared by the Theravada and Vajrayana traditions, however, you engage in meditation for a variety of reasons, one of the most important of which is to overcome such inner obstacles as hatred and anger. Buddhists, therefore, have the reputation of being calm, even-tempered, and unflappable when faced with adversity. Many people, even some Buddhists, think of monks and nuns as being especially incapable of anger.

But keep in mind that merely becoming a Buddhist, or putting on the robe of a monk or a nun, doesn't mean that you suddenly break all the destructive habits of a lifetime (or, as Buddhists would say, countless lifetimes). Spiritual development takes time, and expecting dramatic changes simply because you've adopted a new religion or decided to wear different clothing is unrealistic and unfair.

If you're sincere in your Buddhist practices, you may begin to notice some changes in a relatively short period of time — say six months or a year. You may still get angry, but maybe you don't get angry as often or as violently. And, when you do get angry, you don't stay angry as long as you once did. If you notice such positive signs of change, you can rejoice in them. Eventually you may discover that situations that used to cause you to blow your stack only increase your understanding, love, and tolerance. That's when you know that you're really making progress.

Also remember that avoiding anger doesn't mean allowing others to walk all over you. People do things to one another that are harmful or just plain wrong; if you can do anything to stop or change this behavior, go right ahead. The trick is to be motivated by the positive power of love, compassion, and wisdom (if possible) when you confront the troublemaker. Try to leave the destructive power of hatred and resentment out of the picture.

Finally, we should mention that pretending to be calm and peaceful while you're seething inside with anger is most definitely not a recommended Buddhist practice. Neither, of course, is acting out your anger toward others. The first step is to acknowledge that you're angry; the next step is to work with your anger using one of several Buddhist practices that can help soften and ultimately defuse it. (See Chapter 7 for some ways to handle anger.) If necessary, you may need to express your anger in a clear, responsible way. But merely stuffing it down is like trying to stop a pot of water from boiling by pressing down tightly on its lid: Sooner or later, the pot will explode!

"It's Just Your Karma; There's Nothing You Can Do about It"

The term *karma* crops up often in casual conversation these days, and different people have different ideas of what it means. (If you're interested in exploring this subject in some depth, turn to Chapters 12 and 13.) For some people, karma seems to be unpredictable — kind of like luck. For others, the term means little more than *fate,* and their attitude toward life, therefore, tends to be rather fatalistic: "It's my karma to be short-tempered," they may say. "That's just the way I am; what can I do?"

But Buddhism views karma (which literally means "action") as both more predictable and more dynamic than the uses of the word that we just described. You're continually engaging in actions now that will lead to karmic results in the future, and you're continually experiencing the karmic results now of actions you created in the past. In other words, your karma isn't a fixed, unchanging destiny that you must passively accept, as if it were a single, unchangeable poker hand dealt to you by the universe. Instead, your karmic situation constantly shifts and changes depending on how you act, speak, and think right now. By changing your behavior and transforming your mind and heart through Buddhist practice, you can definitely transform the quality of your life.

Buddhists Don't Know How to Count

For all we know, this statement may be true. After all, this item is the eleventh in a list of ten.

Chapter 17

Ten Ways Buddhism Can Help You Deal with Life's Problems

In This Chapter

▶ Using the dharma to handle life's difficulties

▶ Laying down some general principles

▶ Applying specific advice to your problems

*B*uddha's purpose for teaching the dharma was entirely practical: He wanted people to be free from suffering. Simple as that. He never wanted his followers to just study, debate, and commit the dharma to memory. And he certainly wasn't interested in people learning it just so they could claim to be expert authorities on Buddhism (unless, of course, occupying that kind of position enables them to benefit others). The entire point of the dharma is to help people free themselves from suffering, experience peace, and realize their true nature.

Because the scope of Buddhism is so broad and profound, you can easily lose sight of the fact that the dharma is also a practical, everyday guide. Nearly every tradition emphasizes the importance of regular meditation practice in dealing with life's problems. When you meditate each day, spending some time simply being present for your experience just the way it is, you gradually reduce your inner conflicts and make friends with yourself. In fact, meditation creates a welcoming inner space in which problems often resolve themselves. (For more on meditation, see Chapter 7.)

In this chapter, we share a few hints and suggestions, both general and specific, for using insights from Buddha's teachings to help you deal with the challenges of day-to-day life. You may find that some of the pointers seem more difficult than others to put to use, and some provide nothing more than a temporary fix. But, if you gradually incorporate them into your repertoire of responses, you may find that your problems gradually diminish — and your happiness and peace of mind noticeably increase.

Affirming the Basic Principles

Buddha taught that reality has three basic characteristics:

- Reality is unsatisfactory, in the sense that ordinary existence fails to give you exactly what you want out of life.
- Reality is impermanent, in the sense that things change from moment to moment.
- Reality lacks a concrete, abiding substance, or self-nature.

When you ignore these characteristics, you risk acting according to three corresponding misconceptions, which inevitably prevent you from living in harmony with reality. In brief, these misconceptions are

- Believing that things that are fundamentally unsatisfactory can bring lasting happiness
- Believing that things that change from moment to moment are permanent
- Believing that things that lack a self-nature are concrete and independent

Applying the Basic Principles

Every difficulty you face in life is related, either directly or indirectly, to the three mistaken notions we mention in the previous section. When you find yourself in a situation that makes you upset, frustrated, or downright miserable, try to identify which of these three misconceptions is most responsible. This approach can take the edge off your suffering by giving you a good idea of how to alter your point of view so you're more in tune with the way things actually work in the world. The following ten situations can give you a pretty good idea about how to apply the dharma approach to your problems.

Turning the page on your great expectations

You probably get upset when things go wrong in your life — no big surprise there. Being criticized, losing your job, or breaking up with your sweetheart are just a few examples of painful occurrences that can have you singing the blues (or a sad country-and-western equivalent).

But, even when things go the way you want, you may be left with the nagging thought: "Is this all there is?" Although receiving praise, getting a promotion, or meeting the man or woman of your dreams sure feels good, your initial euphoria is often followed by a letdown. After all, you expected your good fortune to bring you some peace and satisfaction, and you're disappointed when you discover that something deep inside of you remains unfulfilled.

Feeling like something is missing, even in the face of good news, points to the fundamentally unsatisfactory nature of cyclic existence, or samsara (see Chapter 13 for more about samsara and how to break out of it). As long as you permit attachment and craving to rule your mind, you'll continue to live, die, and be reborn in a state of perpetual dissatisfaction, wandering from one disappointing situation to another. That's a fact, Jack — at least according to Buddhism.

But the situation isn't as bleak as it may appear: The reason for following the Buddhist path is to discover an alternative to this round of unsatisfactory existence. This path doesn't require you to leave your present life and go somewhere else; it only requires you to develop the self-awareness necessary to examine and change your point of view. Your disappointments provide one of the strongest motivations for making a change.

When things don't turn out the way you hoped, don't be surprised. Instead, take a close look at your expectations; you may be suffering because you expect too much. Life hasn't signed a contract with you promising to give you everything you want. It just unfolds in its own mysterious and uncontrollable way. The more you stop resisting the way things are, the happier and more peaceful you'll be.

Accepting change gracefully

Why do people lust after other people and material objects? The answer, in part, is that those people and things appear to be so darned attractive, at least from an ordinary point of view. At first, this attractive quality seems to be a permanent, unchanging attribute of the desired objects. But a little reflection reveals that everything you see, hear, smell, taste, and touch is constantly undergoing change. You can save yourself a lot of trouble simply by accepting this reality — the reality of impermanence.

Don't just consider the impermanence of the things you desire; consider your own impermanence as well. Buddhism places great value on the awareness of death (see Chapter 11 for details). A big death waits for you at the end of your life, but you also experience a lot of mini-deaths along the way. In other words, you're constantly changing, and you're never the exact same person you were before.

As you grow older, your likes and dislikes change (think of the foods you love now but would never even think about eating as a kid), along with your looks, abilities, and interests. The objects of your passions change too. Thinking that the object that appeals to you today will always seem that attractive to you is foolish (as we explain in the section "Watching your car rust" later in the chapter). If you can keep this little nugget of info in mind when something screams for your attention (and the contents of your wallet), you can save yourself a lot of hassles.

Remembering the reality of change not only protects you from the dangers of desire and attachment, but it can also be a safeguard against hatred. When you realize that you and the person bothering you will both be pushing up daisies before too long, what's the sense in holding a grudge?

Breaking up the concrete

Buddhism teaches that ignorance is the root cause of all suffering and dissatisfaction — specifically, the ignorance that views things as if they're concrete, separate, self-contained entities (see Chapters 2, 13, and 14 for details). Ultimately, the antidote for this ignorance is wisdom — in particular, the wisdom that realizes the deep meaning of interdependence (as explained in more detail in those chapters). But the question is: How can you apply what you know of this wisdom to the everyday problems you encounter? Consider this situation: A man comes up and insults you by calling you hurtful names, which makes you angry. What can you do to prevent yourself from giving in to this destructive emotional response?

In provocative situations, especially, everything seems very concrete. The words directed at you appear to be a real, solid insult; the person insulting you appears to be a real, solid attacker; and an uncomfortably real and solid sense of yourself as the attackee arises in your heart in response. But, by applying wisdom, you can see that nothing has a concrete existence all to itself, which will save you quite a bit of emotional wear and tear.

If you immediately give in to anger after being insulted, it's too late to apply the wisdom antidote. Delusion and wisdom don't coexist very well. You'll have to be content with insightfully analyzing the situation later when you review the incident in the calm and quiet atmosphere of your meditation session. But, the more you put the following advice into practice in your meditation, the better equipped you become to use your wisdom to defuse potentially dangerous situations as they happen and before they explode and engulf you.

First take a look at the words being hurled at you. Where exactly in this combination of sounds can you find the insult itself? Can you locate it in any of the individual noises coming from the man's mouth? In a certain combination of these noises? Somewhere else? If you analyze the words in this way, taking them apart to look for the self-existent insult, you'll never find one. The insult develops its meaning in your response to the words, not in the words themselves.

In a similar way, where in the man's mental and physical makeup is the attacker himself? Can you find him in the lips and mouth that uttered the words? In some other part of his body? In its overall shape? Can you locate the concrete attacker in any of the millions of thoughts and emotions that course through the man's mind? The more closely you look, the more elusive the bad guy becomes.

Finally, where is the "you" who was insulted? Can you locate that apparently concrete entity in your ears, where the sound waves entered? In some part of your brain that processed these sound signals? In another location of your body or mind? Somewhere, anywhere, else?

As you become more proficient at carefully investigating situations, you begin to realize that things aren't as substantial or as definite as they first appear. Rather than concrete objects with hard edges, all things are actually loosely organized phenomena — feelings, thoughts, sensations, and so on — that are interdependent and rely to a great extent on how you perceive and interpret them. This more open view leaves no place for hatred.

Pretending to be a Buddha

When all other ways of dealing with difficult situations fail, why not pretend that you're a Buddha? Sit quietly and let the situation, including the external circumstances and your own reactions to them, wash over you like a wave. Feel whatever you feel, but don't respond in any way.

In one scene in the movie *Little Buddha,* seductive visions of dancing girls and frightening images of attacking armies confront Keanu Reeves, but he doesn't budge. Imitate Keanu. This technique may lack spiritual sophistication, but it can get you through some difficult situations without making them worse. Besides, who knows? If you imitate a Buddha long enough, you may actually become one.

Watching your car rust

If you're like most people, you often feel disappointed by your material possessions. Cars break down, televisions go on the blink, and your good china gets chipped and cracked. All these experiences can be frustrating and lead to unexpected hassles — as well as unwanted expenses.

The fact is that you can't prevent your possessions from deteriorating. No matter how carefully you handle them or try to keep them shiny and new, they inevitably decay. But you can prevent yourself from experiencing unnecessary grief by realizing that all these material things are impermanent and, therefore, subject to change.

When you first purchase something — a new car, for example — it certainly doesn't appear impermanent. Sitting there all bright and shiny, it doesn't look like it'll ever get old and rusty or fall apart two weeks after its warranty expires. It appears to be solid and permanent as if it'll always look the way it does right now. But this appearance is completely misleading. As Buddha repeatedly pointed out, nothing you perceive through your five senses remains the same from one moment to the next (as we discuss in Chapter 2, unless that has changed too); everything is constantly changing.

The real problem isn't that things *appear* to be permanent but that you *buy into* this false appearance and mistake it for reality. Then, when things begin to fall apart, you experience unnecessary grief and anxiety. The solution is simple: Repeatedly remind yourself of the truth of impermanence, especially when you catch yourself admiring a possession as if it'll last forever.

One of Jon's friends had a grammatical trick he used to help him remain mindful of impermanence. If he owned something he thought was particularly attractive, like a watch, instead of thinking, "This is a fine-looking watch," he would purposely think, "That *was* a fine-looking watch." Referring to the object in the past tense, as if it were already broken, helped him let go of the notion that it was immune to change.

Seeing that what's yours isn't really yours

Besides becoming damaged and broken, material possessions also have the habit of getting lost, which can be quite annoying, especially if the lost item is expensive or hard to replace. A particularly unhelpful attitude exaggerates your sense of loss, reinforces your annoyance, and makes the loss harder to bear. If you can reverse or overcome this attitude, you can eliminate quite a bit of unnecessary pain.

The attitude we're referring to is the notion of possession, which (like all unhelpful notions) is nothing more than a projection of your mind. The idea works this way: When you first see an item in a shop, you may be attracted to it, but you don't think that it belongs to you. However, as soon as you plunk down some cold, hard cash (or swipe some cold, hard plastic) and take the object home with you, your view of it begins to change. You start to think of it as yours. It begins to have something to do with you personally as if it somehow reflects on your importance or worth as a human being. "Because I have this fancy new car or beautiful new dress or cool new pair of shoes," you think to yourself, "I'm finally the person I've always wanted to be."

Eventually, even though you know better, you begin to feel as though this item *always* belonged to you — almost as if it were part of you. Then, losing it is like losing part of yourself. (The same basic pattern holds true for partners or spouses as well. Many people treat them like possessions.)

The antidote to this delusion is to recognize that the things and people you supposedly own don't really belong to you. You're just their temporary care-taker. There was a time in the past when you had no connection with these items, and there will be a time in the future when that'll be true again. The fleeting present occupies the ground between these two points in time, and your association with these items is similarly fleeting. If you can train your-self to look at things in this way, free of all exaggerated notions of possessive-ness, you can live both with them and without them with far less anxiety.

Feeling sorry for a thief

Simply losing something is bad enough, but having it stolen from you feels far worse. If you've ever been a victim of theft, you know that this experience can be painful. In addition to losing an item of value, you also feel the pain of having your personal space invaded, the pain of feeling violated.

When someone takes something from you, being angry with the thief is common. You may also wish that he or she gets caught or has to pay for the crime or that something bad happens to the person. Your mind fills with resentment and thoughts of revenge or retribution. But these thoughts are worse than useless. They don't help you get your stuff back or help the police catch the thief; they only make you more agitated and upset.

But you can do something to make the situation better and calm yourself down: You can give the stolen item to the thief. Although you can't physically give the object to the thief — he or she has already taken it — you can give it to the thief in your mind. Just relinquish all sense of ownership and imagine that you're presenting the object to whoever took it.

Now we know this technique may seem to be a bit illogical — after all, you're upset precisely because you don't want to give up the item. But, by offering to give it up, you're offering to give up your attachment as well. This action may seem like an empty gesture, but if you do it wholeheartedly, with the understanding that it's in the best interest of all concerned, you can replace resentment with generosity, which is definitely helpful in significant ways.

From a karmic point of view, you may have been the victim of theft because you committed a similar theft in the past (check out Chapter 12 for the low-down on karma). Now, you may be reaping the results of your past negative karma and exhausting this past karma in the process. While you're paying off your karmic debt, so to speak, the thief is accumulating his or her own debt and will eventually have to face the consequences.

With this understanding, you may feel some compassion for the thief, know-ing that suffering awaits him or her in future. You may even want to help alle-viate this suffering (and then again, of course, you may not). Because theft is the act of taking something that's not given, you can try to reduce the severity of the thief's future karma by voluntarily giving up the item. After all, you can't steal something that's been given to you. Even if you can't directly affect the thief's karma, generating compassion toward him or her feels a lot better than seething with hatred and resentment, right?

Tendering your resignation to pain

The fact that you have a physical body means that you get to experience pain and discomfort. When this pain inevitably strikes, your mental attitude largely determines how intense the pain will be.

Pain often causes people to get trapped in a "poor me" mentality. You say that life is unfair and complain about your fate. Your suffering is all that you can think about. At times like this, you're not just caught up in your pain, you're imprisoned in the negative story that you create about your condition. This claustrophobic feeling just adds to your discomfort.

The solution is to turn outward and think of something or someone other than yourself. This exercise may not be easy, especially when you're experiencing a throbbing headache or some other form of intense physical pain, but it's definitely possible. The key is to recognize that many other people in the world are experiencing the same type of suffering as you are at that very minute. If you're experiencing a bad headache, for example, you can be sure that millions of others are suffering from the same affliction — and many of them even are probably worse off than you.

Simply realizing that you're not alone in your suffering helps to lighten the burden of your pain and relieve your self-pity. But you can take it to another level. You can generate this compassionate thought: "May my experience of this headache be enough to exhaust the suffering of everyone else." You make the heart-felt decision to use your experience to alleviate the pain of others.

We realize that the headache of Joe from down the street may be the last thing on your mind when you're writhing in agony. And the point isn't to punish yourself. Rather, you're choosing to look at your experience from a different point of view. You still have the same headache, but you're now giving it meaning and purpose by using it to strengthen the bonds of sympathy that connect you with all other beings. Your pain is no longer a personal affliction but an opportunity to connect with others. The main benefit of this practice is that it increases your compassion. But it sometimes brings an unexpected bonus: Your headache goes away.

Turning off the projector

Two types of annoying people exist — people you can avoid and people you can't. How can you deal with the latter?

Suppose that you live near an elderly relative whom you're expected to visit every month. For the sake of this discussion, say this person is your mother. You dread these visits because they generally end with one or both of you becoming upset. No matter how good your intentions are at the beginning, you always seem to get on each other's nerves. What can you do about this situation, short of refusing to visit her?

 First, keep in mind that, from a Buddhist point of view, trying to change yourself is much more effective than trying to change someone else. Second, remember that the underlying cause of most, if not all, problems can be found in the distorted views you project onto situations. Even the habit of seeing other people as annoying, for example, tends to blame them for your unhappiness, when you're the one annoying yourself.

Back to your mother. The way you behave toward her is obviously important, but it's the view you have of her (and ultimately of yourself) that determines your behavior. So ask yourself, "Am I projecting anything onto my mother that makes it difficult for us to get along with each other?"

You may discover that you've stopped regarding her as a person in her own right. Perhaps you've fallen into the habit of thinking of her only in terms of her relationship with you. If so, you're doing her an injustice in at least two ways:

✔ As your mother, she has played a larger role in your life than you selectively remember. You may think of her as someone who's always finding fault with you, complaining about your life, putting unreasonable demands on you, and so on. But, as your mother, she has related to you in many other ways as well. For example, she may have been your nurturer, your protector, your biggest fan, and many other things.

✔ Plus, she's not just your mother. She has had many different relationships with many different people. She has been someone's daughter, friend, lover, rival, wife, neighbor, and so on. In fact, she can't be defined just by her relationships. As a human being, she has had her own hopes and fears, expectations and disappointments, triumphs and challenges, and a history of experiences that you probably know little about. In short, she's a complex, multifaceted person — just like you. Thinking of her only as your mother, and a rather crabby one at that, prevents you from finding out how interesting a person she may be.

So how do you go about improving a relationship? How do you get out of the rut into which you've fallen? You can start by sitting alone in meditation, bringing the other person to mind, and viewing him or her simply as a person, without your accustomed projections. Everyone just wants to be happy and avoid suffering. Spend some time regarding someone who annoys you in this way and allow your heart to open.

If you practice in this way for a while, you can eventually see annoying people — even your mother — in a new light. Then, the next time you visit dear ol' mom, instead of relating to "your mother," try to relate to this intriguing new person you've discovered. If appropriate, ask her about some period or aspect of her life that you don't know much about. Keep the focus on her, not on her relationship to you. See where this exercise takes you.

We can't guarantee that approaching an individual as an individual and not according to his or her relationship with you will immediately patch up a relationship. In fact, the folks may be so taken aback by your new and unaccustomed interest in them that they become suspicious or even defensive. But if your interest is genuine — if it comes from loving concern — this new approach will eventually bear fruit. Just be patient and keep in mind that you can't hope to undo years of bad habits overnight.

Dealing with uninvited houseguests

Although some problems may arise because you take things too personally, others can occur because you don't treat things personally enough. Let us explain.

We've met quite a few people who can't tolerate flies, spiders, and other creepy-crawlies. If one of these insects is brave enough enter their house, they don't hesitate to reach for the bug spray or the newspaper to annihilate it. (Before Jon lived in India, he was the same way himself, so he understands this mentality.) When these folks spot an ant, a bee, or a mosquito, all they see is a threat to their health and well-being, so they feel justified in eliminating it as swiftly as possible.

But, according to the teachings of Buddha, killing insects and other creatures has karmic consequences. Your short-term solution to one problem — swatting an unsanitary fly, for example — may set you up to experience greater problems in the future. (See Chapter 12 for more on the karmic effect of negative actions.) In addition, you get used to the act of killing, which definitely isn't a worthwhile habit to cultivate.

Clearly, if you take the teachings on karma seriously, you'll try not to harm other living beings. If you have to get rid of unwelcome intruders in your house, look for ways to do so without harming them, at least intentionally. Instead of using a chemical that kills bugs, use something that only repels them. Instead of lining your floors with poisonous ant powder, find ways to seal off the cracks that serve as ant-sized entrances. And, instead of swatting mosquitoes, figure out how to catch them and take them outside.

You can find a bunch of ways to remove these critters without killing them. But most of these techniques take a lot more time and energy than simply pressing a button and letting some patented insecticide do the job for you. To convince yourself that these more humane approaches are worth the effort, change your attitude toward insects (and all creatures), recognizing that they have the same desire and right to live as you do. In other words, relate to them in a more personal manner.

If you take the time to look past the annoying buzz and painful sting of a mosquito, for instance, you can find a being who's simply struggling to survive. The little fella isn't purposely bothering you; it just views you as a source of nourishment.

When Jon lived in India, he and his housemate came up with a method that helped them see things from a critter's point of view: They gave them all names. Molly Mosquito had to be escorted out of the room at night; Betty Bee sometimes got confused and came in through a crack in the door; and Waldo Wolf-spider lived on the wall of the latrine. Although they never became pals with these little beings, they certainly never thought of harming them. We're not suggesting that you go around assigning names to all the insects in your house (after all, your friends and family may start wondering when you refer to an ant as Arnold), but you may try looking at the world from their point of view occasionally; you'll no doubt find it easier to share your living space with them.

Part VI
Appendixes

"I'm always endeavoring to become one with all things, however I'm going to make an exception with this fish casserole."

In this part . . .

This part is like a grab bag of helpful odds and ends. Can't remember what that Buddhist term means? Reach into the handy glossary and pull out a definition. Want to know more about some aspect of Buddhism that intrigues you? Glance through the list of books and other useful resources. Go ahead — pick something out.

Appendix A

Brushing Up Your Sanskrit: A Glossary of Useful Buddhist Terms

• •

Any book on Buddhism, even an introductory work like this one, will probably contain a number of words that are unfamiliar to you. You're cruising through the text when, out of the blue, you come across words like *duhkha, avidya,* and *dhyana.* Why, you may wonder, has the author suddenly decided to switch to another language? Isn't English good enough?

The truth is that certain Buddhist terms don't have precise English equivalents — at least not yet. As Buddhism has evolved over the centuries in Asia, a vocabulary has evolved along with it to express complex concepts and subtle experiences. But Buddhism is new to the West and, as a result, hasn't developed a terminology that all Western Buddhists can recognize and accept. So, for the time being, sticking to an Asian language for certain terms is the most accurate way to go.

But sometimes you see the very same unfamiliar terms spelled differently. For example, the three terms we threw out earlier, *duhkha, avidya,* and *dhyana,* are Sanskrit, an ancient Indian language. But you may also see these terms written as *dukkha, avijja,* and *jhana.* In that case, the author is using Pali, another ancient Indian language closely related to Sanskrit. If this language lottery isn't maddening enough, sometimes these same words are adorned with strange markings above or even below some of their letters. These *diacritical marks* (a fancy term for slashes, dots, and squiggles) are supposed to help you pronounce the words more accurately, but unless you're already a student of languages that almost no one speaks anymore, these diacritical marks often do more harm than good. (That's why we do without these marks in *Buddhism For Dummies.*)

As different Buddhist traditions arose in India (see Chapter 4), they transmitted their versions of Buddha's teachings in different Indian languages. Sanskrit and Pali are the two most important of these languages — as far as Buddhism is concerned. That's why many Buddhist technical terms, especially the ones that are difficult to translate precisely, still appear in these ancient languages. (This is similar to the way that certain important terms in Christian theology still appear in Greek.)

In this glossary, we provide useful — but certainly not exhaustive — definitions for the Buddhist terms you're likely to come across often in this book. To simplify matters as much as possible, most of the entries are in Sanskrit (which we signify with an S), without any confusing diacritical marks. We list certain terms in Pali (which we mark with a P) as well, with a smattering of other Asian languages thrown in for good measure. (We use a C for Chinese, a J for Japanese, and a T for Tibetan.) Where appropriate, we also include some of the English terms we use repeatedly in this book.

One more note: When you see words in quotes following the glossary entry, these words are a close approximation of the literal meaning of the entry. After this info, we go on to explain the entry more fully.

Abhidharma: (S) "higher learning"; section of the Buddhist teachings dealing with psychology, philosophy, cosmology, metaphysics, and other matters (P: abhidhamma); **see also *tripitaka***

Amitabha: (S) Buddha of "infinite light," considered by some traditions to have taken a vow to lead all beings to the *pure land* over which he presides (J: Amida)

arhat: (S) "foe-destroyer"; one who has attained *nirvana*

arya: (S) "noble one"; advanced practitioner who has gained direct insight into the true nature of reality

Avalokiteshvara: (S) "he who looks down with compassion"; figure revered in certain traditions as the embodiment of enlightened compassion; known as Chenrezig in Tibet

avidya: (S) "ignorance," the root cause of all suffering (P: avijja)

Bodhi: (S, P) the full enlightenment of a Buddha; the state of supreme spiritual fulfillment, characterized by universal compassion, wisdom, and skill; the goal of the Mahayana practitioner; Buddhahood

bodhichitta: (S) "mind (directed toward) enlightenment"; the altruistic motivation of a *bodhisattva;* the wish to achieve *enlightenment* for the sake of benefiting others

bodhisattva: (S) "enlightenment(-bound) being"; a previous incarnation of *Shakyamuni,* prior to his *enlightenment,* as mentioned in the *Jataka Tales;* anyone who aspires to attain enlightenment to help free others from suffering (P: bodhisatta); one of numerous transcendent awakened beings embodying certain essential qualities of enlightenment, revered in some traditions as objects of devotion

brahmavihara: (S) "heavenly abode"; any one of four essential heart qualities (loving-kindness, compassion, sympathetic joy, and equanimity) cultivated on the path of spiritual fulfillment

Buddha: (S, P) "awakened one"; first of the *Three Jewels of Refuge;* a fully enlightened being; anyone who has overcome all obstacles and developed all good qualities and can therefore be of greatest benefit to others; **see also** *Shakyamuni Buddha*

Buddhahood: complete enlightenment; the attainment or realization of those following the *Mahayana* path to completion

Buddha nature: inner purity; according to some Buddhist traditions, your true nature, indistinguishable from enlightenment; the potential to achieve enlightenment, said to exist within all beings

cyclic existence: see *samsara*

deity yoga: an essential Vajrayana practice in which you identify your pure nature with a figure embodying the qualities of enlightenment

dharma: (S) spiritual teachings, particularly those of an enlightened being; truth that "holds you back" from suffering; second of the *Three Jewels of Refuge* (P: dhamma)

dhyana: (S) meditative concentration (P: jhana; C: ch'an, J: zen)

duhkha: (S) suffering; dissatisfaction; the unsatisfactory nature of mundane *cyclic existence* (P: dukkha)

eight-fold path: path taught by *Shakyamuni Buddha* leading to the complete cessation of suffering; consists of right understanding (or view), right thought, right speech, right action, right livelihood, right effort, right mindfulness, and right concentration

emptiness: see *shunyata*

enlightenment: any of various levels of spiritual fulfillment, particularly the full enlightenment of *Buddhahood;* **see also** *Bodhi*

four noble truths: the main subject matter of the first discourse of *Shakyamuni Buddha,* in which he explained the reality of suffering, the cause of suffering, the cessation of suffering, and the path leading to the complete cessation of suffering

geshe: (T) "spiritual friend"; degree awarded to those who've completed an intensive course of monastic study, roughly equivalent to a doctor of divinity

guru: (S) spiritual teacher

Hinayana: (S) "lesser vehicle"; term used in a disparaging way by some *Mahayana* Buddhists to refer to the spiritual path followed by those intent on achieving personal liberation only

Jataka Tales: (S) stories originally told by *Shakyamuni Buddha* about his previous lives, in which he often took the form of an animal

karma: (S) intentional "action"; the workings of cause and effect, whereby virtuous actions lead to happiness and non-virtuous actions lead to suffering (P: kamma)

karuna: (S, P) "compassion"; the wish that others not suffer

kensho: (J) "seeing true nature"; a direct glimpse of your essential (Buddha) nature

klesha: (S) any thought or emotion that disturbs your peace of mind, particularly ignorance, aversion, and attachment; obscuration, afflictive emotion

Kuan Yin: (C) female *bodhisattva* of mercy and compassion (J: Kwannon)

lama: (T) spiritual guide and teacher; guru

lam-rim: (T) "stages of the path"; Buddha's teachings organized into an organic whole according to practitioners' different levels of motivation

liberation: see *nirvana*

Mahayana: (S) "great vehicle"; the path the *bodhisattva* follows on his or her way to supreme *enlightenment;* the vehicle of universal *liberation*

Maitreya: (S) "loving one"; *bodhisattva* disciple of *Shakyamuni,* predicted to be the future *Buddha* who will reintroduce *dharma* to the world after the teachings of Shakyamuni disappear

maitri: (S) see *metta*

Manjushri: (S) "sweet voice"; figure revered in certain traditions as the embodiment of enlightened wisdom

mantra: (S) "mind protection"; words of power; syllables, generally in Sanskrit, recited during certain meditational practices

metta: (P) "loving-kindness"; the wish for others to be happy (S: maitri)

nirvana: (S) state beyond sorrow; personal *liberation* from suffering and the causes of suffering; the attainment of an *arhat* (P: nibbana)

puja: (S) offering ceremony

pure land: state of existence outside *samsara* in which all conditions are favorable for attaining *enlightenment*

roshi: (J) spiritual teacher in Zen

samadhi: (S) state of deep meditative absorption

samsara: (S, P) "wandering"; cyclic existence; the cycle of uncontrolled death and rebirth, rooted in ignorance and full of suffering and dissatisfaction; ordinary life as experienced through unenlightened eyes

sangha: (S) spiritual community; third of the *Three Jewels of Refuge*

satori: (J) sudden flash of insight; a direct glimpse of your essential (Buddha) nature; **see also *kensho***

Shakyamuni Buddha: "sage of the Shakya clan"; the historical Buddha; founder of the teachings now known as Buddhism (approximately 563–483 BCE)

shunyata: (S) "emptiness"; the actual way in which all things exist, empty of all false notions of independent self-existence and ultimately ungraspable by the conceptual mind

stupa: (S) monument holding relics of Buddha or another spiritual master

sutra: (S) discourse, especially of *Shakyamuni Buddha;* section of Buddha's teachings dealing with meditation topics (P: sutta)

tantra: (S) texts forming the basis of the *Vajrayana* tradition, dealing with such esoteric practices as *deity yoga*

Tara: (S) "the savior"; female figure considered by some traditions to embody the enlightened, compassionate activity of all Buddhas

Theravada: "tradition of the elders"; the tradition of Buddhism that relies exclusively on the Pali canon, the discourses of the Buddha compiled in the first few centuries after his death; the predominant tradition in Sri Lanka and Southeast Asia

Three Jewels of Refuge: *Buddha, dharma,* and *sangha* (S: triratna); also known as the Triple Gem or Three Treasures: the teacher, his teachings, and the community of those following these teachings

tripitaka: (S) "three baskets"; the three sections into which Buddha's teachings have been traditionally divided: *sutra, vinaya,* and *Abhidharma* (P: tipitaka)

Vajrayana: (S) "diamond vehicle"; the *tantric* teachings of Buddhism; the tradition of *Mahayana* Buddhism that evolved in India and came to prominence in Tibet

vinaya: (S, P) section of Buddha's teachings dealing with the rules of monastic discipline, ethical behavior, and the *karmic* law of cause and effect

yoga: (S) spiritual practice or discipline to which you "yoke" yourself; skilled male and female practitioner of yoga referred to as a *yogi* and *yogini,* respectively

Zen: (J) "meditation"; the tradition of *Mahayana* Buddhism that arose first in China and then spread to Japan, Korea, and other Asian countries, emphasizing the practice of meditation as a means to sudden awakening

Appendix B

Additional Buddhist Resources to Check Out

• •

*I*n an introductory book like this one, we couldn't possibly do justice to all the many different aspects of Buddhism and its 2,500-year history. But we hope we've sparked your interest and that you want to explore Buddhism further.

If you want to know more about Buddhism, in general, or any of its various traditions, you've come to the right place. This appendix offers a list of books and other resources that can help you. Within the list of magazines, we also include a few Web sites that contain lots of useful and interesting information about all things Buddhist, including the names of dharma centers near you. And, as soon as you start surfing the Web, you're bound to discover many more intriguing sites on your own. (An excellent place to start is www.buddhanet.net, the Web site of the Buddhist Information and Education Network.)

When we first became seriously interested in Buddhism 30 years or so ago, the term *Internet* had never been used, and the number of books on Buddhism suitable for a general reader was quite small — especially in comparison to the embarrassment of riches available today. Today, so many Buddhist publications line bookstore shelves and fill newsstands that our biggest problem in compiling this appendix has been limiting ourselves to a manageable number of entries. From the works we left out, we could easily put together several other excellent lists. Consider this brief catalogue as your entrance into a vast world just waiting for you to explore. Enjoy.

The Story of Buddha

The life of Shakyamuni Buddha has been told and retold numerous times. Here are some of the versions that readers from different backgrounds have found particularly inspiring.

- *Jatakamala, the Marvelous Companion: Life Stories of the Buddha,* by Aryasura (Dharma Publishing). An updated version of a translation that originally appeared in 1895, this title is a collection of 34 stories of the past lives of Shakyamuni Buddha.

- *The Life of the Buddha,* by Venerable H. Saddhatissa (HarperCollins). This compelling account of the life of Shakyamuni Buddha was drawn from original Sanskrit and Pali sources by a highly respected monk-scholar from Sri Lanka.

- *The Light of Asia,* by Sir Edwin Arnold (numerous publishers). Since it first appeared in 1879, this poetic version of Buddha's story has been an international favorite.

- *Old Path White Clouds: Walking in the Footsteps of the Buddha,* by Thich Nhat Hanh (Parallax Press). Drawing from Pali, Sanskrit, and Chinese sources, this evocative work tells the story of Buddha's life as seen in part through the eyes of the fictional buffalo boy Svasti.

- *Prince Siddhartha,* by Jonathan Landaw (Wisdom Publications). This story of the life of Buddha is retold especially for children — and their parents.

- *Siddhartha,* by Hermann Hesse, newly translated by Sherab Chodzin Kohn (Shambhala). Written by the Nobel Prize winning author in 1922, this novel, set at the time of Shakyamuni Buddha, brings the reader into the world of Buddhism's founder. The translator is a longtime student of Buddhism and Eastern philosophy.

Buddhist Classics, Old and New

The following list contains some of the most influential and popular books on Buddhism.

- *Buddhist Scriptures,* by Edward Conze (Penguin Books). This compact volume contains a wide selection of useful material from Indian, Tibetan, Chinese, and Japanese sources.

- *Cutting through Spiritual Materialism,* by Chogyam Trungpa Rinpoche (Shambhala). A contemporary Tibetan lama who had a profound impact on Buddhism in the West clearly addresses the problems and pitfalls faced by spiritual seekers.

- *The Dhammapada* (numerous publishers). This ancient collection (also entitled *The Dharmapada*) contains some of the most famous sayings of Shakyamuni Buddha, and is an excellent introduction to his thought and the spirit of his teachings. The version brought out by Dharma Publishing is of particular interest, for it identifies the exact source in Buddha's discourses of each saying.

- *The Experience of Insight: A Simple and Direct Guide to Buddhist Meditation,* by Joseph Goldstein (Shambhala). As the title implies, this book is a straightforward manual for the practice of Buddhist *vipassana* (insight) meditation. The author is one of the founders of the Insight Meditation Society in Barre, Massachusetts.

- *The Heart of Buddhist Meditation,* Nyanaponika Thera (Red Wheel/Weiser). Originally published in 1962, this classic outlines the practice of meditation in the Theravada tradition.

- *Loving-kindness: The Revolutionary Art of Happiness,* by Sharon Salzberg (Shambhala). Filled with personal anecdotes and insights from one of the founders of the Insight Meditation Society in Barre, Massachusetts, this accessible guidebook offers meditations for cultivating not only loving-kindness but also compassion, sympathetic joy, and equanimity.

- *Masters of Enchantment: The Lives and Legends of the Mahasiddhas,* by Keith Dowman (Inner Traditions International). Richly illustrated by Robert Beer, this work is a fascinating introduction to the ancient and magical world of Indian Vajrayana Buddhism.

- *Mother of the Buddhas: Meditation on the Prajnaparamita Sutra,* by Lex Hixon (Quest Books). More than a mere translation of a major *Perfection of Wisdom Sutra,* this is a work of rare devotional beauty that welcomes the reader to share a glorious vision of insight and compassion.

- *A Path with Heart,* by Jack Kornfield (Bantam Books). Written by the author of numerous works on Buddhist thought and practice, this bestseller provides a friendly, psychologically astute introduction to meditation. Kornfield is a founder of the Insight Meditation Society in Massachusetts and the Spirit Rock Center in California.

- *Three Pillars of Zen: Teaching, Practice, and Enlightenment,* by Philip Kapleau (Anchor Books). The first popular Zen guidebook written by an enlightened westerner for westerners, *Three Pillars* single-handedly introduced a generation to Zen Buddhism.

- *The Tibetan Book of Living and Dying,* by Sogyal Rinpoche (Harper SanFrancisco). Filled with teaching stories, meditations, and time-honored insights from the Tibetan Vajrayana tradition, this bestseller approaches the experience of dying — and living — with compassion and wisdom.

- *The Way of Zen,* by Alan W. Watts (Vintage Books). Written in 1957, this work by one of the most influential commentators on Eastern philosophy and religion is still one of the best introductions to the world of Zen thought and practice. Also see his *Psychotherapy East and West* (Vintage Books) for a thought-provoking discussion of the common ground between Western psychiatry and Eastern philosophy.

- *When Things Fall Apart: Heart Advice for Difficult Times,* by Pema Chodron (Shambhala). This favorite is a warm, lucid, and accessible guide to the practice of compassion, especially toward oneself, by an American Buddhist nun who is the resident teacher at a Vajrayana retreat center in Nova Scotia.

- *Zen Mind, Beginner's Mind,* by Shunryu Suzuki (Weatherhill). A classic collection of talks by the beloved Japanese-American Zen master that covers posture, attitude, and understanding from a Soto Zen perspective.

Well Worth Reading

Here are some additional titles that we think you'll like. Take a look.

- *Buddhism for Beginners,* by Thubten Chodron (Snow Lion Publications). Using a question and answer format, a leading American Buddhist nun addresses some of the most fundamental issues raised by those coming into contact with Buddhism for the first time.

- *Buddhism with an Attitude: The Tibetan Seven-Point Mind-Training,* by B. Alan Wallace (Snow Lion Publications). In this work, Wallace (one of the leading Western translators and writers on Buddhism) brings the traditional techniques of thought transformation directly into the modern world.

- *The Buddhist Handbook: The Complete Guide to Buddhist Schools, Teaching, Practice, and History,* by John Snelling (Inner Traditions). This invaluable resource for anyone wanting to know more about Buddhism past and present contains appendices listing useful addresses of Buddhist organizations in North America, major Buddhist festivals, an extensive selection of further readings, and much more.

- *Cultivating Compassion: A Buddhist Perspective,* by Jeffrey Hopkins (Broadway Books). Interpreter for the Dalai Lama for more than ten years, and translator and editor of numerous works of Buddhism, Hopkins presents a compelling and extremely moving account of the practice of compassion in everyday life.

- *Developing Balanced Sensitivity: Practical Buddhist Exercises for Daily Life,* by Alexander Berzin (Snow Lion Publications). Author, translator and worldwide lecturer, Berzin introduces a series of techniques adapted from traditional Buddhist sources for dealing with both insensitivity and hypersensitivity. Also check out Berzin's *Relating to a Spiritual Teacher* (Snow Lion) for a comprehensive discussion of the all-important, but often misunderstood, relationship between disciples and their spiritual guides.

✔ *Dharma Family Treasures: Sharing Mindfulness with Children,* edited by Sandy Eastoak (North Atlantic Books). This anthology of Buddhist writings offers a wealth of ideas for helping children bring Buddhist principles into their daily lives.

✔ *The Diamond Cutter: The Buddha on Strategies for Managing Your Business and Your Life,* by Geshe Michael Roach (Doubleday). This book, by the first American to complete the rigorous Tibetan *geshe* training, master-fully weaves together commentary on Buddha's profound *Diamond Cutter Sutra* and practical advice for running a business based on the author's experiences in the New York diamond trade. You can also check out Geshe Roach's *The Garden* (Doubleday), a beautiful parable of Buddha's wisdom teachings.

✔ *The Heart of Buddha's Teaching: Transforming Suffering into Peace, Joy, and Liberation,* by Thich Nhat Hanh (Parallax Press). This clear and poetic introduction to the core teachings of Buddhism covers the four noble truths, the eight-fold path, the six perfections, the twelve links, and much more.

✔ *The Illustrated Encyclopedia of Buddhist Wisdom: A Complete Introduction to the Principles and Practices of Buddhism,* by Gill Farrer-Halls (Quest Books). Visually attractive and easy to read, this volume provides an excellent overview of the world of Buddhism.

✔ *Introduction to Tantra: A Vision of Totality,* by Lama Thubten Yeshe (Wisdom Publications). This presentation of the most essential features of Vajrayana Buddhism is told with clarity and engaging humor.

✔ *Living Buddhism,* by Andrew Powell (Harmony Books). Graham Harrison's beautiful photographs richly illustrate this wide-ranging survey of Buddhist thought and practice. This book covers the growth of Buddhism in India and its spread throughout Asia and to the West.

✔ *Lotus in a Stream: Essays in Basic Buddhism,* by Hsing Yun (Weatherhill). This work by the contemporary Chinese monk and Ch'an (Zen) master Hsing Yun is a well-organized and easily readable reference to the major themes of Buddhist thought and practice.

✔ *Mindfulness in Plain English,* by Venerable Henepola Gunaratana (Wisdom Publications). This step-by-step insight meditation manual is accessible to all readers. Of related interest is Ajahn Sumedho's slim volume *Mindfulness: The Path to the Deathless* (Amaravati Publications).

✔ *Moon in a Dewdrop: Writings of Zen Master Dogen,* edited by Kazuaki Tanahashi (North Point Press). These beautiful translations of writings by the Japanese Zen master Dogen (1200–1253), the founder of the Soto school, include a variety of practical instructions as well as philosophi-cal and poetical works.

- *Practical Insight Meditation,* by Mahasi Sayadaw (Unity Press). A revered Burmese master provides an in-depth look at mindfulness meditation: the heart of Buddhist practice.

- *Transforming Problems into Happiness,* by Lama Thubten Zopa Rinpoche (Wisdom Publications). Lama Zopa's commentary on a short thought-transformation text by a past Tibetan master is filled with practical advice that can be valuable to anyone, regardless of his or her spiritual background.

- *Voices of Insight,* edited by Sharon Salzberg (Shambhala). This collection of articles by many of the most well-known and articulate teachers of the Vipassana tradition provides an excellent introduction to the world of Buddhist meditation.

- *The Zen of Seeing: Seeing/Drawing as Meditation,* by Frederick Franck (Vintage Books). This wonderful book approaches the art of seeing/drawing as a spiritual discipline endowed with the Zen flavor of experiencing the world freshly in each moment.

By and about the Modern Masters

In Chapter 15 we introduce you to four teachers who have exerted a great influence of contemporary Buddhism. Here we present a sampling of books written by and about these illustrious teachers.

- *The Art of Happiness: A Handbook for Living,* by the Dalai Lama (Riverhead Books). This best seller, co-authored by the American psychiatrist Howard Cutler, presents many different methods for dealing with the challenges of everyday life.

- *Food for the Heart: The Collected Teachings of Ajahn Chah,* introduced by Ajahn Amaro (Wisdom Publications). This compilation provides an excellent overview of Ajahn Chah's teachings, and its introduction ushers the reader into the Thai Forest Tradition that this beloved Buddhist master did so much to revitalize.

- *The Good Heart: A Buddhist Perspective on the Teachings of Jesus,* by the Dalai Lama (Wisdom Publications). Invited to give his commentary on the Gospels, the Dalai Lama responds with what Huston Smith has called "arguably the best book on inter-religious dialogue published to date."

- *The Jew in the Lotus,* by Rodger Kamenetz (Harper). This engaging and often humorous account of the meeting of Jewish religious leaders and the Dalai Lama throws light on the issues facing Buddhists, Jews, and indeed all people of faith striving to survive in the secular world.

- *Living Buddha, Living Christ,* by Thich Nhat Hanh (Riverhead Books). The Vietnamese Zen master explores the meeting ground of two of the world's major spiritual traditions. Also check out his *Going Home: Jesus and Buddha as Brothers* (Riverhead Books).

✔ *Meeting of Minds: A Dialogue on Tibetan and Chinese Buddhism,* by the Dalai Lama and Chan Master Sheng-yen (Dharma Drum Publications). This historical dialogue between two of the leading exponents of Tibetan and Chinese Buddhism throws much needed light on the similarities and differences between the wisdom teachings of the Vajrayana and Zen traditions.

✔ *An Open Heart: Practicing Compassion in Everyday Life,* by the Dalai Lama (Little, Brown and Company). This easy to comprehend work provides a basic understanding of Buddhism and some of the key methods for cultivating compassion and wisdom in your daily life, no matter what your religious affiliation may be.

✔ "Transformation of a Housewife" by Amy Schmidt, found in *Women's Buddhism, Buddhism's Women,* edited by Ellison Banks Findly (Wisdom Publications). This inspiring biography of Dipa Ma brings to life one of the most beloved and influential Buddhist teachers of the Theravada tradition.

✔ *The World of the Dalai Lama: An Inside Look at His Life, His People, and His Vision,* by Gill Farrer-Halls (Thorsons). This richly illustrated and delightfully written account of the world of the Dalai Lama, both inside and outside Tibet, demonstrates the impact a life of dedication can have on others, no matter what their religious or cultural heritage.

Women and Buddhism

One of the most interesting developments in contemporary Buddhism is the increasing role that women are playing in this traditionally male-dominated sphere. The following books present a variety of points of view on this significant phenomenon.

✔ *Buddhist Women on the Edge: Contemporary Perspectives from the Western Frontier,* edited by Marianne Dresser (North Atlantic Books). This work contains contributions from important authors like Pema Chodron, Jan Willis, Tsultrim Allione, Anne Klein, Thubten Chodron, and Kate Wheeler.

✔ *Dreaming Me: An African American Woman's Spiritual Journey,* by Jan Willis (Riverhead Books). This personal memoir takes the reader along on the author's remarkable journey from an Alabama mining camp, through undergraduate life at Cornell University, to a Tibetan Buddhist monastery, and eventually to her position as professor of religion at Wesleyan University.

✔ *The First Buddhist Women: Translations and Commentary on the Therigatha,* by Susan Murcott (Parallax Press). This look at the early history of women in Buddhism includes the earliest known collection of women's religious poetry.

- *Sakyadhita: Daughters of the Buddha,* edited by Karma Lekshe Tsomo (Snow Lion Publications). This collection of essays is the result of the International Conference of Buddhist Nuns held in Bodh Gaya, India, in 1987, the first such conference ever convened.

- *Turning the Wheel: American Women Creating the New Buddhism,* by Sandy Boucher (Beacon Press). This account of the challenges facing women attempting to create a vital tradition of contemporary Buddhism addresses issues of great importance to both men and women.

- *Women of Wisdom,* by Tsultrim Allione (Routledge & Kegan Paul). These biographies of six extraordinary Tibetan female mystics invite the reader to gain a deeper understanding of women's experiences of Buddhism.

Socially Engaged Buddhism

The practice of Buddhist meditation is, by its nature, a personal, private, and inner-directed activity. But the ultimate purpose of this and all other Buddhist practices is to bring as much benefit to others as possible. This compassionate concern for the welfare of others has given rise to Engaged Buddhism. To find out more about this important trend in contemporary Buddhism, check out the following books.

- *Being Peace,* by Thich Nhat Hanh (Parallax Press). By one of the founders of the Engaged Buddhism movement, this book contains lectures given to activists and meditators about the importance of embodying peace in one's own life.

- *Buddhist Peace Work: Creating Cultures of Peace,* edited by David Chappell (Wisdom Publications). This compilation contains first-person accounts of the ideas and work of illustrious leaders from a wide variety of Buddhist traditions on the subject of creating and maintaining peace. Of related interest are Daisaku Ikeda's *For the Sake of Peace: Seven Paths to Global Harmony, A Buddhist Perspective* (Middleway Press) and Sulak Sivaraksa's *Seeds of Peace: A Buddhist Vision for Renewing Society* (Parallax Press).

- *Dharma Gaia: A Harvest of Essays in Buddhism and Ecology,* edited by Alan Hurt Badiner (Parallax Press). This work contains contributions by such luminaries as the Dalai Lama, Thich Nhat Hanh, Joanna Macy, and Joan Halifax.

- *Engaged Buddhism in the West,* edited by Christopher Queen (Wisdom Publications). The history and teachings of Engaged Buddhism are presented here in terms of the individuals and organizations involved in Buddhist activism.

✔ *World as Lover, World as Self,* by Joanna Macy (Parallax Press). An influ-ential scholar of Buddhism and general systems theory shows how redefining your relationship to the world helps promote not only your own spiritual development but also the health of the planet.

At Your Local Newsstand

If you're interested in the Buddhist perspective on current social and political affairs, you may want to look at some of the following magazines and periodi-cals. They're also an excellent source of up-to-date information on meditation courses and study groups being given in your local area.

✔ *Inquiring Mind.* Born out of the Theravada Buddhist community of insight (vipassana) meditators, this journal is highly regarded for its excellent thought-provoking interviews with Buddhist teachers, philosophers, psychologists, and artists, as well as for its poetry, stories, and humor-ous essays. Each issue includes an extensive international calendar of vipassana retreats and listings of events and sitting groups throughout North America (Internet: www.inquiringmind.com).

✔ *Mandala: Buddhism in Our Time.* Published by the Foundation for the Preservation of the Mahayana Tradition (FPMT), this magazine regu-larly features articles by and about the founder of the FPMT, the late Lama Thubten Yeshe, and its current head, Lama Zopa Rinpoche, in addition to general coverage of the Buddhist scene (Internet: www.mandalamagazine.org).

✔ *Shambhala Sun: Creating Enlightened Society.* This magazine contains articles on all facets of Buddhism and its relationship to contemporary society (Internet: www.shambhalasun.com). You can also take a look at *Buddhadharma: The Pracitioner's Quarterly,* by the same publisher.

✔ *Snow Lion.* The newsletter of Snow Lion Publications is a major source of news, books, tapes, and related material on Buddhism (Internet: www.snowlionpub.com).

✔ *Tricycle: The Buddhist Review.* Executive Director, Helen Tworkov. Read-ing this attractive publication, the most popular Buddhist magazine in America, is an excellent way to keep up on a wide range of issues relating to Buddhist thought and practice (Internet: www.tricycle.com).

✔ *Turning Wheel: The Journal of Socially Engaged Buddhism.* Published by the Buddhist Peace Fellowship, *Turning Wheel* provides a Buddhist per-spective on such current issues as ecology, peace activism, human rights, and much more (Internet: www.bpf.org).

Index

• N •

• Q •

• R •

• S •

Notes